To my wife, Gerri, for her support and patience during the process of writing this book. I couldn't have done it without you. And also to my son, Mike, who inherited my love of games of all types.

IT LRC

3D   1
Usi   ‡

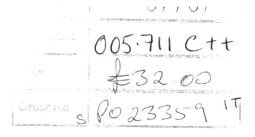
Apress™

Introduction to 3D Game Engine Design Using DirectX 9 and C#
Copyright ©2003 by Lynn T. Harrison

ISBN (pbk): 1-59059-081-3

Printed and bound in the United States of America 12345678910

Technical Reviewer: Patrick DeNardo

Editorial Board: Dan Appleman, Craig Berry, Gary Cornell, Tony Davis, Steven Rycroft, Julian Skinner, Martin Streicher, Jim Sumser, Karen Watterson, Gavin Wray, John Zukowski

Assistant Publisher: Grace Wong

Project Manager: Tracy Brown Collins

Copy Editor: Ami Knox

Production Manager: Kari Brooks

Compositor and Proofreader: Kinetic Publishing Services, LLC

Indexer: Michael Brinkman

Cover Designer: Kurt Krames

Manufacturing Manager: Tom Debolski

Distributed to the book trade in the United States by Springer-Verlag New York, Inc., 175 Fifth Avenue, New York, NY, 10010 and outside the United States by Springer-Verlag GmbH & Co. KG, Tiergartenstr. 17, 69112 Heidelberg, Germany.

In the United States: phone 1-800-SPRINGER, email orders@springer-ny.com, or visit http://www.springer-ny.com. Outside the United States: fax +49 6221 345229, email orders@springer.de, or visit http://www.springer.de.

For information on translations, please contact Apress directly at 2560 Ninth Street, Suite 219, Berkeley, CA 94710. Phone 510-549-5930, fax 510-549-5939, email info@apress.com, or visit http://www.apress.com.

The source code for this book is available to readers at http://www.apress.com in the Downloads section.

Contents at a Glance

Contents

About the Author

LYNN THOMAS HARRISON is both a Microsoft Certified Systems Engineer (MCSE) and Microsoft Certified Solutions Developer (MCSD) and is currently employed as a senior systems engineer for Diamond Visionics Company (a visualization engineering company). He lives in Binghamton, New York, with his wife, Gerri, and son, Michael. Lynn has been active in the simulation and graphics industries for over 22 years.

About the Technical Reviewer

PATRICK DENARDO is a project director and software technical lead at Universal Instruments, Inc., where he architects and develops client-server internationalized software for the Windows platform. He is a Microsoft Certified Professional and has a Bachelor of Science degree in computer science from Binghamton University. Patrick enjoys reading computer books, playing golf, and spending time with his wife, Jennifer, and their dog, Abby.

Acknowledgments

I WOULD LIKE TO THANK ALL of the great people at Apress for their guidance along the way. I really had no idea when I started this book about everything that went into the process. First, thanks to Gary Cornell and Dan Appleman for their enthusiasm in this project and for getting me started. Also thanks to Sofia Marchant and Tracy Brown Collins for keeping everything organized and on track. Big thanks to my wife, Gerri, and to my copy editor, Ami Knox, who helped translate my techie ramblings into English.

I would also like to thank my technical reviewer, Pat DeNardo. Pat not only made sure that the information presented in this book was technically correct, but also that the information was understandable to those new to C# and Managed DirectX.

Lastly, I would like to thank my family for their support over the last 14 months. Too many weekends were spent with my computer rather than with them. Gerri and Mike, thanks for understanding my need to do this. I would also like to thank my parents for always believing me and raising me to believe in myself.

Introduction

I HAVE BEEN EDUCATING MYSELF about game design and 3D visualization for many years. My bookshelves are full of books on programming, game development, and the various graphical application programming interfaces (APIs). Many books have been written that explain every part of DirectX or OpenGL. Quite a few books are also dedicated to creating portions of a game using one or both of these technologies.

The book that I could never find was one on game engine design. I wanted an object-oriented, reusable package of software that was not tightly integrated to one particular game. I knew that I wasn't the only person interested in game engine design. I decided that, as I learned C# and managed DirectX 9 and ported my game engine to this new technology, I would document the process. The fact that you are reading this indicates you share my interest in 3D game engines.

I have kept this book at an introductory level. When I initially began planning the book, I considered including more advanced topics such as animation, networking for multiplayer capability, and the programmable pipeline (shaders). I quickly came to the conclusion that to cover that much material in any depth at all was too much for a single book. I am hoping that at some point in the future I will have the time to do a follow-up volume that includes these and other more advanced areas.

No one book can answer all questions. I encourage you to extend your research to other books and the Internet as you hone your development capabilities. The best resources for getting your questions answered are the Microsoft DirectX newsgroups. There are a number of newsgroups of interest that are prefixed with microsoft.public.win32.programmer.directx. The newsgroup dedicated to Managed DirectX is microsoft.public.win32.programmer.directx.managed. I often monitor this newsgroup, and I will answer any questions that I can.

Chapter 1: Overview

This chapter looks at several types of game engines as well as the distinction between a game and a game engine. Game engine design requires more thought than do hard-coding rendering and game logic within the game itself. The benefit is greater reuse of the underlying technology and a cleaner overall design.

Chapter 2: User Interface

A game's user interface provides the means of giving the player information and obtaining the player's commands. This chapter investigates the presentation of splash screens, option screens, and a console screen. It also looks at the use of DirectInput to obtain player inputs from the keyboard, mouse, and joysticks.

Chapter 3: Hanging Ten: A Ride Through the Rendering Pipeline

Before diving into the actual rendering of three-dimensional objects, it is good to have a basic understanding of the rendering pipeline. This chapter walks you through the typical steps involved in the fixed-function rendering pipeline. This includes the manipulation of cameras to provide the viewpoint in the game. It also describes a base class that will be used for all rendered objects. The process of culling objects and other techniques for improving performance is also investigated. The actual illustration of these steps appears in Chapters 4 through 8.

Chapter 4: Basic 3D Objects

This chapter is the first of two chapters dealing with rendering the various types of objects that are used within a game. These objects include a skybox for providing a view into the distance, terrain rendering to provide a surface to move upon, billboards for simple symmetrical objects, and particle systems. Particle systems are an extremely powerful tool that may be used for dynamic systems of small objects. These include flowing water, fire, fireworks, and blowing sand.

Chapter 5: Complex 3D Objects

Chapter 5 is the second chapter dedicated to the rendering of objects for games. The objects described in this chapter are much more complex, with many polygons per object. These are referred to as *mesh objects* and are used as the primary moving models within a game. The class used to encapsulate meshes includes the capability to adjust the complexity of the mesh as a function of range from the camera to improve performance.

Chapter 6: Camera: The Player's View of the World

To control the view of the action, we need something akin to the cameras used to film a movie. This chapter illustrates the design and use of a camera class that may be employed in a variety of ways. Cameras may be positioned at static locations within the scene and follow objects as they move past or they may be attached to the moving objects themselves. Employing multiple cameras and including logic within a game can provide a cinematic flair to the game.

Chapter 7: Adding Some Atmosphere: Lighting and Fog

All of the rendering performed by the game engine up until this point has been under fully lit and crystal-clear conditions—conditions that are often hard to find in the real world. This chapter explores the four types of lights that may be used to illuminate a scene as well as how to configure fog to improve the realism of a game. Fog may also be used to disguise shortcomings in the ability to render objects at a large distance from the camera.

Chapter 8: Artificial Intelligence: Adding the Competition

Few games are much fun without opponents. Although it is possible to write games that are strictly multiplayer, in which all of the opponents are human, networking is out of the scope of this book. Instead, we will look at the different types of artificial intelligence techniques that can be used within a game. One of these methods will be developed as part of the sample game engine for the book.

Chapter 9: Game Audio: Let's Make Some Noise

Another method to add character to a game is through the use of audio. Background music, if chosen properly, adds mood to the play. This chapter shows you how to develop classes for the game engine that facilitate playing songs. It also includes support for sound effects within a game. Players expect certain sounds to coincide with events within a game. If a car hits another car or a tree, they expect to hear the crash as well as see a reaction between the objects involved in the collision.

Chapter 10: Game Physics: Keeping It Real

As I mentioned when talking about audio, players not only expect to hear noise in a collision, but also to see a more physical reaction. Chapter 10 concentrates on the physics involved primarily with cars. The basic mathematics applied to cars may also be applied to many types of moving objects. This chapter also covers the physics used for cloth dynamics. This type of physics is used for not only cloth, but also for many types of flexible objects such as hair or rope.

Chapter 11: Tools of the Trade

The final chapter of the book looks at a cross-section of tools that are used during game development. If you are just starting out in game development (or just starting out with C#), you may find it useful to check out this chapter before diving into the rest of the book. The first portion of this chapter concentrates on the development environment used to compile and test your software. Other topics covered in the chapter include the manipulation of the artistic content for the game. The artistic content includes the audio files, two-dimensional images, and three-dimensional models.

CHAPTER 1

Overview

THIS BOOK IS WRITTEN FOR people who may or may not have experience with 3D graphics and want to look at the bigger picture of game engine design. This first chapter looks at game engines from a broad perspective. The goal is to provide an overview of game engines that will serve as a foundation for the detailed discussion in the rest of the book. Over the course of the book, we will explore each aspect of game engines and examine the corresponding features in the source code for the example game engine provided with the book (downloadable from the Apress Web site at http://www.apress.com). Each chapter focuses on a major concept or subset of the game engine. Several chapters are dedicated to different types of graphical rendering, since different techniques are employed based on the complexity of the object being rendered.

What Is a Game Engine?

A *game engine* is the very heart of any computer game. Many times the engine is highly coupled to the game and unique to that game. A properly designed engine, however, is modular, reusable, and flexible enough to be used for multiple games that are similar. A game engine is generally designed and optimized for a particular type of game. These types include first-person shooters, real-time strategy games, and vehicle simulations, to name a few of the most popular.

The commercial game engines described here are each highly optimized for their respective games, which were written by teams of highly experienced professionals who spent many man-years developing them. These commercial games must perform well on a wide range of computer hardware. They are written to use either DirectX or OpenGL rendering so that players are free to choose the one that works best for the video card in their system. The commercial software uses advanced methods such as vertex and pixel shaders with proprietary coding in order to provide their respective companies with an edge in the game market.

First-Person Shooter Game Engines

First-person shooter game engines are often based indoors. This places an emphasis on visual detail and animations. Increased visual detail comes at the cost of more textures and increased polygon count across a given game level. To compensate for this (which is necessary to maintain a reasonable frame rate), most of these engines rely on Quadtree, Portal, or Binary Space Partition (BSP) culling. *Culling* is the process of removing polygons from the scene. (More detail on these culling methods appears in Chapter 3.) Examples of this genre include Doom and Quake (in its many versions) from id Software and Half-Life (including the extremely popular Counter-Strike version) from Sierra.

Real-Time Strategy Game Engines

Until recently, real-time strategy games have been two-dimensional, sprite-based games that use a fixed viewpoint and cleverly designed sprites to give the illusion of three dimensions. Newer games such as Empire Earth from Sierra and Age of Mythology from Ensemble Studios have brought this type of game into the 3D environment. Figure 1-1 shows a scene from Age of Mythology.

Figure 1-1. A scene from Age of Mythology

This type of game is generally set outdoors and faces the daunting task of displaying a very large number of objects at one time as well as an expansive terrain. The game engines for these games use an aerial view to reduce the number of objects and the amount of terrain that is within the player's view. These games can also use objects that are somewhat lower in resolution than those we would typically find in a first-person shooter. Since the viewpoint is kept at a fixed distance from the ground, the player doesn't typically get close enough to an object to see the details that would require high-resolution modeling.

Vehicle Simulation Game Engines

The third type of game engine mentioned is the vehicle simulation category. This group includes first-person military combat simulators (planes, helicopters, tanks, etc.), racing games, and other driving games. One example of this type of game is Comanche 4 from NovaLogic.

Since the setting for these games is outdoors and the view angle is relatively unconstrained, special techniques are required to maintain a playable frame rate. These techniques fall primarily in the areas of culling and level of detail (LOD) to reduce the number of polygons that must be textured and drawn. One of the most common methods in outdoor simulation games is to move the far clipping plane nearer to the point of view. This causes any polygons beyond the plane to be culled from the scene. An adverse effect of this is that the player can see objects appearing and disappearing at the far clipping plane as the viewpoint moves. The solution to this problem is the judicious use of fog. Fog or haze allows polygons to fade to the selected fog color as they approach the fog maximum distance (usually at or just short of the far clipping plane). Both LOD and progressive mesh technologies provide a mechanism to reduce the number of polygons in a given object in a controlled manner as a function of range to the viewpoint. LOD techniques replace highly detailed models with less detailed models as they move further from the eye. Progressive mesh, on the other hand, modifies a single mesh based on its range from the eye.

NOTE *Do not confuse game engine design with game design. The game engine is the enabling technology behind the game. Game design needs to take into account many issues that have nothing to do with the game engine. The game engine supports the game by providing the tools the game designer needs to translate a concept or storyline into a game.*

How This Book's Game Engine Project Differs

The purpose of this book is to illustrate all of the basic components of a game engine while demonstrating how to build an example game engine over the course of the book. You may expand the example game engine to create the game of your choice. I have chosen to concentrate on rendering using DirectX 9. If you prefer OpenGL, I leave it to you as a coding exercise to substitute OpenGL API calls in place of the Direct3D API calls. The same basic rendering capabilities are provided by both APIs.

Discussions of the game engine presented in this book will not delve into all of the great things we can do with vertex and pixel shaders. (As a topic, the new High Level Shader Language included in DirectX 9 could fill most of a book itself.) Nor will we explore all of the potential methods of optimizing terrain rendering or character animation.

In developing an example game engine throughout the course of this book, I will concentrate more on an object-oriented, generic approach to game engine design. This game engine is not meant for use in the next blockbuster game to hit the market. Instead, my hope is that, by providing a fundamental, yet flexible game engine, you will learn something new you can use in your own 3D game engine development. This object-oriented approach will produce a modular engine that can be easily modified and extended as you move into more advanced game engine components.

The Object-Oriented Approach

In order to develop a clean, generic design, we will use object-oriented techniques in the design and development of this game engine. Object-oriented design and programming (when done properly) provides a final system that is simple, straightforward, and easy to maintain. I have designated the C# language as the programming language for our game engine, because it provides all of the object-oriented features we desire for this project.

Why C#?

You may be wondering at the choice of the C# language for this game engine. Almost every game in recent history has been developed in C or C++ due to performance considerations. Microsoft has created the C# language in an attempt to bring the rapid application development (RAD) aspect of Visual Basic to the C++ community. As part of the .NET initiative, Microsoft has also increased the performance and object-oriented nature of Visual Basic. Its stated goal for DirectX 9 is to achieve performance values within a couple percent of C++. This makes the choice of using a RAD language very appealing. The point that tips the scales in favor of C# is the fact that C# includes a feature for self-documentation. Developing a game these days is usually a group effort. It is the rare individual who can develop a complete game on his or her own. This makes sharing well-formatted and documented code a high priority. The clean, object-oriented structure available with C#, combined with good commenting and documentation practices, can make the difference in whether or not you meet your schedule.

Starting at the Beginning–Defining a Few Primitives

Before we venture into the working code of this game engine, we will start with a few of the low-level or primitive data structures that we will be using. The C# language has two ways in which data and associated methods may be defined. The first is a structure (struct), which is a value type that is allocated on the stack rather than the managed heap. The structure types do not have the power and flexibility found in the class type, but they are more efficient for small data units such as the primitives that form the foundation of the game engine.

The first primitive is Vector3, a simple structure consisting of three single-precision floating-point variables (X, Y, and Z). This simple structure forms the very foundation of much of the 3D rendering and physical dynamics within the game engine. We will use this type to describe everything from each point in three-dimensional space as well as the speed, acceleration, and forces along each axis for an object. The three-dimensional system that we will use in this game engine is defined with X positive moving to the right of the reference point, Y positive moving up from the reference point, and Z positive moving forward from the reference point. The majority of the code found in this book will use the vector class provided with Microsoft with DirectX. There will be an example in Chapter 10 that employs our own implementation of the class for a dynamics library usable by either DirectX or OpenGL. The C# code to represent this structure is shown in Listing 1-1.

Listing 1-1. Vector3 C# Definition

```
public struct Vector3
{
public float X = 0.0;
public float Y = 0.0;
public float Z = 0.0;
}
```

NOTE   *The units used in this game engine will all be in the English system. All distances will be measured in feet.*

The Vector3 values can be referenced to two basic coordinate systems. The first system is called the *world coordinate system*. This system is centered at a point in the world database chosen by the game author. For the purpose of the game engine developed in this book, the origin of the world coordinate system will be at the southwest corner of the terrain model. With this origin, the X coordinate is positive moving east and the Z coordinate is positive moving north. The other coordinate system is referred to as the *local coordinate system*, or *body coordinate system*. For the terrain model, there is no difference between the two systems. For every other object, the local coordinate system is used in the definitions of the vertices that make up the object. As you will see in Chapter 3, both of these coordinate systems will be transformed to screen coordinates (two-dimensional coordinates) in order to draw properly on the screen.

The second primitive, `Attitude`, is a variation on `Vector3` that describes the rotation around each of these axes. You will often see these referred to as *Euler angles*. For the sake of efficiency, all angles (rotations) are stored in radians. This is the format required by trigonometric math functions. If we use degrees in developing our game engine, it might be a bit more understandable to us as programmers, but not worth the computational cost required to convert each angle every time we build a transformation matrix.

There are a few terms related to the Attitude primitive you need to know before we move on. *Pitch* is the rotation around the X-axis with positive values in the clockwise direction when looking from the origin. *Yaw* is the rotation around the Y-axis with positive values in the counterclockwise direction when looking from the origin. *Roll* is the rotation around the Z-axis with positive values in the clockwise direction. It may seem strange that yaw angles are defined a bit differently from the other two. This is done in order to match up with compass heading angles. As you may know, the compass is defined with zero degrees as north, with angles increasing in the clockwise direction. In our system, that would only be true while looking toward the axis origin. Since all of our rotations are defined as looking along the given axis from the origin, we must rotate in the opposite direction for yaw to match compass angles. The C# code to represent this structure is shown in Listing 1-2.

Listing 1-2. Attitude C# Definition

```
public struct Attitude
{
 public float Pitch = 0.0;
 public float Yaw = 0.0;
 public float Roll = 0.0;
}
```

The third and last primitive that I will define for now is `Vertex`. This structure is an extension of the `Vector3` structure that includes information used in texture mapping. A *vertex* defines a point in three-dimensional space that is part of a definition of a three-dimensional object. You will see later that a *mesh* (3D lingo for the data describing a three-dimensional shape) is made up of a list of vertices with additional information about how they are connected and the textures that cover them. The first component in the structure is a `Vector3` component called `Point` that holds the position in three-dimensional space for the vertex. The next two components (TU and TV) are the two-dimensional coordinates within a texture map that corresponds to a particular vertex's position within the texture map. The texture map is simply a bitmap that describes how the pixels at and between vertices will be rendered. If any of this seems confusing, rest assured that we will discuss this in much greater detail in Chapter 3 as we look at the rendering pipeline. We will not need to develop these vertex structures ourselves though. Microsoft has kindly provided all of the basic vertex structures for us in managed DirectX. The C# code to represent this structure is shown in Listing 1-3.

Listing 1-3. Vertex C# Definition

```
public struct Vertex
{
 public Vector3 Point;
 public Vector3 Normal;
 public Color Diffuse;
 public Color Specular;
 public float TU = 0.0;
 public float TV = 0.0;
}
```

This is the first and most basic version of the `Vertex` structure. Later in the book, you will encounter more complex versions of this structure tailored for specific purposes. These other versions will support features such as multi-texturing as well as nontextured surfaces.

Interfaces: The Integration Contract

As I said earlier, this will be an object-oriented game engine. Traditionally in C++, multiple inheritance would be used to provide a collection of predefined behaviors for the various classes within the engine.

While this is a powerful technique, it does have its dangers. If a class inherits from two base classes that define attributes or methods with the same name, there would be a problem. The duplicated names would "collide" and produce a compiler error. The C# language addresses this problem by not allowing multiple inheritance. C# classes are allowed to inherit from only a single base class. To provide the benefits of multiple inheritance without the dangers, C# uses a mechanism called an *interface*. If you are familiar with C++, you can think of an interface as a pure virtual or abstract base class. A C# interface may define methods and properties but does not include the implementation of either. A C# class may inherit from as many interfaces as it needs. It is the responsibility of the inheriting class to implement each method and property defined by the interfaces it inherits. If it fails to provide a method or property defined in an inherited interface, the compiler will flag an error.

Class instances may be queried at run time to determine if they support a given interface. This allows us to have a collection of objects of different types, iterate through the collection, and call interface methods of those objects that support the interface. Since each class provides its own implementation for the interface methods, it is free to provide an implementation that is unique and appropriate for that class. As an example, let's look at two classes that implement an interface called IRenderable declaring a method called Render. This interface will be discussed in detail shortly. For now, accept that a class uses this method in order to draw the object to the screen appropriately for the current view.

For this example, we will assume that one object is a billboard made from two triangles to represent a tree and that the other object is the terrain model, with hundreds of thousands of triangles for an entire outdoors game. It is easy to see how the requirements and implementation of this method must be different for these two classes. The billboard needs only to draw the two triangles oriented toward the point of view and textured to look like a tree. The terrain class, on the other hand, must first determine which triangles are visible (no current hardware can render a world of this size in real time for every frame), transform the vertices for the texture appropriately for the current view, and draw and texture.

Let's look at a view of the more important interfaces that we will use in this game engine. We will get into various implementations of these interfaces as we progress through the book. The code for these interfaces is shown in Listing 1-4, which appears later in this section.

The first interface is the IRenderable interface mentioned previously. A class that implements this interface is able to render an image of itself to the screen using the Render method. The argument of this method is the camera definition that defines the current view. This is all the information any class implementing this interface requires to render itself.

The second interface, ICullable, is implemented by any class that may not always be rendered to the display. This interface defines two properties. The properties manage the cull state of the object (whether the object should be rendered or not). The first property defined is Culled, which is responsible for clearing the cull state flag to the not culled state. The second property is defined as a read-only Boolean variable that is read with a Get method, IsCulled. It is important for game efficiency that any graphical object support this interface. As mentioned earlier when discussing terrain, the number of triangles in an object would overload the video card if not reduced to only the visible subset.

The next interface is the ICollidable interface. Any class whose object might physically collide with another object should support this interface. The properties and methods of this interface support the testing for collisions between two objects. The interface specifies several properties that expose the object's geometry in several levels of detail. In order for this interface to work, both objects involved must support the interface. The first property is a Vector3 property called CenterOfMass. This property defines the location of the center of the object in world coordinates. The second property of the object is BoundingRadius. This value defines a sphere around the object—the smallest possible sphere centered on the center of mass that completely encloses the object.

The first method defined by the interface is CollideSphere, which takes an object reference as an argument. This method performs a spherical collision check between the two objects. This is the quickest collision check possible, since it only needs to check the distance between the two objects against the sum of the bounding radii of the two objects. This is a low-fidelity collision check, as it is possible to report a false positive if the two objects are close together without any of the polygonal faces intersecting or coming into contact. If neither of the objects is the player's model, and both are far enough from the viewpoint or otherwise out of view, this might be sufficient. Otherwise, we would normally proceed to using the second method of this interface. This method, CollidePolygon, takes three Vector3 variables as arguments. The method is called for each polygon in one of the models until a collision is detected or all polygons have returned a false Boolean value. As you can see, this is far more computationally expensive. Unfortunately, we must go to this extent if we want 100 percent confidence in the collision test.

The next interface that we will look at is the IDynamic interface. This interface supports any object that moves or changes as time progresses. Only one method is defined for this interface: Update. The only argument to this method is a floating-point variable containing the number of milliseconds since the object was last updated. This uses the method for integration of the position and attitude of the object, the step to the proper frame of an animation, or both. The properties of the interface are related to the physical dynamics, which I will address in detail in Chapter 10.

The final interface that we will discuss for now is ITerrainInfo. Any class that may be queried for information about the terrain implements this interface. This information is vital for any object that moves along or over the surface of the terrain. The first method for this interface is HeightOfTerrain, which returns the Y-axis value of the terrain at the supplied location in meters. By preventing an object from moving below this value, the object stays on the surface rather than dropping through. The second method, HeightAboveTerrain, is an extension of the first method that returns the difference between the Y-axis value passed in as part of the location and the height of the terrain at that point. This method is important for objects that are in flight above the terrain and striving not to collide with the surface. The next method is InLineOfSight, which returns a positive (true) value if there is an unobstructed line of sight between the two points that are supplied as arguments. The final method of the interface, GetSlope, is used by any object (such as a ground vehicle) to match its attitude with that of the slope it is resting upon. As you can see in the code in Listing 1-4, this method accepts the location in question and the heading of the object making the call. The heading allows the method to return an attitude that is rotated to match the object's heading.

Listing 1-4. Interface Definitions

```
public interface IRenderable
{
    void Render(Camera cam);
}

public interface ICullable
{
    bool Culled { set; }
    bool IsCulled { get; }
}

public interface ICollidable
{
    Vector3 CenterOfMass { get; }
    float    BoundingRadius { get; }
    bool CollideSphere ( Object3D other );
    bool CollidePolygon ( Vector3 Point1, Vector3 Point2, Vector3 Point3 );
}

public interface IDynamic
{
    void Update( float DeltaT );
}

public interface ITerrainInfo
{
    float    HeightOfTerrain( Vector3 Position );
    float    HeightAboveTerrain( Vector3 Position );
    bool     InLineOfSight( Vector3 Position1, Vector3 Position2 );
    Attitude GetSlope( Vector3 Position, float Heading );
}
```

Process Flow Overview

Although this is not part of the game engine design, we need to look at the typical game application structure and process flow that will employ the engine to provide a framework for the game engine that we will develop. This process flow is based on observations of numerous commercial computer games. The important thing to remember is that the steps in this flow are not hard-and-set requirements. Do not feel bound to include any steps that do not seem appropriate. The implementation of this process for this book's example game will be a simple state machine.

We will have five states in our game process:

- Developer splash screen

- Game splash screen

- Options

- Game play

- After action review

There will be one or more triggers. Each trigger controls the transition from one state to the next. These triggers will be a keystroke, mouse click, or timer expiration as appropriate for whichever state is current.

Developer Splash Screen

The first thing that a player will see when starting this game will be the developer splash screen. Think of this as analogous to seeing the movie studio logo at the beginning of a movie. It lets the viewer know who created the wonderful media production they are about to enjoy. This splash screen could be either a static image or a short video depending on the preferences (and production capabilities) of the game developer. For the purposes of our sample game engine, we will be treating all game resources as separate files rather than building them into the executable as resources. The game engine has a method called ShowSplash, which takes a string argument holding the path to the image to be displayed. The implementation of this method will be described in Chapter 2 as part of the player interface. The method call will look like this:

```
m_Engine.ShowSplash("devsplash.jpg", 8, new CGameEngine.BackgroundTask(LoadOptions));
```

This splash screen will remain displayed until a state change causes it to be replaced by something else. The ShowSplash method does not include the state change logic to transition to the next state. The primary reason for this is that time spent displaying a splash screen can be put to good use. This is a good time to preload other resources the game will need, rather than have the player wait later. My preference is to spend the time during this splash screen to load configuration and option data. This data includes the video resolution to use in the actual playing portion of the game, special-effect filter values to exclude some flashy special effects that the player's computer might not be able to support, and keyboard key mappings that let the player choose how he or she prefers to control the game.

This configuration data will be loaded using another call to an engine method (LoadOptions). Once the time has expired for the splash screen (say 8 seconds), or the player has pressed a key on the keyboard or clicked a mouse button, the game state will be advanced to the game splash screen state.

Game Splash Screen

After reminding players who developed this wonderful game, it is time for a flashy reminder of just what game they are about to play. This splash screen may actually come in two varieties. The very first time the game is played, we want to set the stage for the player so that they understand the premise for the game. A registry entry could be set after the game has run the first time. If this value is not set, we show an extended introduction. Otherwise, we make a short introduction and proceed directly to the game.

Game development studios with large production budgets tend to provide an extended high-quality video (often with live casts) to present the opening story for the game. Other studios with more modest budgets will produce animated videos developed through the same 3D modeling software used to build the 3D models within the game. Garage developers are typically reduced to displaying one or more static images with text as the introduction to their game. Regardless of the source of the media used, the technology to present the media is the same, the ShowSplash method we use when presenting the developer splash screen.

Usually when a longer opening is being presented, the user is not allowed to terminate the presentation before it has completed. A flag stored with the configuration data may be used to record whether this is the first time the game has been played. If this is not the first time, we could program the game to play a shorter opening or allow early termination into the next state, or both.

As with the first splash screen, we have processing time to spare while the player is enjoying the splash screen. This time can be spent loading additional resources, such as texture bitmaps, 3D model files common to all variations of the game, etc., we will need so that once the player hits the Play button there is no significant delay before the fun starts.

Presenting the Options

In all but the simplest games, we are still not ready for the player to start playing the game. The player will likely want to make a few choices before starting to play. What screen resolutions will the game use? What controls and keystrokes will the player use to control the game? What map, level, or scenario will he or she be playing? Will the player be loading a previously saved game? Will he or she be playing a single player game or connecting with a multiplayer game? The number of options that we give the player will determine the screens required to present the options.

If the game requires more than one option screen (our example game does not), we would require a state for each screen. The details on how each screen is presented will be covered in detail in Chapter 2. We will use several different styles of option screens (button oriented and Windows dialog based) to give us the tools we need to develop our own option screens. The code extract in the "Looking at the C#" section at the end of this chapter shows the control structure used for transitioning through the option screen states.

The most important options are the ones that lead into playing the game itself. Once the play game state is entered, the game engine itself takes center stage to control the play.

Playing the Game

Once the primary game state is entered, the game itself starts. The game loop begins executing as soon as the player enters this state. The game loop consists of the following general steps:

- Process player inputs.

- Calculate automated player actions.

- Update the dynamics for all dynamic models.

- If in multiplayer mode, exchange state information with other players (not included in the sample game engine).

- Render the next frame.

These steps that make up the game loop continue to execute as long as the game is in the play state. The first step works with the control preferences defined through one of the option screens. These preferences map mouse, joystick, or keystroke actions to game control functions, which include movement control, weapons control if applicable, and game state control (save game, exit game, activate game console, etc.).

The second step in the game loop provides a similar control function for any computer-controlled models. By controlling the automated models at the same level of fidelity as the player-controlled model, it provides several positive factors. It simplifies the dynamics software by eliminating duplication of creating two separate versions to support both player-controlled and automated models. The other bonus is the degree of fidelity attained by keeping a level playing field between the player and the automated opponents.

Next, we need to update all of the dynamic models. In other words, everything that should move is moved. Objects that support the IDynamic interface have their Update method called in order to calculate new positions or sequence an animation. Once everything has been updated, we are almost ready to redraw the screen. Before we continue on to the rendering phase, we check to see if this is a multiplayer game. If it is, then we must send the state of any local controller objects out to the other players and accept any updates that have been sent to us.

Now we are finally ready to update the screen. The Render method of each object is called. The order in which we make calls is important for some of the objects. As you will see in Chapter 4, the SkyBox object (if it exists for this game) should always be rendered first so that it appears in the background. User interface and console objects should always be rendered last so that they appear on top of the scene. If any of this seems a bit confusing right now, no need for you to worry. As we build up the game engine during the course of the book, each of these steps will be dealt with in detail.

After everything has been rendered, it is time to make a decision. Is the game over? If not, we branch back to the process player inputs step and continue to iterate the game loop. If the game is over, it is time to proceed to the next state—player scoring.

After Action Review: Player Scoring

After the game play has completed, it is good to sum things up for the player. Depending on the game, this summary could come in one of several forms. For simple games, this might be no more than a display of high scores that gives players an indication how they fared against other players (or themselves on another attempt). If there were automated opponents in the game, it could show how players ranked against the automated opponents. If the game was multiplayer, it could show how each player ranked in that game. In a scenario-based game, we could present the option to restart the game to play the same scenario again. This step is optional, but most good games provide some form of feedback to the player on completion.

Once players indicate through some form of user input that they are finished looking at the scoring page, it is time to change states again. The normal procedure is to set the game state back to the main (or only) option screen. This allows players the opportunity to set up and play another game or exit the game entirely.

Looking at the C# Code

The code in Listing 1-5 is from the application class for the sample game. As you will see, the application inherits from another class called CD3DApplication. This class is based on a class supplied by Microsoft with the DirectX 9 SDK. A handy base class takes care of all the initial bookkeeping required to initialize and terminate DirectX. I have modified the Microsoft version slightly to start in full-screen mode and adapted the processing loop to the one used with the game engine. If you are interested in the details of setting up and tearing down DirectX 9, I encourage you to look at the source code downloadable from the Apress Web site.

Listing 1-5. Sample Application

```
//---------------------------------------------------------------------------
// File: App.cs
//
// Desc: Sample code for Introduction to 3D Game Engine Design
//
//       This sample shows the basic application software that sets up the
//        base application and the process flow.  The application uses a version
//        of the CD3DApplication base class provided with the Microsoft
//        DirectX 9 SDK to perform the standard initialization of DirectX.
//
//        Note: This code uses the D3D Framework helper library.
//
// Copyright (c) 2002 Lynn T. Harrison. All rights reserved.
//---------------------------------------------------------------------------
using System;
using System.Drawing;
using System.Collections;
using Microsoft.DirectX;
```

```
using Microsoft.DirectX.Direct3D;
using Microsoft.DirectX.DirectInput;
using GameEngine;
using GameAI;

namespace SampleGame
{
    /// <summary>
    /// Summary description for GameEngine.
    /// </summary>
    class CGameApplication : GraphicsSample
    {
        #region    // Game State enumeration
        /// <summary>
        /// Each member of this enumeration is one possible state for the
        /// application
        /// </summary>
        ///
        /// <remarks>
        /// DevSplash          - Display the developer splash screen
        /// </remarks>
        /// <remarks>
        /// GameSplash         - Display the game splash screen
        /// </remarks>
        /// <remarks>
        /// OptionsMain        - Display and process the primary options screen
        /// </remarks>
        /// <remarks>
        /// GamePlay           - State to actually play the game
        /// </remarks>
        /// <remarks>
        /// AfterActionReview - Display the results of the game
        /// </remarks>
        public enum GameState
        {
            /// <summary>
            /// Display the developer splash screen
            /// </summary>
            DevSplash,
            /// <summary>
            /// Display the game splash screen
            /// </summary>
            GameSplash,
            /// <summary>
```

```
        /// Display and process the primary options screen
        /// </summary>
        OptionsMain,
        /// <summary>
        /// State to actually play the game
        /// </summary>
        GamePlay,
        /// <summary>
        /// Display the results of the game
        /// </summary>
        AfterActionReview,
    }
#endregion

    #region // Application member variables
    /// <summary>
    /// Current state of the application
    /// </summary>
    private GameState         m_State;
    private static CGameEngine m_Engine = new CGameEngine();
    private GraphicsFont       m_pFont = null;
    private GameEngine.Console m_Console;
    private ArrayList          m_opponents = null;
    private OptionScreen       m_OptionScreen = null;
    private bool               m_bShowStatistics = false;
    private bool               m_bScreenCapture = false;
    private bool               m_bUsingJoystick = true;
    private bool               m_bUsingKeyboard = false;
    private bool               m_bUsingMouse = false;
    private Ownship            m_ownship = null;
    private Cloth              m_flag = null;
    private Jukebox            music = null;
    #endregion

    public static CGameEngine Engine { get { return m_Engine; } }

    /// <summary>
    /// Application constructor. Sets attributes for the app.
    /// </summary>
    public CGameApplication()
    {
        // Initialize the game state for the developer splash screen.
        m_State = GameState.DevSplash;
```

```
    m_pFont = new GraphicsFont( "Aerial", System.Drawing.FontStyle.Bold );
    windowed = false;

    m_opponents = new ArrayList();
}


/// <summary>
/// Called during initial app startup, this function performs all the
/// permanent initialization.
/// </summary>
protected override void OneTimeSceneInitialization()
{
    // Initialize the font's internal textures.
    m_pFont.InitializeDeviceObjects( device );

    // Nothing much to do yet - will be used in later chapters.
    m_Engine.Initialize( this, device );

    CGameEngine.Inputs.MapKeyboardAction(Key.Escape,
        new ButtonAction(Terminate), true);
    CGameEngine.Inputs.MapKeyboardAction(Key.A,
        new ButtonAction(MoveCameraXM), false);
    CGameEngine.Inputs.MapKeyboardAction(Key.W,
        new ButtonAction(MoveCameraZP), false);
    CGameEngine.Inputs.MapKeyboardAction(Key.S,
        new ButtonAction(MoveCameraXP), false);
    CGameEngine.Inputs.MapKeyboardAction(Key.Z,
        new ButtonAction(MoveCameraZM), false);
    CGameEngine.Inputs.MapKeyboardAction(Key.P,
        new ButtonAction(ScreenCapture), true);
    CGameEngine.Inputs.MapMouseAxisAction(0,
        new AxisAction(PointCamera));
    CGameEngine.Inputs.MapMouseAxisAction(1,
        new AxisAction(PitchCamera));

    m_Console = new GameEngine.Console( m_pFont, "console.jpg" );

    GameEngine.Console.AddCommand("QUIT", "Terminate the game",
        new CommandFunction(TerminateCommand));
    GameEngine.Console.AddCommand("STATISTICS",
        "Toggle statistics display",
        new CommandFunction(ToggleStatistics));
```

```
    m_OptionScreen = new OptionScreen( "Options1.jpg" );
    m_OptionScreen.AddButton( 328, 150, "PlayOff.jpg", "PlayOn.jpg",
        "PlayHover.jpg", new ButtonFunction(Play) );
    m_OptionScreen.AddButton( 328, 300, "QuitOff.jpg", "QuitOn.jpg",
        "QuitHover.jpg", new ButtonFunction(Terminate) );
    m_Engine.SetOptionScreen( m_OptionScreen );

    music = new Jukebox();
    music.AddSong("nadine.mp3");
    music.AddSong("ComeOn.mp3");
    music.AddSong("Rock.mp3");
    music.Volume = 0.75f;
    music.Play();
}


/// <summary>
/// Called once per frame, the call is the entry point for all game
/// processing. This function calls the appropriate part of the
/// game engine based on the
/// engine based on the current state.
/// </summary>
protected override void FrameMove()
{
    try
    {
        SelectControls select_form = null;
        // get any player inputs
        m_Engine.GetPlayerInputs();

        // Clear the viewport.
        device.Clear( ClearFlags.Target | ClearFlags.ZBuffer,
            0x00000000, 1.0f, 0 );

        device.BeginScene();

        // Determine what needs to be rendered based on the current game state.
        switch ( m_State )
        {
            case GameState.DevSplash:
                if ( m_Engine.ShowSplash("devsplash.jpg", 8,
                        new BackgroundTask(LoadOptions)) )
                {
                    m_State = GameState.GameSplash;
                }
```

```
                break;
            case GameState.GameSplash:
                if ( m_Engine.ShowSplash("gamesplash.jpg", 8, null) )
                {
                    m_State = GameState.OptionsMain;
                    select_form = new SelectControls();
                    select_form.ShowDialog(this);
                    m_bUsingJoystick = select_form.UseJoystick.Checked;
                    m_bUsingKeyboard = select_form.UseKeyboard.Checked;
                    m_bUsingMouse = select_form.UseMouse.Checked;
                    if ( m_bUsingJoystick )
                        GameEngine.Console.AddLine("Using Joystick");
                    if ( m_bUsingKeyboard )
                        GameEngine.Console.AddLine("Using Keyboard");
                    if ( m_bUsingMouse )
                        GameEngine.Console.AddLine("Using Mouse");
                    m_ownship = (Ownship)Engine.GetObject("car1");
                    m_ownship.UseJoystick = m_bUsingJoystick;
                    m_ownship.UseKeyboard = m_bUsingKeyboard;
                    m_ownship.UseMouse = m_bUsingMouse;
                }
                break;
            case GameState.OptionsMain:
                m_Engine.DoOptions();
                break;
            case GameState.GamePlay:
                m_Engine.GetPlayerInputs();
                m_Engine.DoAI( elapsedTime );
                m_Engine.DoDynamics( elapsedTime );
                m_Engine.DoNetworking( elapsedTime );
                m_Engine.Render();
                break;
            case GameState.AfterActionReview:
                m_Engine.DoAfterActionReview();
                break;
        }

        GameEngine.Console.Render();

        if ( m_ownship != null && m_State == GameState.GamePlay )
        {
            m_pFont.DrawText( 200, 560, Color.FromArgb(255,0,0,0),
                    m_ownship.MPH.ToString() );
```

```
        m_pFont.DrawText( 200, 580, Color.FromArgb(255,0,0,0),
                    m_ownship.ForwardVelocity.ToString() );
        m_pFont.DrawText( 200, 600, Color.FromArgb(255,0,0,0),
                    m_ownship.SidewaysVelocity.ToString() );
    }


    // Output statistics.
    if ( m_bShowStatistics )
    {
        m_pFont.DrawText( 2, 560, Color.FromArgb(255,255,255,0),
            frameStats );
        m_pFont.DrawText( 2, 580, Color.FromArgb(255,255,255,0),
            deviceStats );
    }


    if ( m_bScreenCapture )
    {
      SurfaceLoader.Save("capture.bmp",ImageFileFormat.Bmp,
                device.GetBackBuffer(0,0,BackBufferType.Mono));
        m_bScreenCapture = false;
        GameEngine.Console.AddLine("snapshot taken");
    }
}
catch (DirectXException d3de)
{
    System.Diagnostics.Debug.WriteLine(
                "Error in Sample Game Application FrameMove" );
    System.Diagnostics.Debug.WriteLine(d3de.ErrorString);
}
catch ( Exception e )
{
    System.Diagnostics.Debug.WriteLine(
                "Error in Sample Game Application FrameMove" );
    System.Diagnostics.Debug.WriteLine(e.Message);
}
finally
{
    device.EndScene();
}
}


/// <summary>
/// The main entry point for the application
/// </summary>
```

```
[STAThread]
static void Main(string[] args)
{
   try
   {
      CGameApplication d3dApp = new CGameApplication();
      if (d3dApp.CreateGraphicsSample())
         d3dApp.Run();
   }
   catch (DirectXException d3de)
   {
      System.Diagnostics.Debug.WriteLine(
                  "Error in Sample Game Application" );
      System.Diagnostics.Debug.WriteLine(d3de.ErrorString);
   }
   catch ( Exception e )
   {
      System.Diagnostics.Debug.WriteLine(
                  "Error in Sample Game Application" );
      System.Diagnostics.Debug.WriteLine(e.Message);
   }
}


// Action functions

/// <summary>
/// Action to start playing
/// </summary>
public void Play()
{
   m_State = GameState.GamePlay;
   GameEngine.Console.Reset();
}

/// <summary>
/// Action to terminate the application
/// </summary>
public void Terminate()
{
   m_bTerminate = true;
}
```

```
/// <summary>
/// Screen capture
/// </summary>
public void ScreenCapture()
{
   m_bScreenCapture = true;
}


/// <summary>
/// Version of terminate for use by the console
/// </summary>
/// <param name="sData"></param>
public void TerminateCommand( string sData )
{
   Terminate();
}


/// <summary>
/// Toggle the display of statistics information.
/// </summary>
/// <param name="sData"></param>
public void ToggleStatistics( string sData )
{
   m_bShowStatistics = !m_bShowStatistics;
}


/// <summary>
/// Action to transition to the next game state based on a mapper action
/// </summary>
public void NextState()
{
   if ( m_State < GameState.AfterActionReview )
   {
      m_State++;
   }
   else
   {
      m_State = GameState.OptionsMain;
   }
}
```

```
public void PointCamera( int count )
{
   m_Engine.MoveCamera(0.0f, 0.0f, 0.0f, 0.0f, 0.0f, count);
}

public void PitchCamera( int count )
{
   m_Engine.MoveCamera(0.0f, 0.0f, 0.0f, count * 0.1f, 0.0f, 0.0f);
}

public void MoveCameraXP()
{
   m_Engine.MoveCamera(0.5f, 0.0f, 0.0f, 0.0f, 0.0f, 0.0f);
}

public void MoveCameraXM()
{
   m_Engine.MoveCamera(-0.5f, 0.0f, 0.0f, 0.0f, 0.0f, 0.0f);
}

public void MoveCameraY()
{
   m_Engine.MoveCamera(0.0f, 0.5f, 0.0f, 0.0f, 0.0f, 0.0f);
}

public void MoveCameraZP()
{
   m_Engine.MoveCamera(0.0f, 0.0f, 0.5f, 0.0f, 0.0f, 0.0f);
}

public void MoveCameraZM()
{
   m_Engine.MoveCamera(0.0f, 0.0f, -0.5f, 0.0f, 0.0f, 0.0f);
}

/// <summary>
///
/// </summary>
protected override void RestoreDeviceObjects(System.Object sender,
   System.EventArgs e)
{
   // Set the transform matrices (view and world are updated per frame).
   Matrix matProj;
```

```
        float fAspect = device.PresentationParameters.BackBufferWidth /
                        (float)device.PresentationParameters.BackBufferHeight;
        matProj = Matrix.PerspectiveFovLH( (float)Math.PI/4, fAspect,
                        1.0f, 100.0f );
        device.Transform.Projection = matProj;


        // Set up the default texture states.
        device.TextureState[0].ColorOperation = TextureOperation.Modulate;
        device.TextureState[0].ColorArgument1 = TextureArgument.TextureColor;
        device.TextureState[0].ColorArgument2 = TextureArgument.Diffuse;
        device.TextureState[0].AlphaOperation = TextureOperation.SelectArg1;
        device.TextureState[0].AlphaArgument1 = TextureArgument.TextureColor;
        device.SamplerState[0].MinFilter = TextureFilter.Linear;
        device.SamplerState[0].MagFilter = TextureFilter.Linear;
        device.SamplerState[0].MipFilter = TextureFilter.Linear;
        device.SamplerState[0].AddressU = TextureAddress.Clamp;
        device.SamplerState[0].AddressV = TextureAddress.Clamp;


        device.RenderState.DitherEnable = true;
    }


    /// <summary>
    /// Called when the app is exiting, or the device is being changed, this
    /// function deletes any device-dependent objects.
    /// </summary>
    protected override void DeleteDeviceObjects(System.Object sender,
        System.EventArgs e)
    {
        m_Engine.Dispose();
    }


    public void LoadOptions()
    {
        try
        {
          System.Random rand = new System.Random();
          // Loading of options will happen here.
          m_Engine.SetTerrain(200,200,"heightmap.jpg","sand1.jpg", 10.0f, 0.45f);

            for ( int i=0; i<300; i++ )
            {
                float north = (float)(rand.NextDouble() * 1900.0);
                float east  = (float)(rand.NextDouble() * 1900.0);
```

```
        BillBoard.Add( east, north, 0.0f, "cactus"+i, "cactus.dds",
            1.0f, 1.0f);
    }
    for ( int i=0; i<300; i++ )
    {
        float north = (float)(rand.NextDouble() * 1900.0);
        float east  = (float)(rand.NextDouble() * 1900.0);
        BillBoard.Add( east, north, 0.0f, "tree"+i, "palmtree.dds",
            6.5f, 10.0f);
    }
    GameEngine.Console.AddLine("all trees loaded");

     m_Engine.AddObject( new ParticleGenerator("Spray1", 2000, 2000,
                Color.Yellow, "Particle.bmp",
                new ParticleUpdate(Gravity)));

    double j = 0.0;
    double center_x = 1000.0;
    double center_z = 1000.0;
    double radius = 700.0;
    double width = 20.0;

    m_flag = new Cloth("flag", "flag.jpg", 2, 2, 0.1, 1.0f);
    m_flag.Height = 0.6f;
    m_flag.North = 2.0f;
    m_flag.East = 0.1f;
    Cloth.EastWind = -3.0f;

    for ( double i=0.0; i<360.0; i += 1.5 )
    {
        float north = (float)(center_z +
                Math.Cos(i/180.0*Math.PI) * radius );
        float east  = (float)(center_x +
                Math.Sin(i/180.0*Math.PI) * radius );
        BillBoard.Add( east, north, 0.0f, "redpost"+
                (int)(i*2), "redpost.dds",0.25f, 1.0f);
        j += 5.0;
        if ( j > 360.0 ) j -= 360.0;
    }

    j = 0.0;
    for ( double i=0.5; i<360.0; i += 1.5 )
    {
        float north = (float)(center_z +
                Math.Cos(i/180.0*Math.PI) * (radius+width) );
```

```
    float east   = (float)(center_x +
             Math.Sin(i/180.0*Math.PI) * (radius+width) );
    BillBoard.Add( east, north, 0.0f, "bluepost"+
             (int)(i*2), "bluepost.dds",0.25f, 1.0f);
    j += 5.0;
    if ( j >= 360.0 ) j -= 360.0;
}

m_ownship = new Ownship(this, "car1", "SprintRacer.x",
             new Vector3(0.0f, 0.8f, 0.0f),
              new Attitude(0.0f, (float)Math.PI, 0.0f));
m_ownship.AddChild(m_flag);

SoundEffect.Volume = 0.25f;

m_Engine.AddObject( m_ownship );

m_ownship.North = 298.0f;
m_ownship.East = 1000.0f;
m_Engine.Cam.Attach(m_ownship, new Vector3(0.0f, 0.85f,-4.5f));
m_Engine.Cam.LookAt(m_ownship);
m_ownship.Heading = (float)Math.PI * 1.5f;
m_ownship.SetLOD( 10, 3000.0f );

GameEngine.GameLights headlights =
             GameEngine.GameLights.AddSpotLight(
             new Vector3(0.0f,0.0f,0.0f),
   new Vector3(1.0f,0.0f,1.0f), Color.White, "headlight");
headlights.EffectiveRange = 200.0f;
headlights.Attenuation0 = 1.0f;
headlights.Attenuation1 = 0.0f;
headlights.InnerConeAngle = 1.0f;
headlights.OuterConeAngle = 1.5f;
headlights.PositionOffset = new Vector3(0.0f, 2.0f, 1.0f);
headlights.DirectionOffset = new Vector3(0.0f, 0.00f, 1.0f);
m_ownship.AddChild(headlights);
headlights.Enabled = false;

CGameEngine.FogColor = Color.Beige;
CGameEngine.FogDensity = 0.5f;
CGameEngine.FogEnable = true;
CGameEngine.FogStart = 100.0f;
CGameEngine.FogEnd = 900.0f;
CGameEngine.FogTableMode = FogMode.Linear;
}
```

```
      catch ( Exception e )
      {
         GameEngine.Console.AddLine("Exception");
         GameEngine.Console.AddLine(e.Message);
      }
   }

   public void Gravity( ref Particle Obj, float DeltaT )
   {
      Obj.m_Position   += Obj.m_Velocity * DeltaT;
      Obj.m_Velocity.Y += -9.8f * DeltaT;
      if ( Obj.m_Position.Y < 0.0f ) Obj.m_bActive = false;
   }


   public void OwnshipUpdate( Object3D Obj, float DeltaT )
   {
   }

   public void OpponentUpdate( Object3D Obj, float DeltaT )
   {

      Obj.Height = CGameEngine.Ground.HeightOfTerrain(Obj.Position) +
                 ((Model)Obj).Offset.Y;
   }

   }
}
```

Summary

In this chapter, we have looked at what a game engine is in general. Simply restated, a game engine is the underlying technology used in writing a game. By employing a game engine, the game designers are free to concentrate on the game play and any applicable story lines within the game. The chapter has also presented the basic design of this sample game engine at a high level. We have also looked at how the game application interfaces with some of the higher-level game engine functions for controlling the flow of the game.

CHAPTER 2

User Interface

A GAME WOULD NOT BE ANY FUN if the player had no way to interact with it. Although you are probably dying to get right into the 3D graphics part of the game engine, we are going to spend a little time first on the user interface. This will give us the ability to move around in and manipulate the 3D environment once we begin rendering it.

The user interface can be broken down into two major categories: user input and data display. First we will explore the three primary input methods: keyboard, mouse, and joystick. Some high-end systems are capable of doing limited voice input control, but we will not explore that option, since it really hasn't been a factor in game play to date.

After we look at the way we receive our input from the player, we will examine three ways to present information to the player. Two of these were mention in the last chapter: splash screens and option screens. The third choice, consoles, provides a command interface for the application. While you may not feel the need to give players access to the console for a particular game, you will find a console invaluable during your development process.

The final section of this chapter will illustrate how these new classes are used by the game application. The sample game as it stands when we finish the chapter will be our first executable version. It will display the developer and game splash screen, a simple option screen that responds to mouse option selection, and a functional console that understands three commands.

Getting Keyboard Input

DirectX offers a class dedicated to providing access to user input. This class is called DirectInput. Like all other aspects of DirectX, use of DirectInput is centered on a Device object. The DirectInput device is quite flexible in terms of what it interfaces with. When we create a DirectInput device, we must specify what the device will do. C# has an enumeration called `Microsoft.DirectX.DirectInput.SystemGuid` that is used to specify the device. Luckily, in C#, if we specify that we are using `Microsoft.DirectX.DirectInput`, we can refer to the enumeration by just `SystemGuid`. To create a device capable of communicating with the keyboard, we would use the following line:

```
Device KeyboardDev = new Device( SystemGuid.Keyboard );
```

Once we have created the keyboard device, we must configure the way we need it to operate. This includes telling it how it will cooperate with other applications on the computer as well as what data we want it to provide to us. The first is accomplished by a member function called SetCooperativeLevel. This method takes two arguments: a handle to the main window of our application, and a permissions mask that defines how the device will cooperate with the rest of the computer. The window handle must be provided by the application that is using the game engine. It creates the window, so we know that it can provide the handle. The permissions mask is up to us. It is a combination from the enumeration in Table 2-1.

Table 2-1. Cooperative Level Flags

MICROSOFT.DIRECTX.DIRECTINPUT.COOPERATIVELEVELFLAGS
Background
Exclusive
Foreground
NonExclusive
NoWindowsKey

The Background/Foreground pair is mutually exclusive, as is the Exclusive/NonExclusive pair. The Foreground option specifies that we want data only when our application has the focus (i.e., it is the active application). The Background option means we want every keystroke, all the time. If we specify Exclusive, we are saying that we want priority. It is still possible to lose access to the keyboard if another application gets the focus and wants Exclusive access as well, but that is about the only time this loss can occur. The NoWindowsKey value specifies that we want to ignore the Windows logo key if it exists on the keyboard. If our game is running full screen, then it is important to include the NoWindowsKey flag because that key will cause our application to lose the focus. A typical call to this method would look like this:

```
KeyboardDev.SetCooperativeLevel(m_form, CooperativeLevelFlags..NoWindowsKey |
CooperativeLevelFlags.NonExclusive | CooperativeLevelFlags.Foreground);
```

The next thing to do is specify the data we will be getting back from the device. Again, we will pass an enumeration value to the method. For the keyboard, the call will be

```
KeyboardDev.SetDataFormat(DeviceDataFormat.Keyboard);
```

The DeviceDataFormat enumeration is used by all of the devices created by DirectInput. The keyboard format indicates that we want keyboard information, in this case a reference to the KeyboardState class. This class holds the information about which keys are currently pressed.

The configuration of the keyboard device is now complete. The only thing left to do before we can start getting data from the keyboard is to acquire the device. The Acquire method activates the device as we have configured it. To get the key data requires two steps. First we call the Poll method of the device that causes the device to get the data from the hardware. Now that the device has the data, we simply have to ask for a copy. The following statements copy the byte array from the device into a local copy that we can manipulate:

```
private KeyboardState  m_keydata      = null;
m_keydata = KeyboardDev.GetCurrentKeyboardState();
```

To check the current state of a given button, we index into the byte array and check to see if the most significant bit is set. For example, to check to see if the "A" key is pressed, we would use the following:

```
if ( m_keydata[Key.A]  )
```

When our program is exiting, there is one more piece of business to attend to. We must detach our keyboard device from the hardware. This is accomplished by calling the Unacquire method. The common method for doing this is to place the code within a Dispose method of the class implementing the device. Since C# doesn't treat destructors the same way C++ does, the Dispose method is used to explicitly perform cleanup when we are done with a class. In C# object destructors are called when the garbage collection system determines that it is time to reclaim a particular piece of memory. Since we have no control over when this might be, it is preferable to use Dispose from the IDisposable interface.

Getting Mouse Input

Getting input from the mouse is a lot like communicating with the keyboard. DirectInput is very consistent between the two. The same process is used in creating the device; we just specify the mouse in the enumerations rather than the keyboard. The code to create the device looks like this:

```
MouseDev = new Device( SystemGuid.Mouse );
MouseDev.SetCooperativeLevel(m_form,  CooperativeLevelFlags.Exclusive |
CooperativeLevelFlags.Foreground);
MouseDev.SetDataFormat(DeviceDataFormat.Mouse);
```

The biggest difference with working with the mouse comes with working with the mouse data. Instead of the KeyboardState class representing the possible keyboard key states, we have the MouseState class. This class contains the mouse button states as well as three integers for the X, Y, and Z movement values for the mouse. I know that you might be scratching your head and wondering, "Z! Since when is a mouse three dimensional?" Microsoft has dubbed the scroll wheel that comes on many modern mice as Z. This mouse data structure is declared as follows:

```
MouseState  m_mousedata = new MouseState();
```

Just like with the keyboard, we must call the device's Acquire method to attach the device to the hardware and Poll to read the latest data from the hardware. After polling the mouse device we can get a copy of the data with this line:

```
m_mousedata = MouseDev.CurrentMouseState;
```

The button data works just like the keyboard data. The most significant bit gets set if the button is pressed. Button 0 is the primary button. Although this defaults to the left mouse button, don't assume that will always be the case. It is possible through Windows to designate the right mouse button as the primary button (think left-handed users).

The axis data returned in the mouse data structure represents the number of "counts" that the mouse has moved in each direction since the last time the mouse was polled. Following the usual Microsoft axis definitions, the X value is positive to the right and negative to the left. The Y values are positive forward and negative backward. The Z values are positive as the scroll wheel is spun forward and negative when spun backward. It is important to make sure that we poll the mouse only once per frame. Otherwise we will be wondering why our mouse axis data is always zero. Since the axis data is relative to the last time it was polled, the second poll will almost always return zeros unless the mouse is moving very fast during the polling.

Just like with the keyboard, we must also remember to unacquire the device when we are done with it using the Unacquire method. This informs the operating system that we are done with the device.

Getting Joystick Input

The joystick device is the odd duck of the interfaces. Since a joystick or game controller sitting on one or more joystick ports on a player's system could be any of the vast array of such items available, attaching to a joystick becomes more involved. Before we can create and configure a joystick device, we need to discover what joysticks are available and which of them we want to use. The InputObject class that we use in creating the keyboard and mouse devices also has a method for enumerating all of the joysticks configured on the system. The code to enumerate joysticks looks like Listing 2-1.

Listing 2-1. Joystick Enumeration

```
// Enumerate joysticks in the system.
foreach(DeviceInstance instance in Manager.GetDevices(DeviceClass.GameControl,
      EnumDevicesFlags.AttachedOnly))
{
   // Create the device. Just pick the first one.
   JoystickDev = new Device( instance.InstanceGuid );
   break;
}
```

NOTE *Notice that we are selecting the first joystick found. The alternatives would be to present a list of the joysticks found to the user for selection or to compare the capabilities of the joystick against supplied requirements to locate the best fit.*

The cooperative level and the data format are specified just like they are for the mouse:

```
JoystickDev.SetCooperativeLevel(winHandle, CooperativeLevelFlags.Exclusive |
CooperativeLevelFlags.Foreground);
JoystickDev.SetDataFormat(DeviceDataFormat.Joystick);
```

Two possible data formats are available for the joystick. The first format (Joystick) is the simpler of the two. In this case, simpler is definitely a relative term. This data structure includes 3 axes, rotation around 2 axes, 2 sliders, four point of view (POV) inputs, and 32 buttons! The POV inputs are normally wired to a four-direction control on the top of a joystick. It can be used for changing camera direction or selecting weapons. The second format is geared toward force-feedback devices and adds velocities, accelerations, and forces for each of the axes. Needless to say, we are going to use only the first structure for our example.

The m_joystick variable is an instance of the JoystickState structure associated with the Joystick data format. You will also see that we are capturing the actual number of POV inputs out of the device capabilities structure for future reference.

From here on out, the joystick device works just like the other two. We acquire, poll, and unacquire the device the same way. We access the joystick state information using this line of code:

```
m_joystick = JoystickDev.CurrentJoystickState;
```

Unlike the mouse data, the joystick axis data is an absolute value rather than being relative to the last poll.

A Unified Input Interface

Now that we have the basics down on how to communicate with the input hardware, it is time to put this information into the context of the game engine. The game engine will have a single class that encapsulates the three input devices and provides a single unified interface to the game. This class, which we will call GameInput, will inherit from the IDisposable interface. This interface defines a Dispose method to provide the cleanup function normally programmed into the destructor in C++. The constructor for the class will create all of the input devices and will accept a single argument as mentioned earlier, the handle to the applications window.

Although we could force the game to query GameInput for each keystroke it needs every pass through the game loop, there is a better way: We could use an action map. An *action map* associates a keyboard key or mouse button with a specified function. In every frame which the key or button is pressed (or in the transition of being pressed) the function is called. This makes the input system event based rather than query based, which improves performance. DirectInput comes with built-in action mapping capability. This introductory game engine implements a separate action mapping system in order to demonstrate exactly how action mapping works under the covers. Once you understand the concepts, it is straightforward to use Microsoft's imbedded version if you prefer.

Each entry in the action map consists of an instance of the mapping structure or the axis mapping structure shown in Listing 2-2.

Listing 2-2. Mapping Structures

```
struct Mapping
{
    public int key;
    public ButtonAction action;
    public bool bOnTransition;
}
```

```
struct AxisMapping
{
    public int key;
    public AxisAction action;
}
```

The key is an index into the keyboard state data or the mouse button data to indicate which control the action is mapped against. The first 256 values represent keyboard entries and the next 8 are for mouse buttons. The last 32 values are for joystick buttons. The ButtonAction delegate represents a function that takes no arguments and returns no value. The function will typically perform some action within the game such as moving the protagonist, firing a weapon, or anything else the game developer decides that the player can do. The AxisAction delegate is called once per frame with the data for that axis. The definition of the two delegates is shown here:

```
public delegate void ButtonAction();
public delegate void AxisAction(int nCount);
```

The public methods of the GameInput class are shown in Listing 2-3. I will be providing a brief explanation of the methods in the following pages. If you are interested in the details of the implementation, I refer you to the GameInput.cs source file (available as part of the source code, downloadable from the Apress Web site at http://www.apress.com).

Listing 2-3. GameInput Methods

```
GameInput(System.Windows.Forms.Form form)
void Poll()
bool IsMouseButtonDown( int nButton )
bool IsKeyPressed()
bool IsKeyPressed(Key key)
void MapKeyboardAction( Key key, ButtonAction proc, bool bTransition )
void MapMouseButtonAction( int nButton, ButtonAction proc, bool bTransition )
void MapJoystickButtonAction( int nButton, ButtonAction proc, bool bTransition )
void MapMouseAxisAction( int nAxis, AxisAction proc )
void MapJoystickAxisAction( int nAxis, AxisAction proc )
void UnMapKeyboardAction( Key key )
void UnMapMouseButtonAction( int nButton )
void UnMapJoystickButtonAction( int nButton )
void UnMapMouseAxisAction( int nAxis )
```

```
void UnMapJoystickAxisAction( int nAxis )
void ClearActionMaps()
Point GetMousePoint()
int GetMouseX()
int GetMouseY()
int GetMouseZ()
int GetJoystickX( )
int GetJoystickY( )
int GetJoystickNormalX( )
int GetJoystickNormalY( )
int GetJoystickZ( )
bool GetJoystickButton( int nIndex )
int GetJoystickSlider( int nIndex )
void Dispose()
```

The Poll method is called by the game application once per frame. This method polls each of the hardware devices for input. It then checks each entry in the action map to see if the mapped function needs to be called. If it does, the function is called to respond to the player's action. In the case of the actions for a particular axis, the functions are called every time with the current value for that axis. The code in Listing 2-4 resides in the Poll method to process the action maps.

Listing 2-4. Action Map Processing

```
foreach ( AxisMapping map in m_AxisActionMap )
{
    switch ( map.key )
    {
        case 0:
            map.action(m_mousedata.X);
            break;
        case 1:
            map.action(m_mousedata.Y);
            break;
        case 2:
            map.action(m_mousedata.Z);
            break;
        case 3:
            map.action(m_joystick.X);
            break;
        case 4:
            map.action(m_joystick.X);
            break;
        case 5:
            map.action(m_joystick.X);
```

```
        break;
    }
}
// Only process the action map if the console is not visible.
if ( !GameEngine.Console.IsVisible )
{
    foreach ( Mapping map in m_ActionMap )
    {
        // If this mapping is against the keyboard
        if ( map.key < 256 )
        {
            // take the action if the key is down or transitioning.
            if ( m_keydata[(Key)map.key] )
            {
                if ( !map.bOnTransition || oldkeydata[(Key)map.key] )
                {
                    map.action();
                }
            }
        }
        else if ( map.key < 264 )   // Space for 8 mouse buttons
        {
            if ( (m_mousedata.GetMouseButtons()[map.key-256] & 0x80) != 0 )
            {
                if ( !map.bOnTransition ||
                    (oldmousedata. GetMouseButtons() [map.key-256] & 0x80) == 0 )
                {
                    map.action();
                }
            }
        }
        else  // joystick buttons
        {
            if ( (m_joystick.GetButtons()[map.key-264] & 0x80) != 0 )
            {
                if ( !map.bOnTransition ||
                    (oldjoystickdata.Buttons[map.key-264] & 0x80) == 0 )
                {
                    map.action();
                }
            }
        }
    }
}
```

The `Is` and `Get` methods provide low-level access to the input data. If for some reason the game needs to explicitly check an input rather than use a mapped action, these are the methods that would be used.

Drawing Splash Screens

In the first chapter, I mentioned presenting the player with splash screens that credit the developer of the game and serve as an opening for the game. In a more advanced game or a commercial game, either or both of these could be a static image or a short video. The video aspect of this was handled by the DirectShow component of DirectX in previous versions as well as in the current C++ version of DirectX. This is supported by the `AudioVideo` class in Managed DirectX. The video texture sample provided by Microsoft illustrates how this would be done.

Microsoft refers to a structure in memory that holds an image as either a surface or a texture depending on how the image will be used. If the image is being presented in a two-dimensional fashion on the screen, it is called a *surface*. If all or a portion of the image is being applied to a three-dimensional shape, it is called a *texture*. Our splash screens will use textures to hold the image. To make the textures easier to work with, we will wrap the textures in a new class called Image. This class, like the GameInput class discussed earlier, will inherit the `IDisposable` interface so that we can control when and how the class gets cleaned up. The class will hold three attributes: a string with the name of the file from which the image is loaded, an `ImageInformation` structure that provides information about the image, and the texture itself. The attribute definitions are shown in Listing 2-5.

Listing 2-5. Image Class members

```
private Texture     m_image  = null;
private ImageInformation m_info   = new ImageInformation();
private string      m_sFilename;
```

The constructor for the class has one argument, the filename of the image file. The file can be in a number of formats including bitmap (.bmp), JPEG compressed (.jpg), and DirectDraw Surface (.dds). The third format takes a bit more work to set up, but includes alpha channel information for transparency. For now I recommend using JPEG because files in this format are easy to manipulate in most imaging software and are much smaller. The constructor saves a copy of the filename and calls another method, `Load`, to actually load the image from the file onto the surface. We separate the loading into another method because we may need to reload the image later. The `Load` method, shown in Listing 2-6, does the majority of the work for this class.

Listing 2-6. Image Load Method

```
public void Load()
{
   try
   {
      m_info = new ImageInformation();
      m_info = TextureLoader.ImageInformationFromFile(m_sFilename);
      m_image = TextureLoader.FromFile(CGameEngine.Device3D ,m_sFilename);
   }
   catch (DirectXException d3de)
   {
      Console.AddLine("Unable to load image " + m_sFilename);
      Console.AddLine(d3de.ErrorString);
   }
   catch ( Exception e )
   {
      Console.AddLine("Unable to load image " + m_sFilename);
      Console.AddLine(e.Message);
   }
}
```

The first thing that you will notice is that everything is wrapped within a Try/Catch block. Since there are several ways that this function can fail, it is important to catch the exceptions. The file that we are trying to load might not be there to load or it may not be possible to create the texture due to low memory conditions. Our solution to the errors at this point is to just display an error message on the console. I will describe the console in much greater detail later in this chapter in the "Developing the Console" section.

The first thing the Load method does is to create and load an ImageInformation structure for the file. This will give us the size of the image so that we can create a texture that is the proper size to hold the image. The next step is to create the surface for the image. The TextureLoader class has a method, FromFile, that is used for this purpose.

If everything has worked as expected, we now have our image in a texture ready to be rendered to the screen. This class does not handle the rendering itself. Instead, it has two methods that expose the texture and its size as both a Size and a Rectangle structure. This empowers any class that has instantiations of the Image class to render the image as it sees fit.

Now that we have a class to hold our image, we are ready to build a splash screen. The SplashScreen class will provide the required functionality. Like every other class we have built, it too will inherit from IDisposable. The Dispose method in this class simply calls the Dispose method for the image it will load. The constructor for the splash screen will need two arguments: the name of the image file to display and the number of seconds that the splash screen should be displayed. The filename is passed to the image's constructor to create the splash screen image. The duration in seconds is added to the current system time in seconds to set the ending time for the splash screen. A vertex buffer is also created to hold the points used to draw the image to the screen. This much of the SplashScreen class is shown in Listing 2-7.

Listing 2-7. SplashScreen Declaration and Constructor

```
public class SplashScreen : IDisposable
{
    private Image image = null;
    private float m_StartTime;
    private float m_EndTime = 0.0f;
    private VertexBuffer m_vb;
    public bool m_bInitialized = false;
    public float fTimeLeft;

    public SplashScreen( string filename, int nDuration)
    {
        image = new Image( filename );
        m_StartTime = DXUtil.Timer( TIMER.GETABSOLUTETIME );
        m_EndTime = m_StartTime + nDuration;
        m_ vb = new VertexBuffer( typeof(CustomVertex.TransformedTextured), 4,
            CGameEngine.Device3D, Usage.WriteOnly,
            CustomVertex.TransformedTextured.Format,
            Pool.Default );
    }
```

The other major method in this class is the Render method. This is where the splash screen actually gets drawn on the system's screen for the player to see. The method returns false if the splash screen has not timed out yet and true if it has. The first step in rendering the splash screen is to create an array of transformed vertices at the four corners of the screen. Each vertex will include the texture coordinate information for placing the texture on the screen. Once the data structure has been populated, the data is copied into the vertex buffer.

NOTE   *The vertex buffer typically resides in the video card's memory to improve rendering speed.*

Once the vertex data is in the buffer, we need to set up the rendering device to draw the image to the screen. The first step is to capture the current fog state and then turn off fogging. We don't want the fogging to affect the splash screen. We then set our vertex buffer as the current stream source and let the device know the format of the data within the stream. We also need to set the current texture to the one held within the splash screen image. The actual rendering takes place when we command the device to render a strip of two triangles to the screen using the data in the vertex buffer.

After rendering, the only thing left to do is to check the time to see if the splash screen has timed out. The code for all of this appears in Listing 2-8.

Listing 2-8. SplashScreen Render Method

```
public bool Render()
{
    try
    {
        bool fog_state = CgameEngine.Device3D.RenderState.FogEnable;
        CgameEngine.Device3D.RenderState.FogEnable = false;
        CustomVertex.TransformedTextured[] data =
            new CustomVertex.TransformedTextured[4];
        data[0].X =    0.0f;
        data[0].Y =    0.0f;
        data[0].Z =    0.0f;
        data[0].Tu =   0.0f;
        data[0].Tv =   0.0f;
        data[1].X =  CGameEngine.Device3D.Viewport.Width;
        data[1].Y =    0.0f;
        data[1].Z =    0.0f;
        data[1].Tu =   1.0f;
        data[1].Tv =   0.0f;
        data[2].X =    0.0f;
        data[2].Y =  CGameEngine.Device3D.Viewport.Height;
        data[2].Z =    0.0f;
        data[2].Tu =   0.0f;
        data[2].Tv =   1.0f;
        data[3].X =  CGameEngine.Device3D.Viewport.Width;
        data[3].Y =  CGameEngine.Device3D.Viewport.Height;
        data[3].Z =    0.0f;
        data[3].Tu =   1.0f;
        data[3].Tv =   1.0f;

        m_vb.SetData(data, 0, 0);
```

```
            CGameEngine.Device3D.SetStreamSource( 0, m_vb, 0 );
            CGameEngine.Device3D.VertexFormat =
                CustomVertex.TransformedTextured.Format;

            // Set the texture.
            CGameEngine.Device3D.SetTexture(0, image.GetTexture() );

            // Render the face.
            CGameEngine.Device3D.DrawPrimitive( PrimitiveType.TriangleStrip, 0, 2 );
            CgameEngine.Device3D.RenderState.FogEnable = fog_state;
        }
        catch (DirectXException d3de)
        {
            Console.AddLine( "Unable to display SplashScreen " );
            Console.AddLine( d3de.ErrorString );
        }
        catch ( Exception e )
        {
            Console.AddLine( "Unable to display SplashScreen " );
            Console.AddLine( e.Message );
        }

        // Check for timeout.
        float fCurrentTime = DXUtil.Timer( TIMER.GETABSOLUTETIME );

        return ( fCurrentTime > m_EndTime );
    }
```

Drawing Option Screens

The next user interface component to address is the option screen. Depending on the complexity of a game, it is possible to have multiple option screens that are accessed from a primary option screen. This is where players determine what kind of game they wish to play or if they want to exit from the game. The requirements for the option screens will drive the complexity of the controls used on the screens anywhere from simple buttons all the way up to controls reminiscent of MFC dialog boxes.

Building Blocks for the Option Screen

For our initial option screen, we will use a button-style interface. To support this, we will define a small class called ImageButton that will hold our button data.

To add a little flash to our buttons, we will define them as having three possible states: Off, Hover, and On. The Off state will have a basic image of the button. The Hover state will show the button highlighted and will be displayed whenever the mouse cursor is over the button. This helps reinforce for players that they are pointing at a button. The On state can be used for items that they can toggle on and off (e.g., an image with a checked check box). We also need to indicate where on the screen the button should be displayed and potentially a method that should be called when the button is selected.

The declaration of the ImageButton class shown in Listing 2-9 takes these requirements into account.

Listing 2-9. ImageButton Declaration

```
public delegate void ButtonFunction( );

public class ImageButton : IDisposable
{
    private int                 m_X             = 0
    private int                 m_Y             = 0;
    private Image               m_OffImage      = null;
    private Image               m_OnImage       = null;
    private Image               m_HoverImage    = null;
    private bool                m_bOn           = false;
    private bool                m_bHoverOn      = false;
    private ButtonFunction      m_Function      = null;
    private Rectangle           m_Rect;
    private VertexBuffer        m_vb =          null;
    private CustomVertex.TransformedTextured[] data;
```

The Rectangle value within the class holds the size of the button. One assumption that is made about the three images of the button is that all three are the same size. If we mistakenly initialize the class with different-size images, we will have problems that range from only portions of the image being drawn to assertions generated because we are trying to draw a rectangle that is bigger than the image.

NOTE *I recommend that you develop the image for the Off button and then use it as the basis for creating the artwork for the other two.*

The constructor for the ImageButton class is a little more involved than the other classes we have dealt with so far. This constructor needs six arguments: the

X and Y values for positioning the button on the screen, the filenames for the three images, and the delegate function to be called when the button is selected. In code that should look familiar from the SplashScreen class, we also create a vertex buffer with data to draw the button on the screen as a textured rectangle (see Listing 2-10).

Listing 2-10. ImageButton Constructor

```
public ImageButton(int nX, int nY, string sOffFilename, string sOnFilename ,
      string sHoverFilename, ButtonFunction pFunc )
{
   m_X = nX;
   m_Y = nY;
   m_OffImage   = new Image( sOffFilename );
   m_OnImage    = new Image( sOnFilename );
   m_HoverImage = new Image( sHoverFilename );
   m_Rect       = m_OffImage.GetRect();
   m_Rect.X += m_X;
   m_Rect.Y += m_Y;
   m_Function   = pFunc;
   m_vb = new VertexBuffer( typeof(CustomVertex.TransformedTextured), 4,
      CGameEngine.Device3D, Usage.WriteOnly,
      CustomVertex.TransformedTextured.Format, Pool.Default );
}
```

The Render and Dispose methods are shown in Listing 2-11. The Render method works very much like the method used in the splash and option screens. The difference is in the coordinates used in setting up the vertex buffer. Instead of filling the screen, the two triangles that form the button fill the rectangle position assigned to the button. The Dispose method simply calls the Dispose method for each of the button images.

Listing 2-11. ImageButton Render and Dispose Methods

```
      public void Render()
      {
        try
        {
            data = new CustomVertex.TransformedTextured[4];
            data[0].X =    (float)m_Rect.X;
            data[0].Y =    (float)m_Rect.Y;
            data[0].Z =    1.0f;
```

```
     data[0].Tu =    0.0f;
     data[0].Tv =    0.0f;
     data[1].X =  (float)(m_Rect.X+m_Rect.Width);
     data[1].Y =    (float)m_Rect.Y;
     data[1].Z =    1.0f;
     data[1].Tu =   1.0f;
     data[1].Tv =   0.0f;
     data[2].X =    (float)m_Rect.X;
     data[2].Y =  (float)(m_Rect.Y+m_Rect.Height);
     data[2].Z =    1.0f;
     data[2].Tu =   0.0f;
     data[2].Tv =   1.0f;
     data[3].X =  (float)(m_Rect.X+m_Rect.Width);
     data[3].Y =  (float)(m_Rect.Y+m_Rect.Height);
     data[3].Z =    1.0f;
     data[3].Tu =   1.0f;
     data[3].Tv =   1.0f;

     m_vb.SetData(data, 0, 0);

     CGameEngine.Device3D.SetStreamSource( 0, m_vb, 0 );
     CGameEngine.Device3D.VertexFormat =
        CustomVertex.TransformedTextured.Format;

     // Set the texture.
     CGameEngine.Device3D.SetTexture(0, GetTexture() );

     // Render the face.
     CGameEngine.Device3D.DrawPrimitives(
        PrimitiveType.TriangleStrip, 0, 2 );
  }
  catch (DirectXException d3de)
  {
     Console.AddLine( "Unable to display imagebutton " );
     Console.AddLine( d3de.ErrorString );
  }
  catch ( Exception e )
  {
     Console.AddLine( "Unable to display imagebutton " );
     Console.AddLine( e.Message );
  }
}
```

```
    public void Dispose()
    {
        m_OffImage.Dispose();
        m_OnImage.Dispose();
        m_HoverImage.Dispose();
    }
```

Other classes that are rendering the buttons use the remaining methods in the class. The GetTexture method, shown in Listing 2-12, returns the correct image surface depending on the current hover and activation state of the button.

Listing 2-12. ImageButton GetTexture Method

```
public Surface GetTexture()
{
    if ( m_bHoverOn )
    {
        return m_HoverImage. GetTexture ();
    }
    else if ( m_bOn )
    {
        return m_OnImage. GetTexture ();
    }
    else  {
        return m_OffImage. GetTexture ();
    }
}
```

The GetDestRect and GetSrcRect methods get the destination and source rectangles for the button. The two rectangles are the same size with the destination rectangle offset by the position of the button on the option screen. We also need a GetPoint method so that the rendering class knows where to put the button on the screen (see Listing 2-13).

Listing 2-13. ImageButton Size and Position Properties

```
public Rect GetDestRect() { return m_Rect; }
public Rect GetSrcRect() { return m_OffImage.GetRect(); }
public Point GetPoint() { return new Point(m_X, m_Y); }
```

The last three methods in the class are used in the interaction of the button with the mouse. The first is a private method that checks to see if a supplied position is within the button rectangle. The next method sets the hover state for the button based on whether the supplied position is over the button. The last of the ImageButton methods process mouse button clicks on the button. The calling class calls the ClickTest method if the primary mouse button has been clicked. The current mouse position is checked to see if it is within the area of the button. If so, the state of the button is toggled. Finally, if the button is currently on and a function has been supplied for the button, the function is invoked. The code for these functions is shown in Listing 2-14.

Listing 2-14. ImageButton Hit Test Methods

```
private bool InRect( Point p )
{
    return m_Rect.Contains( p );
}
public void HoverTest( Point p )
{
    m_bHoverOn = InRect( p );
}
public void ClickTest( Point p )
{
    if ( InRect( p )  ) m_bOn = !m_bOn;
    if ( m_bOn && m_Function != null ) m_Function();
}
```

Now that we have our ImageButton class for rendering our buttons, it is time to build the option screen itself. The option screen will consist of a background image, an array of buttons that will appear on the screen, and a mouse cursor that will be controlled by mouse movement. The declaration of the OptionScreen class appears in Listing 2-15.

Listing 2-15. OptionScreen Declaration

```
public class OptionScreen
{
#region Attributes
    private Image      m_Background      = null;
    private Image      m_Cursor          = null;
    public  bool       m_bInitialized    = false;
    private ArrayList  m_buttons         = new ArrayList();
    private Point      m_MousePoint      = new Point(0,0);
```

```
    private bool           m_bMouseIsDown     = false;
    private bool           m_bMouseWasDown    = false;
    private VertexBuffer m_vb;
#endregion
```

Designing the OptionScreen Class

The constructor for the option screen will require a single argument: the name
of the file containing the background image for the screen. The constructor will
load the background image and the image for the mouse cursor. The mouse
cursor will use the DDS format since that format can include transparency information. The final step is to create the vertex buffer to be used in rendering the
screen. Listing 2-16 shows the constructor for the option screen.

Listing 2-16. OptionScreen Constructor

```
public OptionScreen( string filename)
{
    try
    {
        m_Background = new Image( filename );
        m_Cursor = new Image("Cursor.dds");
        m_vb = new VertexBuffer( typeof(CustomVertex.TransformedTextured), 4,
               CGameEngine.Device3D, Usage.WriteOnly,
               CustomVertex.TransformedTextured.Format, Pool.Default );
    }
    catch (DirectXException d3de)
    {
        Console.AddLine("Error creating Option Screen " + filename );
        Console.AddLine( d3de.ErrorString );
    }
    catch ( Exception e )
    {
        Console.AddLine("Error creating Option Screen " + filename );
        Console.AddLine( e.Message );
    }
}
```

Now we have the basic option screen, but it doesn't do much for us without
any controls on it. We need a method that allows the game application to add

buttons to the option page. This will be our AddButton method, which will take all of the same arguments as the ImageButton constructor. It will create a new ImageButton and add it to the list of buttons for the option screen as shown in Listing 2-17.

Listing 2-17. OptionScreen AddButton Method

```
public void AddButton(int nX, int nY, string sOffFilename, string sOnFilename ,
    string sHoverFilename, ImageButton.ButtonFunction pFunc )
{
    ImageButton button = new ImageButton( nX, nY, sOffFilename, sOnFilename,
    sHoverFilename, pFunc );

    m_buttons.Add(button);
}
```

We will need another helper method that will be called each frame prior to rendering the option screen. The SetMousePosition method will be used to update the position of the screen's mouse cursor and the primary button status. This is illustrated in Listing 2-18.

Listing 2-18. OptionScreen SetMousePosition Method

```
public void SetMousePosition( int x, int y, bool bDown )
{
    m_MousePoint.X = x;
    m_MousePoint.Y = y;
    m_bMouseIsDown = bDown;
}
```

After creating the option screen and adding some buttons, we are ready to start rendering the screen. Just as in the splash screen, we need to capture the current fog state and disable fogging so that it does not affect the option screen or its buttons. This routine gets a bit involved, so we're going to step through this one a bit at a time. The routine begins by creating and filling an array of vertices for the rectangle used to render the background. The data is then used to render the background image using code similar to that used for the splash screens, as shown in Listing 2-19.

Listing 2-19. OptionScreen Render Method

```
public void Render()
{
    try
    {
        bool fog_state = CgameEngine.Device3D.RenderState.FogEnable;
        CgameEngine.Device3D.RenderState.FogEnable = false;
        CustomVertex.TransformedTextured[] data =
                    new CustomVertex.TransformedTextured[4];
        data[0].X =    0.0f;
        data[0].Y =    0.0f;
        data[0].Z =    0.0f;
        data[0].Tu =   0.0f;
        data[0].Tv =   0.0f;
        data[1].X =   CGameEngine.Device3D.Viewport.Width;
        data[1].Y =    0.0f;
        data[1].Z =    0.0f;
        data[1].Tu =   1.0f;
        data[1].Tv =   0.0f;
        data[2].X =    0.0f;
        data[2].Y =   CGameEngine.Device3D.Viewport.Height;
        data[2].Z =    0.0f;
        data[2].Tu =   0.0f;
        data[2].Tv =   1.0f;
        data[3].X =   CGameEngine.Device3D.Viewport.Width;
        data[3].Y =   CGameEngine.Device3D.Viewport.Height;
        data[3].Z =    0.0f;
        data[3].Tu =   1.0f;
        data[3].Tv =   1.0f;

        m_vb.SetData(data, 0, 0);

        CGameEngine.Device3D.SetStreamSource( 0, m_vb, 0 );
        CGameEngine.Device3D.VertexFormat =
                        CustomVertex.TransformedTextured.Format;

        // Set the texture.
        CGameEngine.Device3D.SetTexture(0, m_Background.GetTexture() );

        // Render the screen background.
        CGameEngine.Device3D.DrawPrimitive( PrimitiveType.TriangleStrip, 0, 2 );
```

Now that the background has been rendered, it is time to add the buttons. We will loop through the array of buttons. Before we render the button image onto the screen, we will call the button's HoverTest method with the current mouse position so that the button can determine if it needs to display the hover state image. Then if the primary mouse button is down, and the mouse button was not down last time, we will call the button's ClickTest method so that it may determine if the player has clicked the button and react accordingly. Finally, we have the button render itself to the screen. This code is shown in Listing 2-20a.

Listing 2-20a. OptionScreen Render Method

```
// Copy on the buttons.
    foreach ( ImageButton button in m_buttons )
    {
        button.HoverTest( m_MousePoint );
        if ( m_bMouseIsDown && !m_bMouseWasDown )
        {
            button.ClickTest( m_MousePoint );
        }
        button.Render();
    }
}
```

After we have repeated this procedure for each button in the array, we save the status of the mouse button down flag for use on the next pass.

```
        m_bMouseWasDown = m_bMouseIsDown;
```

Now that all of the buttons have been rendered, it is time to render the image of our mouse cursor. We do this last, of course, so that the mouse cursor appears to move on top of the buttons. The procedure for rendering the mouse cursor follows the same pattern we just saw with the buttons and is shown in Listing 2-20b. The biggest difference between this code and that used for the buttons is the requirement for portions of the cursor to be transparent. We want the cursor to look like an arrow. To accomplish this, I created the texture image using Microsoft Paint and the Microsoft Texture Tool to include an alpha channel defining the opaque and transparent portions of the image. As you will see in the listing, there are several device settings that control alpha transparency. Once we have finished rendering, we restore the fog state to its previous value.

Listing 2-20b. OptionScreen Render Method (Continued)

```
// Draw cursor.
Rectangle mouserect = new Rectangle(m_MousePoint,m_Cursor.GetSize());
try
{
    data[0].X =     (float)mouserect.X;
    data[0].Y =     (float)mouserect.Y;
    data[0].Z =    0.0f;
    data[0].Tu =   0.0f;
    data[0].Tv =   0.0f;
    data[1].X =  (float)(mouserect.X+mouserect.Width);
    data[1].Y =     (float)mouserect.Y;
    data[1].Z =    0.0f;
    data[1].Tu =   1.0f;
    data[1].Tv =   0.0f;
    data[2].X =     (float)mouserect.X;
    data[2].Y =  (float)(mouserect.Y+mouserect.Height);
    data[2].Z =    0.0f;
    data[2].Tu =   0.0f;
    data[2].Tv =   1.0f;
    data[3].X =  (float)(mouserect.X+mouserect.Width);
    data[3].Y =  (float)(mouserect.Y+mouserect.Height);
    data[3].Z =    0.0f;
    data[3].Tu =   1.0f;
    data[3].Tv =   1.0f;

    m_vb.SetData(data, 0, 0);

    CGameEngine.Device3D.SetStreamSource( 0, m_vb, 0 );
    CGameEngine.Device3D.VertexFormat = CustomVertex.TransformedTextured.Format;

    // Set the texture.
    CGameEngine.Device3D.SetTexture(0, m_Cursor.GetTexture() );

    // Set diffuse blending for alpha set in vertices.
    CGameEngine.Device3D.RenderState.AlphaBlendEnable = true;
    CGameEngine.Device3D.RenderState.SourceBlend = Blend.SourceAlpha;
    CGameEngine.Device3D.RenderState.DestinationBlend = Blend.InvSourceAlpha;

    // Enable alpha testing (skip pixels with less than a certain alpha).
    if( CGameEngine.Device3D.DeviceCaps.AlphaCompareCaps.GreaterEqual )
    {
        CGameEngine.Device3D.RenderState.AlphaTestEnable = true;
        CGameEngine.Device3D.RenderState.ReferenceAlpha = 0x08;
```

```
        CGameEngine.Device3D.RenderState.AlphaFunction = Compare.GreaterEqual;
    }
    // Render the face.
    CGameEngine.Device3D.DrawPrimitive( PrimitiveType.TriangleStrip, 0, 2 );
}
catch (DirectXException d3de)
{
    Console.AddLine( "Unable to display cursor " );
    Console.AddLine( d3de.ErrorString );
}
catch ( Exception e )
{
    Console.AddLine( "Unable to display cursor " );
    Console.AddLine( e.Message );
}
CgameEngine.Device3D.RenderState.FogEnable = fog_state;
}
```

Like any of our code that has a possibility of failure, we have wrapped the rendering code within a Try block. The corresponding Catch block posts a message to the console and continues on. This allows our code to "soft fail" by noting the problem and continuing on (see Listing 2-20c).

Listing 2-20c. OptionScreen Render Method (Conclusion)

```
    catch (DirectXException d3de)
    {
        Console.AddLine( "Error rendering Option Screen" );
        Console.AddLine( d3de.ErrorString );
    }
    catch ( Exception e )
    {
        Console.AddLine( "Error rendering Option Screen" );
        Console.AddLine( e.Message );
    }
```

That concludes our definition of the OptionScreen class. The last section of this chapter will show how our game engine controls the SplashScreen and OptionScreen classes.

Developing the Console

I have referred numerous times to the console for the game. Consoles became popular in recent years through games like Quake and Half-Life that exposed the console to the players. Even if you do not wish your players to have access to a console in your games, you should include a console for your own use. Consoles provide a powerful tool during the development of a game. With a console, we have the ability to display process flow information and statistics from the game to the screen in a logical and controlled manner. We can tweak the game by setting variables on the fly and see immediately what the effect is on game play. If at release time we decide that the player should not have access to the console, we simply unmap the command that displays the console.

The console will be defined as a static class. We want only one console to exist, and we want it existing through the entire game. You've seen in some of the earlier code examples that the console is the place we post any exception data to. By making the console static, we can access the console from anywhere in the game engine without having to get access to a specific instance of the console class.

To access the console, we will map a function that toggles console visibility to the F12 key on the keyboard. You could select any key on the keyboard, but for this example I chose the F12 key because it is common to every modern keyboard, and it is not likely that it will need to be mapped to any other function.

Defining Console Components

Before we get into the design of the console itself, we need to define a class to hold command information for us. For the console to be more than a glorified list box, we need it to be able to accept and execute commands. The GameCommand class will hold the required information for each command. Remember that console commands are not limited to the needs of the game engine itself. Any game that is employing the game engine will need to add their commands. The GameCommand class will need to hold three pieces of information: the command string itself, a help string for the command that explains the use and syntax of the command, and a delegate of the function to be called when the command is entered. Every command processed by the console will accept a string as its only argument. That way the console can be consistent by passing the text following the command to the command's function (even in the case where the string is null because there was no text after the command). Two read-only properties provide external access to the command and help strings. The code for the class declaration is shown in Listing 2-21.

Listing 2-21. GameCommand Declaration

```
public class GameCommand
{
    public delegate void CommandFunction( string sData );

    private string          m_sCommand = null;
    private string          m_sHelp    = null;
    private CommandFunction m_Function = null;
```

```
public string Command { get { return m_sCommand; } }
public string Help { get { return m_sHelp; } }
```

The constructor for a GameCommand (shown in Listing 2-22) will simply accept the three required pieces of information and copy them into its private members.

Listing 2-22. GameCommand Constructor

```
public GameCommand(string sCmd, string sHelp, CommandFunction pFunc )
{
    m_sCommand = sCmd;
    m_sHelp = sHelp;
    m_Function = pFunc;
}
```

The class will have an Execute method that the console will call when it recognizes that this command has been invoked. The argument for the method is the remainder of the entered command string after the command has been extracted. Before calling the function, we will verify that the developer has indeed provided a method delegate. If so, we call the method and give it a string of data. It is the function's responsibility to parse the string to get the information that it expects. See Listing 2-23 for the C# implementation.

Listing 2-23. GameCommand Execute Method

```
public void Execute( string sData )
{
    if ( m_Function != null )
    {
        m_Function( sData );
    }
}
```

Now that we have defined how we will handle the console commands, it is time to create the console itself. The console will have an image as the background for the text. This will not only make the console look better, but serves the purpose of ensuring good contrast between the console text and the image behind it. The image for the console therefore should be quite dark, since we are using a light color for our text. Any variations in the background color should be kept over to the right side of the console, because text will rarely extend all the way across the screen.

We could just pop the console onto the screen when the console is opened and make it disappear when it is closed. Even though this would be the easiest solution, it looks better if the console appears to open onto the screen. For this console, we will have the console appear to slide down from the top of the screen when it opens and slide back up when it closes. The amount of screen that the console covers will also be adjustable. We will set the console to open to half the screen by default and supply the means later to adjust the console size.

Defining the Console Class

The attributes of the Console class are shown in Listing 2-24. You will notice that we are using two different types of container classes for the console. The ArrayList class is a simple dynamic array container that is fine for storing the lines of text that will be displayed on the console. The SortedList class is a little more involved. It stores objects sorted by a key that is associated with each object and can locate the object based on a binary search of the keys. There are two of these SortedList containers, and both will hold instances of the GameCommand class. One set is commands that the console will understand. The other set is parameters that the console will be able to modify. In reality, the parameters will just be more methods that happen to set a variable. Listing 2-24 shows the declaration of the Console class attributes.

Listing 2-24. Console Class Declaration

```
public class Console
{
#region Attributes
    private static bool         m_bVisible = false;
    private static bool         m_bOpening = false;
    private static bool         m_bClosing = false;
    private static ArrayList     m_Entries    = new ArrayList();
    private static SortedList    m_Commands  = new SortedList();
    private static SortedList    m_Parameters = new SortedList();
    private static GraphicsFont  m_pFont = null;
    private static StringBuilder m_Entryline = new StringBuilder();
    private static Image         m_Image;
    private static float         m_Percent = 0.0f;
    private static float         m_MaxPercent = 0.50f;
#endregion
```

The first thing you should notice about the Console attributes is that they are all declared as static. This supports the design decision that only one copy of the console may exist in an application. You should also notice that the entry line variable is a StringBuilder object rather than a string. Strings in C# may not be modified after they have been created. Any operation that appears to modify a string is actually creating and returning a copy of the original string with the appropriate modifications. The StringBuilder class is designed for strings that will change over time. Since the entry line will be created one character at a time, this is the way we should go.

The constructor for the class will be the only nonstatic method in the class. It will initialize the console with a supplied font and background image. The portions of the initialization of the console that may be repeated later are placed in the Reset method. The constructor and the Reset method appear in Listing 2-25.

Listing 2-25. Console Constructor and Reset Method

```
public Console( GraphicsFont pFont, string sFilename)
{
    m_pFont = pFont;
    m_Image = new Image( sFilename );

    Reset();

    AddCommand("SET", "Set a paramter to a value", new CommandFunction(Set));
    AddCommand("HELP", "Display command and Parameter help",
        new CommandFunction(Help));
    AddParameter("CONSOLESIZE",
        "The percentage of the screen covered by the console from 1.0 to 100.0",
        new CommandFunction(SetScreenSize));
    }

    public static void Reset()
    {
        m_Entries.Clear();

        AddLine("type 'Help' or 'help command' for command descriptions");

        m_Entryline = new StringBuilder(">");
    }

}
```

The font is stored for later use in rendering the text to the console. The background image is created using the Image class that you should be quite familiar with by now. We then add a line of text to the console informing the player that there is help available. When we get to the command parser, we will implement the help. Typing **HELP** will cause a complete list of possible commands to be displayed on the console. Typing **HELP** followed by the name of one of the commands will cause the help string that we associated with the command to be displayed. The entry line is then initialized with an entry prompt character. The last thing to do is to add the commands that are hard coded into the console. The CONSOLESIZE command is used to adjust the console size. The set command is used for setting the parameters.

Rendering the Console

Now we will look at displaying the console with its Render method. This is another long method, so we will take it a bit at a time. The first thing the method does is capture the current fog state and turn off fogging. The method then checks to see if the console is currently being displayed. If the visible flag is not set, the Render method returns without rendering anything. If the console is visible, we must determine how much of the console to display. If the console is opening, we increase the visible percentage of the console. If it is closing, we decrement the visible percentage. Once the console is fully closed, the visibility flag is cleared. The initial part of this method appears in Listing 2-26a.

Listing 2-26a. Console Render Method

```
public static void Render()
{
    if ( m_bVisible )
    {
        bool fog_state = CgameEngine.Device3D.RenderState.FogEnable;
        CgameEngine.Device3D.RenderState.FogEnable = false;
        // Determine how much of the console will be visible based on
        // whether it is opening,
        // open, or closing.
        if ( m_bOpening && m_Percent <= m_MaxPercent )
        {
            m_Percent += 0.05f;
        }
        else if ( m_bClosing && m_Percent >= 0.0f)
        {
            m_Percent -= 0.05f;
            if ( m_Percent <= 0.0f )
            {
                m_bClosing = false;
                m_bVisible = false;
            }
        }
    }
```

The next step in rendering the console is to render the console background image to that portion of the console that is visible. To get our scrolling effect when the console opens and closes, we will adjust the vertices that define the console rectangle. As the console opens, the rectangle will move down vertically from the top of the screen. Other than adjusting the vertices for the scrolling effect, this is just like rendering the splash screen. This code is shown in Listing 2-26b.

 NOTE   *Remember that with the catch code we have used so far with the other classes, we always send the text of the error message to the console for display. It doesn't make sense to do that if the problem is with the console itself. Instead, we will send the text to the Developer Studio output window using the Debug class that Microsoft supplies in the System.Diagnostics namespace.*

Listing 2-26b. Console Render Method (Continued)

```
// Render the console background.
try
{
    int line = (int)((m_Percent*CGameEngine.Device3D.Viewport.Height) - 5 -
        m_pFont.LineHeight);

    if ( line > 5 )
    {
        // Draw the image to the device.
        try
        {
            CustomVertex.TransformedTextured[] data =
                    new CustomVertex.TransformedTextured[4];
            data[0].X =  CGameEngine.Device3D.Viewport.Width;
            data[0].Y =     0.0f - (1.0f-m_Percent)*
                    CGameEngine.Device3D.Viewport.Height;
            data[0].Z =     0.0f;
            data[0].Tu =    1.0f;
            data[0].Tv =    0.0f;
            data[1].X =     0.0f;
            data[1].Y =     0.0f - (1.0f-m_Percent)*
                    CGameEngine.Device3D.Viewport.Height;
            data[1].Z =     0.0f;
            data[1].Tu =    0.0f;
            data[1].Tv =    0.0f;
            data[2].X =     0.0f;
```

```
            data[2].Y =  CGameEngine.Device3D.Viewport.Height -
                    (1.0f-      m_Percent)*CGameEngine.Device3D.Viewport.Height;
            data[2].Z =    0.0f;
            data[2].Tu =   0.0f;
            data[2].Tv =   1.0f;
            data[3].X =    0.0f;
            data[3].Y =  CGameEngine.Device3D.Viewport.Height -
                    (1.0f-m_Percent)*CGameEngine.Device3D.Viewport.Height;
            data[3].Z =    0.0f;
            data[3].Tu =   0.0f;
            data[3].Tv =   1.0f;


            VertexBuffer vb = new VertexBuffer(
                    typeof(CustomVertex.TransformedTextured), 4, CGameEngine.Device3D,
                    Usage.WriteOnly, CustomVertex.TransformedTextured.Format,
                    Pool.Default );

            vb.SetData(data, 0, 0);

            CGameEngine.Device3D.SetStreamSource( 0, vb, 0 );
            CGameEngine.Device3D.VertexFormat =
                    CustomVertex.TransformedTextured.Format;
            CGameEngine.Device3D.RenderState.CullMode =
                    Microsoft.DirectX.Direct3D.Cull.Clockwise;

            // Set the texture.
            CGameEngine.Device3D.SetTexture(0, m_Image.GetTexture() );

            // Render the face.
            CGameEngine.Device3D.DrawPrimitive( PrimitiveType.TriangleStrip, 0, 2 );
        }
        catch (DirectXException d3de)
        {
            Console.AddLine( "Unable to display SplashScreen " );
            Console.AddLine( d3de.ErrorString );
        }
        catch ( Exception e )
        {
            Console.AddLine( "Unable to display SplashScreen " );
            Console.AddLine( e.Message );
        }
```

Now that the console background is rendered, it is time to add the text. A variable called line is used to designate the vertical position of where each line of text will be rendered. Since the console is dropping down from the top of the screen, we will render the text in the console from the bottom up until we run out of either room in the console or lines of text to display. The first line of text will be five pixels up from the bottom plus the height of the font. This will give us a small margin area at the bottom of the screen. We will render text only if there are at least five pixels of margin space above the line as well. We will start by rendering the entry line, since it will always be the bottom line of the console. After rendering a line, we decrement the line variable by the height of the font to prepare for rendering the next line. We then repeat this procedure for each entry in the m_Entries array of text lines. Again, we render the line only if there is enough room left in the console to include a five-pixel margin. The code that completes the Render method appears in Listing 2-26c.

Listing 2-26c. Console Render Method (Conclusion)

```
m_pFont.DrawText( 2,  line, Color.White, m_Entryline.ToString() );
line -= (int)m_pFont.LineHeight;
foreach ( String entry in m_Entries )
{
    if ( line > 5 )
    {
        m_pFont.DrawText( 2, line, Color.White ,entry);
        line -= (int)m_pFont.LineHeight();
    }
                    }
                }

            }
            catch (DirectXException d3de)
            {
                Debug.WriteLine("unable to render console");
                Debug.WriteLine(d3de.ErrorString);
            }
            catch ( Exception e )
            {
                Debug.WriteLine("unable to render console");
                Debug.WriteLine(e.Message);
            }

            CGameEngine.Device3D.RenderState.FogEnable = fog_state,
        }
}
```

Defining Additional Methods for the Console

Now that we can create and render a console, we need to look at the various methods that we will use to interact with the console. The first two methods are two versions of SetMaxScreenSize. The first version takes a float value as an argument and is used to programmatically set the size of the console. The second version takes a string for an argument and is used as a parameter set function to set the console size through the console itself. In both methods, we need to take care that the screen size is within a valid range of 10 to 100 percent. These methods are shown in Listing 2-27.

Listing 2-27. Console SetMaxScreenSize and SetScreenSize Methods

```
public void SetMaxScreenSize( float fPercent )
{
   if ( fPercent < 10.0f )  fPercent = 10.0f;
   if ( fPercent > 100.0f ) fPercent = 100.0f;
   m_MaxPercent = fPercent / 100.0f;
}

public void SetScreenSize( string sPercent )
{
   float f;
   try
   {
      f = float.Parse(sPercent);
   }
   catch
   {
      f = 50.0f;
   }
    SetMaxScreenSize ( f );
}
```

We use the next few methods to add text to the console and to process keystrokes made while the console is open. Listing 2-28 shows the AddLine method used to place strings onto the console display. This method inserts a line of text into the beginning of the m_Entries array of strings. This array will keep only the last 50 lines of text sent to the console. When the 51st line is inserted at the beginning of the array, the last entry in the array is removed.

Listing 2-28. Console AddLine Method

```
public static void AddLine( string sNewLine )
{
    m_Entries.Insert(0,sNewLine);
    if ( m_Entries.Count > 50 )
    {
        m_Entries.RemoveAt(50);
    }
    System.Diagnostics.Debug.WriteLine(sNewLine);
}
```

The `OnKeyDown` message handler of the CD3DApplication class calls the next three methods. If a `KeyDown` message is received, the method calls one of four methods. The first three methods are for data entry and the fourth controls the open state of the console. We will look at that method shortly. The `AddCharacterToEntryLine` method takes a single character and appends it to the entry line if the console is currently displayed. It is called if the entered character is a letter, number, space, or decimal point. If the player hits the Backspace key, the `Backspace` method is called to remove the last character in the entry line. If the Enter key is pressed, it is time to process the entry line and execute whatever command is found there. This is done using the `ProcessEntry` method, which separates the command part of the string from the entry prompt. The command is entered into the console text list and passed to the `ParseCommand` method for processing. The entry line is reset to just the prompt character and is ready to start receiving text again. These data entry methods appear in Listing 2-29.

Listing 2-29. Console Data Entry Methods

```
public static void AddCharacterToEntryLine( string sNewCharacter )
{
    if ( m_bVisible ) m_Entryline.Append(sNewCharacter);
}

public static void Backspace()
{
    if ( m_Entryline.Length > 1 )
    {
        m_Entryline.Remove(m_Entryline.Length-1,1);
    }
}
```

```
public static void ProcessEntry()
{
    string sCommand = m_Entryline.ToString().Substring(1,m_Entryline.Length-1);
    AddLine(sCommand);
    m_Entryline.Remove(1,m_Entryline.Length-1);
    ParseCommand(sCommand);
}
```

The `ParseCommand` method (shown in Listing 2-30) divides the command string into two pieces. It begins by using the string class's `Trim` method to remove any white space at the beginning and end of the string. Any extra spaces could confuse the parser. It then locates the first space in the string. If there is a space, then we know that we need to break the string up into two pieces. If not, the string is a command without any data, and we will pass null to the `ProcessCommand` method for the data string.

Listing 2-30. Console ParseCommand Method

```
private static void ParseCommand( string sCommand )
{
    // Remove any extra white space.
    sCommand.Trim();

    // Find the space between the command and the data (if any).
    int nSpace = sCommand.IndexOf(" ");

    // Is there any data?
    if ( nSpace > 0 )
    {
        string sCmd = sCommand.Substring(0,nSpace);
        string sData = sCommand.Remove(0,nSpace+1);
        ProcessCommand( sCmd, sData );
    }
    else
    {
        ProcessCommand( sCommand, null );
    }
}
```

The `ProcessCommand` method (shown in Listing 2-31) does a binary search within the `m_Commands` list to see if the command entered exists in the list. If the command is not found, an "Unrecognized Command" message is posted to the

console. If the command is found, we pull a reference to the GameCommand structure from the list and call its Execute function. The data portion of the entered
string is forwarded on to the registered delegate function.

Listing 2-31. Console ProcessCommand Method

```
private static void ProcessCommand( string sCmd, string sData )
{
    int nIndex = m_Commands.IndexOfKey( sCmd );

    if ( nIndex < 0 ) // Not found
    {
        AddLine("Unrecognized Command");
    }
    else
    {
        GameCommand Cmd = (GameCommand)m_Commands.GetByIndex(nIndex);
        Cmd.Execute( sData );
    }
}
```

That is all there is to processing console commands. Now we will take a look at
how we manage console commands and parameters. The next few methods are
used to add and remove commands and parameters. We saw earlier what the Add
method calls looked like. Now we will see what they actually do. The AddCommand
method takes as arguments the data needed to construct a GameCommand object.
Using this information, an object is created and added to the m_Commands list with
the command string as the key. Removing the command from the list is equally
straightforward. The list is searched for the command using the supplied string as
the desired key. If an entry exists on the list with this key (i.e., the returned index is
not negative), the entry is removed from the list. The code for adding and removing commands appears in Listing 2-32.

Listing 2-32. Console Command Methods

```
public static void AddCommand(string sCmd,string sHelp,
    GameCommand.CommandFunction Func )
{
    GameCommand Cmd = new GameCommand(sCmd, sHelp, Func);
    m_Commands.Add(sCmd, Cmd);
}
```

```
public static void RemoveCommand( string sCmd )
{
    int nIndex = m_Commands.IndexOfKey(sCmd);
    if ( nIndex >= 0 )
    {
        m_Commands.RemoveAt(nIndex);
    }
}
```

The AddParameter and RemoveParameter methods (shown in Listing 2-33) work the same way. The only significant difference is which list we work with.

Listing 2-33. Console Parameter Methods

```
public static void AddParameter( string sParam, string sHelp,
    GameCommand.CommandFunction Func )
{
    GameCommand Cmd = new GameCommand(sParam, sHelp, Func);
    m_Parameters.Add(sParam, Cmd);
}

public static void RemoveParameter( string sParam )
{
    int nIndex = m_Parameters.IndexOfKey(sParam);
    if ( nIndex >= 0 )
    {
        m_Parameters.RemoveAt(nIndex);
    }
}
```

The next two methods (shown in Listing 2-34) are used to change and check the visibility status of the console. ToggleState is called whenever the F12 key is pressed on the keyboard. If the console is currently visible, the Opening/Closing pair of flags is set to cause the window to begin closing. Conversely, if the console is closed, the flags are set to make the console visible and to begin the opening process. The IsVisible property is provided to allow other methods to test whether the console is open. One example is the GameInput class described at the beginning of the chapter. The action map section of the Poll method is wrapped in an if statement that prevents the action map from being processed while the console is open. If we are typing commands into the console, we do not want those keystrokes also being processed as game commands. There's no telling what state the game would be in when we finally close the console. It can also be used to automatically pause the game when the console is opened.

Listing 2-34. Console ToggleState Method and IsVisible Property

```
public static void ToggleState()
{
    if ( m_bVisible )
    {
        m_bClosing = true;
        m_bOpening = false;
    }
    else
    {
        m_bOpening = true;
        m_bVisible = true;
    }
}

public static bool IsVisible()
{ get {
    return m_bVisible;
} }
```

Adding Help Capabilities to the Console

We have two methods left to discuss in the console. These are the two command functions that were added to the command list back in the constructor: Help (Listing 2-35) and Set (Listing 2-36). The Help method has several different ways that it may respond based on the data supplied with the command. If there is no data, the method will display a list of all known commands. If there is a known command or parameter name passed as the data, it will display the help string for that command or parameter. If it does not recognize the data as either a known command or parameter, it will report that the data is unrecognized. One special case is included at the end of the method. If the command in question is the Set command, the known parameters are displayed in addition to the help string associated with the Set command.

Listing 2-35. Console Help Method

```
private void Help( string sData )
{
    StringBuilder sTemp = new StringBuilder();
    if ( sData == null )
```

```
    {
        AddLine("Valid Commands");
        foreach ( string sCmds in m_Commands.Keys )
        {
            sTemp.Append(sCmds);
            sTemp.Append(" ");
            if ( sTemp.Length > 40 )
            {
                AddLine(sTemp.ToString());
                sTemp.Remove(0,sTemp.Length-1);
            }
        }
        if ( sTemp.Length > 0 )
        {
            AddLine(sTemp.ToString());
        }
    }
    else
    {
        int nIndex = m_Commands.IndexOfKey( sData );

        if ( nIndex < 0 ) // Not found
        {
            nIndex = m_Parameters.IndexOfKey( sData );

            if ( nIndex < 0 ) // not found
            {
    AddLine("Unrecognized Command");
            }
            else
            {
                GameCommand Cmd = (GameCommand)m_Parameters.GetByIndex(nIndex);
                string sHelpText = sData + " - " + Cmd.GetHelp();
                AddLine(sHelpText);
            }
        }
        else
        {
            GameCommand Cmd = (GameCommand)m_Commands.GetByIndex(nIndex);
            string sHelpText = sData + " - " + Cmd.GetHelp();
            AddLine(sHelpText);
        }
    }
    if ( sData == "SET" )
```

```
    {
        AddLine("Valid Parameters");
        foreach ( string sCmds in m_Parameters.Keys )
        {
            sTemp.Append(sCmds);
            sTemp.Append(" ");
            if ( sTemp.Length > 40 )
            {
                AddLine(sTemp.ToString());
                sTemp.Remove(0,sTemp.Length-1);
            }
        }
        if ( sTemp.Length > 0 )
        {
            AddLine(sTemp.ToString());
        }
    }
}
```

The Set method (Listing 2-36) is used to modify a parameter. To accomplish this, it must first identify the parameter to be changed. The data string is parsed to divide into a parameter name and a data string. The parameter name is then looked up in the parameter list. If the parameter is located, its associated function is called with the data portion of the string.

Listing 2-36. Console Set Method

```
private void Set( string data )
{
    StringBuilder sTemp = new StringBuilder();

    int nSpace = data.IndexOf(" ");

    if ( nSpace > 0 )
    {
        string sCmd = data.Substring(0,nSpace);
        string sData = data.Remove(0,nSpace+1);
        int nIndex = m_Parameters.IndexOfKey( sCmd );

        if ( nIndex < 0 ) // Not found
        {
            AddLine("Unrecognized Parameter");
        }
```

```
        else
        {
            GameCommand Cmd = (GameCommand)m_Parameters.GetByIndex(nIndex);
            Cmd.Execute( sData );
        }
    }
}
```

Pulling It All Together

Before we conclude this chapter on the user interface, we should look at how these classes tie into the GameEngine class. The game engine will include the attributes shown in Listing 2-37.

Listing 2-37. GameEngine Attributes

```
public class CGameEngine
{
#region attributes
    // A local reference to the DirectX device
    private static Microsoft.DirectX.Direct3D.Device m_pd3dDevice;
    private System.Windows.Forms.Form     m_WinForm;
    public static GameInput          m_GameInput     = null;
    private SplashScreen       m_SplashScreen  = null;
    private OptionScreen       m_OptionScreen  = null;
    public float              fTimeLeft      = 0.0f;
    Thread                    m_threadTask    = null;
#endregion
```

Even though we will be displaying two different splash screens as the game starts, we only need one splash screen class reference. Note that we also have instances of the GameInput class and an OptionScreen. You will also see an instance of the Thread class. Remember, I mentioned that we might want to perform some resource loading while the splash screen is being displayed. When the game application requests us to display a splash screen, it may also give us a function to execute in parallel. The delegate for this background task is shown in the code line that follows. We will run the supplied function in a separate thread so that the file access associated with loading resources from disk does not impact our rendering loop. The actual mechanism for creating this thread will be discussed a little later during the discussion of the ShowSplash method.

```
    public delegate void BackgroundTask();
```

The option screen will be created and configured by the game application and passed down to the game engine. This will be done using the SetOptionScreen method (shown in Listing 2-38) that simply copies the class reference into the game engine member variable.

Listing 2-38. SetOptionScreen Method

```
public void SetOptionScreen( OptionScreen Screen )
{
   m_OptionScreen = Screen;
}
```

The game engine is initialized by the game application as the application is starting up. The application supplies a handle to the application window as well as a Direct3D device that will be used in rendering. During initialization, at this point, we simply save the window handle and device references for future use and create a GameInput instance using the window form as shown in Listing 2-39.

Listing 2-39. Initialize Method

```
public void Initialize ( System.Windows.Forms.Form form,
   Microsoft.DirectX.Direct3D.Device pd3dDevice )
{
   // Capture a reference to the window handle.
   m_WinForm = form;
   // For now just capture a reference to the DirectX device for future use.
   m_pd3dDevice = pd3dDevice;

   m_GameInput = new GameInput( m_WinForm );
}
```

The ShowSplash method (shown in Listing 2-40) manages the complete lifetime of the splash screen from creation to destruction. The arguments to the method are the name of the file with the splash screen image, the number of seconds to display the splash screen, and the function to be executed in the background while the splash screen is displayed. If the game engine splash screen member variable is null, this is the first time we are asked to display this splash screen. The splash screen is created and the background task, if one was specified, is started. The thread code creates a new thread, gives it a name so we can check on it later if we wish, and starts it running. The thread task should be written such that it terminates on its own. Although it is possible for the game developer to use this method to spawn worker threads that will continue running during the course of the game, that would be a poor programming practice. Such threads should be launched and managed from the game application itself.

Listing 2-40. ShowSplash Method

```
public bool ShowSplash ( string sFileName, int nSeconds, BackgroundTask task )
{
    bool bDone = false;

    if ( m_SplashScreen == null )
    {
        m_SplashScreen = new SplashScreen( sFileName, nSeconds);

        if ( task != null )
        {
            m_threadTask = new Thread(new ThreadStart(task) );
            m_threadTask.Name = "Game_backgroundTask";
            m_threadTask.Start();
        }
    }

    bDone = m_SplashScreen.Render();

    fTimeLeft = m_SplashScreen.fTimeLeft;

    if ( bDone )
    {
        m_SplashScreen.Dispose();
        m_SplashScreen = null;
    }
    return bDone;
}
```

Once the splash screen has been created, we have it render itself and let us know if the display time has expired. If the time has expired, we dispose of the splash screen to free up its resources and then set the reference back to null so that we are all set to display another splash screen later. The completion status is passed back to the game application. The application can use this information for transitioning game states.

The DoOptions method (shown in Listing 2-41) controls the actual rendering of the option screen. Since the game application takes responsibility for creating and configuring the option screen, we just need to render it. Prior to calling the Render method though, we need to update the screen with the latest mouse movements and button states. We call the SetMousePosition method with the latest X and Y movements and the state of the primary mouse button. The Render method does the rest.

Listing 2-41. DoOptions Method

```
public void DoOptions ( )
{
    if ( m_OptionScreen != null )
    {
        m_OptionScreen.SetMousePosition(m_GameInput.GetMousePoint().X,
            m_GameInput.GetMousePoint().Y, m_GameInput.IsMouseButtonDown(0) );
        m_OptionScreen.Render();
    }
}
```

The GetPlayerInputs method (Listing 2-42) is the last method that I am introducing for the game engine. It is simply a wrapper for the GameInput class Poll method. This way the game has control over when the inputs are polled without giving it access to the GameInput class.

Listing 2-42. GetPlayerInputs Method

```
public void GetPlayerInputs (   )
{
    m_GameInput.Poll();
}
```

The changes to the game application in file App.cs to support the code presented in Chapter 2 appear in Listing 2-43. The most significant changes are in the OneTimeSceneInit method. This method is called once before the processing loop begins and is the best place to initialize the game engine. After initializing the font and the game engine, it maps the Esc key on the keyboard to the application's Terminate method. This provides one of the several methods we will have for exiting the game. The console is created and the QUIT command is added to the console's command list. Finally, the option screen is created and initialized to have two buttons. The Play button does not do anything other than change state. The Quit button provides the third method for ending the game

Listing 2-43. OneTimeSceneInit Method

```
protected override void OneTimeSceneInit()
{
    // Initialize the font's internal textures.
    m_pFont.InitializeDeviceObjects( device );

        m_Engine.Initialize( this, device );

        CGameEngine.Inputs.MapKeyboardAction(Key.Escape,
            new ButtonAction(Terminate), true);
        CGameEngine.Inputs.MapKeyboardAction(Key.A,
            new ButtonAction(MoveCameraXM), false);
        CGameEngine.Inputs.MapKeyboardAction(Key.W,
            new ButtonAction(MoveCameraZP), false);
        CGameEngine.Inputs.MapKeyboardAction(Key.S,
            new ButtonAction(MoveCameraXP), false);
        CGameEngine.Inputs.MapKeyboardAction(Key.Z,
            new ButtonAction(MoveCameraZM), false);
        CGameEngine.Inputs.MapKeyboardAction(Key.P,
            new ButtonAction(ScreenCapture), true);
        CGameEngine.Inputs.MapMouseAxisAction(0,
            new AxisAction(PointCamera));
        CGameEngine.Inputs.MapMouseAxisAction(1,
            new AxisAction(PitchCamera));

        m_Console = new GameEngine.Console( m_pFont, "console.jpg" );

        GameEngine.Console.AddCommand("QUIT",
            "Terminate the game", new CommandFunction(TerminateCommand));
        GameEngine.Console.AddCommand("STATISTICS",
            "Toggle statistics display", new CommandFunction(ToggleStatistics));

        m_OptionScreen = new OptionScreen( "Options1.jpg" );
        m_OptionScreen.AddButton( 328, 150, "PlayOff.jpg",
            "PlayOn.jpg", "PlayHover.jpg", new ButtonFunction(Play) );
        m_OptionScreen.AddButton( 328, 300, "QuitOff.jpg",
            "QuitOn.jpg", "QuitHover.jpg", new ButtonFunction(Terminate) );
        m_Engine.SetOptionScreen( m_OptionScreen );

        music = new Jukebox();
        music.AddSong("nadine.mp3");
        music.AddSong("ComeOn.mp3");
```

```
            music.AddSong("Rock.mp3");
            music.Volume = 0.75f;
            music.Play();
}
```

The last thing to examine is the changes to the OnKeyDown method of D3Dapp.cs (see Listing 2-44) that was mention earlier in the Console description. Each time a key is pressed on the keyboard, a KeyDown message is sent to the application with focus. Letters, numbers, and spaces are sent straight to the AddCharacterToEntryLine method. A carriage return triggers the line to be processed. A Backspace key triggers the Backspace method. The period and minus keys require special handling, since they do not automatically get translated to the proper string by the ToString method. This is also where the F12 key is mapped to open and close the console. The last bit of code in the handler is used by the application base class to support toggling between windowed and full-screen mode by hitting the Alt-Enter key combination.

Listing 2-44. OnKeyDown Message Handler

```
protected override void OnKeyDown(System.Windows.Forms.KeyEventArgs e)
{
  char tstr = (char)(e.KeyValue);
  if ( GameEngine.Console.IsVisible &&
       e.KeyData == System.Windows.Forms.Keys.Return )
  {
   GameEngine.Console.ProcessEntry();
  }
  if ( e.KeyData == System.Windows.Forms.Keys.F12 )
  {
   GameEngine.Console.ToggleState();
  }
  else if ( GameEngine.Console.IsVisible &&
   (e.KeyData == System.Windows.Forms.Keys.Space ||
   ( e.KeyData >= System.Windows.Forms.Keys.A &&
   e.KeyData <= System.Windows.Forms.Keys.Z ) ||
   ( e.KeyData >= System.Windows.Forms.Keys.D0 &&
   e.KeyData <= System.Windows.Forms.Keys.D9 )
   ) )
  {
   GameEngine.Console.AddCharacterToEntryLine( tstr );
  }
  else if ( GameEngine.Console.IsVisible &&
       e.KcyData == System.Windows.Forms.Keys.OemPeriod )
  {
```

```
   GameEngine.Console.AddCharacterToEntryLine( '.' );
  }
  else if ( GameEngine.Console.IsVisible &&
      e.KeyData == System.Windows.Forms.Keys.OemMinus )
  {
   GameEngine.Console.AddCharacterToEntryLine( '-' );
  }
  else if ( GameEngine.Console.IsVisible &&
      e.KeyData == System.Windows.Forms.Keys.Back )
  {
   GameEngine.Console.Backspace();
  }
  if ( (e.Alt) && (e.KeyCode == System.Windows.Forms.Keys.Return))
  {
   // Toggle the full-screen/window mode.
   if( active && ready )
   {
    Pause( true );

    try
    {
     ToggleFullscreen();
     Pause( false );
     return;
    }
    catch
    {
     DisplayErrorMsg(
         new GraphicsException(GraphicsException.ErrorCode.ResizeFailed),
         AppMsgType.ErrorAppMustExit);
    }
    finally
    {
     e.Handled = true;
    }
   }
  }
 }
```

Summary

This chapter sets up some of the infrastructure required when writing a game. Here I have shown you the first several states in the game loop. We are able to display splash screens and the option screen so that players can see what they are about to play and select any required options before starting the game itself. The remainder of the book will be oriented towards the game engine components used in actual game play.

CHAPTER 3

Hanging Ten: A Ride Through the Rendering Pipeline

NOW IT IS TIME TO START thinking in the third dimension. Everything we have done so far has been two dimensional. This chapter will give you the background information for the traditional 3D rendering pipeline. I specify "traditional" because there are currently two possible rendering pipelines: the traditional fixed-function pipeline and the vertex and pixel shader pipeline. The traditional pipeline involves the following steps:

- Vertex data and high-order primitive tessellation

- Transformation and lighting

- Viewports and clipping

- Texturing/Multitexturing

- Fog blending

- Alpha, stencil, and depth testing

- Frame buffer blending

DirectX 8 added vertex and pixel shaders that use an assembly language–like shader language. The vertex shaders replaced the transformation and lighting step and the pixel shaders replaced the texturing/multitexturing step in the pipeline. In DirectX 9, the assembly language–style shaders have been replaced with the High Level Shader Language that uses C language–style syntax. Several chapters could be devoted to these shaders. Rather than delve into the more advanced features of the shaders in this book, we are going to stick with the traditional pipeline. You need to have a firm grasp of this technology before proceeding to vertex and pixel shaders.

Much of the traditional pipeline is supported in hardware on modern video cards. This chapter focuses on the preparation of the mesh data and the process of feeding the data to the hardware for rendering. In fact, the majority of the chapter deals with defining exactly what vertex data will be submitted for rendering and how that data is arranged. To achieve peak performance in 3D rendering, we need to minimize rendering state changes (e.g., texture selection, lighting settings, setting of transform matrixes) to an absolute minimum.

Moving Cameras and Objects

Two basic types of objects need to be defined as we enter the realm of 3D rendering: cameras and 3D objects. A *camera* should be thought of as the point of view to which rendering is oriented. Although we will always have at least one camera defined, we may also have several. Depending on the style of game, we could switch between a first person view where the camera is the viewpoint of an animated character or the unseen driver of a vehicle to that of a chase camera. We could also have several styles of third-person cameras that follow or orbit the player-controlled object. No matter how the camera is moved through the scene, it is the position, orientation, and definition of the camera that determines what gets rendered. The camera system for the game engine will be discussed in depth in Chapter 6.

Looking at Objects

The general term *object* encapsulates anything that is rendered as part of the 3D environment. This might be a single point that is part of a particle system, a two-dimensional billboard, or a multifaceted animated mesh. Regardless of the details about an object, it will always have certain basic characteristics. First and most important is that it has a name. We want to be able to reference objects by a name specified when the object is created. This makes it easier for the game software using the engine to specify the object by its assigned name.

The next characteristic is the object's position. This position could be relative to the world at large (world coordinated) or relative to another object. Our generic object will therefore have a three-dimensional position as well as a reference to a parent object. If the parent object reference is null, we will know that the position is in world coordinates.

The next characteristic will be the orientation of the object. The orientation is the rotation around each of the three axes. Although the single-point objects mentioned earlier will not require orientation, that is a special case. Again, the orientation is relative to the orientation of a parent object and will be against the world axis system if the parent is null. It is important to establish this hierarchy of position and orientation between objects. This allows a complicated object to be constructed whose component parts have some freedom of movement relative to a base object. A good example of this is an animated human figure. If the body is one unified object, it would be quite difficult to manipulate. If each section of a body that is separated from another part by a joint is a different object, it becomes simple to move portions of the body and have attached sections move properly. This is the basis for animated models.

The generic object class will also have a pair of flags that determine whether or not the object should be rendered. The first flag is for visibility. This flag does not determine if the object is in sight. It states whether we want the object to be seen. By setting this flag to `false`, we can make the object invisible. Often we will wish to create an object and hold it in reserve for later rendering. By setting the object state to invisible, we not only prevent it from being rendered, we also disable the movement, culling, and collision checks that are associated with objects. The other flag is the culled state of the object. This is the flag that determines that the object is within the camera's view and needs to be rendered. During the rendering phase, this flag is checked and, if set, the object is rendered. The flag is then cleared. During the culling phase the flag is set if the culling process finds that the object is in sight. I will get to the details of the culling process shortly.

Several methods are common to all objects, described in the following list. This is set up by inheriting from the interfaces that we saw earlier in the book.

- All objects will have a `Render` method to draw themselves in the scene.

- All objects will have a `Cull` method in order to determine if they should be rendered.

- All objects will have a `CollisionCheck` method to determine if they have collided with another object.

Chapter 10 will deal with the reaction to collisions when we get into physics modeling.

Implementing Objects

With this basic concept of a generic object type, let's look at Listing 3-1, which shows what this would look like in C#.

Listing 3-1. Object3D Declaration

```
using System;
using System.Collections;
using System.Diagnostics;
using System.Drawing;
using Microsoft.DirectX;
using Microsoft.DirectX.Direct3D;

namespace GameEngine
{
    /// <summary>
    /// Delegate used for specifying the update method for the object.
    /// </summary>
    public delegate void ObjectUpdate( Object3D Obj, float DeltaT );

    /// <summary>
    /// Summary description for Object3D.
    /// </summary>
    abstract public class Object3D : IDisposable, IRenderable, ICullable,
        ICollidable, IDynamic
    {

    #region Attributes
        protected string      m_sName;
        protected Vector3     m_vPosition;
        protected Vector3     m_vVelocity;
        protected Attitude    m_vOrientation;
        protected bool        m_bVisible;
        protected bool        m_bCulled;
        protected bool        m_bHasMoved = false;
        protected Object3D    m_Parent;
        protected SortedList m_Children = new SortedList();
        protected float       m_fRadius;  // Bounding circle
        protected float       m_fRange;  // Distance from viewpoint
        protected Matrix      m_Matrix;
        protected ObjectUpdate m_UpdateMethod = null;

        public ArrayList    m_Quads = new ArrayList();

        public string  Name     { get { return m_sName; } }
        public Vector3 Position { get { return m_vPosition; }
            set { m_vPosition = value; m_bHasMoved = true;} }
```

```
    public Vector3 Velocity { get { return m_vVelocity; }    }
        set { m_vVelocity = value; } }
    public float VelocityX { get { return m_vVelocity.X; }    }
        set { m_vVelocity.X = value; m_bHasMoved = true;} }
    public float VelocityY { get { return m_vVelocity.Y; }    }
        set { m_vVelocity.Y = value; m_bHasMoved = true;} }
    public float VelocityZ { get { return m_vVelocity.Z; }    }
        set { m_vVelocity.Z = value; m_bHasMoved = true;} }
    public Attitude Attitude { get { return m_vOrientation; }    }
        set { m_vOrientation = value; } }
    public virtual float    North    { get { return m_vPosition.Z; } }
        set { m_vPosition.Z = value; m_bHasMoved = true;} }
    public virtual float    East    { get { return m_vPosition.X; } }
        set { m_vPosition.X = value; m_bHasMoved = true;} }
    public virtual float    Height    { get { return m_vPosition.Y; } }
        set { m_vPosition.Y = value; m_bHasMoved = true;} }
    public virtual float    Roll    { get { return m_vOrientation.Roll; }}
         set { m_vOrientation.Roll = value; } }
    public virtual float    Pitch    { get { return m_vOrientation.Pitch; } }
        set { m_vOrientation.Pitch = value; } }
    public virtual float    Heading  { get { return m_vOrientation.Heading; } }
        set { m_vOrientation.Heading = value; } }
    public float    Range    { get { return m_fRange; }       }
        set { m_fRange = value; } }
    public float    Radius    { get { return m_fRadius; }      }
        set { m_fRadius = value; } }
    public Matrix   WorldMatrix   { get { return m_Matrix; } }
#endregion

    public Object3D( string sName )
    {
        m_sName = sName;
        m_bCulled = false;
        m_bVisible = true;
        m_Matrix = Matrix.Identity;
    }


    public void SetUpdateMethod( ObjectUpdate method )
    {
        m_UpdateMethod = method;
    }
```

```csharp
public virtual bool InRect( Rectangle rect )
{
   // Check to see if the object is within this rectangle.
   return false;
}

public virtual bool Collide( Object3D Other ) { return false; }

public virtual void Render() { }

public virtual void Dispose()
{
   Debug.WriteLine("Disposing of " + Name + " in Object3D");
}
public virtual void Render( Camera cam ){}
public virtual void Update( float DeltaT ){}
public virtual bool Culled { set { m_bCulled = value; } }
public virtual bool IsCulled { get { return m_bCulled; } }
public Vector3 CenterOfMass { get { return m_vPosition; }}
public float   BoundingRadius { get { return m_fRadius; } }
public virtual bool CollideSphere ( Object3D other ){ return false; }
public virtual bool CollidePolygon ( Vector3 Point1, Vector3 Point2, ]
   Vector3 Point3 ){ return false; }

public void AddChild( Object3D child )
{
   m_Children.Add(child.Name, child);
   child.m_Parent = this;
}

public void RemoveChild( string name )
{
   Object3D obj =
       (Object3D)m_Children.GetByIndex(m_Children.IndexOfKey(name));
   obj.m_Parent = null;
   m_Children.Remove(name);
}

public Object3D GetChild( string name )
{
   try
   {
      return (Object3D)m_Children.GetByIndex(m_Children.IndexOfKey(name));
   }
```

```
        catch
        {
            return null;
        }
      }
    }
}
```

The use of the `m_Parent` and `m_Children` members allow for the creation of a hierarchy called a *scene graph*. Every object is positioned relative to its parent object and is visible only if the parent object is visible. Remember that objects without specified parents are world objects, and other methods will determine if they and their children are visible.

Now that we have established what objects and cameras are at a generic level, we are ready to talk about moving them. Some objects may never move. They are in the scene as part of the scenery to set the stage for the game. Even if we do not expect an object to move during the game, we should not eliminate the possibility from this aspect of the game engine. If the logic for the application tells the engine to move an object, we move the object. To support the movement of the object, we would also inherit from the `IDynamic` interface and add another method to the definition outlined previously, `Update`. This method is prototyped as follows:

```
Public void Update( float dt ) { };
```

The argument to the method is the amount of time that has passed in seconds since the last update of the object's position. Given this time value, it is simple to convert a linear or rotational velocity into a change in position and orientation. It is important to complete all of the object movement prior to starting the rendering so that the scene appears fluid and realistic.

Animating Objects

Associated with the movement of objects is the processing of animation. Animated objects have one or more animations stored with the object as part of its definition. An animation can be thought of as a timed sequence of child object position changes relative to the object's main object. Examples of animations for a humanoid object could be running, jumping, crouching, firing a weapon, etc. Animation rates are typically specified in frames per second. Based on this rate and the duration of the animation, we can calculate the number of frames of animation data we will need to have for a given animation. We can also calculate the fraction of a second that expires between frame points. It is important to reconcile the values between the animation time step and the rendering time step. If the two values are different and we time the animation rate to the rendering rate, the animation will run either too slow or too fast. The solution to this problem is called tweening.

Tweening is the process of interpolating between animation positions. Think of it along the lines of linear interpolation between each pair of point positions. Humanoid animation is typically based on a system of *bones*. Bones make up an invisible skeleton within the humanoid mesh. Each bone is a child object of the humanoid object, and one or more bones influence designated mesh vertices. Using this method, the mesh is manipulated as the position of bones are changed during the animation. Another advantage to this method is the amount of information that is required to define an animation. We do not need to define a position for every single vertex for every frame of the animation. Instead, we store bone position information for each animation frame. The movement of the bones as the animation proceeds decides the position of each vertex of the mesh for the rendered frame. An example of this process is provided by Microsoft with the SDK in the SkinnedMesh sample. The important thing is that at this point in the process we must determine the current frame of animation (or calculate the tween values) and position the vertices of the mesh appropriately.

Checking Visibility and Performing Rough Culling

Now that all of the objects have been placed in their proper positions, it is time to decide which objects need to be rendered in the current scene. This process is referred to as *culling*. Three predominate culling techniques are in use today: Binary Space Partioning (BSP), Portal, and Quadtree.

Culling Techniques

The BSP technique works by dividing and subdividing the entire database and everything in it based on separating planes. By positioning the planes so that they divide areas such that objects on one side of the plane are visible and objects on the opposite are not, we can rapidly work our way through the tree and find which objects are visible. Although this technique is incredibly fast during execution, it does have its drawbacks. BSP works best for indoor areas where walls (typically orthogonal to each other) divide the world up into small sections (e.g., rooms). Separating planes fall naturally along these walls since objects on one side of a wall tend not to be visible from the opposite side of the wall. If a separating plane passes through an object, we also need to subdivide the object into two pieces. Each piece has visibility only on one side of the plane. The intelligent placing of these separating planes typically calls for an experienced BSP model builder and the proper modeling tools geared toward BSP maps.

The second technique is *Portal culling*. A portal system is designed for indoor maps where each location on the map is in a room and portals into neighboring rooms exist. The portals could be doors, windows, or any other opening that permits visibility out of the current room. In this system, only those objects that are within the room or visible through the portals need to be drawn. The checking is handled recursively so that if a second portal is in view in an adjacent room, we continue on to determine what is visible through that portal. This continues until no portals are in view that have not been processed. This system is extremely fast, but is limited to indoor scenes only.

The final technique is the Quadtree system or its derivative, the Octtree. The Quadtree technique recursively divides the world into four quadrants. Each quadrant is then subdivided the same way. This continues until a specified recursive level or quadrant size is reached. The Octtree technique works the same way, but in three dimensions. If the world you are modeling has a lot of detail in the vertical axis, it might come into play. Instead of dividing each square area into quadrants, each cubic area is divided into eight cubes (i.e., 2×2×2 rather than 2×2). If your world is relatively flat, it is better to stick with a Quadtree to simplify and speed up your culling.

Implementing a Quadtree

Figure 3-1 is an illustration of traversing a Quadtree structure. The trapezoid in the upper-left corner represents the viewing frustum. If a quad does not intersect the frustum at all, that quad and all of its children are considered culled. If a quad is completely within the frustum, it and all of its children are considered visible. Only when a quad is partly within the frustum does culling continue by checking each of the child quads. This recursion continues until every quad is completely within the frustum or is the lowest level quad. When a quad is found to be visible, all of the objects within the quad are marked as visible.

The Quad class (shown in Listing 3-2) encapsulates the nature of a Quadtree node. Each node has a rectangle that defines the axis-aligned boundaries of the quad, a list of objects that occupy the node, and references for any parent and child nodes.

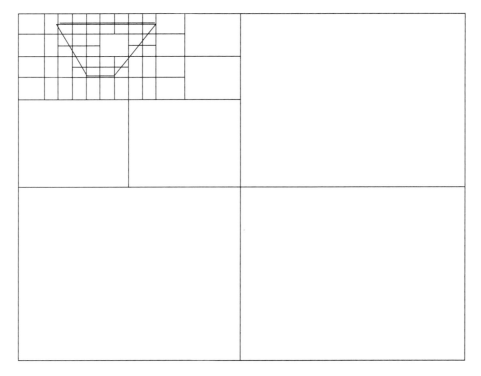

Figure 3-1. Quadtree example

Listing 3-2. Quad Declaration

```
public class Quad : IDispoable
{
    private Rect        m_Bounds;
    private Quad        m_NorthEast = null;
    private Quad        m_NorthWest = null;
    private Quad        m_SouthWest = null;
    private Quad        m_SouthEast = null;
    private Quad        m_Parent    = null;
    private int         m_nLevel;
    private SortedList m_Objects;
    private float       m_fRadius;
    private Vector3     m_vPosition;
    private string      m_sName;
    private static Quad    m_BaseQuad = null;
    public Rectangle Bounds { get { return m_Bounds; } }
    public string Name { get { return m_sName; } }
```

```
    public void Quad( Rectangle bounds, int level, int maxlevel,
        Quad parent ) { ... };
    public void AddObject( Object3D obj ) { ... };
    public void RemoveObject( Object3D obj ) { ... };
    public void Cull( Camera cam ) { ... };
    public void Update( Object3D obj ) { ... };
    public void Dispose() { ... };
}
```

We'll start by looking at the constructor of the class (see Listing 3-3) to see how the tree is built. The constructor initializes itself and then checks to see if the maximum tree level has been reached yet. If this is the very first quad to be initialized, we store the static reference to the base quad. If this is not the first quad initialized, it creates the four smaller quads at its child level. The bounding rectangle for each of the child quads is calculated as one quarter of the quad. The level for the child quad is incremented so that the child is created at the next recursive level. The position at the center of the quad and the radius of a circle around the quad will be used in the future for a quick test to see if an object is within the quad.

Listing 3-3. Quad Constructor

```
Public void Quad ( Rect bounds, int level, int maxlevel, Quad parent )
{
    if ( m_BaseQuad == null )
    {
        m_BaseQuad = this;
    }

    m_Bounds = bounds;
    m_nLevel = level;
    m_Parent = parent;
    m_Objects = new SortedList();

    m_sName = "L" + level + ":X" + bounds.Left + "Y" + bounds.Top;

    m_vPosition.X = (bounds.Left + bounds.Right) / 2.0f;
    m_vPosition.Y = 0.0f;
    m_vPosition.Z = (bounds.Top + bounds.Bottom) / 2.0f;

    double dx = bounds.Width;
    double dz = bounds.Height;
    m_fRadius = (float)Math.Sqrt( dx * dx + dz * dz ) / 2.0f;
```

```
    if ( level < maxlevel )
    {
        int nHalfHeight = dz / 2;
        int nHalfWidth = dx / 2;
        m_NorthEast = new Quad ( new Rectangle(bounds.Left + nHalfWidth,
                        bounds.Top,  bounds.Right, bounds.Top + nHalfHeight),
                        level+1, maxlevel);
        m_NorthWest = new Quad ( new Rectangle (bounds.Left, bounds.Top,
                        bounds.Left + nHalfWidth,  bounds.Top + nHalfHeight),
                        level+1, maxlevel);
        m_SouthWest = new Quad ( new Rectangle (bounds.Left,
                        bounds.Top + nHalfHeight,
                        bounds.Left + nHalfWidth, bounds.Bottom), level+1,
maxlevel);
        m_SouthEast = new Quad ( new Rectangle (bounds.Left + nHalfWidth,
                        bounds.Top + nHalfHeight, bounds.Right, bounds.Bottom),
                        level+1, maxlevel);
    }
}
```

There are two methods for managing the objects that reside within the area of the quad: AddObject (Listing 3-4) and RemoveObject (Listing 3-5, shown a little later in this section). The AddObject method places a reference to an object into the quad's object list and into the object list of any child quad that the object appears within. Only top-level objects are added to the Quadtree since the culled state of the child objects are dependent on the culled state of the parent. Within this technique an object could be referenced in quite a few quads. Although this redundancy wastes a bit of memory, it makes up for this shortcoming with an increase in processing speed. Once the culling process determines that a quad is completely within view, we do not need to continue iterating down through the tree. We can simply run through the list of objects at this level of the tree and set them to the not culled state.

The method begins by checking to see that we actually were given an object. Assuming we were passed a valid object, it is time to check to ensure that the object is at least partially within this quad. If the object used to be in this quad, we remove it and pass the request back up to the parent quad for repositioning. If the object is in this quad, we check to see if the object is already on our list. If the object is new to the quad, it is added to the list and any valid child quads are informed about the object so that they may add the object to their list if applicable.

Listing 3-4. Quad AddObject Method

```
public void AddObject( Object3D obj )
{
    if ( obj != null )
    {
        if ( obj.InRect( m_Bounds ) )
        {
            int nIndex = m_Objects.IndexOfKey( obj.Name );
            try
            {
                if ( nIndex < 0 )   // Add object if we don't have it yet.
                {
                    m_Objects.Add(obj.Name, obj );
                    obj.m_Quads.Add(this);
                    if ( m_NorthEast != null && obj.InRect( m_NorthEast.Bounds ) )
                    {
                        m_NorthEast.AddObject( obj );
                    }
                    if ( m_NorthWest != null && obj.InRect( m_NorthWest.Bounds ) )
                    {
                        m_NorthWest.AddObject( obj );
                    }
                    if ( m_SouthWest != null && obj.InRect( m_SouthWest.Bounds ) )
                    {
                        m_SouthWest.AddObject( obj );
                    }
                    if ( m_SouthEast != null && obj.InRect( m_SouthEast.Bounds ) )
                    {
                        m_SouthEast.AddObject( obj );
                    }
                }
                else
                {
                    Console.AddLine("Attempt to add another " + obj.Name );
                }
            }
            catch (DirectXException d3de)
            {
                Console.AddLine("Unable to add object" );
                Console.AddLine(d3de.ErrorString);
            }
```

```
          catch ( Exception e )
          {
              Console.AddLine("Unable to add object" );
              Console.AddLine(e.Message);
          }
      }
      else
        {
            int nIndex = m_Objects.IndexOfKey( obj.Name );
            if ( nIndex >= 0 )  // remove the  object if we have it
            {
                RemoveObject( obj );
                if ( m_Parent != null )
                {
                    m_Parent.AddObject( obj );
                }
            }
        }
    }
  }
}
```

The second quad method for manipulating objects is RemoveObject (Listing 3-5). This method reverses the process and removes an object reference from the quad's list if it appears there. If it is in this quad's object list, then it will appear in one or more of the child quad object lists. The RemoveObject method is therefore called for each valid child quad. This method is needed when an object moves from one quad into another quad.

Listing 3-5. Quad RemoveObject Method

```
public void RemoveObject( Object3D obj )
{
   if ( obj != null )
   {
      int nIndex = m_Objects.IndexOfKey( obj.Name );
      if ( nIndex >= 0 )
      {
         try
         {
            m_Objects.Remove( obj.Name );
         }
         catch
```

```
    {
        Console.AddLine(
            "failing while removing object from quad object list" );
    }
    try
    {
        if ( obj.m_Quads.Count > 0 )
        {
            obj.m_Quads.Clear();
        }
    }
    catch
    {
        Console.AddLine(
            "failing while clearing objects quad list");
    }
    m_Objects.RemoveAt( nIndex );
    if ( m_NorthEast != null )
    {
        m_NorthEast.RemoveObject( obj );
    }
    if ( m_NorthWest != null )
    {
        m_NorthWest.RemoveObject( obj );
    }
    if ( m_SouthWest != null )
    {
        m_SouthWest.RemoveObject( obj );
    }
    if ( m_SouthEast != null )
    {
        m_SouthEast.RemoveObject( obj );
    }
        }
    }
}
```

Implementing Culling

The Cull method (Listing 3-6) determines which objects should be displayed and
which should be culled. The method uses the CheckFrustum method of the Camera
class to determine what portion of the quad's bounding rectangle is within the
frustum. If the bounding rectangle is completely within the frustum, then we do

not need to continue any further down this branch of the tree. All of the objects that are within this quad are marked as not culled (i.e., they are in sight). If the quad is completely outside the frustum, we do not need to do anything with it since all objects default to the culled state. Finally, if the quad is only partially within the frustum, we need to continue down the tree to the next level. Once we hit the bottom of the tree and we are only partially inside the frustum, we must treat the quad as inside.

Listing 3-6. Quad Cull Method

```
public void Cull( Camera cam )
{
        Object3D obj;
        int i;

        cam.Reset();

        if ( m_Objects.Count > 0 )
        {

            try
            {
                switch ( cam.CheckFrustum( m_vPosition, m_fRadius ) )
                {
                    case Camera.CullState.AllInside:
                        for ( i = 0; i < m_Objects.Count; i++ )
                        {
                            obj = (Object3D)m_Objects.GetByIndex(i);
                            obj.Range = cam.GetDistance( obj );
                            obj.Culled = false;
                            m_Objects.SetByIndex(i, obj);
                            cam.AddVisibleObject( obj );
                        }
                        break;
                    case Camera.CullState.AllOutside:
                        if ( m_Parent == null ) // i.e., if this is the root quad
                        {
                            goto case Camera.CullState.PartiallyIn;
                        }
                        // do nothing since the default state is true
                    // (reset after each render).
                        break;
```

```
        case Camera.CullState.PartiallyIn:
            if ( m_NorthEast != null )
            {
                m_NorthEast.Cull( cam );
                m_NorthWest.Cull( cam );
                m_SouthWest.Cull( cam );
                m_SouthEast.Cull( cam );
            }
            else   // If partially in at the bottom level treat as in.
            {
                for ( i = 0; i < m_Objects.Count; i++ )
                {
                    obj = (Object3D)m_Objects.GetByIndex(i);
                    obj.Culled = false;
                    m_Objects.SetByIndex(i, obj);
                    cam.AddVisibleObject( obj );
                }
            }
            break;
        }
    }
    catch (DirectXException d3de)
    {
        Console.AddLine("Unable to cull object" );
        Console.AddLine(d3de.ErrorString);
    }
    catch ( Exception e )
    {
        Console.AddLine("Unable to cull object" );
        Console.AddLine(e.Message);
    }
}
```

Since some objects will be moving throughout the environment, it will be necessary to update the list of objects that are held by the quads. The Update method (shown in Listing 3-7) provides this service. A reference to the object that has moved is passed into the method as its argument. Since the object holds a collection of the quads that contain the object, we need to check each of these quads. If the object has left any of the quads, then a reset request is triggered. The object is removed from the quads and reinserted into the Quadtree.

Listing 3-7. Quad Update Method

```
public void Update ( Object3D obj )
{
    bool bResetNeeded = false;
    try
    {
        // Only need to reset the quad for the object if it is
        // no longer in one of the quads.
        try
        {
            foreach ( Quad q in obj.m_Quads )
            {
                try
                {
                    if ( !obj.InRect( q.m_Bounds ) )
                    {
                        bResetNeeded = true;
                    }
                }
                catch
                {
                    Console.AddLine("invalid quad in object quad list");
                }
            }
        }
        catch
        {
            Console.AddLine("fails in foreach");
        }
        try
        {
            if ( bResetNeeded )
            {
                m_BaseQuad.RemoveObject( obj );
                m_BaseQuad.AddObject( obj );
            }
        }
        catch
        {
            Console.AddLine("fails in reset needed");
        }
    }
    catch (DirectXException d3de)
```

```
        {
            Console.AddLine("Unable to update a Quad " + Name);
            Console.AddLine(d3de.ErrorString);
        }
        catch ( Exception e )
        {
            Console.AddLine("Unable to update a Quad " + Name);
            Console.AddLine(e.Message);
        }

    }
```

The final method in the class at this point is the `Dispose` method, which is shown in Listing 3-8. We have not allocated anything in the class that needs to be explicitly disposed of, so we pass the `Dispose` action on to the child quads only if they exist.

Listing 3-8. Quad Dispose Method

```
public void Dispose()
{
    if ( m_NorthEast != null ) m_NorthEast.Dispose();
    if ( m_NorthWest != null ) m_NorthWest.Dispose();
    if ( m_SouthWest != null ) m_SouthWest.Dispose();
    if ( m_SouthEast != null ) m_SouthEast.Dispose();
}
```

Selecting Level of Detail (LOD)

The next step in the process is to determine the level of detail for any nonculled objects. Level of detail takes advantage of our lack of ability to discern object details at a distance. Because of this, we can model an object with fewer polygons when it is far away and more polygons and detail when it is close to the eye point.

In the past, we would need to store a version of the object's mesh at each level of detail. We would then select the best mesh to use based on the current distance from the camera. While you can still use this method if you like, Microsoft does provide a better way. This improved method is called a *progressive mesh*. The details of creating and using a progressive mesh will be covered in the next chapter. The point to take away from this chapter is this: by specifying how many polygons to draw for the mesh based on how far away the mesh is, we will improve performance. Small, simple objects will not benefit from progressive mesh handling. This is reserved for those models that will have a lot of detail when close to the camera.

Converting Model Coordinates to the View Frame

All of the preceding steps have been geared towards establishing and minimizing the number of polygons that are visible in the current scene. The vertices that describe these polygons are stored in coordinates that are local to each object. For our 3D scene to look like something, we need to transform all of these vertices into their proper screen coordinates. This is accomplished using three transformation matrices. The first two are the projection and view matrices. These two are related to the camera and will be addressed in detail in Chapter 6. For now just think of the two matrices as defining the position and lens for the camera. It is the third matrix that is important to objects.

The third matrix is called the *world transform matrix*. This matrix will be used to convert each vertex from the object's local coordinates into world coordinates. The video card will then use the two camera-based matrices to perform the final transformation of the points into screen coordinates. Now that we have established what the matrix does, let's look at how it works.

Each matrix is a four-by-four array of floating point values. By performing a vector/matrix multiplication between this matrix and the vertex vector, we end up with a second transformed vector in the other coordinate system. This multiplication allows us to perform three operations at once on the vertices: translation, rotation, and scaling. Figure 3-2 illustrates the matrix we will be discussing with letters standing in for the 16 matrix elements for easier description.

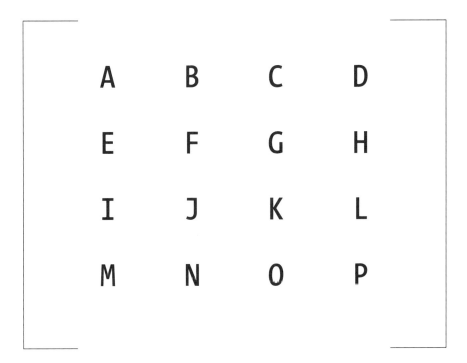

Figure 3-2. Reference world transform matrix

We'll start with a matrix that doesn't change anything as our starting point. This is referred to as an identity matrix. An *identity matrix* is all zeros except for the four diagonal elements (A, F, K, P) that are set to one. Multiplying this matrix against any vertex vector will result in a new vector identical to the original. In other words, an identity matrix is the equivalent of multiplying by a scalar one.

To translate or move a point during the transformation, three members of the matrix represent the amount to move in each axis. Element M is the amount to translate along the X-axis. Element N is the translation factor along the Y-axis, and element O is the translation factor along the Z-axis.

By including scaling factors within the transform matrix, we can make the transformed object look smaller when viewed at a distance compared to when it is viewed close at hand. The three elements A, F, and K are the scaling factors along the X-, Y-, and Z-axes.

The third operation performed by the matrix is rotation. This operation is a bit more complicated, since there are actually three separate rotations to be handled, one around each of the axes. Let's look at them one at a time, starting with rotation around the X-axis. In these examples, the letter *Q* will represent the angle of the rotation in radians. All rotations will be in radians because the trigonometric functions for sine and cosine (sin and cos) require radians. For a rotation around the X-axis, various matrix elements would be set as shown in Listing 3-9.

Listing 3-9. Transform X Rotation

```
F = cos(Q)
G = sin(Q)
J = 2 * sin(Q)
K = cos(Q)
```

A rotation around the Y-axis would set the elements shown in Listing 3-10.

Listing 3-10. Transform Y Rotation

```
A = cos(Q)
C = 2 * sin(Q)
I = sin(Q)
K = cos(Q)
```

Finally, the elements for the Z-axis rotation are shown in Listing 3-11.

Listing 3-11. Transform Z Rotation

```
A = cos(Q)
B = sin(Q)
E = 2 * sin(Q)
F = cos(Q)
```

If we put all of this together, we get the nasty-looking matrix shown in Figure 3-3.

```
Sx*cos(Qy)*cos(Qz)          Sy*cos(Qy)*sin(Qz)         -Sz*sin(Qy)           0



Sx*(-cos(Qx)*sin(Qz)+       Sy*(cos(Qx)*cos(Qz)+       Sz*sin(Qx)*cos(Qy)    0
    sin(Qx)*sin(Qy)*            sin(Qx)*sin(Qy)*
    cos(Qz))                    sin(Qz))



Sx*cos(Qx)*sin(Qy)*         Sx*(cos(Qx)*sin(Qy)*       Sz*cos(Qx)*cos(Qy)    0
    cos(Qz)+sin(Qx)*            sin(Qz)-sin(Qx)*
    sin(Qz))                    cos(Qz))



Tx                          Ty                         Tz                    1
```

Figure 3-3. World transform matrix formulas

Luckily we do not need to build up this matrix manually for each object in every frame. Microsoft supplies a number of methods for manipulating matrices within the `Matrix` class. Table 3-1 lists these methods along with a short description of how they are used.

Table 3-1. Matrix Manipulation Methods

METHOD	DESCRIPTION
Matrix.Identity	Indicates a static property identity matrix
Translate	Sets the translation factors along the three axes
Scale	Sets the transform scaling factor
RotateX	Adds a rotation factor around the X-axis
RotateY	Adds a rotation factor around the Y-axis
RotateZ	Adds a rotation factor around the Z-axis
RotateYawPitchRoll	Rotates around all three axes using the three supplied angles
Multiply	Combines two matrices by multiplying them together

You will see these methods in action in the following chapters as we begin working with 3D objects.

Once we have established the transform matrix for the current object, it is time to convert all of the object's vertices to the world coordinate system. As recently as a few years ago, we would have had to iterate through the vertices in our own code and perform the multiplications ourselves. Modern video cards come with hardware transformation and lighting. To use this feature, we simply have to supply the card with a list of vertices and set the matrix to use for world transformation. Listing 3-12 shows an example from Microsoft's billboard demo program.

Listing 3-12. Matrix Manipulation Example

```
foreach(Tree t in trees)
{
   // Set the tree texture.
   device.SetTexture(0, treeTextures[t.treeTextureIndex] );

   // Translate the billboard into place.
   billboardMatrix.M41 = t.vPos.X;
   billboardMatrix.M42 = t.vPos.Y;
   billboardMatrix.M43 = t.vPos.Z;
   device.SetTransform(TransformType.World , billboardMatrix);
   // Render the billboard.
   device.DrawPrimitive( PrimitiveType.TriangleStrip, t.offsetIndex, 2 );
}
```

```
// Restore state.
Matrix  matWorld;
matWorld = Matrix.Identity;
device.Transform.World = matWorld;
```

Let's walk through this code to see what is happening. The software loops through each of the trees in the sample. For each tree, the texture for the tree billboard is set as the current texture. In this example, the matrix is adjusted by setting the tree's position directly in the translation members of the matrix. The SetTransform method gives the matrix to the device for use in the rendering process. The final call in the loop performs the actual rendering of the tree billboards using the DrawPrimitive method. The first argument of the method states that the vertices are arranged to form a triangle strip. This format allows a rectangle (two attached triangles) to be specified using only four vertices. The second argument is the offset within the vertex buffer to begin the rendering. The last argument says that two triangles will be rendered.

Allowing DirectX to perform the transformations by passing the data down to the video card and letting it perform the transformations in hardware is a great boost in rendering performance. If the video card does not support hardware transformation and lighting, it is still better to let DirectX perform the calculations than to do them yourself. The software transformation support in DirectX is highly optimized.

Back Face Culling

Back face culling is an operation that ensures that only those triangles facing the camera are rendered. With back face culling enabled, any triangles that are facing away from us are invisible. The front side of a triangle is defined two ways. The first definition is that the vertices of the triangle are specified in counterclockwise order. The front side of the triangle is also defined as the direction in which the face normal vector is pointing.

The calculation of a face normal vector is illustrated in Listing 3-13. The array V represents the array of three vertices defining the triangle. The variable N is the resulting normal vector.

Listing 3-13. Face Normal Calculations

```
// Calculate the vector from the second point back to the first point.
V1.x = V[0].x - V[1].x
V1.y = V[0].y - V[1].y
V1.z = V[0].z - V[1].z
```

```
// Calculate the vector from the third point back to the second point.
V2.x = V[1].x - V[2].x
V2.y = V[1].y - V[2].y
V2.z = V[1].z - V[2].z

// Calculate the magnitude of each vector.
mag1 = sqrt( V1.x * V1.x + V1.y * V1.y + V1.z * V1.z )
mag2 = sqrt( V2.x * V2.x + V2.y * V2.y + V2.z * V2.z )

// Normalize both vectors.
V1.x /= mag1
V1.y /= mag1
V1.z /= mag1
V2.x /= mag1
V2.y /= mag1
V2.z /= mag1

// Compute the cross product of the two vectors which is the normal of the vectors.
N.x = V1.y * V2.z - V1.z * V2.y
N.y = V1.Z * V2.y - V1.x * V2.z
N.z = V1.x * V2.y - V1.y * V2.x
```

We will need to calculate the face normal vector only if we are programmatically creating a 3D object. Modeling software normally includes the face normal information in the saved data format. The normal vector is not only used to determine the lighting characteristics for the face; when we know the direction a face is pointing, we can also calculate the angle of incidence of light striking the face.

We have established what back face culling is and how it is determined. Since culling back faces is the default, why would we ever want to turn it off? By turning off the back face culling for some objects, we can make a two-dimensional object visible from both sides. One example of using this technique would be a checkered banner over the finish line of a race. Since both sides of the banner look the same, there is no reason we cannot have one set of triangles do double duty and make the simple banner visible from either side. The code to turn off back face culling is shown here:

```
Device.SetRenderState( RS.CullMode, Cull.None );
```

We must make sure that when we are done rendering that object we restore the culling state to its previous value. This is true with any of the rendering states. Forgetting to restore rendering states is a sure recipe for strange things happening on the screen.

Clipping

Clipping is the process of discarding the portions of the objects or their polygons that fall outside the current view. This is a part of the rendering pipeline that is handled for us by DirectX and the video card with no help required. Certain commands let us modify the clipping planes, but these are needed only for advanced tweaking of the clipping process, and therefore will not be covered in this book.

Setting Up the Vertex Buffer

As I touched on briefly in the "Converting Model Coordinates to the View Frame" section earlier, the point data for the objects that will be rendered get packed into a vertex buffer. The DrawPrimitive method called in the rendering phase will employ the vertex buffer to render using this information. The type of primitive specified must match the way in which the vertices are placed in the buffer to get the desired results.

Five basic primitive types can be used for rendering: point, line, triangle list, triangle strip, and triangle fan. The point primitive is used for rendering individual pixels onto the screen, such as when you want to depict stars in a night sky or in outer space. Another more prevalent use is for rendering point particles in a particle system. (Particle systems will be covered as part of Chapter 4.) Each vertex in the vertex buffer for points is the three-dimensional position of the point as well as the color information for that point. The number of primitives of this type will match the number of vertices in the buffer.

The second primitive, line, is used for drawing single-pixel-wide lines between two points in three-dimensional space. This is probably one of the least used primitive types. Its only utility is to render "heads-up" display information as part of an overlay. The primitive actually comes in two types: LineList and LineStrip. This list version declares that for every two points in the vertex buffer there will be a line drawn. Note that there must be an even number of points in the vertex buffer if we are rendering a line list. The strip version renders one multisegment line using the points in the buffer.

The remaining primitives are the ones that see the most usage in 3D games. These render triangles, with specific relationships between the triangles. The first and most common is the triangle list. For each set of three vertices in the buffer, one triangle will be rendered. This method requires the least amount of setup of the three triangle types. If the triangles of the object being rendered are adjacent to one another, we can take advantage of this fact and the fact that the adjacent polygons share common vertices.

The triangle strip primitive is used if the last two vertices of each triangle are also part of the next triangle in the buffer. This provides a roughly 66 percent performance gain over the triangle list since only about a third as many vertices need to be transformed to screen coordinates. In order to use this primitive, we must model the object in this manner and make sure that the vertex buffer is packed properly. Triangle strips are most commonly used when rendering a rectangular region. Figure 3-4 gives an example of a triangle strip.

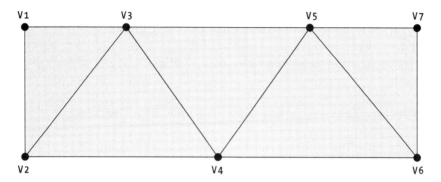

Figure 3-4. Triangle strip

The last primitive is the triangle fan. The fan has the same benefits as the strip, but serves a slightly different purpose. In a triangle fan, the first vertex in the buffer is common to all triangles in the fan. The last vertex in each triangle is also common with the next triangle. Figure 3-5 gives an example of a triangle fan.

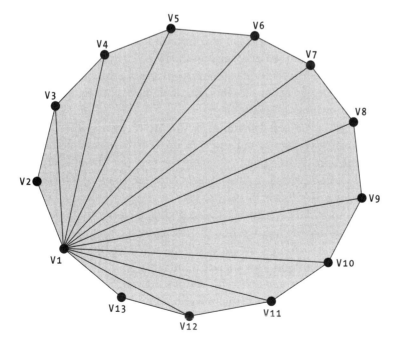

Figure 3-5. Triangle fan

Shading, Texturing, and Fog

Up to this point, the rendering process has been concerned with the shape of the objects that will be rendered. Now it is time to discuss how the shapes will look from the color aspect. A number of factors determine the color of each pixel as it is rendered to the screen. These factors include the material applied to the triangle, any texture applied to the triangle, the current light shining on the object, and any current fog effects.

Objects may have four basic color properties—diffuse, ambient, specular, and emissive:

- *Diffuse color:* The basic color for a particular portion of the object

- *Ambient color:* The minimum level of brightness of the color

- *Specular color:* The shininess of the color (i.e., how reflective the color is)

- *Emissive color:* The color that the object emits at a particular point

This color information is held in the vertices of the object. If all three vertices of a triangle have the same color value, then that triangle will have that same color. If the color values at the vertices differ, then the color of the triangle will transition from one color to the next as we look across the triangle from one vertex to another.

Another factor that determines the color at a given pixel in a triangle is the type of shading that is being performed. There are two shading methods that we can select from in the standard pipeline: flat and Gouraud. The flat shading method is the quickest and uses the color value at the first vertex for the entire polygon. The drawback with this method is that the outline of each polygon tends to be quite visible. Unless you desire this look to achieve a particular effect, I recommend against using flat shading.

The preferred method is Gouraud shading. This method uses the color data at each vertex as well as the vertex normal and lighting data to determine the colors to use. It also interpolates the colors between the vertices. The end effect is that the object looks smoother and more natural. Since the shading is being done in the video card anyway, this is the way to go.

Vertex coloring, or material coloring, as it is sometimes referred to, is one way to color our objects. Another method that provides much better apparent level of detail is texturing. Texturing is the process by which a portion of a bitmap is applied to each triangle. The image on the bitmap supplies the added detail. There are also alternate texturing options that apply predetermined lighting and bump information to the polygon. This allows the flat surface to appear to have shadows and an irregular surface. Depending on the capabilities of your video card, it is possible to combine up to eight textures to a polygon in a single pass. Each texture may also have multiple mipmaps. *Mipmaps* are a set of versions of a given texture at different resolutions. Each mipmap level is half the size of its parent texture. If mipmapping is being used, the smaller textures are automatically used as the textured polygons move further from the eye point.

This multitexturing is accomplished using texture stages. A texture is set to each stage through the SetTexture method as well as the stage index (which is zero based). A texture blending operation is also set for each stage using the SetTextureStageState method. The blending operation specifies how each texture is combined with the previous stage to produce the new texture that will be passed to the next stage or the renderer. The operation applied to the first stage typically specifies how the first texture is combined with the material color of the polygon. Table 3-2 lists the various texture stage operations and a brief description of what they do, and Table 3-3 lists the states that may be set for each stage.

Table 3-2. Texture Stage Operations

OPERATION	DESCRIPTION
ADD	Adds the components of the two arguments
ADDSIGNED	Adds the components of the two arguments and subtracts 0.5
ADDSIGNED2X	Functions the same as ADDSIGNED, with a 1 bit shift left
ADDSMOOTH	Performs the operation (argument 1 + argument 2) − (argument 1 $\times$ argument 2)
BLENDCURRENTALPHA	Blends arguments using the alpha from the previous stage
BLENDDIFFUSEALPHA	Blends the arguments using alpha data from vertices
BLENDFACTORALPHA	Blends arguments using a scalar alpha
BLENDTEXTUREALPHA	Blends arguments using alpha data from this stage texture
BLENDTEXTUREALPHAM	Blends arguments using a premultiplied alpha
BUMPENVMAP	Performs per-pixel bump mapping without luminance
BUMPENVMAPLUMINANCE	Performs per-pixel bump mapping with luminance
DISABLE	Disables output from the texture stage
DOTPRODUCT3	Modulates all color channels including alpha
LERP	Performs linear interpolation between two arguments proportioned by a third argument

Table 3-2. (continued)

OPERATION	DESCRIPTION
MODULATE	Multiplies the components of the two arguments
MODULATE2X	Multiplies the two arguments and shifts left 1 bit
MODULATE4X	Multiplies the two arguments and shifts left 2 bits
MODULATEALPHA_ADDCOLOR	Modulates the color of the second argument with the alpha from the first argument
MODULATECOLOR_ADDALPHA	Modulates color of the arguments and adds alpha from the first argument
MODULATEINVALPHA_ADDCOLOR	Functions the same as MODULATEALPHA_ADDCOLOR, but uses inverse of alpha
MODULATEINVCOLOR_ADDALPHA	Functions the same as MODULATECOLOR_ADDALPHA, but uses inverse of color
MULTIPLYADD	Multiplies the second and third argument and adds in the first argument
PREMODULATE	Modulates this texture stage with the next stage
SELECTARG1	Uses the first color or alpha argument as the output
SELECTARG2	Uses the second color or alpha argument as output
SUBTRACT	Subtracts the components of argument 2 from argument 1

Table 3-3. Texture Stage States

OPERATION	DESCRIPTION
ADDRESSU	Specifies the addressing mode for the U coordinate (wrap, clamp, etc.)
ADDRESSV	Specifies the addressing mode for the V coordinate (wrap, clamp, etc.)
ADDRESSW	Selects the texture addressing method for the W coordinate
ALPHAARG0	Selects the setting for the third alpha argument for triadic operations
ALPHAARG1	Designates the first argument for the alpha operation
ALPHAARG2	Designates the second argument for the alpha operation
ALPHAOP	Specifies that this stage is a texture-alpha blending operation

Table 3-3. (continued)

OPERATION	DESCRIPTION
BORDERCOLOR	Specifies the color to use for out-of-range texture coordinates
BUMPENVLOFFSET	Indicates offset value for bump map luminance
BUMPENVLSCALE	Indicates scale value for bump map luminance
BUMPENVMAT00	Specifies the [0][0] coefficient for the bump mapping matrix
BUMPENVMAT01	Specifies the [0][1] coefficient for the bump mapping matrix
BUMPENVMAT10	Specifies the [1][0] coefficient for the bump mapping matrix
BUMPENVMAT11	Specifies the [1][1] coefficient for the bump mapping matrix
COLORARG0	Selects the setting for the third color argument for triadic operations
COLORARG1	Designates the source for the first argument for the operation
COLORARG2	Designates the source for the second argument for the operation
COLOROP	Specifies texture-color blending operation (values for which appear in Table 3-2)
MAGFILTER	Specifies the type of filtering to use for texture magnification
MAXANISOTROPY	Specifies the maximum level of anisotropy
MAXMIPLEVEL	Specifies the highest level of mipmap that will be used
MINFILTER	Specifies the type of filtering to use for texture minification
MIPFILTER	Specifies the type of filtering to use between mipmap levels
MIPMAPLODBIAS	Specifies a bias factor in selecting mipmap levels
RESULTARG	Selects the destination for the stage's operation (default is the next stage)
TEXCOORDINDEX	Specifies which texture coordinates out of a possible eight sets to use
TEXTURETRANSFORMFLAGS	Controls the transformation of texture coordinates for this stage

The texture coordinates stored at each of the polygon's vertices determine the portion of the resulting texture that is applied to the polygon. The texture coordinates are stored in the U and V variables of the vertex. Think of U as the texture X coordinate and V as the texture Y coordinate. The texture coordinates are floating-point numbers in the range of 0.0 to 1.0. With this range, it does not matter if the texture is 16×16 pixels or 512×512 pixels. The portion of the image specified by the coordinates will be applied to the polygon. There are also filtering options that can be set to specify how the images are compressed or expanded to fit the size of the polygon. It is usually safe to let DirectX determine which filtering method to use. If the default method is causing problems, we will then need to determine what other method (if any) provides a better result.

NOTE   *Notice in the preceding paragraph that the texture sizes are a power of two. This is important! Video cards tend to expect that textures will always be a power of two in size. Although some texture operations appear to accept odd-sized textures, it is not recommended that you use odd-sized textures. Internally the operations are resizing the textures to be a power of two. Make it a practice to create your textures in power-of-two sizes, and you will stay out of a lot of trouble.*

Although we have applied our texture to the polygon, we still do not have the final colors that will be rendered to the screen. Now we need to consider lighting effects. The ambient light color and intensity, as well as any other light specified in the scene, are combined with the pixel colors based on the difference between the face normal and the direction of any directional lights.

Three types of lights can be defined in our scene: point lights, directional lights, and spotlights:

- *Point lights* radiate in all directions from a specified location (like the light emitted from a lightbulb).

- *Directional lights* behave as if they are at an infinite distance in a given direction (like sunlight).

- *Spotlights* produce a cone of light similar to a car's headlights.

For all of these lights, we are able to define diffuse, specular, and ambient colors just like we did for the vertices. The color of each light shining on a surface is added to the color value of the surface to calculate the resulting color.

It is possible that we still do not have the final color for our pixels. If we have defined fog for the scene, it makes a final adjustment to the color values. Fog works by fading the color of objects from their otherwise calculated values to the fog color as a function of the distance from the viewpoint. The exact rate of transition to the fog color is based on the minimum fog distance, the maximum fog distance, and the falloff formula for the fog. All of these attributes are defined when we set up fog for our scene. You will learn the details of lighting and fog in Chapter 7.

Rendering

The final step in the rendering pipeline is the actual rendering to the screen. At this point, every pixel of every object has been determined and transformed to a screen coordinate. As each pixel is about to be drawn to the screen, its Z (or W) value is checked against the corresponding value at that location in the Z buffer. If the pixel's depth value is greater than the value currently stored for that position, the pixel is not rendered. If the depth value is less (i.e., the pixel is closer to the viewpoint), the pixel is rendered to that location and the depth value is stored in the buffer.

Summary

This chapter gives you a quick look at the traditional fixed-function rendering pipeline. If we were to examine in detail each of the DirectX classes that are used during 3D rendering, there would be enough material to span several chapters. Rather than delve into that level of detail, I will present the information as we apply it in the following chapters. The DirectX documentation as well as the Visual Studio help and code completion features are always available to fill in the details along the way.

CHAPTER 4

Basic 3D Objects

THIS CHAPTER CONCENTRATES ON the portions of the game engine that provide the setting for the game. Every game is set in a particular environment, which could be the dark and winding corridors of a dungeon, the great outdoors, the depths of space, and so on. The genre of the game as well as any story line usually decides what this setting will be. The sample game we are developing over the course of this book will be an outdoor driving game. To set the scene for this game, we will want to provide the feeling of being outdoors: the illusion of seeing to the horizon, rolling landscape, static objects that dot the land, and some environmental effects.

Seeing to the Horizon: The Skybox

In an outdoor game, we should include a sense of being able to see for miles in all directions. Since the hardware does not exist to render three-dimensional terrain at these distances, a shortcut was developed to give the illusion of seeing to the horizon. This technique relies on a skybox or a sky dome, depending on the implementation. A *skybox* is a textured cube that is displayed around the viewpoint. All of the textures on the cube are displayed on the inside facing the viewpoint.

The top of the cube has a texture of the sky we would see if we were looking straight up. The bottom of the cube is a texture of the ground. The textures on each of the sides represent the view looking north, south, east, and west. These textures are created so that they meet with no visible seams to produce a sense of immersion within a scene. The tools for creating these textures are discussed in Chapter 11.

To create the illusion that the skybox is at a great distance from the viewer, we disable the Z-buffering for the skybox. Since the rendering of the skybox does not write to the Z-buffer, everything rendered after it is drawn on top of the skybox. We also want to prevent the player from getting closer to any of the images that make up the cube, so the cube is always centered on the current viewpoint.

What Makes Up a Skybox?

Now that we have established the basics of what makes up a skybox, it is time to look at an implementation and discuss the details. We will start with the vertex

113

structure for storing the points used to construct the cube for the skybox. Managed DirectX offers two different ways to define our vertex formats. The first method is reminiscent of the method used in the previous versions of DirectX. We define a structure for our vertex data and use the VertexFormat enumerations to inform the device as to what the structure looks like. Managed DirectX provides a second method by predefining a number of vertex formats that are commonly used. These structures appear in the CustomVertex namespace. All we need is the vector to define the point, normal vector, and the texture coordinates that dictate how the texture map is drawn. The CustomVertex PositionNormalTextured structure fits the bill.

Now that we have a structure defining a point for the corner of the cube, it is time to move up to a class defining a cube face. A *cube face* is one side of the skybox consisting of the four points that define the corners of the face and the texture that is drawn on the face. The other information that the class will hold includes the name of the file containing the texture, the vertex buffer used for rendering, and a flag indicating that the class has been properly initialized and may be rendered. The final attribute in the class is a read-only accessor to allow other classes to check the face's validity. Listing 4-1 shows these attributes as they appear in the C# source code.

Listing 4-1. SkyFace Class Attribute Definition

```
public class SkyFace : IDisposable
{
#region Attributes
    private CustomVertex.PositionNormalTextured[]  m_Corners;
    private VertexBuffer m_VB = null;  // Vertex buffer
    private Texture      m_Texture; // Image for face
    private bool         m_bValid = false;
    private string       m_sName;

    public bool Valid { get { return m_bValid; } }
#endregion
```

The constructor sets the points for the four corners and loads the texture for that face. The arguments for the constructor are the name of the file holding the structure and an enumerated value declaring which face of the cube to build. The constructor begins by saving the filename for future reference and creating an array of four vertices, one for each corner. The next three listings (Listing 4-2a, shown here, and Listings 4-2b and 4-2c, shown a little later) cover the source code for the constructor.

Listing 4-2a. SkyFace Constructor Definition

```
public SkyFace( string sName, SkyBox.Face face )
{
    m_sName = sName;
    // Create the vertices for the box.
    m_Corners = new CustomVertex.PositionNormalTextured[4];
```

A switch statement is then used to establish which face to build based on the value passed into the constructor. Each face is 200 units on a side centered on zero. The texture coordinates are set up so that the face texture occupies the complete face. The normal vector at each corner is set to point toward the inside of the cube. The code snippet in Listing 4-2b shows the initialization for the face at the top of the cube. The code for the other faces is nearly identical except for the coordinates used for the corner locations. To see the details for the other faces, check out SkyBox.cs in code downloadable from the Apress Web site.

Listing 4-2b. SkyFace Constructor Definition (Continued)

```
    switch ( face )
    {
    case SkyBox.Face.Top:
        m_Corners[0].X = -100.0f;
        m_Corners[0].Y =  100.0f;
        m_Corners[0].Z = -100.0f;
        m_Corners[0].Tu = 0.0f;
        m_Corners[0].Tv = 1.0f;
        m_Corners[0].Nx = 0.0f;
        m_Corners[0].Ny = -1.0f;
        m_Corners[0].Nz = 0.0f;
        m_Corners[1].X =  100.0f;
        m_Corners[1].Y =  100.0f;
        m_Corners[1].Z = -100.0f;
        m_Corners[1].Tu = 0.0f;
        m_Corners[1].Tv = 0.0f;
        m_Corners[1].Nx = 0.0f;
        m_Corners[1].Ny = -1.0f;
        m_Corners[1].Nz = 0.0f;
        m_Corners[2].X = -100.0f;
        m_Corners[2].Y =  100.0f;
        m_Corners[2].Z =  100.0f;
```

```
    m_Corners[2].Tu = 1.0f;
    m_Corners[2].Tv = 1.0f;
    m_Corners[2].Nx = 0.0f;
    m_Corners[2].Ny = -1.0f;
    m_Corners[2].Nz = 0.0f;
    m_Corners[3].X =  100.0f;
    m_Corners[3].Y =  100.0f;
    m_Corners[3].Z =  100.0f;
    m_Corners[3].Tu = 1.0f;
    m_Corners[3].Tv = 0.0f;
    m_Corners[3].Nx = 0.0f;
    m_Corners[3].Ny = -1.0f;
    m_Corners[3].Nz = 0.0f;
  break;
```

Now that the data for the corner positions has been defined, it is time to load the texture to apply to the face, as shown in Listing 4-2c. The call to create the texture from the image file is enclosed in a Try/Catch block. This protects against trying to load a file that doesn't exist. If the call fails, a message is posted to the console so that the developer is alerted to the problem. The CreateTexture method will create the texture using video memory if enough is available. Failing this, it will create the texture in System memory, which will allow the texture to be used at the cost of performance. If the call to CreateTexture succeeds, the valid flag is set to true so that the rendering code knows that the face is ready to be rendered. The final thing to do is the allocation and setup of the vertex buffer for the face. An event handler is used to place the data into the vertex buffer. This allows the system to automatically refill the vertex buffer if it needs to be re-created later.

 NOTE *If the game application loses focus (i.e., another application gets input focus), the resources on the video card may be lost. When the game regains the focus, we will need to restore these resources. DirectX provides events and event handlers for this situation.*

Listing 4-2c. SkyFace Constructor Definition (Conclusion)

```
// Load the texture for the face.
try
{
    m_Texture = GraphicsUtility.CreateTexture(CGameEngine.Device3D, sName);
    m_bValid = true;
```

```
    }
    catch
    {
        Console.AddLine("Unable to create skybox texture for " + sName);
    }
    // Create a quad for rendering the face.
    m_VB = new VertexBuffer( typeof(CustomVertex.PositionNormalTextured), 4,
            CGameEngine.Device3D, Usage.WriteOnly,
            CustomVertex.PositionNormalTextured.Format, Pool.Default );
    m_VB.Created += new System.EventHandler(this.CreateQuad);
    CreateQuad(m_VB, null);

}
```

The `CreateQuad` message handler is used to populate the vertex buffer. This message handler is called anytime the vertex buffer needs to be re-created. This simple message handler only needs to copy the contents of the `m_Corners` array into the vertex buffer as shown in Listing 4-3.

Listing 4-3. SkyFace CreateQuad Message Handler

```
public void CreateQuad(object sender, EventArgs e)
{
    VertexBuffer vb = (VertexBuffer)sender;

    // Copy tree mesh data into vertex buffer.
    vb.SetData(m_Corners, 0, 0);
}
```

The drawing of a face of the `SkyBox` object is performed by the `SkyFace Render` method. Before we actually try to render anything, we need to make sure that the face is valid. Remember that back in the constructor we set the valid flag to true at the end of the construction steps. If an exception had been thrown at any point in the constructor, the setting of the flag to true would have been skipped. Assuming that the face is valid, the normal rendering steps are followed. The stream source, vertex format, and texture are set. The `DrawPrimitives` method is then called to render the face as a triangle strip of two triangles. The method is show in Listing 4-4.

Listing 4-4. SkyFace Render Method

```
public void Render()
{
    if ( m_bValid )
    {
        Material mtrl = new Material();
        mtrl.Ambient = Color.White;
        mtrl.Diffuse = Color.White;
        CGameEngine.Device3D.Material = mtrl;
        CGameEngine.GetDevice().SetStreamSource( 0, m_VB, 0 );
        CGameEngine.Device3D.VertexFormat =
                        CustomVertex.PositionNormalTextured.Format;
        // Set the texture.
        CGameEngine.GetDevice().SetTexture(0, m_Texture );

        // Render the face.
        CGameEngine.GetDevice().DrawPrimitives(
                        PrimitiveType.TriangleStrip, 0, 2 );
    }
}
```

The last method in the class is the `Dispose` method shown in Listing 4-5. The assets of this class to dispose of consist of the texture and the vertex buffer.

 NOTE *Remember that textures, vertex buffers, and index buffers are allocated from memory on the video card. Failing to dispose of them as soon as you no longer need them could get you into a situation where you do not have enough memory left on the card to allocate new textures and buffers. You cannot wait for the .NET garbage collector to do this for you. It does not distinguish between system memory and video card memory and may not free the memory until the application exits.*

Listing 4-5. SkyFace Dispose Method

```
public void Dispose()
{
    m_Texture.Dispose();

    if( m_VB != null )
        m_VB.Dispose();
}
}
```

Building the Skybox

Now that we have a class that defines and handles a given face of the skybox, we are ready to construct the box itself. Listing 4-6 shows the definition of the SkyBox class. The box is composed of the six faces of the cube, and there is also an enumeration to describe each of the six faces. The enumeration value is passed into the constructor of each face so that it knows its position within the cube. This defines the correct vertices for that face.

Listing 4-6. SkyBox Class Definition

```
public class SkyBox : Object3D, IDisposable
{
#region Attributes
    private SkyFace[] m_faces = new SkyFace[6];

    public enum Face { Top, Bottom, Front, Right, Back, Left }
#endregion
```

The constructor for the SkyBox accepts six arguments. Each argument is a string containing the complete path to a texture file that will be used for one of the box faces. These strings are used along with values from the face enumeration to construct each of the SkyFace members. Listing 4-7 shows the constructor and Figure 4-1 shows the six image files that will be used for the six textures.

Listing 4-7. SkyBox Constructor

```
public SkyBox( string sFront, string sRight, string sBack, string sLeft,
   string sTop, string sBottom ) : base( "SkyBox" )
{
    // Create the faces for the box.
    m_faces[0] = new SkyFace( sFront,  Face.Front );
    m_faces[1] = new SkyFace( sLeft,   Face.Right );
    m_faces[2] = new SkyFace( sBack,   Face.Back );
    m_faces[3] = new SkyFace( sRight,   Face.Left );
    m_faces[4] = new SkyFace( sTop,    Face.Top );
    m_faces[5] = new SkyFace( sBottom, Face.Bottom );
}
```

The Dispose method for the class (shown in Listing 4-8) calls the Dispose method for each of the faces. This ensures that the faces have the chance to free the textures and buffers as described earlier.

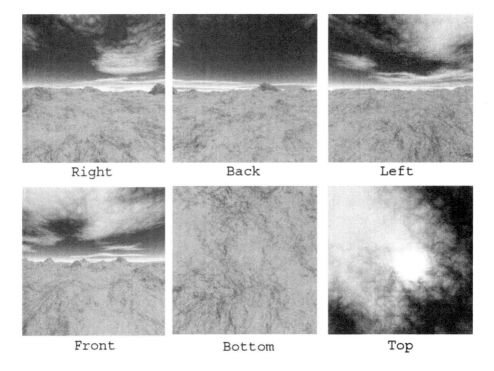

Right   Back   Left

Front   Bottom   Top

Figure 4-1. Skybox faces

Listing 4-8. SkyBox Dispose Method

```
public override void Dispose()
{
    for ( int i = 0; i < 6; i++ )
    {
        m_faces[i].Dispose();
    }
}
```

The heart of the class is its Render method shown, in Listing 4-9. The SkyBox object has several unique features that will not be found in any other object that will be rendered. The viewpoint must always be in the center of the box; therefore the box must move as the camera moves. Even though the box is built with a finite size, it must appear to be a very long distance away. To give the illusion that the box is very far away, we will turn off writing to the Z-buffer. By doing this, everything else that is rendered will be drawn on top of the box and appear to be closer.

Listing 4-9. SkyBox Render Method

```
public void Render( Camera cam )
{
   try
     {
     // Set the matrix for normal viewing.
     Matrix matWorld = new Matrix();
     matWorld = Matrix.Identity;

     // Center view matrix for skybox.
     Matrix matView;
     matView = cam.View;
     matView.M41 = 0.0f;
     matView.M42 = -0.3f;
     matView.M43 = 0.0f;
     CGameEngine.Device3D.Transform.View = matView;

     CGameEngine.Device3D.Transform.World = matWorld;
     CGameEngine.Device3D.RenderState.ZbufferWriteEnable = false;
     CGameEngine.Device3D.RenderState.CullMode =
         Microsoft.DirectX.Direct3D.Cull.None;

      // Pick faces based on camera attitude.
      if ( cam.Pitch > 0.0f )
      {
         m_faces[4].Render();
      }
      else if ( cam.Pitch < 0.0f )
      {
         m_faces[5].Render();
      }

      if ( cam.Heading > 0.0f && cam.Heading < 180.0 ) m_faces[1].Render();
      if ( cam.Heading > 270.0f || cam.Heading < 90.0 ) m_faces[0].Render();
      if ( cam.Heading > 180.0f && cam.Heading < 360.0 ) m_faces[3].Render();
      if ( cam.Heading > 90.0f && cam.Heading < 270.0 ) m_faces[2].Render();
```

```
        // Restore the render states.
        CGameEngine.Device3D.Transform.View = cam.View;
        CGameEngine.Device3D.RenderState.ZbufferWriteEnable = true;
}
catch (DirectXException d3de)
{
    Console.AddLine("Unable to render skybox ");
    Console.AddLine(d3de.ErrorString);
}
catch ( Exception e )
{
    Console.AddLine("Unable to render skybox ");
}
```

The method begins by creating a world matrix for itself that is set to the identity matrix. This ensures that the box (whose vertices are all offset around a zero position) is not translated from that position. Copying the camera's matrix and adjusting the position down slightly creates a view matrix. Experience has shown me that by adjusting the position down, we get a better-looking horizon than if we were dead center in the box. These matrices are passed to the device, and the Z-buffer write enable flag is cleared in the render state so that the buffer will not be altered as we render the box. The culling in the render state is turned off by setting the state to None. Since we are only drawing the few faces that are in view, there is no sense having the device check for face culling. The pitch and heading of the camera are checked, and only the faces of the box that might be visible are rendered. Once the faces have been rendered, the view matrix and Z-buffer render states are restored to their normal conditions.

This completes the SkyBox class. If we run the game now, we see something like Figure 4-2. We can move the camera using our mouse, and can look in all directions. Because we are near the center of the box, it appears that we are floating above the ground. As we turn full circle, it appears that we can see to the horizon in all directions. Mission accomplished.

Figure 4-2. Skybox only

Traveling the Rolling Landscape

Now that we have our horizon and sky, it is time to put some ground under our feet. The class that will provide the ground for our game will be the `Terrain` class. There are many different ways to create the ground surface in a game, ranging from a detailed mesh created in a 3D modeling package at the high end down to a single textured square at the low end. We are going to use a solution that is somewhere in the middle of these two extremes by creating a regular grid mesh. This means that each point in the rectangular mesh will be a constant distance from each of its neighbors.

   The easiest way to model the shape of the terrain in a regular grid system like this is to use an image as a height map. Each pixel in the image will represent one of the points in the grid. The blue color channel for each pixel will represent the height at that point. In a normal image where each color is represented by an 8-bit value, this gives us 256 possible values for each height. A vertical scale factor will define how many feet each value represents. A horizontal scale factor will determine how far apart each of the points will be. In Chapter 11, during our investigation of applicable tools, we will look at how this height map is created.

The Building Blocks for the Terrain

Each square area within the grid will be represented by an instance of the TerrainQuad class. Breaking the terrain up in this manner allows us to display only those portions of the terrain that are currently visible in the viewing frustum.

The TerrainQuad class (shown in Listing 4-10) indicates that the class inherits from the Object3D class to give each quad the basic characteristics of a 3D object. The class also has an array of vertices that will be used in rendering the quad. It also has a validity flag and two vectors (one for each triangle of the quad) for the normal vectors. A property called FaceNormals returns the average of the two triangle normal vectors as the average normal for the quad.

Listing 4-10. TerrainQuad Class Definition

```
public class TerrainQuad : Object3D, IDisposable
{
    #region Attributes
    private  CustomVertex.PositionNormalTextured[] m_Corners;
    private bool        m_bValid = false;
    public Vector3      m_Face1Normal;
    public Vector3      m_Face2Normal;

    public bool Valid { get { return m_bValid; } }
    public Vector3 FaceNormals { get {
      Vector3 sum = Vector3.Add(m_Face1Normal, m_Face2Normal);
      sum.Normalize();
      return sum; } }
#endregion
```

NOTE   *A shortcut for averaging two vectors is to add them and then normalize (assuming the original vectors were normalized in the first place).*

Each terrain quad is going to be made up of two triangles. While some would argue that it is more efficient to do this with four points and a triangle strip, we will not. Because we will be batching the triangles together, it is actually more efficient to use the larger buffer a triangle list requires than to break the rendering calls up so that there is one call per strip. Therefore the constructor (shown in Listing 4-11) will define six vertices using the four positions that are passed as arguments. These vertices will use the PositionNormalTextured vertex format. As the name implies, this format holds the three components of the position, the three components of the normal vector, and the two texture coordinates for each vertex. A helper method in the `GameMath` class `ComputeFaceNormal` is used to calculate the normal vector for each triangle.

Listing 4-11. TerrainQuad Constructor

```
public TerrainQuad( string sName, Vector3 p1, Vector3 p2,
   Vector3 p3, Vector3 p4 ) : base( sName )

{
    m_sName = sName;

    // Create the vertices for the box.
    m_Corners = new CustomVertex.PositionNormalTextured[6];

    m_Corners[0].X = p3.X;   // nw
    m_Corners[0].Y = p3.Y;
    m_Corners[0].Z = p3.Z;
    m_Corners[0].Tu = 0.0f;
    m_Corners[0].Tv = 1.0f;
    m_Corners[1].X = p1.X;   // sw
    m_Corners[1].Y = p1.Y;
    m_Corners[1].Z = p1.Z;
    m_Corners[1].Tu = 0.0f;
    m_Corners[1].Tv = 0.0f;
    m_Corners[2].X = p4.X;   // ne
    m_Corners[2].Y = p4.Y;
    m_Corners[2].Z = p4.Z;
    m_Corners[2].Tu = 1.0f;
    m_Corners[2].Tv = 1.0f;
    m_Corners[3].X = p2.X;   // ne
    m_Corners[3].Y = p2.Y;
    m_Corners[3].Z = p2.Z;
    m_Corners[3].Tu = 1.0f;
    m_Corners[3].Tv = 0.0f;

    m_vPosition.X = (p4.X + p3.X) / 2.0f;
    m_vPosition.Y = (p1.Y + p2.Y + p3.Y + p4.Y) / 4.0f;
    m_vPosition.Z = (p1.Z + p3.Z) / 2.0f;
    double dx = p4.X - p3.X;
    double dz = p3.Z - p1.Z;
    m_fRadius = (float)Math.Sqrt( dx * dx + dz * dz ) / 2.0f;
```

```
    m_Face1Normal = GameMath.ComputeFaceNormal(
        new Vector3(m_Corners[0].X,m_Corners[0].Y,m_Corners[0].Z),
        new Vector3(m_Corners[1].X,m_Corners[1].Y,m_Corners[1].Z),
        new Vector3(m_Corners[2].X,m_Corners[2].Y,m_Corners[2].Z) );
    m_Face2Normal = GameMath.ComputeFaceNormal(
        new Vector3(m_Corners[1].X,m_Corners[1].Y,m_Corners[1].Z),
        new Vector3(m_Corners[3].X,m_Corners[3].Y,m_Corners[3].Z),
        new Vector3(m_Corners[2].X,m_Corners[2].Y,m_Corners[2].Z) );

    // Default the vertex normals to the face normal value.
    m_Corners[0].SetNormal( m_Face1Normal );
    m_Corners[1].SetNormal( FaceNormals );
    m_Corners[2].SetNormal( FaceNormals );
    m_Corners[3].SetNormal( m_Face2Normal );
    m_Corners[4].SetNormal( FaceNormals );
    m_Corners[5].SetNormal( FaceNormals );

     m_Corners[4].X = m_Corners[2].X;
     m_Corners[4].Y = m_Corners[2].Y;
     m_Corners[4].Z = m_Corners[2].Z;
     m_Corners[4].Tu = m_Corners[2].Tu;
     m_Corners[4].Tv = m_Corners[2].Tv;
     m_Corners[5].X = m_Corners[1].X;
     m_Corners[5].Y = m_Corners[1].Y;
     m_Corners[5].Z = m_Corners[1].Z;
     m_Corners[5].Tu = m_Corners[1].Tu;
     m_Corners[5].Tv = m_Corners[1].Tv;

    m_bValid = true;
}
```

Once all of the quads for the terrain have been created, the `Terrain` class will go back and compute a new normal for each of the vertices. This normal vector will be the average of all of the triangle normal vectors that include that vertex. This will make the terrain look smooth as it is rendered. If the default normal vectors were used for each vertex, the terrain would tend to look faceted and angular. The `SetCornerNormal` method shown in Listing 4-12 provides the interface for the `Terrain` class to alter a vertex normal. Since this function cannot be sure that vector is properly normalized, we will normalize the vector prior to saving it.

Listing 4-12. TerrainQuad SetCornerNormal Method

```
public void SetCornerNormal( int Corner, Vector3 Normal )
{
   Normal.Normalize();
   m_Corners[Corner].SetNormal( Normal );
}
```

The `Dispose` method (shown in Listing 4-13) is an empty method at this time. I am including it for completeness. Future versions of the `TerrainQuad` class may require that we dispose of allocated objects. One example might be the use of a specific texture per quad. For now, we will be using one texture common to all quads. For this reason, it is defined and maintained by the `Terrain` class rather than by each quad.

Listing 4-13. TerrainQuad Dispose Method

```
public override void Dispose()
{
}
```

The `RenderQuad` method (shown in Listing 4-14) will not actually render anything to the screen. Instead, it will copy the vertices for this quad into a buffer supplied by the calling method. This is part of the batching process that is used to improve rendering efficiency. The video cards can render the triangles quicker if given several thousand vertices at a time whenever possible. To fill the buffer, this method accepts the buffer (an array of vertices) and the current offset within the buffer. If the quad is valid and has not been culled (i.e., it should be visible), each of the six vertices is copied to the buffer. The offset is incremented by six and returned to the calling method.

NOTE *Notice that the culled flag is reset to the true state after the data has been copied. In this game engine, all objects are set to the culled state after they have been rendered. The culling software assumes that the objects are not visible. If the object is within the viewing frustum, the culled flag is cleared to false to allow the object to be rendered.*

Listing 4-14. TerrainQuad RenderQuad Method

```
public int RenderQuad( int Offset,
        CustomVertex.PositionNormalTextured [] vertices )
{
    int newOffset = Offset;

    if ( Valid && !IsCulled )
    {
        for ( int i=0; i<6; i++ )
        {
            vertices[Offset+i] = m_Corners[i];
        }
        newOffset += 6;
        Culled = true;
    }
    return newOffset;
}
```

The InRect method (shown in Listing 4-15) is used when an object is being inserted into the Quadtree. A bounding rectangle is passed in as the argument. The method returns a false if the quad is not within the rectangle and a true if it is. The Rectangle class supplied by Microsoft includes a method called Contains that checks a point against the rectangle. We will loop through the four corners of the quad, checking to see if the rectangle contains that point. If it does, we set the return value to true and break out of the loop. If any point is within the rectangle, we do not need to waste time checking any of the other corners.

Listing 4-15. TerrainQuad InRect Method

```
public override bool InRect( Rectangle rect )
{
    bool inside = false;

    // Check to see if the object is within this rectangle by checking each
corner.
    for ( int i=0; i<4; i++ )
    {
        if ( rect.Contains((int)m_Corners[i].X,(int)m_Corners[i].Z) )
        {
            inside = true;
            break;
        }
    }
    return inside;
}
```

Assembling the Terrain

The TerrainQuad instances will be used in a two-dimensional array to form our terrain. The Terrain class needs to support more than just the visible effect of having some ground below us. It must also supply us with information about that terrain so that we may interact with it as we move along. The ITerrainInfo interface is used to define the various queries that we will want to make against the terrain. It allows us to know what the altitude is below us so that we do not sink through the surface. The interface also returns the slope of the terrain under us so that we are properly oriented on the surface.

Listing 4-16 shows the definition of the Terrain class. The class contains a two-dimensional array of vectors that holds the raw data points that make up the terrain. There is also a two-dimensional array of the TerrainQuad instances that define the surface mapped over these points. The class will also remember the dimensions of the arrays using the m_xSize and m_ySize integers. The distance between points in the grid is stored in the variable m_Spacing. The other members of the class are the texture and the array of vertices to be rendered in a given pass.

Listing 4-16. Terrain Class Definition

```
public class Terrain : IDisposable, ITerrainInfo
{

    private Vector3[,]       m_Elevations;
    private VertexBuffer m_VB = null;   // Vertex buffer
    private TerrainQuad[,] m_Quads = null;
    private int m_xSize;
    private int m_ySize;
    private Texture       m_Texture; // Image for face
    private bool m_bValid = false;
    private CustomVertex.PositionNormalTextured [] m_Vertices;
    private float m_Spacing;
```

The class constructor (shown in Listings 4-17a through 4-17e in a bit) has the job of building the terrain structure from the supplied data. The first two arguments are the dimensions of the grid of elevations. The third argument is the fully qualified path name of the image file holding the height map. The dimensions of this image must be equal to or greater than the dimensions specified in the first two arguments. If the image is not big enough, an exception will be thrown and the terrain will be considered invalid. The next argument is the fully qualified path to the image that will be used as the texture on each quad. For the sample game engine we are developing, this will be an image of a sandy surface. The final two arguments are used to scale the data from the height map to calculate the elevation posts. The spacing data specifies how far apart each post is in meters. The elevation factor is the vertical scaling to convert the blue color value to an elevation in meters.

The constructor begins by allocating the arrays for the elevation data and the quads (Listing 4-17a). Note that the dimensions for the quad array are one smaller in each dimension. This is because the quads lay between the elevation points. A vertex array is allocated to hold three thousand vertices. This is the size of the vertex batch that we will pass to the 3D device with each DrawPrimitive call.

Listing 4-17a. Terrain Class Constructor

```
public Terrain(int xSize, int ySize, string sName, string sTexture,
    float fSpacing, float fElevFactor)
{
    int nTemp;

    m_Elevations = new Vector3[xSize,ySize];
    m_xSize = xSize-1;
    m_ySize = ySize-1;
    m_Quads = new TerrainQuad[m_xSize,m_ySize];
    m_Vertices = new CustomVertex.PositionNormalTextured [3000];
    m_Spacing = fSpacing;
```

The next step in the constructor is to extract the elevation information from the height map (Listing 4-17b). The Bitmap class in the System.Drawing namespace is a handy tool for this. It knows how to read many of the common image formats and includes a method to examine individual pixels within the image. To calculate the elevation data, we will loop through the pixels of the height map using the size information passed into the constructor. The X dimension of each elevation point will start at zero and increment east by the spacing value. The Z dimension will operate the same way but in the northern direction. The Y dimension is the elevation at each point. It is calculated by taking the blue component of the pixel's color and multiplying it by the elevation factor. Once we have operated on all of the desired pixels, we call the bitmap's Dispose method. Any exceptions thrown will be sent to the console for display.

Listing 4-17b. Terrain Class Constructor (Continued)

```
    try
    {
        System.Drawing.Bitmap bmp = new System.Drawing.Bitmap(sName);
        for ( int i=0; i<xSize; i++ )
        {
```

```
        for ( int j=0; j<ySize; j++ )
        {
            nTemp = bmp.GetPixel(i,j).ToArgb() & 0x000000ff;
            m_Elevations[i,j].X = i * fSpacing;
            m_Elevations[i,j].Z = j * fSpacing;
            m_Elevations[i,j].Y = nTemp * fElevFactor;
        }
    }
    bmp.Dispose();
}
catch (DirectXException d3de)
{
    Console.AddLine("Unable to load terrain heightmap " + sName);
    Console.AddLine(d3de.ErrorString);
}
catch ( Exception e )
{
    Console.AddLine("Unable to load terrain heightmap " + sName);
    Console.AddLine(e.Message);
}
```

The next portion of the constructor (shown in Listing 4-17c) creates the TerrainQuads for the terrain. This time we loop through the dimensions of the m_Quads array and create the quad instances to populate the array. The data from the elevations array is passed to the TerrainQuad constructor. Each quad is also added to the Quadtree for culling when we are rendering the terrain.

Listing 4-17c. Terrain Class Constructor (Continued)

```
try
{
    for ( int i=0; i<m_xSize; i++ )
    {
        for ( int j=0; j<m_ySize; j++ )
        {
            string sQuadName = "Quad" + i + "-" + j;
            m_Quads[i,j] = new TerrainQuad(sQuadName, m_Elevations[i,j],
              m_Elevations[i+1,j], m_Elevations[i,j+1], m_Elevations[i+1,j+1]);
            CGameEngine.QuadTree.AddObject((Object3D)m_Quads[i,j]);
        }
    }
    Console.AddLine("Done creating quads");
}
```

```
catch (DirectXException d3de)
{
    Console.AddLine("Unable to create quads " );
    Console.AddLine(d3de.ErrorString);
}
catch ( Exception e )
{
    Console.AddLine("Unable to create quads " );
    Console.AddLine(e.Message);
}
```

Now that we have created all of the quads, it is time to do a little housekeeping. When we create the quads, we set the vertex normals to be the same as the face normals for that quad. Now we can go back and calculate the correct normals at each vertex. Listing 4-17d shows the section of the constructor that accomplishes this. In each quad corner (except those along the outside edge of the terrain), four quads come together at that point. To get the normal vector for that point, we need to average the four face normals to get the correct vertex normal. Remember that the easy way to average normalized vectors is to add the vectors and then renormalize. The SetCornerNormal method takes care of the normalizing of the vector.

Listing 4-17d. Terrain Class Constructor (Continued)

```
for ( int i=1; i<m_xSize-1; i++ )
{
    for ( int j=1; j<m_ySize-1; j++ )
    {
        // Assign normals to each vertex.
        Vector3 Normalsw =
            m_Quads[i,j].FaceNormals + m_Quads[i-1,j-1].FaceNormals +
            m_Quads[i-1,j].FaceNormals + m_Quads[i,j-1].FaceNormals;
        m_Quads[i,j].SetCornerNormal( 0, Normalsw );

        Vector3 Normalse =
            m_Quads[i,j].FaceNormals + m_Quads[i,j-1].FaceNormals +
            m_Quads[i+1,j].FaceNormals + m_Quads[i+1,j-1].FaceNormals;
        m_Quads[i,j].SetCornerNormal( 1, Normalse );

        Vector3 Normalnw =
            m_Quads[i,j].FaceNormals + m_Quads[i-1,j].FaceNormals +
            m_Quads[i-1,j+1].FaceNormals + m_Quads[i,j+1].FaceNormals;
        m_Quads[i,j].SetCornerNormal( 2, Normalnw );
```

```
      Vector3 Normalne =
          m_Quads[i,j].FaceNormals + m_Quads[i,j+1].FaceNormals +
          m_Quads[i+1,j+1].FaceNormals + m_Quads[i+1,j].FaceNormals;
      m_Quads[i,j].SetCornerNormal( 3, Normalne );
   }
}
```

The final portion of the constructor (shown in Listing 4-17e) initializes the
texture and vertex buffer used to render the terrain. The texture is created using
the utility function CreateTexture. We wrap it in a Try/Catch block in case there is
not enough video memory to hold the texture or the texture file is not found. The
vertex buffer is created to hold 3000 vertices. If we succeed in creating the vertex
buffer, it is safe to set the valid flag to true. As a final step, we post a message to
the console that the loading of the terrain has been completed.

Listing 4-17e. Terrain Class Constructor (Conclusion)

```
      try
      {
          m_Texture = GraphicsUtility.CreateTexture(CGameEngine.Device3D,
              sTexture);
      }
      catch
      {
          Console.AddLine("Unable to create terrain texture using " + sTexture);
      }

      try
      {
          // Create a vertex buffer for rendering the terrain.
          m_VB = new VertexBuffer( typeof(CustomVertex.PositionNormalTextured),
              3000, CGameEngine.Device3D, Usage.WriteOnly,
              CustomVertex.PositionNormalTextured.Format, Pool.Default );
          m_bValid = true;
      }
      catch
      {
          Console.AddLine("Unable to create terrain vertex buffer");
      }

      Console.AddLine("terrain loaded");
}
```

There are two methods (shown in Listing 4-18) in the Terrain class for querying the elevation at a given point on the terrain. The first method is HeightOfTerrain, which accepts a position vector and returns the floating-point elevation in feet. It simply passes the X and Z components of the position to the other method, TerrainHeight. The TerrainHeight method accepts an east and a north position and returns the elevation at that point. This is the method that actually calculates the elevation. The method calculates the indices of the four elevation points that surround the position in question. Once we have the four elevation points, it is simply a matter of doing a four-way interpolation between the points to get the elevation.

Listing 4-18. Terrain Class HeightOfTerrain and TerrainHeight Methods

```
public float HeightOfTerrain( Vector3 pos )
{
    return TerrainHeight( pos.X, pos.Z );
}

public float TerrainHeight( float east, float north )
{
    int x1 = (int)(east/m_Spacing - 0.5);
    int x2 = (int)(east/m_Spacing + 0.5);
    int z1 = (int)(north/m_Spacing - 0.5);
    int z2 = (int)(north/m_Spacing + 0.5);

    // Interpolation between the corner elevations
    float height;

    float dx = (east - x1 * m_Spacing) / m_Spacing;
    float dy = (north - z1 * m_Spacing) / m_Spacing;
    height = m_Elevations[x1,z1].Y + dx * (m_Elevations[x2,z1].Y -
        m_Elevations[x1,z1].Y) + dy * (m_Elevations[x1,z2].Y -
        m_Elevations[x1,z1].Y) + dx * dy * (m_Elevations[x1,z1].Y -
        m_Elevations[x2,z1].Y - m_Elevations[x1,z2].Y +
        m_Elevations[x2,z2].Y);
    return height;
}
```

The HeightAboveTerrain method (shown in Listing 4-19) proves useful in a flight simulation. The height above the terrain is simply the difference between the height of the supplied point and the elevation of the terrain beneath that point. As this method accepts a position vector as an argument, it simply uses that same vector as the argument for the HeightOfTerrain method.

Listing 4-19. Terrain Class HeightAboveTerrain Method

```
public float HeightAboveTerrain( Vector3 Position )
{
    return HeightOfTerrain( Position ) - Position.Y;
}
```

Another important query that would be made against the terrain is a line of sight (LOS) check. This query traverses a line connecting two points to see if the line passes through the terrain at any point. There are several ways to address the problem. If it were vital that this check be extremely accurate, we would need to do a line polygon intersection test with every polygon along the path from one point to the other. This would be computationally expensive. We will take a slightly lower fidelity approach to the problem. We will step a test point along the line connecting the two points in question. If the terrain height at that point is below the interpolated point's height, we will assume that we still have line of sight. The first tested point that is below the terrain surface will determine that the line of sight has been broken.

NOTE *There is a small chance that this method will return a false positive if a ridge occurs in the terrain between two of the test points. Decreasing the increment step will decrease the chance of this happening (with a corresponding increase in processing time).*

Listing 4-20 shows the code for the InLineOfSight method. The method begins by assuming that we do have line of sight between the two points. The slope of the line between the two points is then calculated in both the horizontal and vertical axes. The slope will be used to move the test point between the two points being tested. The increment on the east/west axis is calculated at 75 percent of the spacing between elevation data points. This is to ensure that each quad in the terrain grid is checked with at least one test point.

Listing 4-20. Terrain Class InLineOfSight Method

```
public bool InLineOfSight( Vector3 Position1, Vector3 Position2 )
{
    bool los = true;
    float north;

    float dx = Position2.X - Position1.X;
    float dy = Position2.Y - Position1.Y;
    float dz = Position2.Z - Position1.Z;
```

```
        float dp = dz / dx;

        float dist = (float)Math.Sqrt(dx*dx + dz*dz);
        float de = dy / dist;

        float IncX = m_Spacing * 0.75f;
        float y = Position1.Y;
        float east = Position1.X;

        while ( east < Position2.X && los )
        {
            north = Position1.Z + ( east - Position1.X ) * dp;
            los = TerrainHeight(east, north ) <= y;
            east += IncX;
            y += (IncX*dp) * de;
        }
        return los;
    }
```

The next terrain information query that we will look at is the GetSlope method (shown in Listing 4-21). This method takes advantage of the fact that the slope of a terrain polygon is equal to the difference between the face normal vector of the polygon and a vector in the vertical direction. The arguments to the method consist of the position in question and a heading in radians. The heading is important since we need to rotate the vector so that the pitch and roll that is calculated corresponds to the heading. The method begins by creating an attitude variable to hold the results and a matrix to rotate the vector. The quad in question is calculated from the X and Z components of the supplied position. Subtracting a vertical vector from the normal vector and transforming it by the rotation matrix calculates the slope vector. The pitch and roll components of the attitude are calculated using standard trigonometric formulas. The X and Z components of the slope vector are checked against zero to prevent divide-by-zero errors.

Listing 4-21. Terrain Class GetSlope Method

```
public Attitude GetSlope( Vector3 Position, float Heading )
{
    Attitude attitude = new Attitude();
    Matrix matrix = Matrix.Identity;

    matrix.RotateY(Heading);
```

```
int x1 = (int)(Position.X/m_Spacing);
int z1 = (int)(Position.Z/m_Spacing);

Vector3 normal = m_Quads[x1,z1].FaceNormals;
normal.TransformCoordinate(matrix);

if ( normal.Z == 0.0f )
{
    attitude.Pitch = 0.0f;
}
else
{
    attitude.Pitch = -(float)Math.Atan(normal.Y/normal.Z);
    if ( attitude.Pitch > 0.0 )
    {
        attitude.Pitch = (float)(Math.PI/2.0) - attitude.Pitch;
    }
    else
    {
        attitude.Pitch = -((float)(Math.PI/2.0) + attitude.Pitch);
    }
}
if ( attitude.Pitch > (Math.PI/4.0) || attitude.Pitch < -(Math.PI/4.0) )
{
    Console.AddLine("Pitch " + attitude.Pitch*180.0/Math.PI + " " +
        normal.ToString());
}

if ( normal.X == 0.0f )
{
    attitude.Roll = 0.0f;
}
else
{
    attitude.Roll = -(float)Math.Atan(normal.Y/normal.X);
    if ( attitude.Roll > 0.0 )
    {
        attitude.Roll = (float)(Math.PI/2.0) - attitude.Roll;
    }
    else
    {
        attitude.Roll = -((float)(Math.PI/2.0) + attitude.Roll);
    }
```

```
    }
    if ( attitude.Roll > (Math.PI/4.0) || attitude.Roll < -(Math.PI/4.0) )
    {
        Console.AddLine("Roll " + attitude.Roll*180.0/Math.PI + " " +
            normal.ToString());
    }


    attitude.Heading = Heading;

    return attitude;
}
```

The drawing of the terrain is done in the Render method (shown in Listing 4-22). This is where we will take any of the TerrainQuads that are visible and render them to the screen. The very first thing to do, of course, is to check whether the terrain is valid. If an error occurred while creating the terrain, we might not have anything valid to render. Checking the validity flag allows us to bypass all of the rendering code if there is a problem. If everything is OK, we ensure that the culling mode is correct and let the device know the vertex format that we are using for the terrain triangles that we are about to send. We need to set up a material for inclusion in the rendering device context. If a material is not set, the lighting effects we will look at in Chapter 7 will not work properly. Materials are required for the lighting calculations in the fixed-function pipeline. Since we are using a single texture for all terrain quads, we will set the texture into the first texture position.

 NOTE *The rendering code appears twice. The second set of lines are required since it is quite unlikely that we will fill the array a fixed number of times with no vertices left over.*

Listing 4-22. Terrain Class Render Method

```
public void Render( Camera cam )
{
    int nQuadsDrawn = 0;
    if ( m_bValid )
    {
        CGameEngine.GetDevice().RenderState.CullMode = Cull.Clockwise;
        CGameEngine.Device3D.VertexFormat =
            CustomVertex.PositionNormalTextured.Format;
        Material mtrl = new Material();
```

```
mtrl.Ambient = Color.White;
mtrl.Diffuse = Color.White;
CGameEngine.Device3D.Material = mtrl;

// Set the texture.
CGameEngine.GetDevice().SetTexture(0, m_Texture );

// Set the matrix for normal viewing.
Matrix matWorld = new Matrix();
MatWorld = Matrix.Identity;

CGameEngine.GetDevice().Transform.World = matWorld;
CGameEngine.GetDevice().Transform.View = cam.View;

 int Offset = 0;

for ( int i=0; i<m_xSize; i++ )
{
    for ( int j=0; j<m_ySize; j++ )
    {
        try
        {
        Offset = m_Quads[i,j].RenderQuad( Offset, m_Vertices );
        if ( Offset >= 2990 )
        {
            CGameEngine.Device3D.VertexFormat =
                CustomVertex.PositionNormalTextured.Format;
            m_VB.SetData(m_Vertices, 0, 0);
            CGameEngine.Device3D.SetStreamSource( 0, m_VB, 0 );
            CGameEngine. Device3D.DrawPrimitives(
                PrimitiveType.TriangleList, 0, Offset/3 );
            nQuadsDrawn += Offset / 6;
            Offset = 0;
        }
        catch
        {
            Console.AddLint("Error rendering quad "+I+","+j);
        }
        }
    }
}
if ( Offset > 0 )
```

```
        {
            try
            {
                CGameEngine.Device3D.VertexFormat =
                    CustomVertex.PositionNormalTextured.Format;
                m_VB.SetData(m_Vertices, 0, 0);
                CGameEngine.GetDevice().SetStreamSource( 0, m_VB, 0 );
                CGameEngine.GetDevice().DrawPrimitives(
                    PrimitiveType.TriangleList, 0, Offset/3 );
                nQuadsDrawn += Offset / 6;
                Offset = 0;
            }
            catch (DirectXException d3de)
            {
                Console.AddLine("Unable to render terrain " );
                Console.AddLine(d3de.ErrorString);
            }
            catch ( Exception e )
            {
                Console.AddLine("Unable to render terrain" );
                Console.AddLine(e.Message);
            }
        }
    }
}
```

The next thing to do is set up the transformation matrices. Since all of the positions are already in world coordinates, we will set the world matrix to the identity state (since no change needs to occur in the coordinates). The view matrix comes from the active camera. For efficiency, we will accumulate the terrain data into a vertex array. The Direct3D device is at its best when given large numbers of vertices at a time. We loop through all of the terrain quads and have their Render methods add data to the vertex array if the quad has not been culled from the scene. When the array is full or we run out of quads, the vertex data is transferred to the vertex buffer and the vertices are drawn with a call to DrawPrimitives. The final method in the Terrain class is Dispose (shown in Listing 4-23). This method disposes of each of the terrain quads as well as the texture and the vertex buffer.

Listing 4-23. Terrain Class Dispose Method

```
public void Dispose()
{
    for ( int i=0; i<m_xSize; i++ )
    {
        for ( int j=0; j<m_ySize; j++ )
        {
            if ( m_Quads[i,j] != null ) m_Quads[i,j].Dispose();
        }
    }
    if ( m_Texture != null ) m_Texture.Dispose();
    if ( m_VB != null ) m_VB.Dispose();
}
```

Now that we have added terrain to the scene, it is starting to look better. Figure 4-3 shows the terrain and skybox. We currently have a scene of rolling sand dunes with mountains off in the distance. This is better, but still a bit empty. The next section of this chapter will help us dress up the scene a bit by adding more objects to the scene.

Figure 4-3. Skybox and terrain

Populating the Landscape: Billboards

Now that we have some ground under our feet, it is time to start adding more objects to the scene. One of the tricks for adding many objects to a 3D scene without a corresponding reduction in rendering speed is to use two-dimensional objects. These objects are referred to as *billboards* due to their similarity to the billboard signs found along the highway. The billboard is a two-dimensional image on a vertical quad positioned within the scene.

A combination of tricks gives our billboards the illusion of being three dimensional. The first trick is the use of transparency. Portions of an image used for a billboard are flagged as being transparent. This gives the billboard an irregular outline so that it does not appear rectangular like the original image. The second and even more important trick is the orientation of the billboard. The billboard quad is always oriented so that it is vertical and facing the camera. This way, no matter what direction we are looking from, we see the same image.

The obvious drawback to this technique is that the object being portrayed should be fairly symmetrical about the vertical axis. By being symmetrical, the observer is not bothered by the fact that the object looks the same from all directions. Trees and shrubs are common uses for billboards. Even though trees in real life do not tend to look exactly the same from all directions, the typical observer ignores this fact. Most people will perceive the billboard as a three-dimensional tree and think no more about it. To truly model a tree in three dimensions would require thousands of polygons. Billboards allow us to add a tree to the scene using only two.

For our sample game, we will use a number of different billboards to dress up the scene. We will add palm trees, cacti, and course markers. The course markers will be a series of red or blue posts. The posts will work like those seen in slalom racing, where the drivers in the race must stay to the right of the red posts and to the left of the blue posts. Placing the posts will allow us to lay out the course among the dunes.

The BillBoard class will provide the implementation of the billboard concept. The definition of the BillBoard class is shown in Listing 4-24. One of the features of this class that should jump out at you is the fact that several of the class members are defined as static, which means that these variables will be shared by all instances of the class. One of these static variables is a list of all of the billboards. A static Render method provides rendering of all of the visible billboards with a single call.

Listing 4-24. BillBoard Class Definition

```
public class BillBoard : Object3D, IDisposable
{
 #region Attributes
 private CustomVertex.PositionNormalTextured[]  m_Corners;
 private Texture              m_Texture;     // Image for face
 private bool                m_bValid = false;
 private string              m_sTexture;

 private static string       m_sLastTexture;
 private static VertexBuffer m_VB;
 private static Matrix       m_TheMatrix;

 private static ArrayList m_List = new ArrayList();
     public static ArrayList  Objects { get { return m_List; } }

 public bool Valid { get { return m_bValid; } }
 #endregion
```

The SetupMatrix method (Listing 4-25) generates a rotation matrix that will
orient any billboard in the scene so that it faces the camera. This orientation is
based on the difference between the camera's LookAt vector and Eye vector. This
difference gives us an idea as to how much we need to rotate the billboard and
in what direction. The angle from the viewpoint to the billboard is an arctangent
function of the ratio of the Z and X components of the vector. The sign of the
X component determines which direction we need to rotate 90 degrees in order
to have the billboard facing the camera. If the X component is zero, we need to
use the camera heading angle to determine the proper rotation. This method is
called by the static Render method prior to rendering the billboards.

Listing 4-25. BillBoard SetupMatrix Method

```
 private static void SetupMatrix( Camera cam )
 {
  // Set up a rotation matrix to orient the billboard towards the camera.
  Vector3 vDir = Vector3.Subtract(cam.LookAtVector, cam.EyeVector);
  if( vDir.X > 0.001f )
   m_Matrix = Matrix.RotationY( (float)(-Math.Atan(vDir.Z/vDir.X)+Math.PI/2) );
  else if( vDir.X < -0.001f )
   m_Matrix = Matrix.RotationY( (float)(-Math.Atan(vDir.Z/vDir.X)-Math.PI/2) );
  else
```

```
      if ( cam.Heading < 179.0f || cam.Heading > 181.0f )
         m_TheMatrix = Matrix.Identity;
      else
         m_TheMatrix = Matrix.RotationY( (float)Math.PI );
   }
```

The static Add method (shown in Listing 4-26) is used to place a billboard into the scene. This method works most efficiently if all billboards that use a common texture image are loaded sequentially. This allows the method to load only one copy of the image to the video card to be shared by all instances of the type of billboard. The method takes the position, size, name, and texture name as arguments. It begins by comparing the texture name with the name of the last texture used. If the two names match, we can clone the last billboard and reuse the texture. The last entry in the list is passed to a copy constructor to create the new billboard. If the texture names do not match, the normal constructor is called.

Listing 4-26. BillBoard Add Method

```
public static void Add( float north, float east, float altitude, string sName,
  string sTextureName, float fWidth, float fHeight)
{
  BillBoard obj;

  if ( sTextureName.CompareTo(m_sLastTexture) == 0 )
  {
   BillBoard lastObject = (BillBoard)m_List[m_List.Count-1];
   obj = new BillBoard(sName,lastObject);
  }
  else
  {
   obj = new BillBoard(sName, sTextureName, fWidth, fHeight);
  }
  m_sLastTexture = sTextureName;

  float height = CGameEngine.Ground.TerrainHeight(east,north);

  if ( altitude < height )
  {
   altitude = height;
  }

  obj.m_Pos.X = east;
  obj.m_Pos.Y = altitude;
  obj.m_Pos.Z = north;
```

```
  try
  {
   m_List.Add( obj );
   CGameEngine.QuadTree.AddObject((Object3D)obj);
  }
  catch (DirectXException d3de)
  {
   Console.AddLine("Unable to add billboard " + sName);
   Console.AddLine(d3de.ErrorString);
  }
  catch ( Exception e )
  {
   Console.AddLine("Unable to add billboard " + sName);
   Console.AddLine(e.Message);
  }
 }
```

The next thing to do is set the position of the billboard. The terrain height at the billboard's position is queried to ensure that the billboard is not placed below ground level. You may place the billboard so that it appears to be floating above the ground if you wish. Once the position is saved into the object, the object is placed into the billboard list for future use and added to the Quadtree for culling.

The copy constructor for the class (shown in Listing 4-27) creates a new billboard that is a complete copy of the supplied billboard except for the name. The name is saved into the new instance and the Copy method is used to perform the member variable data copying.

Listing 4-27. BillBoard Class Copy Constructor

```
  public BillBoard(string sName, BillBoard other) : base( sName )
  {
   m_sName = sName;
   Copy(other);
  }
```

The normal constructor for the class (shown in Listing 4-28) creates the billboard at the supplied size and using the supplied texture filename. A radius value of half the width is used as the bounding radius for the object. Setting up the vertices for the billboard quad looks much like the quad we used for the terrain. The difference is that the size of the quad is based on the height and width passed into the constructor. The billboard is considered valid once the texture is successfully loaded.

Listing 4-28. BillBoard Class Constructor

```
public BillBoard(string sName, string sTextureName, float fWidth,
    float fHeight) : base( sName )
{
 m_sName = sName;
 m_sTexture = sTextureName;

 m_fRadius = fWidth / 2.0f;

 // Create the vertices for the box.
 m_Corners = new CustomVertex.PositionNormalTextured[4];

 m_Corners[0].X = m_fRadius;  // Upper left
 m_Corners[0].Y = fHeight;  // Upper left
 m_Corners[0].Z = 0.0f;  // Upper left
 m_Corners[0].Tu = 1.0f;
 m_Corners[0].Tv = 0.0f;
 m_Corners[0].Nx = 0.0f;
 m_Corners[0].Ny = 0.0f;
 m_Corners[0].Nz = -1.0f;
 m_Corners[1].X = -m_fRadius;  // Upper right
 m_Corners[1].Y = fHeight;  // Upper right
 m_Corners[1].Z = 0.0f;  // Upper right
 m_Corners[1].Tu = 0.0f;
 m_Corners[1].Tv = 0.0f;
 m_Corners[1].Nx = 0.0f;
 m_Corners[1].Ny = 0.0f;
 m_Corners[1].Nz = -1.0f;
 m_Corners[2].X = m_fRadius;  // Lower left
 m_Corners[2].Y = 0.0f;  // Lower left
 m_Corners[2].Z = 0.0f;  // Lower left
 m_Corners[2].Tu = 1.0f;
 m_Corners[2].Tv = 1.0f;
 m_Corners[2].Nx = 0.0f;
 m_Corners[2].Ny = 0.0f;
 m_Corners[2].Nz = -1.0f;
 m_Corners[3].X = -m_fRadius;  // Lower right
 m_Corners[3].Y = 0.0f;  // Lower right
 m_Corners[3].Z = 0.0f;  // Lower right
 m_Corners[3].Tu = 0.0f;
 m_Corners[3].Tv = 1.0f;
```

```
m_Corners[3].Nx = 0.0f;
m_Corners[3].Ny = 0.0f;
m_Corners[3].Nz = -1.0f;

// Load the texture for the face.
try
{
  m_Texture = GraphicsUtility.CreateTexture(CGameEngine.Device3D,
    sTextureName);
  m_bValid = true;
}
catch
{
  Console.AddLine("Unable to create billboard texture for " + sName);
}
}
```

The Copy method (shown in Listing 4-29) is used by the copy constructor to duplicate the contents of one instance into another. You might have seen this referred to as a *deep copy* elsewhere. It does not reload the texture. Instead, it just creates another reference to the existing texture.

Listing 4-29. BillBoard Copy Method

```
private void Copy(BillBoard other)
{
  m_sTexture = other.m_sTexture;

  m_fRadius = other.m_fRadius;

  // Create the vertices for the box.
  m_Corners = other.m_Corners;

  m_bValid = true;
}
```

The game engine renders the billboards by calling the static method RenderAll shown in Listing 4-30. By being static, we are ensuring that there is a single point for rendering every billboard. Remember that we have placed references to every billboard in a static array list. The first thing to see is if there are any billboards to draw at all. If not, we can just return. If we are going to be drawing billboards, we need to set up the rendering states required.

Listing 4-30. BillBoard RenderAll Method

```
public static void RenderAll( Camera cam )
{
 string currentTexture = "";

 if ( m_List.Count > 0 )
 {
 CGameEngine.Device3D.RenderState.CullMode =
        Microsoft.DirectX.Direct3D.Cull.Clockwise;
  // Set diffuse blending for alpha set in vertices.
  CGameEngine.Device3D.RenderState.AlphaBlendEnable = true;
  CGameEngine.Device3D.RenderState.SourceBlend = Blend.SourceAlpha;
  CGameEngine.Device3D.RenderState.DestinationBlend = Blend.InvSourceAlpha;

  // Enable alpha testing (skips pixels with less than a certain alpha).
  if( CGameEngine.Device3D.DeviceCaps.AlphaCompareCaps.SupportsGreaterEqual )
  {
   CGameEngine.Device3D.RenderState.AlphaTestEnable = true;
   CGameEngine.Device3D.RenderState.ReferenceAlpha = 0x08;
   CGameEngine.Device3D.RenderState.AlphaFunction = Compare.GreaterEqual;
  }

  SetupMatrix( cam );

  CGameEngine.Device3D.VertexFormat =
    CustomVertex.PositionNormalTextured.Format;

  if ( m_VB == null )
  {
   m_VB = new VertexBuffer(typeof(CustomVertex. PositionColoredTextured),
    4, CGameEngine.Device3D, Usage.WriteOnly,
    CustomVertex. PositionNormalTextured.Format,
    Pool.Default );
  }

  CGameEngine.Device3D.SetStreamSource( 0, m_VB, 0 );

  foreach ( BillBoard obj in m_List )
  {

   if ( currentTexture.CompareTo(obj.m_sTexture) != 0 )
   {
     m_VB.SetData(obj.m_Corners, 0, 0);only copy when texture changes
```

```
        // Set the texture.
        CGameEngine.Device3D.SetTexture(0, obj.m_Texture );

        currentTexture = obj.m_sTexture;
      }

      obj.Render( cam );
    }
    foreach ( BillBoard obj in m_List )
    {
        obj.RenderChildren( cam );
    }
    }
  }
```

The first render state we will set is the culling mode. Since the vertices for the billboard have been defined in clockwise order, we will set the culling mode to Clockwise. The next set of render states are concerned with the transparent portion of the billboard image. The portions of the billboard image that should be transparent have a value in the alpha channel of zero. An alpha value of zero indicates a fully transparent pixel. A value of 255 in the alpha channel indicates an opaque pixel. Values between the two extremes indicate a range of transparency between the two extremes. Chapter 11 will show how to create images with the alpha data for transparency.

Setting the AlphaBlendEnable state to true enables transparency. The two states on the following lines, SourceBlend and DestinationBlend, define how the alpha values are interpreted. SourceAlpha for the source blending and InvSourceAlpha for the destination provide the normal transparency behavior. Some video cards provide alpha testing capabilities to improve efficiency. If the card supports alpha testing, we configure the testing so that any alpha value greater or equal to the reference value is a pixel that is kept. All other pixels are ignored and therefore completely transparent.

The SetupMatrix method creates the rotation matrix that makes the billboards face the camera. The vertex format is set to the value for our billboard vertices. The vertex buffer for the billboards is a static member of the class. If the buffer has not been initialized yet, we create one that will hold four vertices. We then set this buffer as the source stream for drawing the billboards. At this point, we are ready to begin rendering billboards.

To draw the billboards, we iterate through the static list of billboards. If the texture for the current billboard is different from the last billboard we drew, we need to update the texture and vertex data. Whenever the texture image for a billboard changes, it is likely that the size and shape of the billboard changes as well. The new billboard texture is set as the current texture and the vertices for the billboard are copied into the vertex buffer. The call to the billboard object's

Render method comes next. Rendering any child objects of the billboards completes the process.

The object's Render method (shown in Listing 4-31) performs the actual rendering of an individual billboard. It begins by checking to see of the billboard is both valid and not culled. If this is the case, the method sets the billboard's position in the world transform matrix. The drawing of the billboard is accomplished with the DrawPrimitives method that renders a strip of two triangles for the billboard quad. The method finishes by setting the billboard as culled. This means that the billboard will not be drawn during the next pass unless it is still visible. The RenderChildren method performs the same processing for any child objects that may be attached to the billboards.

Listing 4-31. BillBoard Render and RenderChildren Methods

```
public override void Render( Camera cam )
{
 if ( Visible && m_bValid && !IsCulled )
  {

   // Translate the billboard into place.
   m_ TheMatrix.M41 = m_vPosition.X;
   m_ TheMatrix.M42 = m_vPosition.Y;
   m_ TheMatrix.M43 = m_vPosition.Z;
   CGameEngine.Device3D. Transform.World = m_TheMatrix;

   // Render the face.
   CGameEngine.Device3D.DrawPrimitives( PrimitiveType.TriangleStrip, 0, 2 );
   Culled = true;
   }
}

public void RenderChildren( Camera cam )
{
   if ( Visible && m_bValid && !IsCulled )
   {

      // Translate the billboard into place.
      CGameEngine.Device3D.Transform.World = m_TheMatrix;

      Culled = true;
      if ( m_Children.Count > 0 )
      {
         Object3D obj;
         for ( int i=0; i<m_Children.Count; i++ )
```

```
        {
            obj = (Object3D)m_Children.GetByIndex(i);
            obj.Render( cam );
        }
    }
  }
}
```

The InRect method (shown in Listing 4-32) is a method required by all 3D objects. It is used by the routine that inserts objects into the Quadtree to determine if an object is within the supplied rectangle. This implementation of the method will not take the size of the billboard into account. We will just look to see if the placement position of the billboard is within the rectangle. If you want to do a more precise test, you could check to see if the circle consisting of the billboard's position and radius intersects the rectangle. We will take advantage of the Rectangle class's Contains method to perform the test.

Listing 4-32. BillBoard RenderAll Method

```
public override bool InRect( Rectangle rect )
{
  return rect.Contains( (int) vPosition.X, (int) vPosition.Z);
}
```

The last billboard method is Dispose (shown in Listing 4-33). As with other object Dispose methods, we will dispose of the texture. We also dispose of the static vertex buffer if it has not been disposed of yet. If the billboard has any children attached, they are also disposed of.

Listing 4-33. BillBoard RenderAll Method

```
public override void Dispose()
{
  m_Texture.Dispose();

  if ( m_VB != null )
  {
      m_VB.Dispose();
      m_VB = null;
  }
  if ( m_Children.Count > 0 )
  {
      Object3D obj;
      for ( int i=0; i<m_Children.Count; i++ )
```

```
    {
        obj = (Object3D)m_Children.GetByIndex(i);
        obj.Dispose();
    }
  }
}
```

Now that we have our `Billboard` class, we can dress up the scene a bit. Figure 4-4 shows the new scene with a number of palm trees and cacti sprinkled across the sand. There are also a number of red and blue colored posts, which will be used in the finished game to mark the racecourse. We can see the difference that the billboards can make. We have a greater sense of the size of the database when we can see small objects off in the distance.

Figure 4-4. Scene with billboards

Adding Environmental Effects: Particle Systems

All of the objects that we have added to the scene so far have been static. They do not change at all as time goes by. The workhorse of 3D game special effects is the particle system. *Particle systems* are composed of two components: a particle generator and particles. A particle generator is an invisible object that creates a given type of particle. The created particles will have an initial position, velocity, size, color, and texture based on settings in the generator. By varying these settings as well as the dynamics of the particle, we can simulate a wide variety of special effects. These effects can include smoke, fire, explosions, water, fireworks, and more. The sample game for this book uses particles to represent the sand kicked up from the tires of the vehicles as they are driving around.

One of the main features of particles is the fact that they are dynamic. They change over time. Possible changes include position, velocity, and color. The particles also cease to exist once certain conditions are met. For the game engine's particle system to be multipurpose, we do not want to hard code a specific set of dynamics for our particles. Instead, we will use the delegate feature of C# to pass an Update method into the particle generator for use by all particles created by that generator. The signature for this delegate is shown here:

```
public delegate void ParticleUpdate( ref Particle Obj, float DeltaT );
```

The ParticleUpdate delegate accepts a particle reference and a float value as arguments. The particle reference specifies the particle that is going to be affected by the method. The float value represents the fractional number of seconds that have occurred since the last update. This value is typically the inverse of the frame rate. For example, if we were running at 30 Hz (frames per second) the DeltaT value would be 0.03333333 (roughly 33 milliseconds). This value is used to integrate velocities from accelerations and positions from velocities. It can also be used to integrate the amount of time left before the particle is deleted (assuming that the dynamics terminate the particle based on time). Listing 4-34 is an example of the update function that we will use with our sand particles. It shows a simple method called Gravity that only applies the effect of gravity on the particles. It does not apply drag or wind effects, but they could be added if we wanted even more fidelity.

Listing 4-34. Example ParticleUpdateMethod

```
public void Gravity( ref Particle Obj, float DeltaT )
{
    Obj.m_Position   += Obj.m_Velocity * DeltaT;
    Obj.m_Velocity.Y += -32.0f * DeltaT;
    if ( Obj.m_Position.Y < 0.0f ) Obj.m_bActive = false;
}
```

The Gravity method integrates a new position for the particle base on its velocity and the time constant. The acceleration of gravity is then applied by integrating the acceleration due to gravity (32.0 feet/second²) into the Y velocity component. The last thing that each `Update` method should do is to determine if the particle should become inactive. This could be based on either the amount of time the particle has been active or the particle's current position. We will simply terminate the particle if its vertical position drops below zero. The particle generator maintains the particles based on the state of the active flag.

The particles are maintained using a structure rather than a class. This reduces some of the overhead for the particles, which is important since we may have thousands of them active at a given time within the scene. The definition of the structure is shown in Listing 4-35. The structure holds all of the information needed to describe a given particle. The only data that is truly required for a particle is the position, color, and active state. Everything else is there to support the dynamics of the particles. The position and color are required for rendering the particle. The active flag is required, of course, so that we will know when the particle should no longer be rendered and is available for reuse.

Listing 4-35. Particle Structure Definition

```
public struct Particle
{
    public Vector3 m_Position;
    public Vector3 m_Velocity;
    public float   m_fTimeRemaining;
    public Vector3 m_InitialPosition;
    public Vector3 m_InitialVelocity;
    public float   m_fCreationTime;
    public System.Drawing.Color m_Color;
    public bool m_bActive;
}
```

As I mentioned earlier, the `ParticleGenerator` is the object that creates and manages a set of particles. The definition for this class is shown in Listing 4-36. This class inherits from the `Object3D` class as well as the `IDisposable` and `IDynamic` interfaces. Inheriting from the `Object3D` class gives the particle generator all of the basic abilities and characteristics of any other 3D object. The most important of these is the ability to be rendered if it is in the currently viewable portion of the scene and the ability to be attached as a child of another object. If we were to use the particle generator for a fire or a fountain, it might simply be placed at a location in the scene and not move from that spot.

Listing 4-36. ParticleGenerator Definition

```
public class ParticleGenerator : Object3D, IDisposable, IDynamic
{
    #region Attributes
    private bool  m_bValid = false;
    private string m_sTexture;
    private Texture m_Texture;
    private int m_BaseParticle = 0;
    private int m_Flush = 0;
    private int m_Discard = 0;
    private int m_ParticlesLimit = 2000;
    private int m_Particles = 0;
    private Color m_Color;
    private float m_fTime = 0.0f;

    private VertexBuffer m_VB;
    private bool m_bActive = false;

    private ArrayList m_ActiveParticles = new ArrayList();
    private ArrayList m_FreeParticles = new ArrayList();
    private ParticleUpdate m_Method = null;
    private System.Random rand = new System.Random();

    public float m_fRate = 22.0f;  // Particles to create per second
    public float m_fPartialParticles = 0.0f;
    public float m_fEmitVel = 7.5f;
    public Attitude m_Attitude;
     // Window around the pitch axis for distribution (radians)
    public float m_PitchWidth = 1.0f;
     // Window around the heading axis for distribution (radians)
    public float m_HeadingWidth = 1.0f;
    public float m_PointSize = 0.02f;
    public float m_PointSizeMin = 0.00f;
    public float m_PointScaleA = 0.00f;
    public float m_PointScaleB = 0.00f;
    public float m_PointScaleC = 1.00f;

    public bool Valid { get { return m_bValid; } }
    public bool Active { set { m_bActive = value; } }
    #endregion
```

We will be using these generators to throw up sand from the rear tires of each of the vehicles. While we could require the programmers using the game engine to manually move the particle generators around as the vehicles move, this would rapidly become tedious and unmanageable, depending on the number of vehicles. By attaching generators to the vehicle objects and providing positional and rotational offsets from the parent object, they will automatically move correctly with the vehicles.

The IDisposable interface specifies that we need a Dispose method for cleanup purposes. The IDynamic interface indicates that we will need an Update method. The members of the class can be considered as two groups. One group of members is used in managing the particles and their creation. The other group is used in the creation and rendering of the particles. The specific uses of these variables will be covered as we explore each of the methods in the class.

The first ParticleGenerator method is the copy constructor (shown in Listing 4-37). Copy constructors are a handy way of duplicating a constructor that we have already configured. In the case of our sand generators, we will need two for each of the vehicles. If we have a total of three vehicles, we will then need six sand particle generators that are configured the same way. The copy constructor allows us to set up the first one and then make five copies. The six generators would then be attached to the vehicles. The method uses the private Copy method to copy all of the member data except the vertex buffer. Each particle generator will have its own vertex buffer that is created after the other data has been copied. The vertex buffer is created to hold as many positioned and colored points as the value of the m_Discard variable. By flagging the buffer as dynamic, we indicate to the driver that we will be changing the data. The particle generator is not set as valid unless the vertex buffer was successfully created.

Listing 4-37. ParticleGenerator Copy Constructor

```
public ParticleGenerator(string sName, ParticleGenerator other)
   : base( sName )
{
  m_sName = sName;
  Copy(other);
  try
  {
    m_VB = new VertexBuffer(
             typeof(CustomVertex. PositionColoredTextured),
             m_Discard, CGameEngine.Device3D,
             Usage.Dynamic | Usage.WriteOnly | Usage.Points,
             CustomVertex. PositionColoredTextured.Format, Pool.Default);
    m_bValid = true;
```

```
        }
        catch (DirectXException d3de)
        {
           Console.AddLine("Unable to create vertex buffer for " + m_sTexture);
           Console.AddLine(d3de.ErrorString);
        }
        catch ( Exception e )
        {
           Console.AddLine("Unable to create vertex buffer for " + m_sTexture);
           Console.AddLine(e.Message);
        }
    }
```

The normal constructor for the class (shown in Listing 4-38) is a bit more involved. The arguments to the constructor are as follows:

- The name for the generator

- The number of particles that are added to the vertex buffer each time prior to flushing the data to the driver

- The number of particles to put into the vertex buffer before starting over at the beginning of the buffer

- The color of the particles that will be created

- The path to the texture image used for the particles

- The delegate function that will be called to do the particle updates.

The argument values are saved into member variables. The constructor then attempts to load the texture image and create the vertex buffer. If both operations are successful, the generator is considered valid. Notice that many of the variables that configure the generator for the particle characteristics default to the values from the class definition. These members are public and are modified by the controlling program if the default values are not appropriate.

Listing 4-38. ParticleGenerator Constructor

```
public ParticleGenerator(string sName, int numFlush, int numDiscard,
    Color color, string sTextureName, ParticleUpdate method )
    : base( sName )
{
    m_sName = sName;
    m_Color = color;
    m_Flush = numFlush;
    m_Discard = numDiscard;
    m_sTexture = sTextureName;
    m_Method = method;
    try
    {
        m_Texture = GraphicsUtility.CreateTexture( CGameEngine.Device3D,
                m_sTexture, Format.Unknown);
        try
        {
            m_VB = new VertexBuffer(
                typeof(CustomVertex. PositionColoredTextured),
                m_Discard, CGameEngine.Device3D,
                Usage.Dynamic | Usage.WriteOnly | Usage.Points,
                CustomVertex. PositionColoredTextured.Format, Pool.Default);
            m_bValid = true;
        }
        catch (DirectXException d3de)
        {
            Console.AddLine("Unable to create vertex buffer for " +
                m_sTexture);
            Console.AddLine(d3de.ErrorString);
        }
        catch ( Exception e )
        {
            Console.AddLine("Unable to create vertex buffer for " +
                m_sTexture);
            Console.AddLine(e.Message);
        }
    }
    catch (DirectXException d3de)
    {
        Console.AddLine("Unable to create texture " + m_sTexture);
        Console.AddLine(d3de.ErrorString);
    }
    catch ( Exception e )
    {
```

```
            Console.AddLine("Unable to create texture " + m_sTexture);
            Console.AddLine(e.Message);
        }
    }
```

The private `Copy` method (shown in Listing 4-39) is used by the copy constructor to copy member variables from the supplied class instance into the calling class. A few of the variables in this method have not been addressed yet. The `m_fRate` value defines the number of particles that should be created each second. The `m_fEmitVel` value specifies the speed in meters per second of the particles at the moment of creation. The `Attitude` value is the angular offset between the parent model's attitude and the angle at which the particles' velocity vector will be oriented at creation time. The pitch and heading width variables define an angular cone around the attitude. Random values are calculated within this cone so that all particles created do not follow the exact same path. It provides a more natural look to the flow of particles. The point size and scale variables are used by the DirectX driver to calculate how the size of the particles are scaled with their distance from the viewpoint.

Listing 4-39. ParticleGenerator Copy Method

```
    private void Copy(ParticleGenerator other)
    {
        m_sName = other.m_sName;
        m_Flush = other.m_Flush;
        m_Discard = other.m_Discard;
        m_sTexture = other.m_sTexture;
        m_Texture = other.m_Texture;
        m_Method = other.m_Method;
        m_fRate = other.m_fRate;
        m_fEmitVel = other.m_fEmitVel;
        m_Attitude = other.m_Attitude;
        m_PitchWidth = other.m_PitchWidth;
        m_HeadingWidth = other.m_HeadingWidth;
        m_PointSize = other.m_PointSize;
        m_PointSizeMin = other.m_PointSizeMin;
        m_PointScaleA = other.m_PointScaleA;
        m_PointScaleB = other.m_PointScaleB;
        m_PointScaleC = other.m_PointScaleC;
        m_bValid = other.m_bValid;
    }
```

The Update method (shown in Listing 4-40) fulfills the interface specified by IDynamic. The method is called by the GameEngine class to provide the dynamics of the particle generator. This method is responsible for generating any new particles and managing the particles that have already been created. The method integrates a time value that will be used as the creation time—the time in seconds since game play began—for each particle. The method then needs to determine how many particles to create during this pass. This is a function of the rate that particles are to be emitted and the amount of time that has passed. Any fractional particles that could not be created last pass are also included. The integer portion of this number is the number of particles to be created during this pass. The remainder is carried forward to the next pass. This allows us to uncouple the particle creation rate from the games frame rate. Otherwise, we would be limited to multiples of the frame rate.

Listing 4-40. ParticleGenerator Update Method

```
public override void Update( float DeltaT )
{
    m_fTime += DeltaT;

    // Emit new particles.
    float TotalNewParticles = (DeltaT * m_fRate) + m_fPartialParticles ;
    int NumParticlesToEmit = (int)TotalNewParticles;
    m_fPartialParticles = TotalNewParticles - NumParticlesToEmit;
    int particlesEmit = m_Particles + NumParticlesToEmit;
    while( m_Particles < m_ParticlesLimit && m_Particles < particlesEmit )
    {
        Particle particle;

        if( m_FreeParticles.Count > 0 )
        {
            particle = (Particle)m_FreeParticles[0];
            m_FreeParticles.RemoveAt(0);
        }
        else
        {
            particle = new Particle();
        }

        // Emit new particle.
        float fRand1 = (float)(rand.NextDouble()-0.5) * m_PitchWidth;
        float fRand2 = (float)(rand.NextDouble()-0.5) * m_HeadingWidth;
```

```
        m_Matrix = Matrix.RotationYawPitchRoll( m_Attitude.Heading+fRand2,
                        m_Attitude.Pitch+fRand1, 0.0f);

    Matrix TotalMatrix;

    if ( m_Parent != null )
    {
        TotalMatrix = Matrix.Multiply( m_Matrix, m_Parent.GetMatrix );
    }
    else
    {
        TotalMatrix = m_Matrix;
    }

    particle.m_InitialVelocity = Vector3.TransformCoordinate(
                    new Vector3( 0.0f, 0.0f, m_fEmitVel ),TotalMatrix);
    particle.m_InitialPosition = Vector3. TransformCoordinate (
                    m_vPosition, TotalMatrix );

    particle.m_Position = particle.m_InitialPosition;
    particle.m_Velocity = particle.m_TnitialVelocity;

    particle.m_Color = m_Color;
    particle.m_fCreationTime = m_fTime;
    particle.m_bActive = true;

    m_ActiveParticles.Add(particle);
    m_Particles++;
}
for ( int i=0; i < m_ActiveParticles.Count; i++ )
{
    Particle p = (Particle)m_ActiveParticles[i];
    m_Method( ref p, DeltaT );
    if ( p.m_bActive )
    {
        m_ActiveParticles[i] = p;
    }
    else
    {
        m_ActiveParticles.RemoveAt(i);
        m_FreeParticles.Add(p);
        m_Particles--;
    }
}
}
```

The method loops while we still have new particles to create and we have not reached the limit of active particles. If any old particles are waiting in the free particles list, they are reused prior to creating any new particles. Regardless of a particle's origins, it needs to be initialized before it is released into the scene. A rotation matrix is calculated using a combination of the generator's attitude, random factors, and the parent object's attitude. This matrix is applied against the particle velocity to create a velocity vector as the particle's initial velocity. The position and initial position of the particle is also transformed using the matrix. Once the particle is initialized, it is activated and added to the active particle list.

Now that the new particles have been added, it is time to update all of the particles. We loop through all of the particles and call the Update method for each particle. If a particle is still active, it is updated within the active particle list.

NOTE   *Referencing an object in a list actually gets a copy of the object. In order for the changes to the object to be maintained, we must copy the object back to the list.*

If the particle is no longer active, it is removed from the active particle list and added to the free particle list for future reuse. The number of active particles is also decremented.

The particles are drawn by the Render method (shown in Listing 4-41). Microsoft has provided support for particle systems in point sprites. *Point sprites* work like small billboards. The advantage is that we do not need to send a strip of two triangles to the video card for each particle. Instead, we just send the position of each particle in the vertex buffer. This is very important because of the large number of particles that will be rendered. Extra render states must be set up when using point sprites. A specific render state flag must be set as well as enabling scaling of the points. If we do not enable scaling, the points will not appear to change size with distance. There are also scaling factors and minimum size values that affect the size of the points.

Listing 4-41. ParticleGenerator Render Method

```
public override void Render( Camera cam )
{
    try
    {
        if ( m_ActiveParticles.Count > 0 )
        {
            // Set the render states for using point sprites.
            CGameEngine.Device3D.RenderState.ZBufferWriteEnable = false;
            CGameEngine.Device3D.RenderState.AlphaBlendEnable = true;
```

```
CGameEngine.Device3D.RenderState.SourceBlend = Blend.One;
CGameEngine.Device3D.RenderState.DestinationBlend = Blend.One;

CGameEngine.Device3D.SetTexture(0, m_Texture );

CGameEngine.Device3D.RenderState.PointSpriteEnable = true;
CGameEngine.Device3D.RenderState.PointScaleEnable = true ;
CGameEngine.Device3D.RenderState.PointSize = m_PointSize;
CGameEngine.Device3D.RenderState.PointSizeMin = m_PointSizeMin;
CGameEngine.Device3D.RenderState.PointScaleA = m_PointScaleA;
CGameEngine.Device3D.RenderState.PointScaleB = m_PointScaleB;
CGameEngine.Device3D.RenderState.PointScaleC = m_PointScaleC;

CGameEngine.Device3D.VertexFormat =
        CustomVertex.PositionColoredTextured.Format;

// Set up the vertex buffer to be rendered.
CGameEngine.Device3D.SetStreamSource( 0, m_VB, 0);

CustomVertex. PositionColoredTextured [] vertices = null;
int numParticlesToRender = 0;

// Lock the vertex buffer. We fill the vertex buffer in small
// chunks, using LockFlags.NoOverWrite. When we are done filling
// each chunk, we call DrawPrim, and lock the next chunk. When
// we run out of space in the vertex buffer, we start over at
// the beginning, using LockFlags.Discard.

m_BaseParticle += m_Flush;

if(m_BaseParticle >= m_Discard)
   m_BaseParticle = 0;

int count = 0;
vertices = (CustomVertex. PositionColoredTextured [])
    m_VB.Lock(m_BaseParticle *
    DXHelp.GetTypeSize(typeof(CustomVertex. PositionColoredTextured)),
  typeof(CustomVertex. PositionColoredTextured),
  (m_BaseParticle != 0) ? LockFlags.NoOverwrite : LockFlags.Discard,
    m_Flush);
foreach(Particle p in m_ActiveParticles)
{
   vertices[count].X     = p.m_Position.X;
   vertices[count].Y     = p.m_Position.Y;
```

```
                    vertices[count].Z      = p.m_Position.Z;
                    vertices[count].Color = p.m_Color.ToArgb();
                    count++;

                    if( ++numParticlesToRender == m_Flush )
                    {
                      // Done filling this chunk of the vertex buffer. Let's unlock and
                      // draw this portion so we can begin filling the next chunk.

                       m_VB.Unlock();

                       CGameEngine.Device3D.DrawPrimitives(
                            PrimitiveType.PointList, m_BaseParticle,
                            numParticlesToRender);

                       // Lock the next chunk of the vertex buffer. If we are at the
                       // end of the vertex buffer, LockFlags.Discard the vertex
                       // buffer and start at the beginning. Otherwise,
                       // specify LockFlags.NoOverwrite, so we can continue filling
                       // the VB while the previous chunk is drawing.
                       m_BaseParticle +- m_Flush;

                       if(m_BaseParticle >= m_Discard)
                          m_BaseParticle = 0;

                       vertices = (CustomVertex.PositionColored[])m_VB.Lock(
                               m_BaseParticle *
                               DXHelp.GetTypeSize(typeof(
                               CustomVertex. PositionColoredTextured)),
                               typeof(CustomVertex. PositionColoredTextured),
                                (m_BaseParticle != 0) ?
                               LockFlags.NoOverwrite : LockFlags.Discard, m_Flush);
                       count = 0;

                       numParticlesToRender = 0;
                    }
                }

            // Unlock the vertex buffer.
            m_VB.Unlock();
            // Render any remaining particles.
```

```
        if( numParticlesToRender > 0)
            CGameEngine.Device3D.DrawPrimitives(
                PrimitiveType.PointList, m_BaseParticle,
                    numParticlesToRender );


        // Reset render states.
        CGameEngine.Device3D.RenderState.PointSpriteEnable = false;
        CGameEngine.Device3D.RenderState.PointScaleEnable = false;

        CGameEngine.Device3D.RenderState.ZBufferWriteEnable = true;
        CGameEngine.Device3D.RenderState.AlphaBlendEnable = false;
    }
    }
    catch (DirectXException d3de)
    {
        Console.AddLine("Unable to Render Particles for " + Name);
        Console.AddLine(d3de.ErrorString);
    }
    catch ( Exception e )
    {
        Console.AddLine("Unable to Render Particles for " + Name);
        Console.AddLine(e.Message);
    }
}
```

Since we do have so many particles, we will send them to the video card in batches. Each batch will be a portion of the vertex buffer. The flush variable defines how many points will be added to the vertex buffer before flushing them to the card for processing. The size of the buffer is defined by the m_Discard variable. When we reach that point in the buffer, it is time to start over at the beginning of the buffer. This lets us use the vertex buffer like a circular buffer.

Since the particle generator has no size, we will treat it just like the billboards when it comes to determining if it is within a rectangle. The InRect method (shown in Listing 4-42) works just like the method in the Billboard class. It uses the Rectangle class's Contains method.

Listing 4-42. ParticleGenerator InRect Method

```
public override bool InRect( Rectangle rect )
{
    return rect.Contains( (int)m_vPosition.X, (int)m_vPosition.Z);
}
```

The last method in the class is the Dispose method (shown in Listing 4-43). Like the other classes, it must dispose of the texture and vertex buffer.

Listing 4-43. ParticleGenerator Dispose Method

```
public override void Dispose()
{
    m_Texture.Dispose();

    if ( m_VB != null )
    {
        m_VB.Dispose();

    }
}
```

There is no image that can do justice to the sand particle generator. You must see the particles in motion to appreciate the dynamics of particles. When you run the sample game for the book, you will see the sand particles streaming from the rear tires of each vehicle as it drives along.

Summary

This chapter has covered the basic requirements for setting the scene for our game. The skybox gives the player the feeling of having a place in a large exterior location. The Terrain class provides the ground that the game vehicles will be driving upon. Without any objects visible on the ground, the player has no sense of scale. The Billboard class gives the ability to place items like palm trees and cacti into the scene. The ability to see these objects off in the distance gives us a sense of scale and distance. The ParticleGenerator class provides the final addition for this chapter. We use the particle generator so that vehicle tires spew sand as they speed across the sand dunes. Remember that this class can be used for almost any special effect that the user of the game engine needs. The next chapter covers the more complex three-dimensional objects.

CHAPTER 5

Complex 3D Objects

IN CHAPTER 4, WE LOOKED at creating and rendering simple objects consisting of only a few polygons. While this is enough to create our basic terrain and sky, it is not enough to create an entire game. The game engine must also support complex models made up of hundreds or even thousands of polygons. Microsoft has included a class called Mesh that supports the manipulation of such objects. This chapter introduces the Model class of the game engine that encapsulates the Mesh class for the engine.

Looking at Mesh Basics

Before we dive into using the Mesh class as part of our own Model class, we should explore exactly what the Mesh class is and what it can do. The capabilities of the class that we are concerned with can be broken down into three categories: loading a mesh, gathering information about the mesh, and rendering the mesh.

Loading a Mesh

A mesh, by Microsoft's definition, is made up of several components. The first component is a list of vertices for all of the points that define the mesh. These vertices are held in a vertex buffer that is normally stored in the video card if there is sufficient memory capacity on the card. The second component is an index buffer that is also loaded into video memory if possible. The index buffer describes how the vertices are combined to form the triangles that make up the object. Since the shape of a mesh object usually is complex, each vertex tends to be part of a number of adjacent triangles. The use of an index buffer allows the system to reuse one instance of a vertex as many times as necessary. This greatly reduces the number of vertices that are needed to describe the object. Reducing the number of vertices increases performance, since each vertex needs to be transformed from a local mesh-oriented value into world coordinates through matrix multiplication.

The combination of the vertex buffer and the index buffer provide the definition of the basic shape of the object. In order for the mesh to look like something, we must also define what colors should be used for each rendered pixel in the object. This information is held in the material definition associated with each vertex. The material is actually a combination of color values (ambient, diffuse, emissive, and specular) and texturing information.

Microsoft provides three methods in the Mesh class for loading. Two methods (FromStream and FromX) are built for loading the mesh from memory in the form of a data stream or an XfileData structure. We will concentrate on the third method, which loads from a disk file. The Mesh class's FromFile method has eight overloaded variations. All of the variations of the method have the first three arguments in common. The signatures of the eight variations are shown in Listing 5-1.

Listing 5-1. Mesh Class FromFile Method Signatures

```
public Mesh FromFile (String, MeshFlags, Device, EffectInstance)
public Mesh FromFile (String, MeshFlags, Device, GraphicsStream, EffectInstance)
public Mesh FromFile (String, MeshFlags, Device, ExtendedMaterial,
    EffectInstance)
public Mesh FromFile (String, MeshFlags, Device)
public Mesh FromFile (String, MeshFlags, Device, GraphicsStream)
public Mesh FromFile (String, MeshFlags, Device, ExtendedMaterial)
public Mesh FromFile (String, MeshFlags, Device, GraphicsStream,
    ExtendedMaterial)
public Mesh FromFile (String, MeshFlags, Device, GraphicsStream,
    ExtendedMaterial, EffectInstance)
```

The string in the first argument is the fully qualified path and filename for the ".X" mesh data file for the object. Chapter 11 will discuss the creation of these data files. The second argument is a combination of one or more flags that lets us tailor where the components of the mesh are stored and how the mesh might be optimized. There are over 30 values in the enumeration. I highly recommend studying the DirectX SDK documentation for the details. The third argument is the Direct3D device to be used with the operation. The other three possible arguments allow us to get extra information about the mesh after it is loaded. The GraphicsStream object provides accessibility to the vertex information for the mesh. The ExtendedMaterial object provides access to the color and texture information for the mesh. The EffectInstance value exposes an Effect class instance associated with the mesh. This is an advanced feature, and therefore I will not cover it in this book.

The FromFile method loads the vertex and index information for the mesh, but it does not load any textures required by the mesh. What it does load is the name of the files containing the textures. Later in the chapter, we will look at how we go about loading the textures for the mesh as we explore the implementation of the Model class.

Gathering Information About a Mesh

Once a mesh has been loaded, we will likely need to query the instance for information about the mesh. At a minimum, we will need to load any textures required by the mesh. The ExtendedMaterial array available in the FromFile method is the preferred way to obtain this information. This argument is an array of ExtendedMaterial class instances. Each instance of the class contains both a `Material` definition and a texture filename. Iterating through the array allows us access to all of the texture filenames that we will need.

The other basic type of information we probably need to access is the vertex information. Because this information is likely to reside in video memory, we are required to lock the vertex buffer before we are allowed to manipulate it. The process of locking the buffer provides a reference to the data that is safe from possible manipulation by other threads in our application. There are two different ways in which we may lock either a vertex or an index buffer. We may acquire a reference to the buffer from the Mesh class and then call its Lock method. However, an easier way is to use either the LockVertexBuffer or the LockIndexBuffer methods of the Mesh class to access the information more directly. Either way, we gain access to the buffer information as a GraphicsStream or an array of values. Which we choose is largely determined by what we will be doing with the buffer once it is locked. The implementation of the `Model` class will demonstrate both approaches.

Once we have a locked vertex buffer, we can establish the extents of the mesh and even modify the mesh by modifying the vertices. We will use the information in the vertex buffer to calculate both a bounding radius around the mesh as well as an object-aligned bounding box (OABB). The radius is useful for determining the placement of the mesh within our Quadtree as well as the first step in determining collisions with other objects in our scene. The OABB is useful for more precise collision detection. If for some reason you need very precise collision detection, you must access both buffers. Precise collision detection requires that we test each edge of one mesh against the other mesh to see if the edge intersects a face. The Mesh class provides the Intersect method to support this process. Precise collision detection is computationally expensive and usually not needed for most games. Most of the time the OABB or a simplified version of the model built specifically for collision detection is used. This book's sample game simply checks for OABB intersection once bounding radius detection has provided an intersection.

Optimizing a Mesh

The mesh as loaded from the data file is ready to be rendered. Unfortunately (depending on the skill of the modeler who created the mesh), it may not be ready to be *efficiently* rendered. During the modeling process, it is possible for multiple vertices to be created at the same position. The Mesh class includes a method called WeldVertices that checks the mesh for any vertices that are the same within a given tolerance. Each vertex that is not needed and can be removed is a small boost to the performance of our game.

 NOTE   *The WeldVertices method operates in a manner similar to some tools that are available to simplify a mesh during the design of the mesh. They are normally referred to as* polygon reduction tools.

The order of the mesh faces also impacts the performance of the rendering process. Anything that causes a state change in the rendering pipeline has an impact on performance. By sorting the faces so that all faces that use a given texture are rendered together, we reduce the state change cost of changing textures. The Mesh class has the Optimize and OptimizeInPlace methods that perform this sort for us. The Optimize method creates a new mesh instance that is properly sorted. The OptimizeInPlace method alters the original mesh.

Another way to improve performance is to reduce the number of vertices used by the mesh as the mesh moves farther from the viewpoint. Microsoft provides the progressive mesh for the development of multiple levels of mesh detail. The ProgressiveMesh class is built from an instance of the Mesh class. It includes methods for retrieving the minimum and maximum number of vertices that the mesh can have. We can then use the TrimByVertices method of the class to create a version of the mesh with fewer vertices. By rendering simpler meshes as the object gets farther from the viewpoint, we increase performance by not transforming and rendering detail that can't be seen at a distance.

Rendering a Mesh

The rendering of a mesh is quite straightforward. The mesh internally has separated itself into a collection of subsets. Each subset has a specific material and texture. To render the mesh, we are required to loop through the list of materials for that mesh. For each material, we simply set that material and texture as the current value for the device and have the mesh draw the associated subset.

Developing the Model Class

The Mesh class provides a fine, low-level means of rendering a complex object in a three-dimensional scene. A game engine needs to look at the problem from a somewhat higher level. Regarding the game engine, we want a simple interface to position and render the desired mesh. In order to avoid a naming collision with the Microsoft classes, we will call our class Model.

Defining the Model Attributes

Our Model class has a number of requirements. The first requirement is that a model must inherit from our Object3D class. The model is just a more complicated three-dimensional object. This allows the game engine to hold a collection of objects without caring whether a given object is a simple billboard with two triangles or a model with hundreds or even thousands of triangles. The Object3D class is our common base class. The next requirement is that the class must support the IDisposable interface. Since the underlying mesh will be allocating memory on the video card, it is mandatory that we implement the Dispose method so that this memory can be freed as soon as it is no longer needed. The final requirement is that the class must implement the IDynamic interface. The models within our game will not be static objects like the billboards are. It is likely that some or all of the models will be capable of moving through the scene. The player's vehicle (typically referred to as *ownship*) is a primary example. The IDynamic interface defines the Update method that is called by the game engine in order to update the state of the object. Listing 5-2 defines the attributes that make up the Model class.

Listing 5-2. Model Class Declaration

```
public class Model : Object3D, IDisposable, IDynamic
{
    #region Attributes
    private Mesh m_mesh = null; // Our mesh object in sysmem
    private Material[] m_meshMaterials; // Materials for our mesh
    private Texture[] m_meshTextures; // Textures for our mesh
    private Vector3  m_vOffset = new Vector3(0.0f, 0.0f, 0.0f);
    private Attitude m_AttitudeOffset = new Attitude();
    private ProgressiveMesh[] m_pMeshes = null;
    private int m_currentPmesh = 0;
    private int m_nNumLOD = 1;
    private float[] m_LODRanges = null;
    private float m_fMaxLODRange = 1.0f;
    private GraphicsStream m_adj = null;

    private Vector3 m_PositiveExtents = new Vector3(-1.0f,-1.0f,-1.0f);
    private Vector3 m_NegativeExtents = new Vector3(1.0f,1.0f,1.0f);
    private Vector3[] m_Corners = new Vector3[8];
    public Vector3 Offset { get { return m_vOffset; } }
    #endregion
```

171

The first four attributes of the class build the basic mesh for the model. These represent the mesh and the textures and materials needed to render the mesh. The m_adj attribute is the adjacency information. This information is held in a GraphicsStream and is used by some of the utility methods of the Mesh class. The next five attributes will be used in the construction of the progressive meshes that form the level-of-detail portion of the model. There is an array of progressive mesh instances and a corresponding array of ranges. The ranges help in determining which of the progressive meshes should be rendered based on the current range between the object and the camera.

The next two attributes adjust the position of the mesh compared with that of the model. Ideally, a mesh would be built such that the reference position would be centered within the object at ground level. The person creating the mesh may decide to place the reference position elsewhere. The solution is to include an offset in both position and attitude that can be applied to the model. With these two attributes, it does not matter where the reference position is or what the basic orientation of the model was when built. When we create a model, we can specify these offsets to get the positioning and orientation we need.

The final three attributes are used in collision detection for the model. In order to be as efficient as possible, collision checking is done in an increasing amount of accuracy. The Object3D class already has a bounding radius for the first and quickest type of collision testing. For the Model class, we will include the next most accurate form of collision checking. This is the object-aligned bounding box described early in the chapter. To create this box, we will need to know the size of the smallest box that completely encloses the object. From these extents we can later calculate the corners of the box based on the position and attitude of the object.

Constructing a Model

We have established the attributes that make up the class. Now it is time to look at how we build an instance of the class in the constructor. The code for the constructor is shown in Listings 5-3a through 5-3e throughout this section. The beginning of the constructor is shown in Listing 5-3a. The constructor requires four arguments. The first argument is the name of the model. This string is passed down into the Object3D base class. The second argument is the path to the mesh data file that will be loaded into the model. The last two arguments are the positional and attitude adjustments that are to be applied to the model.

Listing 5-3a. Model Class Constructor

```
public Model(string name, string meshFile, Vector3 offset, Attitude adjust)
 : base(name)
{
   Mesh pTempMesh = null;
   WeldEpsilons Epsilons = new WeldEpsilons();

   Vector3 objectCenter;           // Center of bounding sphere of object
   m_vOffset = offset;
   m_AttitudeOffset = adjust;
   m_vPosition.X = 100.0f;
   m_vPosition.Z = 100.0f;
   ExtendedMaterial[] materials = null;
```

The first section of the constructor defines some internal variables for later use in the constructor and saves the offset data into the attribute variables. The epsilon values are used in the vertex welding operation. They define the error tolerance for determining if two vertices are in the same position.

The position of the model is set to one hundred units in both the X and Z dimensions. This ensures that the model will default to a position within the terrain. The game application would set the model to its proper initial position after the model has been created. The ExtendedMaterial array is passed back from the method that loads the mesh from the data file.

The next section of the constructor (shown in Listing 5-3b) covers the loading of the mesh and the computation of the bounding radius around the object. The Mesh class provided by Microsoft has a FromFile method for loading meshes stored in the DirectX format. This method also takes a fully qualified path and filename as a parameter. We will use the version of the method that returns both the adjacency information as well as the material definitions for the mesh. A more advanced version of this class would also include support for effects. We will load the mesh into system memory. If we were going to render the model using this mesh, we would use the Managed flag rather than the SystemMemory flag so that the mesh would be placed in video memory if possible. Since we wish to support levels of detail in our rendering, we will use the basic mesh in system memory to create the progressive meshes in managed (usually video) memory.

Listing 5-3b. Model Class Constructor (Continued)

```
try
{
    // Load the m_mesh from the specified file.
    m_mesh = Mesh.FromFile(meshFile, MeshFlags.SystemMemory,
                        CGameEngine.Device3D,  out m_adj, out materials);
    // Lock the vertex buffer to generate a simple bounding sphere.
    VertexBuffer vb = m_mesh.VertexBuffer;
    GraphicsStream vertexData = vb.Lock(0, 0, LockFlags.NoSystemLock);
    m_fRadius = Geometry.ComputeBoundingSphere(vertexData,
                        m_mesh.NumberVertices, m_mesh.VertexFormat,
                        out objectCenter);
    Geometry.ComputeBoundingBox(vertexData, m_mesh.NumberVertices,
                        m_mesh.VertexFormat, out m_NegativeExtents,
                        out m_PositiveExtents );
    vb.Unlock();
    vb.Dispose();
```

Once the mesh has been loaded, our next step is to compute the bounding radius for the model. To do this, we need to access the vertex data that has been loaded in the model's vertex buffer. We obtain a reference to the vertex buffer from the mesh. Once we have a reference to the vertex buffer, we need to lock the buffer to gain access to its data. This form of the Lock method returns a GraphicsStream that we will use next. The arguments of the Lock method specify that we want the entire vertex buffer and we will allow system background processing to continue while we have the buffer locked.

With the buffer locked we can use the ComputeBoundingSphere method of the Geometry class to calculate the radius from the vertex data. It takes as arguments the GraphicsStream from the vertex buffer as well as the number of vertices and the vertex format. The latter two can be obtained from the Mesh class. The final argument is a vector that is also returned from the method that will be filled with the position of the center of the object. We will be assuming for the purposes of this simple game engine that the position of the model with the specified offsets is the center of the object. A second method of the Geometry class provides us with our bounding box data. ComputeBoundingBox accepts the same first three arguments as the previous method. The last two arguments are the minimum and maximum extents of the mesh. Notice in both of these methods that the arguments that pass information back to us are prefixed with the out keyword. This signals to the compiler that these arguments must be passed as references so that they may be modified by the method and return information back to the calling method. Without the out prefix, the argument would not be modified by the method. Once we are done with the vertex buffer, we must remember to call the Unlock and the Dispose methods to release the vertex buffer.

The next section of the constructor (shown in Listing 5-3c) calculates the corners of the bounding box based on the extents obtained from the mesh. The model offset in the Y-axis vertical axis) is set to the inverse of the negative Y extent. This ensures that the bottom of the model will rest against the ground when the model has an altitude that corresponds with the height of the ground at its location.

Listing 5-3c. Model Class Constructor (Continued)

```
m_vOffset.Y = -m_NegativeExtents.Y;

m_Corners[0].X = m_NegativeExtents.X;
m_Corners[0].Y = m_NegativeExtents.Y + m_vOffset.Y;
m_Corners[0].Z = m_NegativeExtents.Z;

m_Corners[1].X = m_PositiveExtents.X;
m_Corners[1].Y = m_NegativeExtents.Y + m_vOffset.Y;
m_Corners[1].Z = m_NegativeExtents.Z;

m_Corners[2].X = m_NegativeExtents.X;
m_Corners[2].Y = m_PositiveExtents.Y + m_vOffset.Y;
m_Corners[2].Z = m_NegativeExtents.Z;

m_Corners[3].X = m_PositiveExtents.X;
m_Corners[3].Y = m_PositiveExtents.Y + m_vOffset.Y;
m_Corners[3].Z = m_NegativeExtents.Z;

m_Corners[4].X = m_NegativeExtents.X;
m_Corners[4].Y = m_NegativeExtents.Y + m_vOffset.Y;
m_Corners[4].Z = m_PositiveExtents.Z;

m_Corners[5].X = m_PositiveExtents.X;
m_Corners[5].Y = m_NegativeExtents.Y + m_vOffset.Y;
m_Corners[5].Z = m_PositiveExtents.Z;

m_Corners[6].X = m_PositiveExtents.X;
m_Corners[6].Y = m_PositiveExtents.Y + m_vOffset.Y;
m_Corners[6].Z = m_PositiveExtents.Z;

m_Corners[7].X = m_PositiveExtents.X;
m_Corners[7].Y = m_PositiveExtents.Y + m_vOffset.Y;
m_Corners[7].Z = m_PositiveExtents.Z;
```

The operations to this point in the constructor have been based on the mesh as it was loaded from the data file. The next section of the constructor (shown in Listing 5-3d) will prepare the mesh for our model so that we can render it with maximum efficiency. The first step is to create a clean version of the mesh. The Clean method of the Mesh class prepares the mesh for simplification. It does this by adding a vertex wherever two fans of triangles originally shared a vertex. The progressive mesh simplification routines are not as effective if we do not perform this operation first. The first argument of the Clean method is the instance of a mesh that we wish to clean. The second and third arguments are GraphicsStream instances. One is the adjacency stream for the original mesh, and the second is the new stream for the cleaned mesh. The method returns a new mesh created by the method.

Listing 5-3d. Model Class Constructor (Continued)

```
        // Perform simple cleansing operations on m_mesh.
        pTempMesh = Mesh.Clean(m_mesh, m_adj, m_adj);
        m_mesh.Dispose();

        m_mesh = pTempMesh;
        //  Perform a weld to try and remove excess vertices.
        //  Weld the mesh using all epsilons of 0.0f.
        //  A small epsilon like 1e-6 works well too.
        m_mesh.WeldVertices( 0, Epsilons, m_adj, m_adj);
        // Verify validity of mesh for simplification.
        m_mesh.Validate(m_adj);

        CreateLod();
    }
    catch (DirectXException d3de)
    {
        Console.AddLine("Unable to load mesh " + meshFile);
        Console.AddLine(d3de.ErrorString);
    }
    catch ( Exception e )
    {
        Console.AddLine("Unable to load mesh " + meshFile);
        Console.AddLine(e.Message);
    }
```

Now that we have a new, improved, "clean" mesh, we no longer need the original mesh. We can dispose of the original mesh now and replace its reference with that of the cleaned mesh. The cleaning process adds vertices that will be required when we create simplified versions of the mesh. The WeldVertices method will remove vertices that are exact duplicates of another vertex. When verifying whether a vertex is duplicated, this method checks more than just the position of the vertex. It also checks the normal, color, and texture coordinate values associated with the vertex. The Epsilons structure defines the tolerances used in comparing each of these values. Since we do not specify any initial values for the structure when it is created, all of its values will be zero. This states that all values must match exactly for a weld to occur.

The first argument for the WeldVertices method is a set of flags that can tailor the behavior of the operation. For a normal operation, a zero works just fine. The second argument is the epsilon structure holding the comparison tolerances. The last two arguments are the original and resulting adjacency streams, just like in the Clean method. Once any duplicated vertices are welded, we are about ready to create the progressive meshes. The last thing required prior to creating the progressive meshes is to validate the mesh. The Validate method verifies that the mesh is properly configured and returns a GraphicsStream that may be used to perform the creation of the progressive meshes. The actual creation of the new meshes is accomplished in the CreateLod method of the Model class. By placing this functionality in a separate method, we allow the user of the game engine to specify how the levels of detail are configured. The default setting for this operation in the constructor is the creation of a single level of detail that would be used for all ranges.

The last portion of the constructor (shown in Listing 5-3e) manages the materials for the model. The material and texture information for the model is returned from the FromFile method in the ExtendedMaterial array called materials. We will separate this information into two arrays, one array for the material information and one array for the textures. The first step is to allocate the arrays based on the number of entries in the material array. The material data is copied from the Material3D member of the ExtendedMaterial array. One thing that Microsoft does not do is set the ambient color as part of the data. We will set the ambient color to be the same as the diffuse color. Loading the textures for the model is a bit more involved.

Listing 5-3e. Model Class Constructor (Conclusion)

```
if (m_meshTextures == null && materials != null )
{
    // We need to extract the material properties and texture names.
    m_meshTextures  = new Texture[materials.Length];
    m_meshMaterials = new Material[materials.Length];

    for( int i=0; i<materials.Length; i++ )
    {
        m_meshMaterials[i] = materials[i].Material3D;
        // Set the ambient color for the material (D3DX does not do this).
        m_meshMaterials[i].Ambient = m_meshMaterials[i].Diffuse;
```

```
                     // Create the texture.
                     try
                     {
                         if ( materials[i].TextureFilename != null )
                         {
                             m_meshTextures[i] =
                                     TextureLoader.FromFile(CGameEngine.Device3D,
                                     materials[i].TextureFilename);
                         }
                     }
                     catch (DirectXException d3de)
                     {
                         Console.AddLine("Unable to load texture " +
                                                     materials[i].TextureFilename);
                         Console.AddLine(d3de.ErrorString);
                     }
                     catch ( Exception e )
                     {
                         Console.AddLine("Unable to load texture " +
                                                     materials[i].TextureFilename);
                         Console.AddLine(e.Message);
                     }
                 }
             }
         }
```

The ExtendedMaterial structure does not hold the texture. It holds only the name of the file that holds the texture. Before trying to load the texture, we need to ensure that the filename is set. It is quite possible for part of a model to have material values without having a texture. If the filename is null, we will skip the loading of the texture. This won't cause any problems when rendering, since DirectX understands that a null texture means that there is no texture to apply to the triangles. The TextureLoader class supplies the FromFile method needed to create a texture from the specified file.

When an instance of the Model class is created, the constructor builds only one level of detail. The game engine should permit the user to specify how many levels to be used for each model. It should also be able to specify the maximum range for the levels of detail. Each level will switch as its range is reached. The individual ranges will be an equal fraction of the maximum range. For example, if the maximum range is 500 feet and ten levels are specified, the levels will switch every 50 feet. The public interface that allows the user to specify the level-of-detail settings is called SetLOD (shown in Listing 5-4).

Listing 5-4. Model Class SetLOD Method

```
public void SetLOD( int numLOD, float MaxRange )
{
    if ( numLOD < 1 ) numLOD = 1;

    m_nNumLOD = numLOD;
    m_fMaxLODRange = MaxRange;

    m_LODRanges = new float[numLOD];

    float rangeDelta = MaxRange / numLOD;

    for ( int i=0; i < numLOD; i++ )
    {
        m_LODRanges[i] = rangeDelta * ( i+1);
    }
    CreateLod();
}
```

The SetLOD method will require two arguments: the number of levels and the maximum range. We must ensure that we do not accept bad inputs. No matter what the user of the game engine specifies, we need to have at least one level of detail. The first line of the method checks to see if the number of levels is at least one. If not, it sets it to a value of one. The number of levels and the maximum range is saved within the class for later reference. A range delta is calculated by dividing the maximum range by the number of levels, which gives us our change of levels at a regular interval. The range array is created large enough to hold range values corresponding with each detail level. The array is then filled with these range values. The final step is to call the CreateLod method. This method was originally called by the constructor to create a single level of detail. Calling the method now will delete the original level-of-detail model and create the requested number of levels.

I have referred to the CreateLod method a couple of times now. The method is shown in Listing 5-5. It begins by creating a temporary ProgressiveMesh from the basic mesh that will be used to create the lower resolution versions for the other levels of detail. The SimplifyVertex flag is specified to instruct the ProgressiveMesh constructor to simplify the mesh's vertex structure if possible. We want to start this process with the simplest mesh structure we can get. The temporary mesh provides us with the range of vertices that can be used with the mesh. The maximum value is, of course, the original number of vertices. An enhanced mesh allows us to increase the number of vertices in a mesh, but a progressive mesh only allows us to reduce the number. The constructor also determines the minimum number of vertices that may be kept in the mesh. This is largely based on the triangulation of the mesh and the number of objects within the mesh.

Listing 5-5. Model Class CreateLod Method

```
private void CreateLod()
{
    ProgressiveMesh pPMesh = null;
    int cVerticesMin = 0;
    int cVerticesMax = 0;
    int cVerticesPerMesh = 0;

    pPMesh = new ProgressiveMesh(m_mesh, m_adj, null, 1,
                    MeshFlags.SimplifyVertex);

    cVerticesMin = pPMesh.MinVertices;
    cVerticesMax = pPMesh.MaxVertices;

    if ( m_pMeshes != null )
    {
        for (int iPMesh = 0; iPMesh < m_pMeshes.Length; iPMesh++)
        {
            m_pMeshes[iPMesh].Dispose();
        }
    }

    cVerticesPerMesh = (cVerticesMax - cVerticesMin) / m_nNumLOD;
    m_pMeshes = new ProgressiveMesh[m_nNumLOD];

    // Clone all the separate m_pMeshes.
    for (int iPMesh = 0; iPMesh < m_pMeshes.Length; iPMesh++)
    {
        m_pMeshes[m_pMeshes.Length - 1 - iPMesh] =
                pPMesh.Clone( MeshFlags.Managed | MeshFlags.VbShare,
                pPMesh.VertexFormat, CGameEngine.Device3D);
        // Trim to appropriate space.
        if ( m_nNumLOD > 1 )
        {
            m_pMeshes[m_pMeshes.Length - 1 -
                    iPMesh].TrimByVertices(cVerticesMin +
                    cVerticesPerMesh * iPMesh, cVerticesMin +
                    cVerticesPerMesh * (iPMesh+1));
        }
```

```
        m_pMeshes[m_pMeshes.Length - 1 - iPMesh]
                .OptimizeBaseLevelOfDetail(MeshFlags.OptimizeVertexCache);
    }
    m_currentPmesh = 0;
    m_pMeshes[m_currentPmesh].NumberVertices = cVerticesMax;
    pPMesh.Dispose();
}
```

If the array of level-of-detail meshes currently exists, we must dispose of those meshes before we replace them. We have created meshes that may likely be stored within video memory. We lose efficiency if we leave them there after we replace them.

Creating the level-of-detail meshes is a three-step process. We begin by cloning the temporary mesh into the level-of-detail mesh array slot we are currently building. The two flags included in the cloning process (Managed and VbShare) specify that the mesh will be in managed memory (in video memory if possible) and that the vertex buffer will be shared with the original. All of our level-of-detail meshes will share the same vertex buffer. In this way, the vertex buffer only needs to exist in video memory once. What will differ between meshes will be the index buffers that specify which vertices are used.

At this point, we have an exact duplicate of the original mesh. If this is not the first (highest) level of detail, there are two more steps to take. The first step is to reduce the number of vertices in the mesh appropriately for the current level that we are building. The TrimByVertices method does this for us. The number of vertices is based on the current level and the difference between the minimum and maximum number of vertices divided by the number of levels. The final step is to call OptimizeBaseLevelOfDetail. This method optimizes the index buffer so that the faces and vertices are processed in the most efficient order. Once we have created all of our level-of-detail meshes, we can dispose of the temporary mesh. We don't need to worry about losing that shared vertex buffer, since the other meshes are still referencing it.

Implementing Required Model Methods

Now that we have established how to create a model, it is time to add methods to the class in order to manipulate the model. The following methods provide the means to control the model.

Checking If a Model Is Within an Area

Remember that every Object3D-based class has an InRect method, which determines whether an object is within the supplied rectangle. The InRect method for the Model class is shown in Listing 5-6. This method will use a simple algorithm to make this determination. We will check to see if the distance between the center of the rectangle and the center of the model is less than the sum of the bounding radii of the rectangle and the model. One assumption that this method makes is that the rectangle will always be a square. The normal calculations for distance use the Pythagorean theorem of the square root of the sum of the squares. Unfortunately, the square root operation is one of the most computationally expensive. Luckily, we do not actually need to know the distance. We only need to know if one distance is less than another. Because of this, we can compare the squares of the distances and achieve the same result—just one more way in which we can buy a bit more speed and efficiency to keep our rendering rate as high as possible.

Listing 5-6. Model Class InRect Method

```
public override bool InRect( Rectangle rect )
{
    // Check to see if the bounding circle around the model
    // intersects this rectangle.
    int center_x = (rect.Left + rect.Right)/2;
    int center_z = (rect.Top + rect.Bottom)/2;

    int delta_x = center_x - (int)m_vPosition.X;
    int delta_z = center_z - (int)m_vPosition.Z;
    int distance_squared = delta_x * delta_x + delta_z * delta_z;
    int combined_radius = (int)(m_fRadius * m_fRadius) +
                                        (rect.Width*rect.Width);
    bool bInside = distance_squared < combined_radius;
    return bInside;
}
```

Testing for Collisions

The next couple of methods concern collision checking for the models. Collision tests for models is a bit more involved. Up until now, our collision tests have been strictly based on bounding radius intersections. Now we will be working with object-oriented bounding boxes to get a higher quality collision test. In order to do this, we will need to be able to query the bounding box corners of one model from the Collide method of another model. The method used to expose the corner is the GetCorner method (shown in Listing 5-7).

Listing 5-7. Model Class GetCorner Method

```
Vector3 GetCorner( int index )
{
   Vector3 WorldCorner =
              Vector3.TransformCoordinate(m_Corners[index],m_Matrix);
   return WorldCorner;
}
```

For the corner to be of value to us, it needs to be in the world coordinate system. The class can do this quickly and easily using the TransformCoordinate method of the Vector3 class. By passing the object-relative position of the corner and the model's matrix to this method, we get back the world-relative position of the corner. You will see this method put to use in the Collide method.

The Collide method (shown in Listings 5-8a through 5-8c in this section) is another of the methods required of an Object3D-based class. It returns true if this model is in a collision situation with the supplied object. This method is more involved than previous Collide methods mentioned earlier. We will start out the same as the other simpler methods by beginning with a bounding radius check (see Listing 5-8a). If the bounding radii do not intersect, then it is not possible that there would be any other type of collision.

Listing 5-8a. Model Class Collide Method

```
public override bool Collide( Object3D Other )
{
   Plane[] planeCollide;      // Planes of the collide box
   Vector3[] WorldCorners = new Vector3[8];

   // Perform bounding sphere collision test.
   float delta_north = Other.North - North;
   float delta_east = Other.East - East;
   float distance_squared = delta_north * delta_north +
      delta_east * delta_east;
   float combined_radius = (Radius * Radius)+(Other.Radius * Other.Radius);
   bool bCollide = distance_squared < combined_radius;
```

If the bounding radii check indicates that there might be a collision, it is time to perform a more detailed collision test. We will do this by testing points from the other object to see if they are within the object-aligned bounding box. The box is formed by the six planes that make up the faces of the box. The `Plane` class has the `FromPoints` method that creates the plane based on three points on that plane. These points come from the corners of the bounding box transformed into world space. The code for building the collision planes appears in Listing 5-8b.

Listing 5-8b. Model Class Collide Method (Continued)

```
// If the bounding spheres are in contact, perform a more
// precise collision test.
if ( bCollide )
{
    planeCollide = new Plane[6];

    for( int i = 0; i < 8; i++ )
        WorldCorners[i] =
                Vector3.TransformCoordinate(m_Corners[i],m_Matrix);

    planeCollide[0] = Plane.FromPoints(WorldCorners[7],WorldCorners[3],
                                    WorldCorners[5]); // Right
    planeCollide[1] = Plane.FromPoints(WorldCorners[2],WorldCorners[6],
                                    WorldCorners[4]); // Left
    planeCollide[2] = Plane.FromPoints(WorldCorners[6],WorldCorners[7],
                                    WorldCorners[5]); // Far
    planeCollide[3] = Plane.FromPoints(WorldCorners[0],WorldCorners[1],
                                    WorldCorners[2]); // Near
    planeCollide[4] = Plane.FromPoints(WorldCorners[2],WorldCorners[3],
                                    WorldCorners[6]); // Top
    planeCollide[5] = Plane.FromPoints(WorldCorners[1],WorldCorners[0],
                                    WorldCorners[4]); // Bottom
```

The final step in the process depends on what type of object we are testing against (shown in Listing 5-8c). If the other object is a `Model` object, we can use its bounding box information in the test. Here is where we will use the `GetCorner` method we examined earlier. We loop through the eight corners of the other model and see if any of them are within this model's box. The dot product of the plane and the point returns the distance from that point and the surface of the plane. If this distance is positive, it indicates that the point is within the box, and we do have a collision.

Listing 5-8c. Model Class Collide Method (Conclusion)

```
if ( Other.GetType() == typeof(Model) )
{
   for( int i = 0; i < 8; i++ )
   {
      float distance;
      Vector3 testPoint = ((Model)Other).GetCorner(i);

      for( int iPlane = 0; iPlane < 6; iPlane++ )
      {
         distance = planeCollide[iPlane].Dot( testPoint );
         if ( distance > 0.0f ) bCollide = true;
      }
   }
}
else
{
   float distance;
   Vector3 testPoint = Other.Position;
   testPoint.Y += 0.1f;

   for( int iPlane = 0; iPlane < 6; iPlane++ )
   {
      distance = planeCollide[iPlane].Dot( testPoint );
      if ( distance > 0.0f )
      {
         bCollide = true;
      }
   }
   for( int i = 0; i < 8; i++ )
   {
      testPoint = Other.Position;

      float angle = ((float)Math.PI / 4) * i;

      testPoint.X += (float)Math.Cos(angle) * Other.Radius;
      testPoint.Y += 0.2f;
      testPoint.Z += (float)Math.Sin(angle) * Other.Radius;

      for( int iPlane = 0; iPlane < 6; iPlane++ )
      {
         distance = planeCollide[iPlane].Dot( testPoint );
         if ( distance > 0.0f )
```

```
                        {
                            bCollide = true;
                        }
                    }
                }
            }
        }
        return bCollide;
    }
```

If the other object is not a `Model`, we will need to perform the test a bit differently. We will start with the simple test to see if the center position of the other model is within the bounding box. We also check eight points around the other object's bounding circle to see if any of those points are within the box. This combination ensures that we can positively determine if we have collided with a billboard, since billboards are the most common objects other than models that we might collide with.

Rendering the Model

The `Render` method (shown in Listing 5-9) handles the drawing of the model on the screen. Even though models are the most complex objects that we have encountered thus far, they are not that difficult to render. The Mesh class supplied by Microsoft does most of the difficult work for us. We begin by setting the culling mode to counterclockwise. This is the standard way in which models are built. You may, if you wish, make this something that the user of the game engine can specify for each model to make the engine even more flexible. We will stick with supporting just the one mode for simplicity's sake. If the culling mode is set incorrectly, the models will not appear in the display. After setting the culling mode, we transfer the model's matrix into the device's world transform matrix so that all of the vertices in the model are properly transformed.

Listing 5-9. Model Class Render Method

```
public override void Render( Camera cam )
{
    // Meshes are divided into subsets, one for each material. Render
    // them in a loop.
    CGameEngine.Device3D.RenderState.CullMode =
        Microsoft.DirectX.Direct3D.Cull.CounterClockwise;
```

```
    if ( m_Parent != null )
    {
       world_matrix = Matrix.Multiply(m_Matrix, m_Parent.WorldMatrix);
    }
    else
    {
       world_matrix = m_Matrix;
    }

CGameEngine.Device3D.Transform.World = world_matrix;

 for( int i=0; i<m_meshMaterials.Length; i++ )
 {
    // Set the material and texture for this subset.
    CGameEngine.Device3D.Material = m_meshMaterials[i];
    CGameEngine.Device3D.SetTexture(0, m_meshTextures[i]);

    // Draw the m_mesh subset.
    m_pMeshes[m_currentPmesh].DrawSubset(i);
 }
    if ( m_Children.Count > 0 )
    {
       Object3D obj;
       for ( int i=0; i<m_Children.Count; i++ )
       {
          obj = (Object3D)m_Children.GetByIndex(i);
          obj.Render( cam );
       }
    }
 Culled = true;
}
```

The actual rendering of the model is performed by looping through the list of materials that make up the model. For each material, we set the material and texture information in the device. The DrawSubset method of the current mesh renders all of the faces of the model that use that material and texture. If the model has any children, we also have each of them render themselves. After rendering the entire model and any children, the Culled flag is set. Remember that the Render method is called next pass only if the culling routine has cleared this flag.

Updating the Model

Since the Model class also supports the IDynamic interface, we need to have an Update method (shown in Listing 5-10). The Update method takes care of any changes that happen to the model as time progresses. The user of the game engine can expand upon the dynamics of a model by specifying an additional Update method that follows the ObjectUpdate delegate definition.

Listing 5-10. Model Class Update Method

```
public override void Update( float DeltaT )
{
    if ( Visible )
    {
    try
    {
        if ( m_UpdateMethod != null )
        {
            m_UpdateMethod( (Object3D)this, DeltaT );
        }
        m_Matrix = Matrix.Identity;
        m_Matrix =
          Matrix.RotationYawPitchRoll(Heading+m_AttitudeOffset.Heading,
            Pitch+m_AttitudeOffset.Pitch,Roll+m_AttitudeOffset.Roll);
        Matrix temp = Matrix.Translation(m_vPosition);
        m_Matrix.Multiply(temp);

        // Determine the proper LOD index based on range from the camera.
        int index = m_nNumLOD;
        for ( int i = 0; i < m_nNumLOD; i++ )
        {
            if ( Range < m_LODRanges[i] )
            {
                index = i;
                break;
            }
        }
        if ( index >= m_nNumLOD ) index = m_nNumLOD-1;
        m_currentPmesh = index;

        if ( m_bHasMoved && m_Quads.Count > 0 )
        {
            Quad q = (Quad)m_Quads[0];
            q.Update( this );
        }
```

```
      }
      catch (DirectXException d3de)
      {
         Console.AddLine("Unable to update a Model " + Name);
         Console.AddLine(d3de.ErrorString);
      }
      catch ( Exception e )
      {
         Console.AddLine("Unable to update a Model " + Name);
         Console.AddLine(e.Message);
      }
         if ( m_Children.Count > 0 )
         {
            Object3D obj;
            for ( int i=0; i<m_Children.Count; i++ )
            {
               obj = (Object3D)m_Children.GetByIndex(i);
               obj.Update( DeltaT );
            }
         }
      }
   }
```

If the user has specified an Update method (i.e., the method reference is not null), it is called and supplied a reference to this model and the update time delta. This external Update method is likely to change the position and attitude of the object. This is, of course, what makes the objects dynamic. Since the object is likely to have moved in some way, we need to recalculate the world transform matrix for the model. This matrix is formed by multiplying a matrix based on the attitude of the model with another matrix based on the position of the model.

The Update method must also determine which of the level-of-detail models is now appropriate. The distance between the current camera and the model is determined during the culling process and saved in the object's Range attribute. We check this distance against each of the level-of-detail ranges. The lowest level of detail that is still within the proper range is used as the current level of detail. Care is taken that if the model is beyond the farthest range we stop at the lowest level of detail and do not try to index past the end of the array.

If the object has moved, it may no longer be in the same portion of the Quadtree used for culling. The position and attitude attributes of the Object3D class Set methods all set the "has moved" flag whenever they are called. If the object has moved and knows that it exists in at least one quad, we will request that the Quadtree update itself. This is accomplished by calling the Update method of the first quad in the object's list. This will always be the highest-level quad of the set and it will ensure that all of the quads beneath it also update properly. If the model has any children, they should be updated as well.

Disposing of the Model

The last method in the class is the Dispose method (shown in Listing 5-11). We have a number of objects allocated by this class that need to be disposed of—the basic mesh for the model and any children of the model. Also, we need to consider each of the level-of-detail meshes that must be freed as well as any textures required by the model.

Listing 5-11. Model Class Dispose Method

```
public override void Dispose()
{
    m_mesh.Dispose();

    if ( m_Children.Count > 0 )
    {
        Object3D obj;
        for ( int i=0; i<m_Children.Count; i++ )
        {
            obj = (Object3D)m_Children.GetByIndex(i);
            obj.Dispose();
        }
    }
    if ( m_pMeshes != null )
    {
        for (int iPMesh = 0; iPMesh < m_pMeshes.Length; iPMesh++)
        {
            m_pMeshes[iPMesh].Dispose();
        }
    }

    if (m_meshTextures != null)
    {
        for( int i=0; i<m_meshMaterials.Length; i++ )
        {
            // Create the texture.
            m_meshTextures[i].Dispose();
        }
    }
}
```

Using a Model in a Game

This chapter has been dedicated so far to the design of the Model class. Now let's take a look at how a user of the game engine might interact with models within a game. To use a model within the game, we need to do several things. We need to create the model and give it to the game engine so that it may be managed and rendered. We must also perform any initial setup of the model. This all comes under the heading of instantiating the model, and will typically be done in the background task started while the developer splash screen is being displayed. This is the same routine that loads the terrain and billboards. Figure 5-1 shows our sandy terrain with billboard trees and cacti. It also shows two cars that we have added using the Model class.

Figure 5-1. Models in our scene

The portion of the background task code dealing with the instantiation of the models is shown in Listing 5-12. The process begins with creating the model and adding to the game engine with the AddObject method. Notice that we can do both operations in one step for each model by placing the call to the constructor as the argument to the AddObject call. Each model must have a unique name associated with it. This allows us to retrieve a reference to the model back from the game engine so that we can manipulate the model.

Listing 5-12. Instantiating Models

```
m_Engine.AddObject( new Model("car1", "SprintRacer.x",
    new Vector3(0.0f, 0.8f, 0.0f), new Attitude(0.0f, (float)Math.PI, 0.0f)) );
m_Engine.AddObject( new Model("car2", "SprintRacer.x",
    new Vector3(0.0f, 0.8f, 0.0f), new Attitude(0.0f, (float)Math.PI, 0.0f)) );

Model ownship = (Model)m_Engine.GetObject("car1");
ownship.North = 60.0f;
ownship.East = 60.0f;
m_Engine.Cam.Attach(m_ownship, new Vector3(0.0f, 0.85f,-4.5f));
m_Engine.Cam.LookAt(m_ownship);
ownship.Heading = (float)Math.PI * 0.25f;
ownship.SetLOD( 10, 3000.0f );
ownship.SetUpdateMethod( new ObjectUpdate(OwnshipUpdate));

Model car2 = (Model)m_Engine.GetObject("car2");
car2.North = 100.0f;
car2.East  = 100.0f;
car2.SetLOD( 10, 300.0f );
car2.SetUpdateMethod( new ObjectUpdate(OpponentUpdate));
```

We use the game engine's GetObject method to get this reference. Once we have the reference, we can set the model's position and heading. We can also do things like attaching a camera to the model and changing the number of levels of detail that are used by the model. Most importantly, we can set the Update method that the model will use. In this example, we have two different Update methods: one method for the car the player will drive and one for a computer-managed vehicle.

The OwnshipUpdate method (shown in Listing 5-13) is the method passed to the model representing the player vehicle. When we get to Chapter 10, we will have physics-based dynamics for the vehicles. At this point, we will just move the model along the terrain surface at a user-controlled speed. The position on the terrain is a simple integration based on the current speed and heading. The height of the model and its pitch and roll are based on information on the terrain surface that the model is resting upon.

Listing 5-13. Sample Update Method 1

```
public void OwnshipUpdate( Object3D Obj, float DeltaT )
{

    Obj.North = Obj.North +
        ownship_speed * (float)Math.Cos(Obj.Heading) * DeltaT;
```

```
Obj.East  = Obj.East +
    ownship_speed * (float)Math.Sin(Obj.Heading) * DeltaT;
Obj.Height = CGameEngine.Ground.HeightOfTerrain(Obj.Position) +
    ((Model)Obj).Offset.Y;
Obj.Attitude = CGameEngine.Ground.GetSlope(Obj.Position, Obj.Heading );
 if ( m_bUsingJoystick )
{
    Obj.Heading = Obj.Heading +
        (CGameEngine.Inputs.GetJoystickNormalX()-1.0f)*DeltaT;
    ownship_speed +=
        (1.0f-(float)CGameEngine.Inputs.GetJoystickNormalY()) * 0.5f;
}
else if ( m_bUsingMouse )
{
    try
    {
        ownship_speed += (float)CGameEngine.Inputs.GetMouseZ() * 0.1f;
        float x = (float)CGameEngine.Inputs.GetMouseX();
        Obj.Heading = Obj.Heading + (x * .10f)*DeltaT;
        if ( CGameEngine.Inputs.IsKeyPressed(Key.DownArrow) )
        {
            ownship_speed -= 0.1f;
        }
        else if ( CGameEngine.Inputs.IsKeyPressed(Key.UpArrow) )
        {
            ownship_speed += 0.1f;
        }
    }
    catch ( Exception e )
    {
        GameEngine.Console.AddLine("Exception");
        GameEngine.Console.AddLine(e.Message);
    }
}
else if ( m_bUsingKeyboard )
{
    if ( CGameEngine.Inputs.IsKeyPressed(Key.LeftArrow) )
    {
        Obj.Heading = Obj.Heading - .50f * DeltaT;
    }
    else if ( CGameEngine.Inputs.IsKeyPressed(Key.RightArrow) )
    {
        Obj.Heading = Obj.Heading + .50f * DeltaT;
    }
```

```
        if ( CGameEngine.Inputs.IsKeyPressed(Key.DownArrow) )
        {
            ownship_speed -= 0.1f;
        }
        else if ( CGameEngine.Inputs.IsKeyPressed(Key.UpArrow) )
        {
            ownship_speed += 0.1f;
        }
    }

    foreach ( Object3D test_obj in m_Engine.Objects )
    {
        if ( test_obj !=  Obj )
        {
            if ( Obj.Collide(test_obj) )
            {
                GameEngine.Console.AddLine( Obj.Name + " collided with " +
                    test_obj.Name);
            }
        }
    }
    foreach ( Object3D test_obj in GameEngine.BillBoard.Objects )
    {
        if ( test_obj !=  Obj )
        {
            if ( Obj.Collide(test_obj) )
            {
                GameEngine.Console.AddLine( Obj.Name + " collided with " +
                    test_obj.Name);
            }
        }
    }
}
```

A joystick, the mouse, or the keyboard may be chosen by the user to control speed and heading. If the user selects a joystick control, the X-axis of the joystick controls the heading and the Y-axis controls the speed. If the mouse was chosen, the side-to-side movement of the mouse (X-axis) controls the vehicle heading. If the mouse has a scroll wheel, it can be used to control the speed. Just in case the mouse doesn't have a scroll wheel, we include keyboard control of the speed using the up and down arrows. Finally, if the keyboard was chosen, we use the four arrow keys to control the speed and heading.

The last thing that we will do in the OwnshipUpdate method is check to see if the vehicle has collided with anything. This is just a matter of iterating through the game engine's list of objects and billboards and checking for a collision. For now, we will just post a message to the console whenever a collision is detected. Once we add physics to the game engine, we can add more realistic reactions.

The Update method for the other vehicle (shown in Listing 5-14) is much simpler. At this point, the vehicle will be stationary. The only thing we need the routine to do is ensure that the vehicle is resting on the terrain. We set the vehicle's height to the terrain height at its position plus any offset specified for the model.

Listing 5-14. Sample Update Method 2

```
public void OpponentUpdate( Object3D Obj, float DeltaT )
{
   Obj.Height = CGameEngine.Ground.HeightOfTerrain(Obj.Position) +
      ((Model)Obj).Offset.Y;
}
```

Summary

This chapter has explored the Model class, which adds support for complex three-dimensional models to the game engine. This allows us to add vehicles, buildings, and even models of people to the game. All of the action within the game is accomplished with these models.

CHAPTER 6

Camera: The Player's View of the World

IN THE LAST FEW CHAPTERS, you have seen me refer to a Camera class. In this chapter, we will take an in-depth look at the Camera class and the important part it plays in the game engine. Three matrices are used to convert three-dimensional object definitions into the two-dimensional data needed to render images to the computer screen. The first is the world matrix that we have been using in the Object3D and derivative classes. That matrix translates positions in object-relative coordinates to world coordinates.

The other two matrices are the view matrix and the projection matrix. These are used to translate the three-dimensional data into two-dimensional screen coordinates. Since these matrices combine to define the view rendered to the screen, let's use the analogy of a video camera for the class that manages them. The view matrix represents the placement and orientation of the camera. The projection matrix represents the lens of the camera.

Looking Through the Lens

The projection matrix is the lens of our camera. Four values define a projection matrix: field of view, aspect ratio, near clipping plane, and far clipping plane. These are used to create not only the projection matrix, but also the viewing frustum. Figure 6-1 is an illustration of a frustum. Only objects that are within the area enclosed by the frustum will be visible on the screen. The smaller square in the foreground is the near clipping plane. Any objects that are closer to the camera origin than the near clipping plane are considered to be behind the lens. Any objects beyond the far clipping plane are not included in the scene.

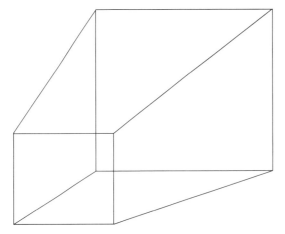

Figure 6-1. Viewing frustum

The width of the frustum is defined by the field of view variable. This is typically set to 45 degrees (or a quarter pi radians, if you prefer). The height of the frustum is defined by the combination of the field of view and the aspect ratio. The aspect ratio is the ratio of the width of the frustum to the height. The standard aspect ratio (assuming that you are rendering a full-screen image) is 1.33 (i.e., 640/480 or 1280/1024).

The near and far clipping planes are ranges in whatever database units that we are using. For example, if all of our positions are defined in meters, the clipping planes will also be defined in meters. The viewing frustum encloses the area that will be rendered to the screen, which is why we use the mathematical definition of the frustum in our culling process. Any object that is completely outside the frustum will not be visible. We would be wasting valuable processing resources rendering those objects.

Adjusting the field of view acts like the zoom feature on a camera. Narrowing the field of view has the same effect as zooming in. Objects in the distance become larger. Widening the field of view is the same as zooming out (up to a point). Widening the field of view much past the 45-degree point will start to create a fishbowl look.

Managing the Camera

Cameras can be used within the game in numerous ways. A camera could be attached to a moving object so that we have a driver's eye view. We could attach a camera so that it is always behind an object, providing a chase view of the action. A camera could also be placed in a fixed location or moved manually by the player. Finally, we can have multiple cameras and switch between them based on player selections or automated switching.

The game engine must provide the flexibility necessary so that the game programmer has all of the tools needed to build the game. This means providing the interfaces required to manage multiple cameras and switch between them.

Remember that any object that is not at least partially within the viewing frustum need not be rendered, since it will not be visible anyway. The camera class will assist in achieving improved efficiency by assisting in the culling process. It will include a method that tests an object or a bounding volume against the camera's frustum. The result returned by this method will be an enumeration value defined with the Camera class. This enumeration (shown in Listing 6-1) includes the three possible results of the test. Any object is either completely within the frustum, completely outside the frustum, or partially inside.

Listing 6-1. Camera Culling Enumeration

```
public class Camera
{
    public enum CullState
    {
        AllInside,
        AllOutside,
        PartiallyIn,
    }
```

Defining the Camera

The Camera class must know certain things about itself. This information is held within the attribute members of the class (shown in Listing 6-2a). First the camera needs to know about any objects that it is either attached to or will be looking at. These may very well be the same object. When a camera is attached to an object, it is likely that it will not be attached to the reference point of the object. The camera will be attached with a positional offset. This offset is held within the class as a vector. If the camera is not attached to an object, it will need its own position and attitude. We will default the camera to a position of one unit north and east of the corner of the terrain (to ensure that it is somewhere within the terrain). The class will also hold the two matrices that it must manage: the view matrix and the projection matrix.

Listing 6-2a. Camera Class Definition (Attributes)

```
#region Attributes
private Object3D  m_AttachedObject = null;
private Object3D  m_LookAtObject = null;
private Vector3   m_Offset;
```

```
private Attitude m_Attitude;
private Matrix m_matProj;
private Matrix m_matView;
private float m_X = 1.0f;
private float m_Y = 1.0f;
private float m_Z = 1.0f;
private Vector3[] vecFrustum;      // Corners of the view frustum
private Plane[] planeFrustum;      // Planes of the view frustum
private Vector3 m_Eye;
private Vector3 m_LookAt;
private string m_name = "default";
private float m_fFOV = (float)Math.PI/4.0f;
private float m_fAspect = 1.33f;
private float m_fNearPlane = 1.0f;
private float m_fFarPlane = 800.0f;
private ArrayList m_VisibleObjects = null;
```

Three vectors are used in the creation of the view matrix. One of the vectors is the Up vector, and this defines which way is "up" for the camera. This vector is useful only if we wish to have the camera be able to achieve attitudes in which the image is rolled to the side or upside down. For this simple engine, we will constrain the camera so that it is always right-side up. Because our Up vector is always pointing straight up, we do not need to have an attribute for it. We will need the other two vectors , which are the Eye and the LookAt vectors. The Eye vector defines the position from which the camera is looking. For an attached camera, this will be the position of the object to which the camera is attached (with any specified offsets). The LookAt vector specifies the direction in which the camera is pointing. This can be used to point the camera at an object or just a specific direction, depending on how the camera is being used.

Each camera must also be given a unique name. This allows the user of the game engine to retrieve a reference to a camera by specifying its name. The default camera that is always created by the game engine will be given the name "default."

The next four attributes of the class will be the values used to create the projection matrix. They will default to the standard 45-degree field of view and an aspect ratio of 1.33. The near clipping plane will default to 1 unit in front of the camera, and the far clipping plane will default to 800 units. Anything that is more than 800 units from the camera will not be visible. The final attribute is a collection of objects that are currently in view for the camera.

All of the attributes of the class will be declared as private so that the game engine or any user of the game engine may not directly access them. Public properties will be defined to provide access in a controlled manner as shown in Listing 6-2b.

Listing 6-2b. Camera Class Definition (Properties)

```
Public ArrayList VisibleObjects { get { return m_VisibleObjects; } }
public float Heading {
    get { return (float)(m_Attitude.Heading*180.0/Math.PI); } }
public float Pitch {
    get { return (float)(m_Attitude.Pitch*180.0/Math.PI); } }
public string Name { get { return m_name; } }
public float X { get { return m_X; } }
public float Y { get { return m_Y; } }
public float Z { get { return m_Z; } }
public Matrix View { get { return m_matView; } }
public Vector3 EyeVector { get { return m_Eye; } }
public Vector3 LookAtVector { get { return m_LookAt; } }
public float FieldOfView
{
    set
    {
        m_fFOV = value;
        m_matProj = Matrix.PerspectiveFovLH( m_fFOV, m_fAspect,
            m_fNearPlane, m_fFarPlane );
    }
}
public float AspectRatio
{
    set
    {
        m_fAspect = value;
        m_matProj = Matrix.PerspectiveFovLH( m_fFOV, m_fAspect,
            m_fNearPlane, m_fFarPlane );
    }
}
public float NearClipPlane
{
    set
    {
        m_fNearPlane = value;
        m_matProj = Matrix.PerspectiveFovLH( m_fFOV, m_fAspect,
            m_fNearPlane, m_fFarPlane );
    }
}
public float FarClipPlane
```

```
    {
        set
        {
            m_fFarPlane = value;
            m_matProj = Matrix.PerspectiveFovLH( m_fFOV, m_fAspect,
                m_fNearPlane, m_fFarPlane );
        }
    }
    #endregion
```

The first two properties concern the attitude of the camera. While the heading and pitch of the camera appear within the Camera class in radians, that is not the most readable format for us humans. These properties are read-only and provide the heading and pitch in degrees. The name of the camera and the position of the camera are exposed as read-only properties as well. We will allow the game engine or the engine's user to look at these values, but the name must not be changed, and there are other ways to alter the position of the camera.

The view matrix and the two vectors used to create it are also made available as read-only properties. You can see how we are using the features of properties to control access to our attributes. In the same way, we will be making the last four properties of the class write-only. These properties are used in setting the values that form the projection matrix. By making them properties, we are able to add the automatic recalculation of the projection matrix anytime one of the four values is changed.

Creating a Camera

There are two constructors for our Camera class, shown in Listing 6-3. The first constructor is the default that should be used only by the game engine. It creates the default camera (i.e., it leaves the name of the camera as "default"). The second constructor is the one that will normally be used by anyone building a game with the game engine. It allows us to specify the name for the camera. Both constructors initialize the two matrices that are held by the class. The view matrix is set to the identity matrix. The identity matrix is a safe default, since it equates to a position and attitude of all zeros. The projection matrix is built from the four values described earlier in the chapter. The only other thing required by the constructors is to allocate the arrays that will be used to hold the points defining the corners of the viewing frustum and the six planes that define the sides of the frustum.

Listing 6-3. Camera Constructors

```
public Camera()
{
   m_matView = Matrix.Identity;
   m_Offset = new Vector3(0.0f, 0.0f, 0.0f);
   vecFrustum = new Vector3[8];    // Corners of the view frustum
   planeFrustum = new Plane[6];    // Planes of the view frustum
   m_matProj = Matrix.PerspectiveFovLH( fFOV, fAspect,
                                 fNearPlane, fFarPlane );
}

public Camera(string name)
{
   m_matView = Matrix.Identity;
   m_Offset = new Vector3(0.0f, 0.0f, 0.0f);
   vecFrustum = new Vector3[8];    // Corners of the view frustum
   planeFrustum = new Plane[6];    // Planes of the view frustum
   m_matProj = Matrix.PerspectiveFovLH( fFOV, fAspect,
                                 fNearPlane, fFarPlane );
   m_name = name;
}
```

Positioning the Camera

Since the camera will be flexible in the way it is positioned and pointed, we need to include a number of methods to provide for all options. The first three methods are concerned with manual control of camera position and attitude. The first of these, AdjustHeading, is used for pointing the camera. The AdjustHeading method (shown in Listing 6-4) takes a heading adjustment value in degrees. This value is converted to radians and added to the camera's current heading. We want to keep the range of the heading within 0 to 360 degrees. Whenever adjusting an attitude angle like this, it is a good idea to ensure that the angles stay within a reasonable range. Microsoft's trigonometric routines tend to lose accuracy when the values get too far from this nominal range.

Listing 6-4. Camera AdjustHeading Method

```
public void AdjustHeading( float deltaHeading )
{
   m_Attitude.Heading += (deltaHeading * (float)Math.PI / 180.0f);
```

```
        if ( m_Attitude.Heading > (2.0f * Math.PI) )
        {
           m_Attitude.Heading -= (float)(2.0f * Math.PI);
        }

        if ( m_Attitude.Heading < 0.0f )
        {
           m_Attitude.Heading += (float)(2.0f * Math.PI);
        }
    }
```

Just like the method for adjusting the heading, we have the `AdjustPitch` method (shown in Listing 6-5) for adjusting the pitch angle up and down. The only difference (other than which attribute is being adjusted) is the range that the angle is kept within. The valid range for a pitch angle is plus or minus 90 degrees, or one-half pi radians.

Listing 6-5. Camera AdjustPitch Method

```
    public void AdjustPitch( float deltaPitch )
    {
       m_Attitude.Pitch += (deltaPitch * (float)Math.PI / 180.0f);

       if ( m_Attitude.Pitch > (0.5f * Math.PI) )
       {
          m_Attitude.Pitch = (float)(0.5f * Math.PI);
       }

       if ( m_Attitude.Pitch < (-0.5f * Math.PI) )
       {
          m_Attitude.Pitch = (float)(-0.5f * Math.PI);
       }
    }
```

The last method for manually controlling the camera is the `MoveCamera` method (shown in Listing 6-6). The three arguments to this method dictate the amount to adjust the camera position in the forward, vertical, and sideways directions. The amount to move the camera in the world X direction (east) is based on the heading and the forward and sideways movement distances. The movement in the world Z direction (north) works the same way, only at right angles to the heading. We also want to make sure that the camera is not moved below the surface of the terrain. We query the terrain for the current terrain height at the camera's position. If the camera is less than one unit above the terrain, it is raised to be one unit above the ground. Notice that the query of the terrain height is placed in a Try/Catch block. If the camera is moved so that it is not over the terrain, it is possible that the HeightOfTerrain method would throw an exception. If the exception is thrown, we will assume a terrain height of zero.

Listing 6-6. Camera MoveCamera Method

```
public void MoveCamera( float x, float y, float z )
{
    float ty;
    m_X += x * (float)Math.Cos(m_Attitude.Heading) + z *
                    (float)Math.Sin(m_Attitude.Heading);
    m_Y += y;
    m_Z += z * (float)Math.Cos(m_Attitude.Heading) + x *
                    (float)Math.Sin(m_Attitude.Heading);
    try
    {
        ty = CGameEngine.Ground.HeightOfTerrain(
                        new Vector3(m_X, m_Y, m_Z));
    }
    catch {ty=0;}
        m_Y = ty + 1.0f;
}
```

The next two methods relate to associating the camera to one or more objects. The camera may be attached to an object so that it moves along with the object. Normally, the camera is attached to the player-controlled vehicle or character. The Attach method (shown in Listing 6-7) associates the camera with an object, with an offset from the object's reference position. It is a simple method that just saves the object reference and offset to attribute variables for use by the rendering method.

Listing 6-7. Camera Attach Method

```
public void Attach( Object3D parent, Vector3 offset )
{
    m_AttachedObject = parent;
    m_Offset = offset;
}
```

The second object-related method is LookAt (shown in Listing 6-8). This method saves the reference to the object that is passed to it and into an attribute variable. The rendering method will orient the camera so that it points toward this object. There are two good uses for this feature. The first is for the camera that is attached to an object. Setting the camera to look at the same object as it is attached to works well for a chase camera that is offset behind the object. No matter how the object moves, the camera will always being centered on the object. The second is for cameras that are at fixed points around the path that the objects will follow (like camera towers at a racetrack). By having cameras sprinkled around the course and always switching to the closest camera, we would get an effect similar to television coverage of a race.

Listing 6-8. Camera LookAt Method

```
public void LookAt( Object3D obj )
{
   m_LookAtObject = obj;
}
```

Culling with the Camera

As I mentioned earlier in the chapter, the camera is a vital part of the culling process. It is the camera, after all, that knows whether an object will be in view or not. The camera will actually have two methods dedicated to culling. One will be oriented towards working with objects. The other will just check a position and radius against the frustum. Both methods will be called CheckFrustum, and the difference will be in the arguments supplied to the method (its signature). The method that works with a position and radius (shown in Listing 6-9) will check to see if any point on the sphere defined by the position and radius lies within the culling frustum.

Listing 6-9. Camera CheckFrustum Method 1

```
public CullState CheckFrustum( Vector3 pos, float radius )
{

   float distance;
   int count = 0;
    // Don't check against top and bottom.
   for( int iPlane = 0; iPlane < 4; iPlane++ )
   {
      distance = planeFrustum[iPlane].Dot( pos );
      if( distance <= -radius )
      {
         return CullState.AllOutside;
      }
```

```
      if ( distance > radius ) count++;
   }

   if ( count == 4 ) return CullState.AllInside;

   return CullState.PartiallyIn;
}
```

These methods will only check to see if the spheres are within the horizontal footprint of the frustum. They will not check to see if the points are above or below the frustum. Due to the nature of the game we are developing, it is unlikely that any object will be above or below the frustum. Any objects that are will be rendered, but this is a small price to pay when balanced against a 30 percent increase in culling speed.

To determine if a sphere intersects the frustum, we will take the dot product of the position versus each of the vertical planes of the frustum. The value returned by the dot product is actually the distance from the surface of the plane to that point, with a positive value indicating a position inside the frustum. Therefore, if the distance is negative and greater than the radius away from any of the planes, it must be completely outside of the frustum. If all of the distances are positive and greater than the radius of the sphere, the sphere is completely inside of the frustum. If the sphere is not completely inside or outside, it defaults to being partially inside the frustum.

The version of CheckFrustum that checks objects (shown in Listing 6-10) works much like the previous version. It gets its position and radius information from the object's position and bounding radius. The fourth plane of the frustum is the near clipping plane. It just so happens that the distance returned by the dot product for the near clipping plane is also the distance that the object is from the camera (minus the near clipping distance).

Listing 6-10. Camera CheckFrustum Method 2

```
public CullState CheckFrustum( Object3D obj )
{
   float distance = 0.0f;
   int count = 0;
     // Don't check against top and bottom.
   for( int iPlane = 0; iPlane < 4; iPlane++ )
   {
      distance = planeFrustum[iPlane].Dot( obj.Position );
      if( distance <= -obj.Radius )
      {
         return CullState.AllOutside;
      }
```

```
        if ( distance > obj.Radius ) count++;
    }

    if ( count == 4 ) return CullState.AllInside;

    return CullState.PartiallyIn;
}
```

There may be times when we need to get the distance between an object and the camera. One possible scenario in which this would happen is for objects that are attached to another object as children. The parent object will have its range set automatically by the culling routines. The same is not true for the child objects. The GetDistance method (shown in Listing 6-11) provides the means of getting this distance. This method performs the same dot product operation used in the CheckFrustum method.

Listing 6-11. Camera GetDistance Method

```
public float GetDistance( Object3D obj )
{
    return (planeFrustum[3].Dot( obj.Position ) + m_fNearPlane);
}
```

Using the Camera

We have covered all of the methods required to put the camera where we need it to be and to extract necessary information from the camera. The one thing that we have not done with the camera is to actually use it in the rendering process. The Render method (shown in Listings 6-12a through 6-12d in this section) takes the current state of the camera and builds the matrices required for rendering the scene.

In order to create the two matrices, it is necessary to first create the vectors that are used to generate the view matrix. The Up matrix is easy. It only needs to be a simple vector pointing up in the Y-axis. The Eye and LookAt vectors depend on whether the camera is attached to an object or not. The code for creating the vector when attached to an object is shown in Listing 6-12a. If an object has been specified as the object to look at, its position is used as the LookAt vector. The object's pitch and heading constitute the camera's attitude. A transpose matrix is created through this attitude for use later in the method. If the camera is not looking at an object, then the vector is set to the camera's position, offset ten units in the camera's current attitude. The Eye vector is set to the object's position with an offset. The offset is transposed to the proper place relative to the attached object using the transpose matrix created earlier.

Listing 6-12a. Camera Render Method

```
public void Render()
{
    Vector3 Up = new Vector3(0.0f, 1.0f, 0.0f);
    if ( m_AttachedObject != null )
    {
        if ( m_LookAtObject != null )
        {
            m_LookAt = m_LookAtObject.Position;
        }
        else
        {
            m_LookAt = m_AttachedObject.Position;
            m_LookAt.X += (float)Math.Sin(m_Attitude.Heading)*10.0f;
            m_LookAt.Y += (float)Math.Sin(m_Attitude.Pitch)*10.0f;
            m_LookAt.Z += (float)Math.Cos(m_Attitude.Heading)*10.0f;
        }
        Matrix transpose = Matrix.Identity;

        m_Attitude.Heading = Attitude.Aepc(m_AttachedObject.Heading);
        m_Attitude.Pitch = m_AttachedObject.Pitch;
        m_Attitude.Roll = 0.0f;
        transpose.RotateYawPitchRoll(m_Attitude.Heading,
            m_Attitude.Pitch,m_Attitude.Roll);

        m_Eye = m_AttachedObject.Position +
            Vector3.TransformCoordinate(m_Offset, transpose);
    }
}
```

If the camera is not attached to an object, the vectors are set based on the camera's position and attitude (shown in Listing 6-12b). The Eye vector is set to the camera's position. If the camera is set to look at an object, then that object's position is used for the LookAt vector. Otherwise, the LookAt vector is set to the Eye vector's position with a ten-unit offset in the direction that the camera is pointing.

Listing 6-12b. Camera Render Method (Continued)

```
else
{
    m_Eye = new Vector3( m_X, m_Y, m_Z);
    if ( m_LookAtObject != null )
```

```
            {
               m_LookAt = m_LookAtObject.Position;
            }
            else
            {
               m_LookAt = m_Eye;
               m_LookAt.X += (float)Math.Sin(m_Attitude.Heading)*10.0f;
               m_LookAt.Y += (float)Math.Sin(m_Attitude.Pitch)*10.0f;
               m_LookAt.Z += (float)Math.Cos(m_Attitude.Heading)*10.0f;
            }
         }
```

Once the vectors are created, it is time to generate the view matrix and to
pass the matrices to the device as shown in Listing 6-12c. The view matrix is
created using a static method of the Matrix class called LookAtLH. This method
employs the three vectors to create a matrix based on a left-hand coordinate system. This is the most commonly used coordinate system and the one that we
will apply throughout this game engine. Once we have created the view matrix,
we pass it and the projection matrix to the device using its view and projection
transformation properties. The device now has all of the transformation information that it needs from the camera.

Listing 6-12c. Camera Render Method (Continued)

```
        // Set the app view matrix for normal viewing.
         m_matView = Matrix.LookAtLH(m_Eye, m_LookAt, Up);

        CGameEngine.Device3D.Transform.View = m_matView;

        CGameEngine.Device3D.Transform.Projection = m_matProj;
```

Even though we are done using the camera to prepare for rendering, we still
have one more thing to do. We need to set up the frustum information that will
be used in the culling process (shown in Listing 6-12d). To create the frustum
data, we will need a matrix that is a combination of the view matrix and projection matrix. Multiplying them together combines matrices. The eight corners of
the frustum are initialized as a cube just in front of the camera. Transforming
each of these points using the combined view/projection matrix creates the
transformed corners. The final step in the process is to generate the six planes
that form the sides of the frustum using the points at the corners. The Plane
class's FromPoints method is used to create each of the planes.

Listing 6-12d. Camera Render Method (Conclusion)

```
        Matrix mat = Matrix.Multiply(m_matView, m_matProj);
        mat.Invert();

        vecFrustum[0] = new Vector3(-1.0f, -1.0f,  0.0f); // xyz
        vecFrustum[1] = new Vector3( 1.0f, -1.0f,  0.0f); // Xyz
        vecFrustum[2] = new Vector3(-1.0f,  1.0f,  0.0f); // xYz
        vecFrustum[3] = new Vector3( 1.0f,  1.0f,  0.0f); // XYz
        vecFrustum[4] = new Vector3(-1.0f, -1.0f,  1.0f); // xyZ
        vecFrustum[5] = new Vector3( 1.0f, -1.0f,  1.0f); // XyZ
        vecFrustum[6] = new Vector3(-1.0f,  1.0f,  1.0f); // xYZ
        vecFrustum[7] = new Vector3( 1.0f,  1.0f,  1.0f); // XYZ

        for( int i = 0; i < 8; i++ )
            vecFrustum[i] = Vector3.TransformCoordinate(vecFrustum[i],mat);

        planeFrustum[0] = Plane.FromPoints(vecFrustum[7],
                vecFrustum[3],vecFrustum[5]); // Right
        planeFrustum[1] = Plane.FromPoints(vecFrustum[2],
                vecFrustum[6],vecFrustum[4]); // Left
        planeFrustum[2] = Plane.FromPoints(vecFrustum[6],
                vecFrustum[7],vecFrustum[5]); // Far
        planeFrustum[3] = Plane.FromPoints(vecFrustum[0],
                vecFrustum[1],vecFrustum[2]); // Near
        planeFrustum[4] = Plane.FromPoints(vecFrustum[2],
                vecFrustum[3],vecFrustum[6]); // Top
        planeFrustum[5] = Plane.FromPoints(vecFrustum[1],
                vecFrustum[0],vecFrustum[4]); // Bottom
    }
}
```

You will see in Chapter 8 that it can be useful to know what objects are currently within the camera's view. The visible object collection held by the camera contains this information. It is populated during the culling process for a given camera. To manage this collection, we will need two methods to clear and populate it with objects. The Reset method (shown in Listing 6-13) handles the clearing part. It empties the collection by calling the ArrayList Clear method.

Listing 6-13. Camera Reset Method

```
public void Reset()
{
   m_VisibleObjects.Clear();
}
```

The population of the collection is done using the AddVisibleObject method shown in Listing 6-14. It takes a reference to an object as an argument. We are not concerned with pieces of the terrain for this collection. If the object is not a TerrainQuad, it is added to the collection.

Listing 6-14. Camera AddVisibleObject Method

```
public void AddVisibleObject( Object3D obj )
{
   if ( ! (obj is TerrainQuad) )
   {
      m_VisibleObjects.Add( obj );
   }
}
```

Summary

This chapter has covered the creation and capabilities of the Camera class, which provides control over the scene that is rendered on the screen for the player. It is analogous to the video cameras employed to capture the action in televised events. This class can be used for a stationary camera that follows the action or a camera mounted on a moving object that gives the driver's eye view.

CHAPTER 7

Adding Some Atmosphere– Lighting and Fog

SO FAR, ALL OF THE RENDERING that we have done has been with DirectX lighting turned off. With lighting turned off, every pixel drawn is colored strictly based on the texture or material colors defined for each object. Lighting and fog adjust the rendered color of each pixel based on different factors.

The lighting system combines the colors of any lights illuminating a pixel with the base colors specified for the pixel by the material and texture definitions. Fog, on the other hand, integrates the color of the pixels between this base color (as altered by any lighting) and a selected fog color. The integration is based on the range between the pixel's position and the viewpoint.

Shedding Some Light on the Subject

We can define several types of lights within our game scene. Each type of light behaves somewhat differently in how it illuminates the pixels. The four types of light are ambient, directional, point, and spot. We will discuss each type of light in the text that follows.

Ambient Light

Ambient light is unique among the four light types. A given scene may include multiple lights of the other three types, but it can have only one ambient light. As such, it is the one type of light that is implemented as a rendering state rather than a light. This rendering state is simply the color of the ambient light. Ambient light by definition exists everywhere and illuminates in all directions.

The color of the ambient light is used to modulate the base color of the pixels. If the ambient color for a scene is set to black and there are no other lights, then the scene will be completely black. This reflects a total lack of illumination. Figure 7-1 shows a scene from our game engine with the ambient light set to a dark gray.

Figure 7-1. Low ambient light

As you can see from the picture, the entire scene is quite dark. This is a good basis for working with the other lights as we progress through the rest of the chapter. Although keeping the three components of the color the same (i.e., shades of gray from black to white) is most natural, this is not a requirement. Let's say that we are doing a game based on Mars instead of Earth. We might want the ambient light to have a reddish tint to it so that everything takes on a reddish cast. Only objects that are illuminated by a separate white light would lose the tinted look.

NOTE *For any of the lighting to work at all, there must be a material active in the current rendering state. For the mesh objects, this is done for us. Looking back at the other objects, you will see that a default white material is set for the billboards and skybox objects.*

Directional Light

While ambient light is the same everywhere at once and does not come from any one direction, it does not provide everything we need for realistic lighting. *Directional light* behaves like light from the sun. It is light coming from a specified direction, with all of the rays of light traveling parallel. Since directional light behaves like light from the sun, a scene tends to have just one directional light. Again, if we were doing a science fiction game set on another planet, we might simulate the effects of multiple suns with different colors. Since each of these suns would give light from a different direction, we would get changes in object color depending on the angle from which we are looking.

Figure 7-2 shows our scene lit by a directional light. One thing we must do when adding lights other than ambient light is to render the skybox with the lights deactivated. Since only ambient light is directionless, we do not want the other lights to affect the skybox. Otherwise, we will begin to see the seams where the sides of the skybox meet. This breaks the illusion the skybox is there to provide. Therefore, remember that the ambient light sets the basic lighting conditions for the scene, including the skybox, and all other lights add to the look of the terrain and other objects within the scene.

Figure 7-2. Directional light

Point Light

Ambient and directional lights provide the illumination for the simulated world at large. The two remaining light types provide localized light sources within the scene. The first of these is the *point light,* which is a point in space where light originates in all directions equally. Think of point lights as things like bare lightbulbs and torches. The parameters that configure a point light determine how far the light shines and how quickly the light intensity falls off as we get farther from the light. Unlike with the first two light types, it is quite possible to have a large number of point lights within a scene. Unfortunately, there are no video cards on the market that can support an unlimited number of such lights within a scene.

To cope with the limitations of video cards, we will need to do two things. The first is to know exactly what these limitations are. We need to find how many lights we can have at once. It is possible to query the capabilities of the video card to get this information. The other thing that our game engine must do is select which lights to include in the scene on a given pass so that we do not exceed the limits of the video card. You will see later in the chapter, when we get into the implementation of the GameLights class, how we will choose the lights to use.

Figure 7-3 shows our desert scene in a low-light condition with a number of point lights distributed around the scene. You can't see the lights themselves. What you will see is the illumination of the terrain surface below each light. Notice that not all areas around the lights are illuminated in the circular pattern that we would expect from a point light. This is due to the fact that the fixed function graphics pipeline performs vertex-based lighting. The colors are determined at each vertex based on the lighting information and then integrated between the vertices. To get pixel-based lighting (which is far more precise and realistic looking) would require the use of a pixel shader. Since the use of shaders is not being covered in this book, we will stick with what the fixed function pipeline provides.

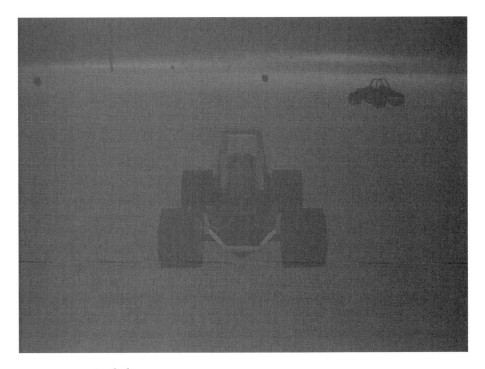

Figure 7-3. Point lights

Spot Light

The final light type is the spot light. *Spot lights* are used to provide light that shines in a cone shape in the specified direction from a given position. Actually, this type of light is implemented as two cones, one inside the other, which mimics the way that spotlights, flashlights, and vehicle headlights work in the real world. A point light has an inner cone within which the light is at its brightest. It also has an outer cone that surrounds the inner cone, and the intensity of the light falls off as we move from the inner cone to the outside edge of the outer cone.

Figure 7-4 shows our night scene with a spot light configured as the headlight of our car. Again, notice that the footprint of the light on the ground is not the cone shape that we would expect in an ideal situation. This is the same vertex versus pixel lighting issue mentioned in the discussion of the point lights.

Figure 7-4. Spot lights

Implementing the GameLights Class

The game engine requires a class to manage the lights in the scene. The class will be organized into two sections. The first section will be the attributes, properties, and methods that configure an individual light. The second section will be the static attributes, properties, and methods that are used to create and manage the lights.

The attributes for the class (shown in Listing 7-1) closely follow the attributes that Microsoft has defined for its Light class. This is not a coincidence. The rendering device's array of lights will be configured using the data in the GameLights instances. The only nonstatic attributes that are unique to the GameLights class are m_DirectionOffset and m_PositionOffset. These attributes will be used when we attach a GameLights object to another object. The class also inherits from the Object3D class so that each light can be treated like any other object in the scene when it comes to positioning and updating the lights.

Listing 7-1. GameLights Attributes

```
public class GameLights : Object3D, IDisposable, IDynamic, IComparable
{
    #region Attributes
    private LightType m_Type = LightType.Point;
    private Vector3   m_Direction = new Vector3(0.0f,0.0f,0.0f);
    private Vector3   m_DirectionOffset = new Vector3(0.0f,0.0f,0.0f);
    private Vector3   m_PositionOffset = new Vector3(0.0f,0.0f,0.0f);
    private Color     m_Diffuse = Color.White;
    private Color     m_Specular = Color.White;
    private float     m_EffectiveRange = 1000.0f;
    private float     m_Attenuation0 = 0.0f;
    private float     m_Attenuation1 = 1.0f;
    private float     m_Attenuation2 = 0.0f;
    private float     m_FallOff = 1.0f;
    private float     m_InnerConeAngle = 0.5f;
    private float     m_OuterConeAngle = 1.0f;
    private bool      m_Deferred = true;
    private bool      m_Enabled = true;

    // A static array that will hold all lights
    private static Color     m_Ambient = Color.White;
    private static ArrayList m_ActiveLights = new ArrayList();
    private static ArrayList m_InactiveLights = new ArrayList();
    private static int m_max_lights = 1;
    private static int m_num_activated = 0;
    #endregion
```

The interfaces that are used in the class should be familiar by now, with the exception of the IComparable interface. We are going to want to sort an array of lights as part of deciding which lights will be active. The IComparable interface declares the CompareTo method that is called by the ArrayList's Sort method.

The static attributes are used for managing the instances of the lights that we will create. We will keep two arrays of lights. One array is for the lights that are on and another array for lights that are currently turned off. We also want to keep track of how many lights have been activated within the video card and how many lights the card can manage. The color value for the ambient light is also managed as a static property, since there can only be one value for the ambient light.

The properties of this class (shown in Listing 7-2) provide controlled access to the attributes of the class. Most of the properties are basic Get/Set methods that simply provide access and nothing more. The Type property is one exception, since it is read-only. We wish to allow the light type to be queried, but we don't want anyone changing the light's type once it has been created. The one property that is significantly more complex is the Enabled property. When the enabled state of a light changes, we need to do more than change the state of the Boolean attribute. We must ensure that the light is on the proper list for its current state. We will remove the light from both lists prior to adding it back onto the proper list to ensure that a light does not end up on a list more than once. This is safe to do since the Remove method of the ArrayList class does not throw an exception if we ask it to remove something that it does not have. If we only remove the light from one list and add it to another, we would get into trouble if the light were set to the same state twice in a row.

Listing 7-2. GameLights Properties

```
#region Properties
public LightType Type { get { return m_Type; } }
public Vector3   Direction {
    get { return m_Direction; }
    set { m_Direction = value; }}
public Vector3   DirectionOffset {
    get { return m_DirectionOffset; }
     set { m_DirectionOffset = value; }}
public Vector3   PositionOffset {
    get { return m_PositionOffset; }
    set { m_PositionOffset = value; }}
public Color     Diffuse {
    get { return m_Diffuse; }
    set { m_Diffuse = value; }}
public Color     Specular {
    get { return m_Specular; }
    set { m_Specular = value; }}
public float     EffectiveRange {
    get { return m_EffectiveRange; }
    set { m_ EffectiveRange = value; }}
public float     Attenuation0 {
    get { return m_Attenuation0; }
    set { m_Attenuation0 = value; }}
```

```csharp
public float      Attenuation1 {
   get { return m_Attenuation1; }
   set { m_Attenuation1 = value; }}
public float      Attenuation2 {
   get { return m_Attenuation2; }
   set { m_Attenuation2 = value; }}
public float      FallOff {
   get { return m_FallOff; }
   set { m_FallOff = value; }}
public float      InnerConeAngle {
   get { return m_InnerConeAngle; }
   set { m_InnerConeAngle = value; }}
public float      OuterConeAngle {
   get { return m_OuterConeAngle; }
   set { m_OuterConeAngle = value; }}
public bool       Deferred {
   get { return m_Deferred; }
   set { m_Deferred = value; }}
public bool Enabled
{
   get { return m_Enabled; }
   set
   {
      m_Enabled = value;
       // Remove from both lists to ensure it does not get onto a list twice.
      m_ActiveLights.Remove( this );
      m_InactiveLights.Remove( this );
     if ( m_Enabled ) // Move from inactive list to active list.
     {
         m_ActiveLights.Add( this );
     }
     else // Move from active list to inactive list.
     {
         m_InactiveLights.Add( this );
     }
   }
}

public static Color Ambient {
                          get { return m_Ambient; }
                   set { m_Ambient = value; } }
#endregion
```

The constructor for the class (shown in Listing 7-3) is quite simple. It accepts the name of the light as an argument and passes that name on to the base class constructor for the Object3D base class. It sets a default range of a thousand units in the range attribute (m_EffectiveRange) and copies that same value to the radius. The bounding radius for a light will be the same as its range. In other words, if the light could be shining on polygons that are in the current view, it is a candidate for inclusion in the list of active lights.

Listing 7-3. GameLights Constructor

```
public GameLights(string name) :base(name)
{
    m_EffectiveRange = 1000.0f;
    m_fRadius = m_EffectiveRange;
}
```

Remember that we added the IComparable interface to our class so that we can easily sort a list of lights based on the criterion of our choice. The CompareTo method (shown in Listing 7-4) is the required method for implementing this interface. This method returns an integer that is negative if the supplied object is less than the object owning the method, zero if the objects are equal, and positive if the supplied object is less than this one. In our case, we wish to be able to sort the lights based on the distance between the current camera and the origin of the light. This makes the result of the comparison just the integer value of the difference between the two ranges. When we get to the SetupLights method, you will see how implementing this interface simplifies our code.

Listing 7-4. GameLights CompareTo Method

```
public int CompareTo( object other )
{
    GameLights other_light = (GameLights)other;
    return (int)(Range - other_light.Range);
}
```

It is quite possible that the user of the game engine will need to get a reference to a light at some point based on the light's name. We will provide the GetLight method (shown in Listing 7-5) to retrieve a reference based on a supplied name. We begin by setting a reference of the correct type to a null condition. If we do not find the requested light, we wish to return a null value. We then iterate through each of the lists (the light may be active or inactive) and set the reference if we find the light.

Listing 7-5. GameLights GetLight Method

```
public static GameLights GetLight( string name )
{
    GameLights light_found = null;
    foreach ( GameLights light in m_ActiveLights )
    {
        if ( light.Name == name )
        {
            light_found = light;
        }
    }
    foreach ( GameLights light in m_InactiveLights )
    {
        if ( light.Name == name )
        {
            light_found = light;
        }
    }
    return light_found;
}
```

The next three methods will be used for the creation of lights. One static method exists for each type of light. Remember that we do not create lights for ambient light—it just "is." The first of these construction methods is AddDirectionalLight (shown in Listing 7-6). For directional light, we will need to know the color of the light and a direction vector so that we know the direction in which the light is shining. We also need a string with the name for the light because every object in the game engine needs a name for later reference.

Listing 7-6. GameLights AddDirectionalLight Method

```
public static GameLights AddDirectionalLight(Vector3 direction,
                 Color color, string name)
{
    GameLights light = new GameLights(name);
    light.m_Diffuse = color;
    light.m_Direction = direction;
    light.m_Type = LightType.Directional;
    m_ActiveLights.Add( light );
    return light;
}
```

We instantiate a new light using the supplied data and set its type to Directional. The light is then added to the active light list. All lights default to active. A reference to the new light is also returned so that the calling method has instant access to the light for additional configuration.

The AddPointLight method (shown in Listing 7-7) is quite similar to the method used for directional lights. Instead of supplying a direction vector, we need to supply a position. The only other difference is the obvious change of setting the light's type to Point before adding the light to the active list.

Listing 7-7. GameLights AddPointLight Method

```
public static GameLights AddPointLight(Vector3 position,
                    Color color, string name)
{
    GameLights light = new GameLights(name);
    light.m_Diffuse = color;
    light.Position = position;
    light.m_Type = LightType.Point;
    m_ActiveLights.Add( light );
    return light;
}
```

The AddSpotLight method (shown in Listing 7-8) is the last of the light creation methods. Because spot lights have an origin location and a direction, both must be supplied as arguments to the method. The attenuation of the light as we go from the origin to its maximum range is based on the attenuation formula that follows. The Attenuation0 variable provides a constant attenuation. The other two attenuation variables are factors multiplied by the range from the origin and the square of the range from the origin.

$$Attenuation = \frac{1}{Attenuation0 + \delta * Attenuation1 + \delta^2 * Attenuation2}$$

This equation is used for both the point and spot lights. It is important that all three attenuation factors are not zero at the same time, which, as you can see from the equation, would generate a divide-by-zero exception.

Listing 7-8. GameLights AddSpotLight Method

```
public static GameLights AddSpotLight(Vector3 position,
                    Vector3 direction, Color color, string name)
{
    GameLights light = new GameLights(name);
    light.m_Diffuse = color;
    light.m_Direction = direction;
```

```
        light.Position = position;
        light.m_Type = LightType.Spot;
        light.Attenuation0 = 0.0f;
        light.Attenuation1 = 1.0f;
        m_ActiveLights.Add( light );
        return light;
    }
```

Before we can manage the lights, we need to call the InitializeLights method (shown in Listing 7-9). This is where we will query the device capabilities to establish how many lights can be active at once. The rendering device has a property named DeviceCaps that exposes all of the capabilities of the video card. The MaxActiveLights property is the one that we are interested in.

Listing 7-9. GameLights InitializeLights Method

```
    public static void InitializeLights()
    {
        m_max_lights = CGameEngine.Device3D.DeviceCaps.MaxActiveLights;
    }
```

I mentioned earlier that we need to deactivate all active lights prior to rendering the skybox so that it is not affected by any lighting values other than ambient light. The DeactivateLights method (shown in Listing 7-10) provides this functionality. It loops through all of the activated lights and disables them within the context of the rendering device. The lights within the device can be modified in two different ways. If the deferred flag for the light is set to false, all changes to that light take effect as the values are set. If the flag is true, none of the changes for that light are passed to the video card until the Commit method for that light is called. It is best to operate with the flag set to true. Otherwise, it is possible for an invalid set of parameters to corrupt the device. A prime example of this situation would be when altering the attenuation factors.

Listing 7-10. GameLights DeactivateLights Method

```
    public static void DeactivateLights()
    {
        try
        {
            for ( int i=0; i< m_num_activated; i++ )
            {
                CGameEngine.Device3D.Lights[i].Enabled = false;
                CGameEngine.Device3D.Lights[i].Commit();
            }
```

```
      }
      catch (DirectXException d3de)
      {
         Console.AddLine("Unable to Deactivate lights ");
         Console.AddLine(d3de.ErrorString);
      }
      catch ( Exception e )
      {
         Console.AddLine("Unable to Deactivate lights ");
         Console.AddLine(e.Message);
      }
   }
}
```

The key to the GameLights class is found in the SetupLights static method (shown in Listing 7-11). This is where we will decide which lights will be shown in the scene for this pass and transfer the information for those lights to the rendering device. The rendering device has an array of the Microsoft Light class, which is where we will store the information for each active light.

Listing 7-11. GameLights SetupLights Method

```
public static void SetupLights()
{
   int num_active_lights = 0;

   CGameEngine.Device3D.RenderState.Lighting = true;
   CGameEngine.Device3D.RenderState.Ambient = m_Ambient;
   CGameEngine.Device3D.RenderState.SpecularEnable = true;

   // Sort lights to be in range order from closest to farthest.
   m_ActiveLights.Sort();

   try
   {
      foreach ( GameLights light in m_ActiveLights )
      {
         if ( !light.IsCulled && num_active_lights < m_max_lights )
         {
            Light this_light =
               CGameEngine.Device3D.Lights[num_active_lights];
            this_light.Deferred = light.m_Deferred;
            this_light.Type = light.m_Type;
            this_light.Position = light.m_vPosition;
```

```
                        this_light.Direction = light.m_Direction;
                        this_light.Diffuse = light.m_Diffuse;
                        this_light.Specular = light.m_Specular;
                        this_light.Attenuation0 = light.m_Attenuation0;
                        this_light.Attenuation1 = light.m_Attenuation1;
                        this_light.Attenuation2 = light.m_Attenuation2;
                        this_light.InnerConeAngle = light.m_InnerConeAngle;
                        this_light.OuterConeAngle = light.m_OuterConeAngle;
                        this_light.Range = light. m_EffectiveRange;
                        this_light.Falloff = light.FallOff;
                        this_light.Enabled = true;
                        this_light.Commit();
                        num_active_lights++;
                    }
                }

                if ( m_num_activated > num_active_lights )
                {
                    for ( int i=0; i< (m_num_activated - num_active_lights); i++ )
                    {
                        Light this_light =
                            CGameEngine.Device3D.Lights[num_active_lights+i];
                        this_light.Enabled = false;
                        this_light.Commit();
                    }
                }
                m_num_activated = num_active_lights;
            }
            catch (DirectXException d3de)
            {
                Console.AddLine("dx Unable to setup lights ");
                Console.AddLine(d3de.ErrorString);
            }
            catch ( Exception e )
            {
                Console.AddLine("Unable to setup lights ");
                Console.AddLine(e.Message);
            }
        }
```

The method begins by setting up the rendering state for lighting using the ambient light value set for the scene. We will set the specular enable flag so that any specular colors that are specified for a light will show up as specular high-lights on the objects. If we knew that we were never going to use specular lighting within our game, we could change this to default to the disabled state, thereby providing a slight increase in rendering performance.

The next step is to sort the active lights array so that it goes from the closest light to the one that is the farthest away. This is why we implemented the IComparable interface earlier in the class. It is also why we split the lights up into two arrays. We want this sort to run as quickly as possible, and keeping the inactive lights in a separate array helps with this.

Once the sort is completed, it is just a matter of iterating through the active lights array and transferring data to the rendering device. We will transfer the information only if the light has not been culled and the video card can handle additional lights. We transfer all of the class attributes, regardless of whether or not they are needed for this particular type of light. It would take more processing time to include flow control to check for each light type and transfer a subset.

If there were more lights active during the last pass than we have active now, we need to deactivate the remaining lights. This is done using a simple loop that clears the enable flag for the extra lights and then commits the changes.

The SetupLights method checks the culling state of each light so that we don't use any lighting slots in the video card for lights that would not be visible in the current scene. This culling state is determined in the CheckCulling method (shown in Listing 7-12), which is a static method of the class that is called prior to the SetupLights method. It takes a reference to the current camera as an argument, since the camera is needed to perform the actual culling check. The method loops through the array of active lights. There is no need to check the culling status of inactive lights.

Listing 7-12. GameLights CheckCulling Method

```
public static void CheckCulling ( Camera cam )
{
    foreach ( GameLights light in m_ActiveLights )
    {
        if ( light.m_Type == LightType.Directional )
        {
            light.Culled = false;  // Can't cull a directional light.
            light.Range = 0.0f;
        }
        else
        {
            if ( cam.CheckFrustum( light ) != Camera.CullState.AllOutside )
            {
                light.Culled = false;
```

```
            // We want the absolute value of the range.
            light.m_fRange = Math.Abs(light.m_fRange);
        }
        else
        {
            light.Culled = true;
           // Big range to sort to end of list
            light.Range = 1000000000.0f;
        }
      }
    }
   }
  }
```

If the light is directional, then it cannot be culled. We don't bother with checking against the camera. We just set the culling status to false and the range to zero so that it will be sorted to the beginning of the list. For the point lights and spot lights, we call the camera's CheckFrustum method to see if the light shines on any points within the current view of the scene. If the light is not completely outside of the frustum, then we set the culling state to false. Since we are sorting based on the range, we want to use the absolute value of the range provided by the CheckFrustum method. We don't want a light that is a thousand units behind us from taking preference over a light ten units in front of us.

If the light is completely outside of the frustum, we will set the culling state to true and the range to a large number. This will force the culled lights to the end of the list when it is sorted.

Since our GameLights class inherits from Object3D, our lights can be attached as children to another object. This allows us to attach a spot light to a vehicle to act as its headlights. The Update method (shown in Listing 7-13) is used to keep the light updated properly as objects move around the scene.

Listing 7-13. GameLights Update Method

```
public override void Update( float DeltaT )
{
   m_fRadius = m_EffectiveRange;

   if ( m_Parent != null )
   {
      Matrix matrix = Matrix.Identity;
```

```
        matrix.RotateYawPitchRoll(m_Parent.Heading,
            m_Parent.Pitch,m_Parent.Roll);
        Vector3 pos_offset =
                    Vector3.TransformCoordinate(m_PositionOffset,matrix);
        m_vPosition = m_Parent.Position + pos_offset;
        m_Direction.X = (float)Math.Sin(m_Parent.Attitude.Heading);
        m_Direction.Y = (float)Math.Sin(m_Parent.Attitude.Pitch);
        m_Direction.Z = (float)Math.Cos(m_Parent.Attitude.Heading);
        m_Direction +=
Vector3.TransformCoordinate(m_DirectionOffset,matrix);
        }
    }
  }
}
```

Regardless of whether the light is attached to another object, we must ensure that the radius value for the light remains equal to the effective range of the light. The game may be adjusting the range of the light. If the radius were not changed to match, the culling would not return the proper state for the light.

If the light is attached to another object, then we need to update the position and direction vector of the light based on the position and attitude of the parent object. A rotation matrix is created using the attitude of the parent. This is used to rotate both the position offset and the directional offset, which are then applied to the parent's data and stored for this light.

Using the GameLights Class

So far in the chapter we have discussed some theory behind lights as used in the game engine as well as the implementation of the GameLights class for the game engine. Now we will see how easy it is to actually use the lights. The example code in Listing 7-14 illustrates how the lighting is set up in the game application's LoadOptions routine. Setting the ambient light is done simply by setting the Ambient property of the GameLights class to the desired value. An RGB value of all 20s gives a fairly dark scene. We will then create a spot light and attach it to the ownship. The ownship is a reference to the vehicle model that we will be driving around the scene. The term comes from the simulation and training world, where the vehicle being simulated was traditionally an aircraft. Once the light is created, configured, and attached to a vehicle, there is nothing else we need to do with it. It will automatically travel around the scene with the vehicle and illuminate the terrain and other objects before it as it moves along.

Listing 7-14. GameLights Example

```
GameEngine.GameLights.Ambient = Color.FromArgb(20,20,20);

GameEngine.GameLights headlights =
        GameEngine.GameLights.AddSpotLight(new Vector3(0.0f,0.0f,0.0f),
        new Vector3(1.0f,0.0f,1.0f), Color.White, "headlight");
headlights.EffectiveRange = 200.0f;
headlights.Attenuation0 = 1.0f;
headlights.Attenuation1 = 0.0f;
headlights.InnerConeAngle = 1.0f;
headlights.OuterConeAngle = 1.5f;
headlights.PositionOffset = new Vector3(0.0f, 2.0f, 1.0f);
headlights.DirectionOffset = new Vector3(0.0f, 0.00f, 1.0f);
ownship.AddChild(headlights);
```

Piercing the Fog

In the real world, the view is rarely crystal clear as we look off into the distance. There always tends to be some haze in the air, whether that is water vapor or blowing sand. The fog capability built into Direct3D and video cards provides an easy implementation for fog and haze. Technically speaking, the fog is simply the integration between the colors defined for objects and a fog color based on the range between the pixel in the scene and the eye point.

The great thing about the use of fog in games is its ability to soften the image. The human eye is not used to seeing crisp images of objects that are far off in the distance. It also helps hide artifacts caused by the far clipping plane. Remember that any object beyond the far clipping plane is not rendered. Without some way of transitioning distant objects into view, they would seem to pop into place as they come within the far clipping distance. The proper use of fog hides this popping effect.

To hide this popping, we should configure fog so that it is fully opaque (i.e., fully fogged) at the far clipping distance. By adjusting the fog starting range and the fog mode and density, we can adjust how abruptly the scene transitions from no fog to fully fogged.

The Managed DirectX 9 implementation for fog is very clean and concise. Only seven attributes of the rendering state need to be adjusted to do anything we wish with fog. Therefore, there is no reason for the game engine to implement a special class just for managing fog. Instead, we will create seven static properties of the CGameEngine class that provide access to the rendering device's fog attributes. Listing 7-15 illustrates these seven properties.

Listing 7-15. Fog Properties

```
public static Color FogColor {
    set { m_pd3dDevice.RenderState.FogColor = value; } }
public static FogMode FogTableMode {
    set { m_pd3dDevice.RenderState.FogTableMode = value; } }
public static FogMode FogVertexMode {
    set { m_pd3dDevice.RenderState.FogVertexMode = value; } }
public static float FogDensity {
    set { m_pd3dDevice.RenderState.FogDensity = value; } }
public static float FogStart {
    set { m_pd3dDevice.RenderState.FogStart = value; } }
public static float FogEnd {
    set { m_pd3dDevice.RenderState.FogEnd = value; } }
public static bool FogEnable {
    set { m_pd3dDevice.RenderState.FogEnable = value; } }
```

The color we use for fog should ideally blend well with the sky color at the horizon. We can also use the fog for an environmental look. Let's say we are creating an underwater game. Aqua-green fog would help to give an underwater look. The code in Listing 7-16 shows how we could configurc fog through the game engine's static properties. We will use some beige fog for that windblown sand look. Figure 7-5 shows what our scene looks like with these fog settings. We've gone back to day lighting so that we can properly see the fog.

Listing 7-16. Using Fog

```
CGameEngine.FogColor = Color.Beige;
CGameEngine.FogDensity = 0.5f;
CGameEngine.FogEnable = true;
CGameEngine.FogStart = 100.0f;
CGameEngine.FogEnd = 500.0f;
CGameEngine.FogTableMode = FogMode.Linear;
```

Figure 7-5. The scene with fog

Summary

This chapter has looked at lighting and fog. These are two operations that modify the colors of the rendered pixels. Both provide means for improving the realism of the rendered scene. One thing to remember is that both lighting and fog are highly subjective. Achieving the effect that you are looking for is often just a case of adjusting the parameters for either of these items.

CHAPTER 8

Artificial Intelligence–Adding the Competition

UP TO THIS POINT, our game engine has concentrated on the visual aspects of playing a game. A game is more than just the images on the screen, though. In order for a game to be exciting and have any chance at being popular, there must be a challenge to playing it. Although some people may find it interesting (for a short period of time) to move a dune buggy around in a desert, this provides no real challenge to keep players coming back to the game. The challenge in most games comes in the form of competition. Although that competition could be against their own past performance (as in such games as Solitaire), it usually comes in the form of opponents. If the game supports networking, these could be other humans playing in a networked game. Not everyone is in a position to network with other people in order to play, however. Those without the network option need a computerized opponent to play against, and this is where artificial intelligence comes into play.

For many people, the term *artificial intelligence* conjures up images of lifelike robots and machines that think as well as humans. So far this is only found in science fiction. Universities that have computer science departments doing research in the subject have large complex programs that can learn and make some decisions based on data presented to them. While these programs can go a long way at mimicking what we consider intelligence, they are far too large and slow to be used in a game engine. Instead, game engines concentrate on providing as realistically as possible the illusion of intelligence by the computer opponents. This chapter presents a look at the different technologies typically used within a game engine as well as the approach chosen for our sample game engine.

Looking at Our AI Options

There are a number of approaches to game artificial intelligence (AI) that vary in both complexity and performance in terms of the level of "intelligence" provided. All of these systems have several features in common. The first and most common feature is the ability to cause an opponent to move. The intelligence behind the movement and the opponent's reactions to outside stimulation vary from approach to approach, as you will see later in this section. Second, the opponent must interact with the player and preferably other computer-controlled objects. The opponents are just window dressing in the scene if they do not react and interact with the player. Finally, we would like the opponents to learn or improve as we play. This way the game remains challenging even as players become more skilled in the game. However, not all game AI approaches support this particular ability. It is also a plus if the system can save this acquired knowledge for use the next time the game is started so that the opponents are not forced to relearn the game each time it is played.

Scripted Action

The opponents in early games did not have anything approaching artificial intelligence driving them. Instead, they relied on heavily scripted action with the possibility of a few hard-coded reactions built in. One example of this approach is the Pac-Man series of games. The path followed by each ghost is predetermined for each level of the game. Each ghost has some low-level, hard-coded approach/flee logic, but other than that there is no intelligence in the movement or reactions of the ghosts. Another even more drastic version of this approach was the original, two-dimensional version of the game Dragon's Lair. In this game, all action was prerendered with multiple paths through each scene based on player actions. In this case, the scripted action was entirely done through the prerendered scenes and path switching logic. This approach is rarely acceptable in today's games. Players are looking for opponents that do the unexpected.

Hard-Coded Rules

The next most powerful approach is hard-coded logic. Given enough If/Else statements, we can create a strong appearance of intelligence in our computer-controlled opponents. This approach is also quite straightforward to develop. Regardless of what we want the opponents to do, it is just a matter of coding the logic within the game. Although this approach is quite powerful and was used for many years, it does have several drawbacks. Making changes to the opponent's logic requires a code change and a recompile. This might not be too bad if you are a one-person game studio and are both the programmer and the game designer. In a larger shop where these functions are distributed among a number of people, this can become a major issue. Every time someone modifies a line of code, he or she risks introducing bugs into software that had been working. This also makes it difficult to change the logic from level to level in a game or for multiple games that share the same game engine. If we wish the logic to change from level to level, we must include all of this logic in the program and switch between the sections depending on the level. Not a very flexible system.

Neural Networks

One technology that has been evolving over the last few years is *neural networks*. Neural networks are strong in the learning ability side of artificial intelligence. In fact, this strength is also a major weakness when it comes to using neural networks in games. Neural networks are not programmed in the traditional sense. They are trained by providing each input as well as the desired output. A neural network adjusts itself until it automatically gives the correct output when it sees a particular input signal again. Although this system can learn and adjust itself to changing situations, it can be difficult to guarantee deterministic behavior. This system can also consume much of your CPU. The power of the neural network is a function of the size of the network. Unfortunately, the amount of processing required to run the network goes up as well with this system.

Inference Engines

The solution to these various shortcomings is a technique I refer to as an *inference engine*. This is a knowledge- and logic-based approach that provides all of the power of the hard-coded system without the logic being programmed as part of the game engine software. Instead, the logic is held in a file that is loaded and processed by the inference engine code within the game engine. A truly powerful inference engine would employ a common scripting language and an interpreter for that language. The Python language is a popular choice for this function in the gaming industry.

The logic or scripting portion of the inference engine is only part of the solution. The inference engine needs information to work with. We need an initial store of knowledge that defines the opponent's reactions as well as a means of adding knowledge of the environment. Sensor methods provide the environmental knowledge. The next piece of the puzzle is a set of action methods that can be triggered by the logic in order to carry out actions. The decisions made by the inference engine are useless unless they trigger an action or reaction to the current situation. A *state system* ties all of this together. A system of states and transitions between those states serves to put everything into a context. Figure 8-1 shows an example of a state diagram. State diagrams are used to illustrate a set of states and the conditions required to transition between the states.

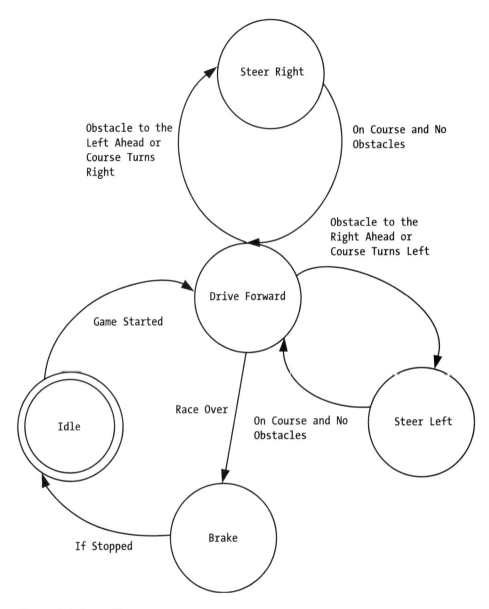

Figure 8-1. State diagram

A state diagram consists of circles that represent the states and directional lines that represent transitions from one state to another. Each of the lines is labeled with the logic that determines if that transition should be made. In this example, the software begins in the Idle state. When the game begins, a transition is made to the Drive Forward state. When the game is over, it transitions to the Brake state and back to Idle once stopped. Each state has a number of methods that are executed while that state is active. These actions, which can control speed (accelerating and braking) and steering (right or left) in this example, move the opponent and cause it to interact with the player and the environment.

Implementing the Artificial Intelligence System

The inference engine for the game will be an implementation of this state and transition system. We will not go to the length of adding a Python interpreter to our game engine. Instead, we will implement a simple logic evaluation system. This will allow us to define all of our transition logic in terms of this logic system. The file format that we will use to hold our inference engine data will be XML. The XML file format has become something of a standard in recent years. The .NET Framework provides a collection of classes to facilitate the reading and writing of XML files.

Our inference engine will be implemented using six interrelated classes. The highest-level class is `Thinker`. This class encapsulates the entire inference engine, and an instance of this class will be instantiated for each opponent. Each `Thinker` contains a collection of facts (the information that the opponent knows) and a collection of states (`AIState`). Each state contains a collection of methods that it will call and a collection of transitions (`Transitioner`) that, when triggered, will change the current state. Each `Transitioner` holds a collection of expressions (`Expression`) that, when evaluated as `true`, will activate the transition. Each expression in turn holds a collection of `Logic` class instances. The `Logic` class is a comparison between two facts that returns a Boolean result. Each of these classes will know how to read and write its contents to an XML file.

Thinking About Facts

The basis for all decisions made by the `Thinker` will be the facts that the `Thinker` knows. Each fact is a named floating-point value. By holding only floating-point values, we simplify the architecture. Holding and manipulating different types of values would add complications that can be avoided at this stage in game engine development. Integer values lend themselves quite easily to being represented as floats. Boolean values are represented by nonzero values. Some of the facts may be loaded from the XML file and never modified. These constants could represent threshold values or comparison against facts acquired from the environment. By using different base facts for different opponents, we can in effect give them different personalities.

The operations that can be used to compare facts are defined in the `Operator` enumeration (shown in Listing 8-1). You can see from the listing that the enumeration contains the common numerical comparison operations. It also contains two Boolean comparison operations and two Boolean test operations.

The True and False operations work on a single fact. As you will see later in the discussion of the Logic class, the second fact is ignored if presented with these operations.

Listing 8-1. Operator Enumeration

```
namespace GameAI
{
    public enum Operator {
        Equals,
        LessThan,
        GreaterThan,
        LessThanEquals,
        GreaterThanEquals,
        NotEqual,
        And,
        Or,
        True,
        False
    };
```

The Fact class has two attributes per instance of the class (shown in Listing 8-2). The name attribute allows us to find and reference the facts by only knowing their names. You will see in the higher-level tasks describe later in this chapter how this is used. The value attribute is a float as described earlier. The final attribute, m_Epsilon, is a static attribute used as a constant. It is the tolerance that we will use when checking to see if a floating-point value should be considered true or false.

Listing 8-2. Fact Attributes

```
    public class Fact
    {
        #region Attributes
        private string m_Name;
        private float m_Value;

        private static float m_Epsilon = 0.001f;
        #endregion
```

Access to the class is through its properties (shown in Listing 8-3). The Name property provides read-only access to the property's name. The Value property, on the other hand, is read/write so that full access is provided for the value of the fact. The IsTrue property provides an evaluation of the fact's value against the epsilon. The final property, Epsilon, is a static property that allows the epsilon value to be set programmatically if a different threshold value is desired.

Listing 8-3. Fact Properties

```
#region Properties
public string Name { get { return m_Name; } }
public float Value { get { return m_Value; } set { m_Value = value; } }
public bool IsTrue { get { return (Math.Abs(m_Value) > m_Epsilon); } }

public static float Epsilon { set { m_Epsilon = value; } }
#endregion
```

The constructor for the Fact class (shown in Listing 8-4) is very simple. It just takes a supplied string and saves it into the m_Name attribute.

Listing 8-4. Fact Constructor

```
public Fact(string name)
{
    m_Name = name;
}
```

The final method in the class is the Write method shown in Listing 8-5. The reading of Fact data from an XML data file will be done in the Thinker class that holds the collection of facts. The class just needs to know how to write itself out to a file. The argument to the method is a reference to XmlTextWriter. The XmlTextWriter class provides the means to opening a file and writing properly formatted XML tags and data to the file. The Thinker class will create the instance of this class and provide a reference to the objects it holds that must be preserved in the XML file.

Listing 8-5. Fact Write Method

```
public void Write( XmlTextWriter writer )
{
    writer.WriteStartElement("Fact");
    writer.WriteElementString("name", m_Name);
    writer.WriteElementString("Value", XmlConvert.ToString(m_Value));
    writer.WriteEndElement();
}
}
}
```

Here we use three members of the `XmlTextWriter` class. The WriteStartElement method places the opening tag for this element into the file. `Fact` elements will contain the name of the fact as well as its current value. This data is written using the WriteElementString method, which takes two strings as arguments. The first string is the field's name within the file and the second is its value. We will use the ToString method of the XmlConvert helper class to change the floating point `m_Value` data into a string for writing to the file. The writing of the XML element will be concluded with the WriteEndElement method. This method writes out the proper closing tag for the most recent open element, which in this case is a `Fact` element.

By providing a method to save facts out to a file for loading the next time the game plays, we give our inference engine a way to learn and remember between sessions. By including methods and logic that modifies the behavior-defining facts, we have made it possible for the system to adapt and change over time.

Maintaining a State

The `AIState` class is the central pillar of our inference engine architecture. It relies on the `Transitioner`, `Expression`, and `Logic` classes to determine the current state. We will work our way up from the most basic of these classes, `Logic`, to the `AIState` class itself.

Down to Basics—the Logic Class

The attributes for the `Logic` class are shown in Listing 8-6. Each instantiation of the class holds two `Fact` objects and an operation that will be performed on the facts when the logic is evaluated. The operation is defined using the `Operator` enumeration you saw earlier in the chapter.

Listing 8-6. Logic Attributes

```
using System;
using System.Xml;

namespace GameAI
{
    /// <summary>
    /// Summary description for Logic
    /// </summary>
    public class Logic
    {
```

```
#region Attributes
private Fact m_first;
private Fact m_second;
private Operator m_operator;
#endregion
```

The class's properties (shown in Listing 8-7) provide the public interface with the attributes. All three of the properties provide read and write access to their corresponding attributes.

Listing 8-7. Logic Properties

```
#region Properties
public Fact FirstFact {
        get { return m_first; }
        set { m_first = value; } }
public Fact SecondFact {
        get { return m_second; }
        set { m_second = value; } }
public Operator Operation {
        get { return m_operator; }
        set { m_operator = value; } }
#endregion
```

The first constructor for the class (shown in Listing 8-8) does not require that any data be passed in. This is the class's default constructor. It sets the references for both Fact objects to null and defaults the operation to Operator.Equals. This allows us to create an instance of the class even if we don't know yet what data it will hold. This becomes important when we get to the Read method later in the chapter.

Listing 8-8. Logic Default Constructor

```
public Logic()
{
   m_first = null;
   m_second = null;
   m_operator = Operator.Equals;
}
```

The second constructor for the class (shown in Listing 8-9) assumes that we know what the data will be when the instance is being created. References to the two Fact objects are passed in as well as the Operator enumeration for the class's logic operation. Remember, a null reference is valid for some of the operations that work only against the first fact.

Listing 8-9. Logic Constructor

```
public Logic(Fact first, Fact second, Operator op)
{
    m_first = first;
    m_second = second;
    m_operator = op;
}
```

The real work of the Logic class is done in the Evaluate method (shown in Listing 8-10). This is where we will perform the operation on the facts referenced by the logic. We need to ensure that the software doesn't fail if a fact has not been properly referenced. All operations require that the first fact exists. If it does not, we won't bother trying to do the operation. Instead, we will just return the default return value of false and post a message to the debug console. Any operations that require a second fact will be tested and reported the same way.

Listing 8-10. Logic Evaluate Method

```
public bool Evaluate()
{
    bool result = false;

    if ( m_first != null )
    {
        switch ( m_operator )
        {
            case Operator.And:
                if ( m_second != null )
                {
                    result = m_first.IsTrue && m_second.IsTrue;
                }
                else
                {
                    Debug.WriteLine("second fact missing in Logic");
                }
                break;
            case Operator.Equals:
```

```
        if ( m_second != null )
        {
            result = m_first.Value == m_second.Value;
        }
        else
        {
            Debug.WriteLine("second fact missing in Logic");
        }
        break;
    case Operator.GreaterThan:
        if ( m_second != null )
        {
            result = m_first.Value > m_second.Value;
        }
        else
        {
            Debug.WriteLine("second fact missing in Logic");
        }
        break;
    case Operator.GreaterThanEquals:
        if ( m_second != null )
        {
            result = m_first.Value >= m_second.Value;
        }
        else
        {
            Debug.WriteLine("second fact missing in Logic");
        }
        break;
    case Operator.LessThan:
        if ( m_second != null )
        {
            result = m_first.Value < m_second.Value;
        }
        else
        {
            Debug.WriteLine("second fact missing in Logic");
        }
        break;
    case Operator.LessThanEquals:
        if ( m_second != null )
        {
            result = m_first.Value <= m_second.Value;
        }
```

```
                else
                {
                    Debug.WriteLine("second fact missing in Logic");
                }
                break;
            case Operator.NotEqual:
                if ( m_second != null )
                {
                    result = m_first.Value != m_second.Value;
                }
                else
                {
                    Debug.WriteLine("second fact missing in Logic");
                }
                break;
            case Operator.Or:
                if ( m_second != null )
                {
                    result = m_first.IsTrue || m_second.IsTrue;
                }
                else
                {
                    Debug.WriteLine("second fact missing in Logic");
                }
                break;
            case Operator.True:
                result = m_first.IsTrue;
                break;
            case Operator.False:
                result = !m_first.IsTrue;
                break;
        }
    }
    else
    {
        Debug.WriteLine("first fact missing in Logic");
    }

    return result;
}
```

The Write method for this class (shown in Listing 8-11) is very similar to the method in the Fact class. For this class, the element name will be Logic and we will save the names of the two facts plus the string value of the Operator enumeration.

The ToString method of an enumeration gives us the enumeration name so that
Operator.And gets stored as "And".

Listing 8-11. Logic Write Method

```
public void Write( XmlTextWriter writer )
{
   writer.WriteStartElement("Logic");
   writer.WriteElementString("Fact1", m_first.Name);
   writer.WriteElementString("Operator", m_operator.ToString());
   writer.WriteElementString("Fact2", m_second.Name);
   writer.WriteEndElement();
}
```

Reading a Logic class from XML is a bit more complicated. The Read method
(shown in Listing 8-12) will get the three strings that were saved into the XML
file. It must then associate those strings with the proper facts and enumeration
value. The arguments to the method are an instance to the XmlTextReader that
was used to open the data file as well as the instance of the Thinker we are loading data for. The Thinker holds the collection of facts that the logic will reference.
Therefore we need to get the references from it.

Listing 8-12. Logic Read Method

```
public void Read ( XmlTextReader reader, Thinker thinker )
{
   bool done = false;

   while ( !done )
   {
      reader.Read();

      if ( reader.NodeType == XmlNodeType.EndElement &&
         reader.Name == "Logic" )
      {
         done =true;
      }
         // Process a start of element node.
      else if (reader.NodeType == XmlNodeType.Element)
      {
         // Process a text node.
         if ( reader.Name == "Fact1" )
         {
```

```
            while (reader.NodeType != XmlNodeType.Text)
            {
                reader.Read();
            }
            m_first = thinker.GetFact(reader.Value);
        }
        if ( reader.Name == "Fact2" )
        {
            while (reader.NodeType != XmlNodeType.Text)
            {
                reader.Read();
            }
            m_second = thinker.GetFact(reader.Value);
        }
        if ( reader.Name == "Operator" )
        {
            while (reader.NodeType != XmlNodeType.Text)
            {
                reader.Read();
            }
            switch ( reader.Valuc )
            {
                case "And":
                    m_operator = Operator.And;
                    break;
                case "Equals":
                    m_operator = Operator.Equals;
                    break;
                case "GreaterThan":
                    m_operator = Operator.GreaterThan;
                    break;
                case "GreaterThanEquals":
                    m_operator = Operator.GreaterThanEquals;
                    break;
                case "LessThan":
                    m_operator = Operator.LessThan;
                    break;
                case "LessThanEquals":
                    m_operator - Operator.LessThanEquals;
                    break;
                case "NotEqual":
                    m_operator = Operator.NotEqual;
                    break;
```

```
                    case "Or":
                        m_operator = Operator.Or;
                        break;
                    case "True":
                        m_operator = Operator.True;
                        break;
                    case "False":
                        m_operator = Operator.False;
                        break;
                }
            }
        }
    }// End while loop.
    }
    }
}
```

The method will loop through the lines in the XML file until it reaches
a Logic end element. If it finds an element node, it checks the name of that element. It then reads until it finds the next text node. The string at the text node is
the value for that element. If this is one of the two Fact nodes, it will call the
Thinker's GetFact method to get a reference for that fact and store it within the
corresponding attribute.

To evaluate the operation, we are forced to use a switch statement to find
the correct enumeration value associated with the string. Unfortunately, C# enumerations do not include a Parse method to complement the ToString method
we used when writing the XML file.

Stepping Up a Level—the Expression Class

The Logic class is our first step hierarchy. The next level is the Expression class. The
attributes for this class are shown in Listing 8-13. An Expression is a means of com-
bining a number of Logic instances together. To accomplish this, it maintains
a collection of the Logic that forms the expression as well as a Boolean value that
specifies whether the values of the individual logic instances are combined with
a logical And or a logical Or operation.

Listing 8-13. Expression Attributes

```
using System;
using System.Collections;
using System.Xml;
```

```
namespace GameAI
{
    /// <summary>
    /// Summary description for Expression
    /// </summary>
    public class Expression
    {
        #region Attributes
        private ArrayList m_logic_list;
        private bool m_and_values = true;
        #endregion
```

There is only one property in the Expression class (shown in Listing 8-14). The CombineByAnding property is used to set the state of the m_and_values attribute.

Listing 8-14. Expression Property

```
        #region Properties
        public bool CombineByAnding { set { m_and_values = value; } }
        #endregion
```

The Expression class (shown in Listing 8-15) has a simple default constructor. The constructor allocates the ArrayList that will hold the logic for the expression.

Listing 8-15. Expression Constructor

```
        public Expression()
        {
            m_logic_list = new ArrayList();
        }
```

We will include a couple of methods to give the ability to change the expression programmatically. The first is the Clear method shown in Listing 8-16. This method simply removes all of the logic from the list.

Listing 8-16. Expression Clear Method

```
        public void Clear()
        {
            m_logic_list.Clear();
        }
```

Once the Clear method has been used to reset the list of logic, it is ready for new logic to be inserted. The AddLogic method (shown in Listing 8-17) accepts the passed Logic reference and adds it to the collection.

Listing 8-17. Expression AddLogic Method

```
public void AddLogic( Logic logic )
{
   m_logic_list.Add(logic);
}
```

The Evaluate method is the key for the Expression class, just as it was for was the Logic class. The Evaluate method is shown in Listing 8-18. It works by iterating through the Logic list and accumulating the answer in the result flag. If the results of evaluating the logic are for the first entry in the collection, the result is assigned to the result variable. The remaining results are combined with this one based on the status of the m_and_values attribute. The final accumulated result is the evaluation of the complete expression and returned as the result.

Listing 8-18. Expression Evaluate Method

```
public bool Evaluate()
{
   bool result = false;
   bool first_logic = true;

   foreach ( Logic logic in m_logic_list )
   {
      bool val = logic.Evaluate();

      if ( first_logic )
      {
         result = val;
      }
      else
      {
         if ( m_and_values )
         {
            result = result && val;
         }
         else
         {
            result = result || val;
         }
```

```
        }
      }

      return result;
    }
```

The `Expression` class must also be able to write itself and restore itself to an XML file. The `Write` method for the class is shown in Listing 8-19. This method follows the same pattern as the `Write` method in the previous classes. It begins by storing the Boolean value. Then it is just a matter of iterating through the list of `Logic` instances and having each one write itself to the file.

Listing 8-19. Expression Write Method

```
public void Write( XmlTextWriter writer )
{
    writer.WriteStartElement("Expression");
    writer.WriteElementString("AndValues", m_and_values.ToString());
    foreach ( Logic logic in m_logic_list )
    {
        logic.Write( writer );
    }
    writer.WriteEndElement();
}
```

The `Write` method for the `Expression` class (shown in Listing 8-20) follows a pattern similar to that of the `Logic` class's `Write` method. It also takes a reference to the `XmlTextReader` class and the `Thinker` associated with this `Expression`. It loops reading and processing the XML lines until the `Expression` end element is encountered. Whenever it encounters a logic element, it creates an instance of the class. This method has the class load itself from the XML file and adds it to its collection.

Listing 8-20. Expression Read Method

```
public void Read ( XmlTextReader reader, Thinker thinker )
{
    bool done = false;

    while ( !done )
    {
        reader.Read();
```

```
        if ( reader.NodeType == XmlNodeType.EndElement &&
           reader.Name == "Expression" )
        {
           done =true;
        }
           // Process a start of element node.
        else if (reader.NodeType == XmlNodeType.Element)
        {
           // Process a text node.
           if ( reader.Name == "Logic" )
           {
              Logic logic = new Logic();
              logic.Read( reader, thinker );
              m_logic_list.Add( logic );
           }
           else if ( reader.Name == "AndValues" )
           {
              while (reader.NodeType != XmlNodeType.Text)
              {
                 reader.Read();
              }
                m_and_values = bool.Parse(reader.Value);
           }
        }
     }// End while loop.
   }
  }
}
```

Putting the Logic to Work—the Transitioner Class

The Transitioner class is where we put all of this logic evaluation to work. This is the class that handles those lines that ran between the circles in the state diagram (refer back to Figure 8-1). To accomplish this, the class needs the expression that defines the condition required to make the transition as well as the state it will transition into. The Transitioner class attributes shown in Listing 8-21 illustrate this.

Listing 8-21. Transitioner Attributes

```
using System;
using System.Xml;

namespace GameAI
{
    /// <summary>
    /// Summary description for Transitioner
    /// </summary>
    public class Transitioner
    {
        #region Attributes
        private Expression m_expression = null;
        private AIState    m_target_state;
        #endregion
```

There is no default constructor for the `Transitioner` class. The constructor (shown in Listing 8-22) requires both the `Expression` and the target state. References to both are passed in and stored in the class's attributes.

Listing 8-22. Transitioner Constructor

```
        public Transitioner(Expression expression, AIState target_state)
        {
            m_expression = expression;
            m_target_state = target_state;
        }
```

The `Evaluate` method (shown in Listing 8-23) is where we decide whether the state should change or not. The current state is passed into the method. This way we can pass the current state back to the calling method if the state isn't changing. If for some reason there is no expression, we have nothing to evaluate and the state will not change. Otherwise, we evaluate the expression. If the expression evaluates to true, then we will return the target state and the transition will take place.

Listing 8-23. Transitioner Evaluate Method

```
        public AIState Evaluate( AIState old_state )
        {
            AIState new_state = old_state;
```

```
    if ( m_expression != null )
    {
        if ( m_expression.Evaluate() )
        {
            new_state = m_target_state;
        }
    }

    return new_state;
}
```

The `Transitioner` class's `Write` method (shown in Listing 8-24) writes the attributes out to the XML file. The name of the target state is saved in the file. We will use this name when we read in the XML and query the `Thinker` for the corresponding class reference. The `Expression` is written using its `Write` method.

Listing 8-24. Transitioner Write Method

```
public void Write( XmlTextWriter writer )
{
    writer.WriteStartElement("Transitioner");
    writer.WriteElementString("Target", m_target_state.Name);
    m_expression.Write( writer );
    writer.WriteEndElement();
}
```

The `Read` method for the `Transitioner` class (shown in Listing 8-25) loads the expression used by the class. Each `AIState` holds a collection of `Transitioner`s. When an `AIState` is loading itself from the XML file, it will call this method and pass in the `XmlTextReader` and the `Thinker` reference. The `Read` method will read the target state and use it when creating the `Transitioner` instance before having to load its expression.

Listing 8-25. Transitioner Read Method

```
public void Read ( XmlTextReader reader, Thinker thinker )
{
    bool done = false;

    while ( !done )
    {
        reader.Read();
```

```
                    if ( reader.NodeType == XmlNodeType.EndElement &&
                        reader.Name == "Transitioner" )
                    {
                        done =true;
                    }
                        // Process a start of element node.
                    else if (reader.NodeType == XmlNodeType.Element)
                    {
                        // Process a text node.
                        if ( reader.Name == "Expression" )
                        {
                            m_expression.Read( reader, thinker );
                        }
                    }
                }// End while loop.
            }
        }
}
```

Getting to the Top—the AIState Class

The Transitioner class gives us the means to sequence from one state to another. Now it is time to look at the AIState class we will use for the states themselves. The attributes for the class are shown in Listing 8-26. Each state will know its name so that it can be referenced by name. It will also hold a collection of Transitioners to the states that it is connected with. Finally, it will hold a collection of action methods. These methods are executed each pass that the state is active.

Listing 8-26. AIState Attributes

```
using System;
using System.Collections;
using System.Xml;

namespace GameAI
{
    /// <summary>
    /// Summary description for AIState
    /// </summary>
    public class AIState
    {
        #region Attributes
        private string m_name;
```

```
private ArrayList m_transition_list;
private ArrayList m_actions;
#endregion
```

The class has a single property (shown in Listing 8-27). It is a read-only property that returns the state's name so that any class holding a reference to the state can access its name.

Listing 8-27. AIState Properties

```
#region Properties
public string Name { get { return m_name; } }
#endregion
```

The constructor for the class (shown in Listing 8-28) takes a string for the state's name as an argument. The string is saved in an attribute for future reference. We also need to initialize the collections so that they are ready to receive data.

Listing 8-28. AIState Constructor

```
public AIState(string name)
{
    m_name = name;
    m_transition_list = new ArrayList();
    m_actions = new ArrayList();
}
```

The AddAction method (shown in Listing 8-29) is used to add action methods to the class. The ActionMethod delegate of the Thinker class is a void method that takes a Thinker reference as an argument. The supplied method is added to the m_actions collection.

Listing 8-29. AIState AddAction Method

```
public void AddAction( Thinker.ActionMethod method )
{
    m_actions.Add( method );
}
```

The DoActions method (shown in Listing 8-30) provides the means for the Thinker to execute the state's methods. A reference to the Thinker that called the function is passed in as an argument to each action method held in the collection.

By giving each action method this reference, the DoActions method has the ability to query the Thinker for any information it needs about the object it is working on, including a reference to the object itself.

Listing 8-30. AIState DoActions Method

```
public void DoActions( Thinker thinker )
{
   foreach ( Action act in m_actions )
   {
      act(thinker);
   }
}
```

The Think method (shown in Listing 8-31) is where the class decides if the current state should change based on current conditions. This method is called by the Thinker class and returns a reference to the desired state. To accomplish this, the method iterates through the collection of Transitioners, calling the Evaluate method for each one. If any Transitioner returns a state other than the current state, we stop evaluating and return that state. Therefore, even if multiple transitions could have been made, only the first transition is actually made.

Listing 8-31. AIState Think Method

```
public AIState Think()
{
   AIState new_state;

   foreach ( Transitioner trans in m_transition_list )
   {
      new_state = trans.Evaluate( this );
      if ( new_state != this )
      {
         return new_state;
      }
   }
   return this;
}
```

We need a programmatic means of adding Transitioners to the state so that we can modify the logic on the fly. The AddTransitioner method (shown in Listing 8-32) provides this capability by adding the supplied Transitioner reference to the Transitioner list.

Listing 8-32. AIState AddTransitioner Method

```
public void AddTransitioner ( Transitioner trans )
{
   m_transition_list.Add( trans );
}
```

Due to the way the states interrelate, we need to instantiate all instances of AIState before we populate them with Transitioners. This way we can establish the references to them in the Transitioner by name lookup as the Transitioners are created and loaded from the XML file. To simplify this procedure, we will make two entries into the XML file for each state. The first set of entries will be only the name of the state. This is accomplished by the WriteStateName method, shown in Listing 8-33, which writes StateName elements with the state name as the value.

Listing 8-33. AIState WriteStateName Method

```
public void WriteStateName( XmlTextWriter writer )
{
   writer.WriteStartElement("StateName");
   writer.WriteElementString("name", m_name);
   writer.WriteEndElement();
}
```

The WriteFullState method (shown in Listing 8-34) writes the second entry for the state. This entry includes all of the information required to re-create the state. It begins with the name of the state so that we can retrieve the correct state to populate. It then iterates through the collection of Transitioners and has each write itself to the file. Once all of the Transitioners have been written to the file, the method then iterates through the collection of action methods for the state and writes the name of the methods to the XML file.

Listing 8-34. AIState WriteFullState Method

```
public void WriteFullState( XmlTextWriter writer )
{
   writer.WriteStartElement("StateDefinition");
   writer.WriteElementString("name", m_name);
   foreach ( Transitioner trans in m_transition_list )
   {
      trans.Write( writer );
   }
```

```
        foreach ( Thinker.ActionMethod act in m_actions )
        {
           writer.WriteStartElement("StateAction");
           writer.WriteElementString("name", Thinker.GetActionName( act ));
           writer.WriteEndElement();
        }
        writer.WriteEndElement();
    }
```

The last two methods provide for the saving of an AIState to an XML file. The Read method (shown in Listing 8-35) repopulates an AIState based on this saved information. The Read method of the Thinker class will create the state. This Read method then populates it from the data in the file. The method reads the XML file until it encounters the StateDefinition end element marking the end of the data for that state.

Listing 8-35. AIState Read Method

```
    public void Read ( XmlTextReader reader, Thinker thinker )
    {
        bool done = false;
        Transitioner trans = null;
        Expression exp = null;

        while ( !done )
        {
            reader.Read();

            if ( reader.NodeType == XmlNodeType.EndElement &&
                 reader.Name == "StateDefinition" )
            {
                done =true;
            }
            // Process a start of element node.
            else if (reader.NodeType == XmlNodeType.Element)
            {
                // Process a text node.
                if ( reader.Name == "Target" )
                {
                    while (reader.NodeType != XmlNodeType.Text)
                    {
                        reader.Read();
                    }
```

```
                    AIState state = thinker.GetState(reader.Value);
                    exp = new Expression();
                    trans = new Transitioner( exp, state );
                    AddTransitioner( trans );
                    trans.Read( reader, thinker );
                }
                if ( reader.Name == "StateAction" )
                {
                    while (reader.NodeType != XmlNodeType.Text)
                    {
                        reader.Read();
                    }
                    Thinker.ActionMethod method = Thinker.GetAction(reader.Value);
                    m_actions.Add( method );
                }
            }
        }// End while loop.
    }
  }
}
```

The `Target` nodes in the file denote `Transitioners` to a target state. When this node is encountered, we need to get a reference to the target state. The `Thinker` class's `GetState` method gives us this reference. We have the `Transitioner` that we create to target this state load itself from the file and we add the `Transitioner` to the state's collection.

The `StateAction` nodes in the XML file contain the name of the action methods that will be called while this state is active. We will need references to the methods themselves to call them while the state is active. The `Thinker` class has a `GetAction` method that returns a reference to an action method when supplied with the method's name.

Our Opponent—the Thinker

The `Thinker` class brings it all together. This is the class that encapsulates our inference engine and provides the artificial intelligence for our computer opponents. It consists of a collection of sensor methods that run continually, collecting information (`Facts`) that will be used to make decisions regarding what the object should do. It also has a collection of states (`AIState`) with their `Transitioner` and action methods that define the behavior.

Defining the Thinker Class

The Thinker class uses two delegates (shown in Listing 8-36) that define the method prototypes that will be used for the sensors and actions. Both methods accept a reference to the Thinker that is calling the method. This provides the method with the context that it will need to work within. Each Thinker holds a reference to the Model that the Thinker is attached to. The only real difference in the delegates is the use to which the methods are put.

Listing 8-36. Thinker Delegates

```
using System;
using System.Collections;
using System.Threading;
using System.Xml;
using GameEngine;

namespace GameAI
{
    /// <summary>
    /// Summary description for Thinker
    /// </summary>
    public class Thinker : IDisposable
    {
        #region delegates
        public delegate void SensorMethod( Thinker the_thinker );
        public delegate void ActionMethod( Thinker the_thinker );
    #endregion
```

The attributes for the Thinker class are shown in Listing 8-37. A static collection of methods is shared by all instances of the Thinker class. This is the collection that is queried when setting up an instantiation of the class and its states. This collection needs to be populated before any Thinkers are created. The static AddAction method that we will look at shortly is used to populate this collection.

Listing 8-37. Thinker Attributes

```
        #region Attributes
        private ArrayList     m_state_list = null;
        private ArrayList     m_sensor_methods = null;
        private AIState       m_current_state = null;
```

```
private SortedList     m_fact_list;
private Thread          m_think_thread;
private Model          m_model = null;
private bool            m_thread_active = true;

private static SortedList m_methods = null;
#endregion
```

Each instance of the `Thinker` class contains the following:

- Attributes that are specific to that `Thinker`.

- A collection of the states that define the logic for that instance.

- A collection of the facts that the `Thinker` knows and a collection of sensor methods that are used to keep those facts up to date.

- A reference to the current state. This is the state that will be executed each pass until one of its `Transitioners` fires to change the current state.

- A `Thread` reference. This is because each `Thinker` will execute in its own separate thread. This allows each `Thinker` to take an extended amount of time each iteration to make its decisions without impacting the rendering rate of the application.

- A m_thread_active flag, which provides a means of signaling the thread that it should be terminated. It defaults to the `true` state and is set to `false` when the thread should terminate.

- A reference to the `Model` that is using this `Thinker` for control. This makes the model available to both the sensor methods that will need to know where they are in the world and the action methods that will modify the model's attributes in order to control the model's actions.

The class will have one property. The `Self` property (shown in Listing 8-38) provides read-only access to the `Model` reference held by the class. This is how the methods that need the model will be able to access it.

Listing 8-38. Thinker Properties

```
#region Properties
  public Model Self { get { return m_model; } }
  #endregion
```

Constructing a Thinker

The Thinker constructor (shown in Listing 8-39) does a bit more than the typical constructor that we have seen so far. It accepts the reference to the Model that is controlled by this Thinker. This is saved in an attribute and the three collections are initialized. The novel portion of the constructor is found in the final three lines of the method, which is where we set up the thread that will execute the class and perform the "thinking." A thread is created with the Execute method of the class used as the method executed by the thread. The IsBackground flag for the thread is set to indicate that this thread will execute with background priority. The final line starts the new thread executing. By placing this thread creation and management within the constructor, we automatically create new threads each time we create a new Thinker.

Listing 8-39. Thinker Constructor

```
public Thinker( Model model )
{
    m_model = model;
    m_state_list = new ArrayList();
    m_sensor_methods = new ArrayList();
    m_fact_list = new SortedList();

    m_think_thread = new Thread(new ThreadStart(Execute));
    m_think_thread.IsBackground = true;
    m_think_thread.Start();
}
```

Earlier I mentioned a static method that we would use to populate the static collection of action methods to be shared by all instances of the class. The AddAction method (shown in Listing 8-40) is that method. By being a static method, it can be used before any of the Thinkers are created. It takes as arguments a string holding the name of the method and a reference to the method. The method must adhere to the ActionMethod delegate structure. The collection of methods uses the SortedArray collection type, which provides quick access to the stored data based on a key value. We will use the string name of the method as our key. By its nature, this collection does not allow entries with duplicate keys. Before we add the method reference to the collection, we will use the Contains method of the collection to check if the key already exists. If it does not, we are free to add the reference and its name to the collection.

Listing 8-40. Thinker AddAction Method

```
public static void AddAction( string action_name, ActionMethod method )
{
    if ( !m_methods.Contains( action_name ) )
    {
        m_methods.Add(action_name, method);
    }
}
```

Since the methods are of little use unless we can provide them upon request, we also need a method for supplying the action methods. This is provided using the static GetAction method shown in Listing 8-41. A string with a reference name is passed in as an argument and the reference pointer is returned as the result. We start with a method reference set to null. If the calling method asks for a method that is not found in the collection, this is what will be returned. We first check to see if the method's name is found in the collection. If it is, we will use the IndexOfKey method to find the index in the collection for that entry. The method reference is set using the GetByIndex method.

Listing 8-41. Thinker GetAction Method

```
public static ActionMethod GetAction( string action_name )
{
    ActionMethod method = null;

    if ( m_methods.Contains( action_name ) )
    {
        int index = m_fact_list.IndexOfKey( action_name );
        method = (ActionMethod)m_methods.GetByIndex(index);
    }
    return method;
}
```

There will be times when we will need to get the name of a method when given a reference to that method. The static GetActionName method (shown in Listing 8-42) provides a lookup similar to that found in the previous GetAction method. Instead of getting the index of the entry based on its key, we get the index based on the stored value (the method reference) using the IndexOfValue method of the collection. The GetKey method of the collection will give us the string with the method's name at that index.

Listing 8-42. Thinker GetActionName Method

```
public static string GetActionName( ActionMethod method )
{
    string action_name = null;

    if ( m_methods.Contains( method ) )
    {
        int index = m_methods.IndexOfValue( method );
        action_name = (string)m_methods.GetKey(index);
    }

    return action_name;
}
```

When we discussed the Thinker constructor, we showed the creation of a thread that would be spawned for the execution of the Thinker. This thread uses the Execute method (shown in Listing 8-43) as the method to be executed. The method will loop as long as the m_thread_active flag is set. Once the method completes, the thread is automatically terminated. The current state is set once the Thinker is fully configured. When the thread sees the reference become non-null, it will start executing that state. It begins by calling the sensor methods of each of the Thinkers. Remember, these are the methods that provide the information state transitions are based upon. Once all sensor methods have been called, the state is commanded to perform its action methods. Lastly, the Think method of the state is called to determine what state will execute during the next iteration. Since all of this is done in a lower priority background thread, it is quite possible that the image on the screen may be updated several times for each loop through this method. This is fine. In fact, in some games you may find that the computer opponents are simply too good to beat. One of the solutions to that problem would be to lower the thread priority further or add a short delay in this method's iterations so that the opponent is not thinking too fast.

Listing 8-43. Thinker Execute Method

```
public void Execute()
{
    while ( m_thread_active )
    {
        if ( m_current_state != null )
        {
            foreach ( SensorMethod method in m_sensor_methods )
            {
                method( this );
            }
```

```
            m_current_state.DoActions( this );
            m_current_state = m_current_state.Think();
        }
    }
}
```

We have made the Thinker class inherit from the IDisposable interface. This provides us with the Dispose method (shown in Listing 8-44) to perform cleanup when the class is no longer needed. In the case of the Thinker class, we need to stop the thread that was created. Since the thread method is looping based on the state of the m_thread_alive flag, we need to clear the flag by setting it to false. The flag will only be checked when the execution of the thread loops back to the beginning, so we will pause until the thread reports that it has terminated by clearing its IsAlive property. The Sleep method allows us to pause for one millisecond after each check until the thread has terminated.

Listing 8-44. Thinker Dispose Method

```
public void Dispose()
{
    m_thread_active = false;

    while ( m_think_thread.IsAlive ) Thread.Sleep(1);
}
```

Getting Information from the Thinker

We will give the class a number of helper methods so that other methods and classes may query this class for information about the data it holds. The first of these methods is the GetState method shown in Listing 8-45. This method provides the means of finding a state reference based on the name of the state. Since the state collection is a simple ArrayList rather than a SortedList, we handle the lookup a little differently. We will use the more brute-force method of looping through the states in the collection and checking to see if each state is the one we want. If we find the desired state, we will save its reference. After we finish looping, we will return the reference if we found it. Otherwise, we will return a null to indicate that the state was not found. Since this function is only used when loading or saving a state, we do not need to use a more complicated system just to save the small performance penalty of this type of search.

Listing 8-45. Thinker GetState Method

```
public AIState GetState( string name )
{
   AIState the_state = null;

   foreach ( AIState state in m_state_list )
   {
      if ( state.Name == name )
      {
         the_state = state;
      }
   }
   return the_state;
}
```

The GetFact method (shown in Listing 8-46), on the other hand, will be used often during the execution of the game. This is a good reason to use the somewhat larger but much faster SortedList collection. If the fact exists in the collection, we will return a reference to the fact to the calling method. If it does not, then we will add a new fact to the collection with that name and set its initial value to zero. This allows us to check for facts that have not been set yet without throwing an exception.

Listing 8-46. Thinker GetFact Method

```
public Fact GetFact( string name )
{
   Fact the_fact = null;

   if ( m_fact_list.Contains( name ) )
   {
      int index = m_fact_list.IndexOfKey( name );
      the_fact = (Fact)m_fact_list.GetByIndex(index);
   }
   else
   {
      the_fact = new Fact(name);
      the_fact.Value = 0.0f;
      m_fact_list.Add( name, the_fact );
   }
   return the_fact;
}
```

The complement to the GetFact method is the SetFact method shown in Listing 8-47. This method takes a string with the Fact's name as well as the value that the fact should take. We look up the fact in the collection and set the value. If the Fact does not exist yet, we will create a new fact with the supplied value and add it to the collection.

Listing 8-47. Thinker SetFact Method

```
public void SetFact( string name, float value )
{
    if ( m_fact_list.Contains( name ) )
    {
        int index = m_fact_list.IndexOfKey( name );
        Fact fact = (Fact)m_fact_list.GetByIndex(index);
        fact.Value = value;
    }
    else
    {
        Fact fact = new Fact(name);
        fact.Value = value;
        m_fact_list.Add( name, fact );
    }
}
```

The AddSensorMethod method (shown in Listing 8-48) is used to populate the collection of sensor methods. It takes a method reference that was passed in as an argument and adds it to the collection that is called by the Execute method each iteration.

Listing 8-48. Thinker AddSensorMethod Method

```
public void AddSensorMethod( SensorMethod method )
{
    m_sensor_methods.Add( method );
}
```

The AddState method (shown in Listing 8-49) is used to add AIState references to our collection of states. Through this method we can programmatically add states to the class. It is also used by the Read method as we are creating the states based on the XML data.

Listing 8-49. Thinker AddState Method

```
public void AddState( AIState state )
{
   m_state_list.Add( state );
}
```

Serializing the Thinker

This is all the functionality we need in the Thinker class. All that is left is the ability to read and write the contents of the class to an XML file. The Write method (shown in Listing 8-50) provides the output portion of this capability. All of the XML Write methods that we have investigated from the other classes worked with an XmlTextWriter that was supplied by the calling method. The Thinker's Write method is the source of the XmlTextWriter that is used. This Write method is supplied with a string that holds the fully qualified path to the XML file that will be written.

Listing 8-50. Thinker Write Method

```
public void Write( string filename )
{
   XmlTextWriter writer = new XmlTextWriter( filename, null );

   writer.WriteStartDocument();
   writer.WriteStartElement("Knowledge");

   //Use indentation for readability.
   writer.Formatting = Formatting.Indented;
   writer.Indentation = 4;

   int num_facts = m_fact_list.Count;

   for ( int i=0; i<num_facts; i++ )
   {
      Fact fact = (Fact)m_fact_list.GetByIndex(i);
      fact.Write( writer );
   }

   foreach ( AIState state in m_state_list )
   {
      state.WriteStateName( writer );
   }
```

```
        foreach ( AIState state in m_state_list )
        {
            state.WriteFullState( writer );
        }

        writer.WriteEndElement();
        writer.WriteEndDocument();
        writer.Close();
    }
```

The writer is created using this path as an argument to the constructor. The WriteStartDocument method of the writer puts the standard XML header into the file. The overall element name for the data is "Knowledge". We have the writer use tab indenting for the information as it is written to the file. This has no effect on the data itself, but makes the data more legible if we look at the file in a text editor.

The first information written to the file is the collection of facts. We iterate through the collection of facts and have each write itself to the file. We can't use the foreach loop architecture for a SortedList. Instead, we use a standard for loop. The collection of AIStates is an ArrayList. This allows us to use foreach. We will loop through the collection of states twice. The first time through, we will have each state write its name to the file. The second pass we will have each state write its complete state using the WriteFullState method.

Once all of the states have been written to the file, we have captured all of the information for a Thinker. To close the file, we will call WriteEndElement to close the "Knowledge" element in the file. We will then call WriteEndDocument to finalize the XML and Close to actually close the file itself.

The Read method (shown in Listing 8-51) re-creates the contents of a Thinker based on the XML data. This is the method that creates the XmlTextReader that is used by the other class's Read methods. Just like the Write method, the Read method takes a string with the fully qualified path for the XML file. Once the file is opened, this method reads the file and processes the element and text nodes that hold our data. The name and value nodes hold our Fact data, and they are written to the file in that order. When we read in the value, we have everything we need to create a Fact, and we then use the SetFact method to create the Fact. The StateName nodes hold the names of all of the states. Each time we hit one, we create a new AIState and add it to our collection of states. The StateDefinition nodes hold the full definitions of the states. When we hit one of these nodes, we get the associated state from our collection. We then have that state load itself from the file. Once we have finished reading the file, we are ready to begin "thinking." Remember that the thinking thread does not begin doing actual work until the current state has been set. Assuming that we load at least one state from the file, we set the current state to the first state in the collection. This should always be the default state. A Try/Catch block wraps the entire method so that any errors in loading the file (including not finding the file to load) will result in an appropriate message being displayed.

Listing 8-51. Thinker Read Method

```
public void Read( string filename )
{
    XmlTextReader reader = new XmlTextReader( filename );
    string name = "unknown";
    float float_value;
    AIState state = null;

    try
    {
        reader.Read();
        // If the node has value
        while ( reader.Read() )
        {
            // process a start of element node.
            if (reader.NodeType == XmlNodeType.Element)
            {
                // Process a text node.
                if ( reader.Name == "name" )
                {
                    while (reader.NodeType != XmlNodeType.Text)
                    {
                        reader.Read();
                    }
                    name = reader.Value;
                }
                else if ( reader.Name == "Value" )
                {
                    while (reader.NodeType != XmlNodeType.Text)
                    {
                        reader.Read();
                    }
                    float_value = float.Parse(reader.Value);
                    SetFact(name, float_value);
                }
                else if ( reader.Name == "StateName" )
                {
                    while (reader.NodeType != XmlNodeType.Text)
                    {
                        reader.Read();
                    }
                    state = new AIState(reader.Value);
                    AddState( state );
```

```
                }
                else if ( reader.Name == "StateDefinition" )
                {
                    while (reader.NodeType != XmlNodeType.Text)
                    {
                        reader.Read();
                    }
                    state = GetState(reader.Value);
                    state.Read( reader, this );
                }
            }
        }// End while loop.

    if ( m_state_list.Count != 0 )
    {
        m_current_state = (AIState)m_state_list[0];
    }
        reader.Close();
    }
    catch ( Exception e )
    {
        System.Diagnostics.Debug.WriteLine (
            "error in thinker read method/n");
        System.Diagnostics.Debug.WriteLine (e.Message);
    }
    }
  }
}
```

Supplying Data to the Thinker

With the completion of the Thinker class, we have the complete encapsulation of
our artificial intelligence inference engine. Listing 8-52 gives an example of an
XML data file that would be read by the class when creating an instance of
a Thinker. Notice that the tags within the data match the element names that we
defined within each of the classes that make up a Thinker.

Listing 8-52. Example XML Data File

```
<?xml version="1.0"?><Knowledge>
    <Fact>
        <name>race started</name>
        <Value>0.0</Value>
    </Fact>
```

```
<Fact>
    <name>collision ahead</name>
    <Value>0.0</Value>
</Fact>
<Fact>
    <name>race over</name>
    <Value>0.0</Value>
</Fact>
<StateName>
    <name>Idle</name>
</StateName>
<StateName>
    <name>Race</name>
</StateName>
<StateName>
    <name>Evade</name>
</StateName>
<StateDefinition>
    <name>Idle</name>
    <Transitioner>
        <Target>Race</Target>
        <Expression>
            <AndValues>true</AndValues>
            <Logic>
                <Fact1>race started</Fact1>
                <Operator>True</Operator>
                <Fact2>null</Fact2>
            </Logic>
        </Expression>
    </Transitioner>
</StateDefinition>
<StateDefinition>
    <name>Race</name>
    <Transitioner>
        <Target>Idle</Target>
        <Expression>
            <AndValues>true</AndValues>
            <Logic>
                <Fact1>race over</Fact1>
                <Operator>True</Operator>
                <Fact2>null</Fact2>
            </Logic>
        </Expression>
    </Transitioner>
```

```
        <Transitioner>
            <Target>Evade</Target>
            <Expression>
                <AndValues>true</AndValues>
                <Logic>
                    <Fact1>collision ahead</Fact1>
                    <Operator>True</Operator>
                    <Fact2>null</Fact2>
                </Logic>
                <Logic>
                    <Fact1>race started</Fact1>
                    <Operator>True</Operator>
                    <Fact2>null</Fact2>
                </Logic>
                <Logic>
                    <Fact1>race over</Fact1>
                    <Operator>False</Operator>
                    <Fact2>null</Fact2>
                </Logic>
            </Expression>
        </Transitioner>
    </StateDefinition>
    <StateDefinition>
        <name>Evade</name>
    </StateDefinition>
</Knowledge>
```

Detecting the World Around Us—Sensor Systems

The Thinker as we have designed it so far can think but has limited information to think about. The opponent for our sample game needs to see the vehicles, obstacles, and course markings in order to steer around the racecourse. We might also want to give it a sense of hearing to detect other cars that are nearby but not in sight. In a military-oriented game, we might also have radar or sonar systems that would detect our opponents. All of these are examples of sensor systems.

Our sensor systems will be implemented as the sensor methods that we provide to the Thinker class. These methods are game specific and not part of the game engine itself. This is why the game engine was built so that the methods are supplied to the engine rather than hard coded. This allows the sensor methods to be specifically targeted to what is needed for that game.

The results of the sensor method will be facts that are set within the Thinker. These facts can then be used by the state transition logic as well as the action methods that put the decisions into effect. For our sample game, we need an opponent that can see the world around him or her in order to drive his or her car. Luckily, we happen to have a class handy that can provide sight to our Thinker. Although the class was designed to assist in culling and rendering, it also has capabilities that we can exploit for this purpose. A camera attached to an opponent vehicle will hold a collection of the objects that are within the viewing frustum of that camera.

The DriverView method (shown in Listing 8-53) is an example of a sensor method. This method belongs to the Opponent class within the game application that uses the game engine. For this example, we are interested in sensing three types of objects. We want to know the closest red and blue posts that are in sight. These are the course markers, and the logic for the opponent is to stay within these borders, with the red posts to the right and the blue posts to the left. The opponent also needs to know of any obstacles directly in front of his or her car. We will define "in front" to mean within an arc of ±5 degrees in front of the car.

Listing 8-53. DriverView Method

```
public void DriverView( Thinker thinker )
{
    ArrayList objects = new ArrayList();

    Opponent self = (Opponent)thinker.Self;
    Camera eyes = self.Eyes;

    // Get a local copy of the objects that the camera can see.
    objects.Clear();
    foreach ( Object3D obj in eyes.VisibleObjects )
    {
        objects.Add( obj );
    }

    float range_to_nearest = 10000.0f;
    float bearing_to_nearest = 0.0f;
    Object3D nearest_object = null;

    // Nearest red post
    foreach ( Object3D obj in objects )
    {
        if ( obj.Name.Substring(0,3) == "red" )
        {
            float range = eyes.GetDistance(obj);
            if ( range < range_to_nearest )
```

```
            {
                range_to_nearest = range;
                nearest_object = obj;
            }
        }
    }
    if ( nearest_object != null )
    {
        bearing_to_nearest = GetBearing( self, nearest_object );
        thinker.SetFact("red_post_in_sight", 1.0f );
        thinker.SetFact("red_post_range", range_to_nearest );
        thinker.SetFact("red_post_bearing", bearing_to_nearest );
    }
    else
    {
        thinker.SetFact("red_post_in_sight", 0.0f );
    }


    // Nearest blue post
    range_to_nearest = 10000.0f;
    foreach ( Object3D obj in objects )
    {
        if ( obj.Name.Substring(0,4) == "blue" )
        {
            float range = eyes.GetDistance(obj);
            if ( range < range_to_nearest )
            {
                range_to_nearest = range;
                nearest_object = obj;
            }
        }
    }
    if ( nearest_object != null )
    {
        bearing_to_nearest = GetBearing( self, nearest_object );
        thinker.SetFact("blue_post_in_sight", 1.0f );
        thinker.SetFact("blue_post_range", range_to_nearest );
        thinker.SetFact("blue_post_bearing", bearing_to_nearest );
    }
    else
    {
        thinker.SetFact("blue_post_in_sight", 0.0f );
    }
```

```
            // Nearest obstacle (vehicles and trees)
            range_to_nearest = 10000.0f;
            foreach ( Object3D obj in objects )
            {
                if ( obj.Name.Substring(0,4) == "tree" ||
                     obj.Name.Substring(0,3) == "car" )
                {
                    float bearing = GetBearing( self, nearest_object );
                    float range = eyes.GetDistance(obj);

                    // Only accept nearest object within +/- 5 degrees.
                    if ( Math.Abs(bearing) < 0.0872664625997164788846184538424431
                             && range < range_to_nearest )
                    {
                        range_to_nearest = range;
                        nearest_object = obj;
                        bearing_to_nearest = bearing;
                    }
                }
            }
            If ( nearest_object != null )
            {
                thinker.SetFact("obstacle_in_sight", 1.0f );
                thinker.SetFact("obstacle_range", range_to_nearest );
                thinker.SetFact("obstacle_bearing", bearing_to_nearest );
            }
            else
            {
                thinker.SetFact("obstacle_in_sight", 0.0f );
            }
        }
```

The method begins by creating a collection to hold the objects currently in view and references to the opponent and its "eyes." Since the Thinker is running in a separate thread, we will capture a copy of the references held by the camera. We can then iterate through this list, looking for objects that meet our needs. In the first pass through the collection, we will look for the red posts. The names for all of the posts begin with the color of the post. If we find an object whose name starts with "red", we have a candidate object. The camera class provides the GetDistance method that will give us the range from the camera to the object. If the range is less than the closest object encountered so far, we capture that range and the reference to the object. Once we have finished iterating through the objects, we check to see if we have found any red posts. If we have, we calculate the relative bearing to the object and set three facts in the Thinker. The first fact is a flag that indicates we can see a red post by being set to one. The other two facts are the range and bearing that we calculated. If no red posts were seen, then the flag fact is set to zero to indicate the fact.

The next section of code provides the same check for the nearest blue post. After that, we want to look for the nearest obstacle. We will consider the trees and other vehicles as obstacles for this example. We will not worry about the posts or bushes. These will not cause any damage to our vehicle if we hit them. The loop to check for obstacles is similar to the one we used for posts. The major difference is that we calculate the bearing to the object for each object and only include the object as a candidate if the absolute value of the bearing is within 5 degrees.

Putting Decisions to Work–Action Methods

The sensor methods provide the inputs to the Thinker. To put the decisions of the Thinker into action requires the action methods that are executed within the current state. These methods may be as simple or complex as required to do a specific task. The key is that the task should be quite specific. If we overgeneralize the tasks, we are actually embedding the decision logic within the task itself. Although this may achieve the desired results in the short-term, it reduces the effectiveness of being able to tailor the Thinker through the knowledge files.

The car dynamics model that we will be using for both the player and opponent vehicles requires three control inputs: steering, brake pedal, and accelerator. The player will be using a joystick, mouse, or keyboard to control these inputs. For the opponents, we will use action methods that adjust these values within the dynamics model. The five action methods are shown in Listing 8-54. These methods (SteerLeft, SteerStraight, SteerRight, HitTheBrakes, and Accelerate) will be called every iteration that the associated state remains active. This allows us to adjust the values gradually over time, thereby making the control changes more natural. When we are driving and decide to turn the steering wheel to the left, the wheel does not move immediately to the left extreme. It moves gradually toward the desired position. If the reason we were turning goes away (our state changes), we stop moving the wheel in that direction and move it back to center. These actions behave the same way. Each of these methods is a member of the Opponent class of the game application.

Listing 8-54. Action Methods

```
void SteerLeft( Thinker thinker )
{
    Opponent self = (Opponent)thinker.Self;

    if ( self.Steering > -1.0 ) self.Steering = self.Steering - 0.01f;
```

```
    }
    void SteerStraight( Thinker thinker )
    {
        Opponent self = (Opponent)thinker.Self;

        if ( self.Steering > 0.0 ) self.Steering = self.Steering - 0.01f;
        else if ( self.Steering < 0.0 ) self.Steering = self.Steering + 0.01f;
    }

    void SteerRight( Thinker thinker )
    {
        Opponent self = (Opponent)thinker.Self;

        if ( self.Steering < 1.0 ) self.Steering = self.Steering + 0.01f;
    }
    void HitTheBrakes( Thinker thinker )
    {
        Opponent self = (Opponent)thinker.Self;

        self.Gas = 0.0f;

        if ( self.Brake < 1.0 ) self.Brake = self.Brake + 0.1f;
    }
    void Accelerate( Thinker thinker )
    {
        Opponent self = (Opponent)thinker.Self;

        self.Brake = 0.0f;

        if ( self.Gas < 1.0 ) self.Gas = self.Gas + 0.1f;
    }
```

Initializing the Opponent

Earlier in this chapter, I mentioned the Opponent class. This class is not part of the
game engine. It is a class within the game application that uses the engine. Since
it is part of the game, it is allowed to have game-specific logic and code. This
class inherits from the Car class, which is also defined in the game application.
We will look more closely at the Car class in Chapter 10 when we discuss physics.
Suffice it to say at this point that the Car class inherits from the game engine's
Model class and controls the movement of the model with a car physics class.

   The Opponent class extends the Car class even further by adding Thinker control of the physics inputs. You have already seen the sensor method and action

methods that are defined within this class. The remainder of the class is shown in Listing 8-55. The attributes of this class are a `Thinker` object and a `Camera` object. An `Eyes` property provides external access to this opponent's camera.

Listing 8-55. Opponent Class

```
public class Opponent : Car
{
    #region Attributes
    private Thinker m_thinker;
    private Camera  m_camera;
    #endregion

    #region Properties
    public Camera Eyes { get { return m_camera; } }
    #endregion

    public Opponent(string name, string meshFile, Vector3 offset,
        Attitude adjust,   string knowledge )
        : base (name, meshFile, offset, adjust)
    {
        m_camera = new Camera(name + " cam");
        m_camera.Attach( this, new Vector3(0.0f, 0.0f, 0.0f ));

        Thinker.AddAction( "SteerLeft",
                    new Thinker.ActionMethod( SteerLeft ) );
        Thinker.AddAction( "SteerStraight",
                    new Thinker.ActionMethod(SteerStraight) );
        Thinker.AddAction( "SteerRight",
                    new Thinker.ActionMethod( SteerRight ) );
        Thinker.AddAction( "HitTheBrakes",
                    new Thinker.ActionMethod( HitTheBrakes ) );
        Thinker.AddAction( "Accelerate",
                    new Thinker.ActionMethod( Accelerate ) );

        m_thinker = new Thinker( this );

        m_thinker.AddSensorMethod( new Thinker.SensorMethod( DriverView) );

        m_thinker.Read( knowledge );
    }
```

The camera is created and attached to the class's model so that it moves with the car. Each of the action methods is registered with the `Thinker` class so that references to the methods can be associated with the states as they are created. The `Thinker` for the class is created with a reference of this instance of the class. The sensor method is provided to the `Thinker` and its knowledge is loaded from the XML file. When a `"RaceStarted"` fact is set to true by the main game application, this car will be off and running.

Summary

This chapter has provided an initial look at artificial intelligence as applied to a game engine. Far more powerful and flexible systems are available and in use in most commercial game engines. This chapter provides the first step toward working with game artificial intelligence. The next step beyond what is covered in this book is the use of a language such as Python to control the opponent's logic. Systems such as these allow more complicated logic structures than we can form with our simple logical expression.

CHAPTER 9

Game Audio:
Let's Make Some Noise

ALL GAMES USE AUDIO TO set their tone and to provide cues that an event has occurred. Music often sets the mood in a game. Most of us expect to hear something when a collision occurs or a motor is running. Without these aural cues, something is missing and everything feels less real. Microsoft included the DirectSound and AudioVideo namespaces within DirectX to address this part of the game experience.

Making Beautiful Music Together

We will begin with the musical portion of our program. Prior to DirectX 9, this capability was part of the DirectShow interface. This interface was not included in the Managed DirectX available to C#. Instead, Microsoft provided the AudioVideo namespace, which furnishes some of the functionality that was lost when DirectShow became unavailable. The Video class in this namespace includes the ability to stream video to either the screen or a texture. The Audio class provides the ability to play music files and supports the audio portion of a video file. We will use this ability within the game engine to play music.

The music files that are used within a game setting normally rely on one or both of two file formats. The first format is the MIDI format. This format holds a musical score in the form of the notes required to play the music. The files are typically created using composing software or a MIDI-capable keyboard attached to a computer. MIDI music was the original format used within games, and it is supported within the Audio class.

A more popular format these days is MP3. This format allows for quality music with near CD-quality sound at a decent compression to save disk space. This is another of the many formats supported by the Audio class.

Controlling the Music

The Audio class is very capable but does have a few limitations. We will address these limitations by creating the `Music` class that inherits from Audio. Listing 9-1 shows the attributes and properties that we will use to extend the class. The first of these limitations is the ability for a song to repeat. This allows a properly written MIDI song to repeat over and over in the background. If the beginning and end of the MIDI song are written to flow together, we can make the transition without it being noticeable. To support looping, we will have a Boolean attribute that signals that looping is required and a property to expose this flag to the user.

Listing 9-1. Music Class Attributes and Properties

```
using System;
using System.Drawing;
using Microsoft.DirectX;
using Microsoft.DirectX.AudioVideoPlayback;

namespace GameEngine
{
    /// <summary>
    /// Summary description for music
    /// </summary>
    public class Music : Microsoft.DirectX.AudioVideoPlayback.Audio
    {
        #region Attributes
        private bool  loop = false;
        #endregion

        #region Properties
        public bool  Loop { get { return loop; } set { loop = value; } }
        public float MusicVolume {
            set { base.Volume = (int)(-4000 * (1.0f - value)); } }
        #endregion
```

The second limitation is the way Microsoft designed the control of the music's volume. They provided a Volume property for the Audio class that is a bit misleading. Although they named the property Volume, it is really an attenuation factor. A value of 0 in the property represents full volume. A value of –10,000 is stated to be complete silence. This attenuation is in decibels, though, which makes it nonlinear. A value of –4000 is silent for all intents and purposes. To address this, we will provide a MusicVolume property that contains a floating-point value, where a 0 represents silence and a 1 represents full volume. Since there is no reason to query the volume, this is defined as a read-only property.

The constructor for the Music class (shown in Listing 9-2) is responsible for loading the song file. It does this by passing the supplied filename on to the base class constructor. Since we want our class to be able to loop and repeat the song, we will need to know when the song is finished. The Audio class provides the Ending event that is triggered when the song completes. In order to be notified when the event has occurred, we need to register an event handler with the event. The handler will be the ClipEnded method of our class. We will provide a Try/Catch block around this code, but this will not detect the problem of trying to load a file that can't be found. Unfortunately, the base class will throw an exception before our constructor code has a chance to execute. To protect against this occurrence, any class that instantiates copies of the Music class must safeguard against failing to load the file.

Listing 9-2. Music Constructor

```
/// <summary>
/// Music constructor
/// </summary>
public Music( string filename ) : base(filename)
{
   try
   {
      Ending += new System.EventHandler(this.ClipEnded);
   }
   catch (DirectXException d3de)
   {
      Console.AddLine("Unable to create music ");
      Console.AddLine(d3de.ErrorString);
   }
   catch ( Exception e )
   {
      Console.AddLine("Unable to create music ");
      Console.AddLine(e.Message);
   }
}
```

The ClipEnded event handler (shown in Listing 9-3) is used to repeat songs that are selected for looping. Remember, we registered to have this method called when the song finishes. When this method is called, we check to see if the looping attribute has been set. If it has, we call the Audio class's Stop method to put the class into the stopped state. We then call the Play method to start the song playing again.

Listing 9-3. Music Class ClipEnded Event Handler

```
    private void ClipEnded(object sender, System.EventArgs e)
    {
        // The clip has ended, stop and restart it.
        if ( loop )
        {
            Stop();
            Play();
        }
    }
  }
}
```

Playing Multiple Songs

It would quickly become repetitious and boring if the same song were played over and over for the duration of the game. We need the means to play a number of songs one after another as an ongoing soundtrack for our game engine. To accomplish this, we will create the Jukebox class. This class will hold a collection of songs contained within instances of our Music class. Listing 9-4 shows the attributes and properties that will be needed for the class.

Listing 9-4. Jukebox Attributes and Properties

```
using System;
using System.Drawing;
using System.Collections;
using Microsoft.DirectX;
using Microsoft.DirectX.AudioVideoPlayback;

namespace GameEngine
{
    /// <summary>
    /// Summary description for Jukebox
    /// </summary>
    public class Jukebox : IDisposable
    {
        #region Attributes
        private ArrayList  playlist = null;
        private int        current_song = 0;
        private int        volume = 0;
        #endregion
```

```
#region Properties
public float Volume { set { volume = (int)(-4000 * (1.0f - value)); } }
#endregion
```

We will use an ArrayList as our playlist of songs. We will add songs to the list as they are added to the jukebox. An index to the collection provides the selection of the song being played. We will also include an attribute and property for setting the master volume for the jukebox. This volume will work the same as the volume we used for the Music class. As each song is played, this volume value will be passed on to that song.

The constructor for the Jukebox class (shown in Listing 9-5) is quite simple. All the constructor needs to do is prepare the playlist collection to hold the music.

Listing 9-5. Jukebox Constructor

```
/// <summary>
/// Jukebox constructor
/// </summary>
public Jukebox( )
{
    playlist = new ArrayList();
}
```

Music is added to our jukebox through the AddSong method shown in Listing 9-6. A string with the full path and filename for the song file is passed into the method. Remember that this can be any combination of MIDI, MP3, or even WAV files that we wish to play during the game. When we defined the Music class, I stated that the Try/Catch block in the constructor would not catch cases where the song could not be loaded because the file was not found or was not of an acceptable format. The Try/Catch block in this method is to safeguard against these types of errors.

Listing 9-6. Jukebox AddSong Method

```
public void AddSong( string filename )
{
    try
    {
        Music song = new Music(filename);
        song.Ending += new System.EventHandler(this.ClipEnded);
        playlist.Add(song);
    }
    catch (DirectXException d3de)
    {
```

```
        Console.AddLine("Unable to add " + filename +
                " to the jukebox playlist ");
        Console.AddLine(d3de.ErrorString);
    }
    catch ( Exception e )
    {
        Console.AddLine("Unable to add " + filename +
                " to the jukebox playlist ");
        Console.AddLine(e.Message);
    }
}
```

A new instance of the Music object is created for the requested file. Assuming that an exception was not thrown and the song was loaded, we will need to register a handler for the Ending event so that we will be notified when this song finishes. All songs will notify the same event handler when they finish. Finally, we will add the song to our playlist collection. If any exceptions occur along the way, we will post an error to the console. If we are running in debug mode, the message will also appear in the debug output window.

The constructor and the AddSong method take care of setting up the jukebox. Now it is time to put the jukebox to work. We will need several methods to control the playing of the songs stored within the jukebox. The Play method (shown in Listing 9-7) will start the current song playing. The current song is initially the first song stored in the playlist. Before we try to play the song, we need to make sure that the current song index is a valid value. The only time it might not be is if no songs have been loaded into the jukebox.

Listing 9-7. Jukebox Play Method

```
public void Play()
{
    if ( current_song < playlist.Count )
    {
        Music song = (Music)(playlist[current_song]);
        song.Volume = volume;
        song.Play();
    }
}
```

Assuming that the current song index is valid, we need to get a copy of the class's reference from the collection. The collections hold all objects as instances of the general Object base class. This requires that we cast the object back to the proper type before we do anything with it. Once we have the song, we will set its volume to the jukebox volume. This allows the game to set the master volume for all songs in one place. Typically this would be an option screen that is accessed before the game is started or possibly even while the game is in play. Since it is possible for the volume to change at any time, we will reset the song's volume each time the song is started. We will then command the song to start playing itself.

There may be times when the person writing the game does not want a song playing. The Stop method (shown in Listing 9-8) provides the means for stopping whatever song is currently playing. This method is just an alias for the Next method shown in Listing 9-9.

Listing 9-8. Jukebox Stop Method

```
public void Stop()
{
    Next();
}
```

Listing 9-9. Jukebox Next Method

```
public void Next()
{
    Music song = (Audio)(playlist[current_song]);
    song.Stop();
    song.SeekCurrentPosition(0.0, SeekPositionFlags.AbsolutePositioning );
    current_song++;
    if ( current_song >= playlist.Count )
    {
        current_song = 0;
    }
}
```

The Next method obtains a reference to the song that is currently playing. It stops that song and resets the current playing position within the song back to the beginning. This is to ensure that the song is ready to play again next time it comes around in the playlist. The current song index is incremented and checked to see if it has been advanced past the end of the playlist. If the method has passed the end of the collection, it is reset back to the first song in the list. When this method is used as the Stop method, it not only stops the current song, but also prepares to play the next song in the list the next time the Play command is issued.

The ClipEnded event handler (shown in Listing 9-10) is called each time the current song finishes. The handler calls the Next method to reset the song that just completed. It then calls the Play method to start the next song in the playlist.

Since all songs in the playlist have registered for this handler, calling `Play` on the first song is all that is required to keep music playing for the entire time that the game is being played.

Listing 9-10. Jukebox ClipEnded Event Handler

```
private void ClipEnded(object sender, System.EventArgs e)
{
    Next();
    Play();
}
```

The final method in the `Jukebox` class is the `Dispose` method shown in Listing 9-11. Since each instance of the `Music` class is disposable, we need to call the `Dispose` method for each one. We will use the `foreach` command to iterate through the collection and call each song's `Dispose` method.

Listing 9-11. Jukebox Dispose Method

```
public void Dispose()
{
    foreach (Music song in playlist )
    {
        song.Dispose();
    }
}
}
```

Hearing in Three Dimensions

The `Music` class has the ability to play the WAV files that are typically used for sound effects within a game. Unfortunately, there is limited control over the audio that can be played this way. The Audio class that we used for the music has the ability to manually change the volume and the balance through method calls. Using this capability to control sound effects would be incredibly painful. Microsoft provides a better solution using the classes within the DirectSound namespace.

DirectSound provides the concept of three-dimensional sound. By defining the position of the object listening for the sounds, and the positions of the objects generating sounds, the DirectSound classes have the ability to mix multiple sounds into a single buffer with the balance and volume of each sound appropriate for the relative position. The DirectSound documentation gives a detailed explanation on how three-dimensional sound works. We will concentrate on how we can take advantage of the capabilities that it gives us.

Listening for Noise

The first half of the equation is the ability to listen for the sounds that we will be making. All listening will take place wherever the player is within the game. It is important that there only be one active listener at any point in time. We will provide a `Listener` class that encapsulates all of the required functionality. The game application will create and hold one copy of this class.

The attributes and properties that define our `Listener` class are shown in Listing 9-12. This class has three attributes that hold the required information for the class. The first is an instance of `Listener3DSettings` that holds the parameters, defining the way in which the class will be able to listen. The second is an instance of `Listener3D` that is the actual buffer within which the sounds will be mixed. The third is a reference to `Object3D` that defines the position and orientation of the listener at any point in time. There is also a static attribute holding the DirectSound device that will be shared with all of the sound effects. This ties the entire system together. A static property (`Device`) provides the access to this attribute by other classes.

Listing 9-12. Listener Class Attributes and Properties

```
using System;
using System.Drawing;
using Microsoft.DirectX;
using Microsoft.DirectX.DirectSound;
using Sound = Microsoft.DirectX.DirectSound;
using Buffer = Microsoft.DirectX.DirectSound.Buffer;

namespace GameEngine
{
    /// <summary>
    /// Summary description for Listener
    /// </summary>
    public class Listener : IDisposable
    {

        #region Attributes
        private Sound.Listener3DSettings listenerParameters =
                    new Sound.Listener3DSettings();
        private Sound.Listener3D applicationListener = null;
        private Object3D m_listener = null;
```

```
private static Sound.Device applicationDevice = new Sound.Device();
#endregion

#region Properties
public static Sound.Device Device { get { return applicationDevice; } }
#endregion
```

The constructor for the Listener class (shown in Listing 9-13) is a vital part of the class. This class is largely passive. It defines the properties and capabilities of the listener and collects and mixes the sounds as they occur. The arguments of the constructor are the reference to a Windows Form and to the object that we will be listening from. We need the Windows Form in order to create the DirectSound device. All of the DirectX devices need knowledge of the main application's form so that they can receive Windows messages and have knowledge of the current state of the application.

Listing 9-13. Listener Class Constructor

```
public Listener(System.Windows.Forms.Form form, Object3D object_listening)
{
    m_listener = object_listening;
    Sound.BufferDescription description = new Sound.BufferDescription();
    Sound.WaveFormat fmt = new Sound.WaveFormat();
    description.PrimaryBuffer = true;
    description.Control3D = true;
    Sound.Buffer buff    = null;

    fmt.FormatTag = Sound.WaveFormatTag.Pcm;
    fmt.Channels = 2;
    fmt.SamplesPerSecond = 22050;
    fmt.BitsPerSample = 16;
    fmt.BlockAlign = (short)(fmt.BitsPerSample / 8 * fmt.Channels);
    fmt.AverageBytesPerSecond = fmt.SamplesPerSecond * fmt.BlockAlign;

    applicationDevice.SetCooperativeLevel( form,
            Sound.CooperativeLevel.Priority);

    // Get the primary buffer and set the format.
    buff = new Buffer(description, Device);
    buff.Format = fmt;

    applicationListener = new Listener3D(buff);
    listenerParameters = applicationListener.AllParameters;
}
```

The BufferDescription and WaveFormat classes provide the means of configuring the DirectSound device. The description defines how the sound buffer will be used, and the format defines how the data in the buffer will be organized. It is important that the format defined for this buffer matches the formats used in the sound effect files. DirectSound will be mixing the active sounds into this buffer. If the formats differ between the buffer in the Listener object and the buffer in the SoundEffect object, the mixing software is forced to perform additional manipulation of the source data before it can be mixed into the Listener object's buffer. This will adversely affect our game's performance.

We will designate the Listener object's buffer as the primary buffer on the sound card and flag that we will be using the buffer for three-dimensional sound. If performance is a problem or three-dimensional sound is not appropriate for the games that the engine will be used for, we could set this to false. The format settings shown in the example code are common for WAV files and produce reasonable quality.

We will set the cooperative level for the sound at the priority level. This gives our device priority for the sound hardware whenever our game application has the focus. If the application loses the focus, it will surrender the device to the application that has gained focus. The actual Listener object's buffer is created using the DirectSound device and the description that we set up earlier. The buffer is supplied with the format description and is passed to the Listener3D class for final construction. The final step is to get a reference to the configuration parameters for the Listener3D class. These parameters provide the means of controlling the position and orientation of the listener.

The dynamic portion of the Listener class is held within the Update method shown in Listing 9-14. Assuming that an Object3D instance was supplied, we will be able to update the position and orientation of our listener. The position is easy. We can just set the listener position to that of the object that we are attached to. The orientation is a bit more complicated. The listener requires a pair of vectors that define the orientation. One vector is the front vector that defines the direction in which the listener is looking. The second is the top vector that defines which way is up. Although these vectors exist for the camera that is usually attached to the player, we will not assume that this is always the case. To calculate the vectors that we need, we start with two unit vectors. One vector is in the Z direction that is the untransformed front vector. The other is a unit vector in the Y direction for the untransformed top vector. Rotating these vectors for the actual orientation of the object will require a rotation matrix. We can create this using the object's attitude and the RotationYawPitchRoll method of the Matrix class. The TransformCoordinate method of the Vector3 class takes care of multiplying the vector and the matrix and producing the new vectors that are passed to the listener. The application of the new listener parameters is held until we flag that we have finished changing parameters. The CommitDeferredSettings method notifies the listener that we are done.

Listing 9-14. Listener Update Method

```
public void Update()
{
   if ( m_listener != null )
   {
      listenerParameters.Position = m_listener.Position;

      Vector3 front = new Vector3( 0.0f, 0.0f, 1.0f );
      Vector3 top   = new Vector3( 0.0f, 1.0f, 0.0f );
      Matrix transform = Matrix.RotationYawPitchRoll(
         m_listener.Attitude.Heading,
         m_listener.Attitude.Pitch,
         m_listener.Attitude.Roll);

      listenerParameters.OrientFront =
         Vector3.TransformCoordinate( front, transform );
      listenerParameters.OrientTop   =
         Vector3.TransformCoordinate( top, transform );
   }
   applicationListener.CommitDeferredSettings();
}
```

That is everything we need for the Listener class aside from cleaning up after ourselves. The Dispose method (shown in Listing 9-15) handles this cleanup by disposing of both the listener and the DirectSound device.

Listing 9-15. Listener Dispose Method

```
public void Dispose()
{
   applicationListener.Dispose();
   applicationDevice.Dispose();
}
   }
}
```

Making Noise in Three Dimensions

So far, we have prepared to listen to three-dimensional sound. Now it is time to make noise. For some reason Microsoft decided to refer to the structure holding the sounds that will be played as SecondaryBuffer. While this may hold some reasoning somewhere in the history of DirectX, it is not a very descriptive name. We will encapsulate all of the pieces required to make three-dimensional sound into the SoundEffect class.

NOTE *In order for three-dimensional sound to work, all WAV files used must be mono rather than stereo. The three-dimensional algorithms built into the Buffer3D class will determine how loud this sound will be in each speaker. Chapter 11 will identify utilities to convert stereo sound files into the mono format.*

The SecondaryBuffer's soundBuffer holds the WAV file that we will be using. In order to be three dimensional, we need to wrap this buffer with a Buffer3D object. This adds the three-dimensional capability. Just like in our listener, all sound effects will be tied to an object to provide the source position for each effect. The class will also remember the file that the sound was loaded from in case we need to reload the sound.

Some of the advantages of using these DirectSound classes for sound effects over the Audio class include some powerful low-level control over the sounds. Rather than having to catch a completion event and restart a sound to have it loop, we can provide a looping flag when a sound is played. When this flag is set, the sound will continue to play until explicitly stopped. For some sounds, we may also wish to modify the frequency of a sound while it is playing. The sound our engine makes, for example, will change in frequency as a function of the engine speed. To facilitate this capability, we will provide a minimum and maximum valid frequency as well as a floating-point current frequency value where zero represents the minimum frequency and a one represents the maximum frequency. Values in between zero and one will be linearly interpolated between these extremes. The final parameter is a static integer that is shared among all sound effects. This is the master volume for sound effects. Just like how the volume within the jukebox works across all songs, this volume can be used to control all sound effects.

The attributes for the SoundEffect class are shown in Listing 9-16. These attributes include the buffers used in playing the sound as well the attributes we will need to adjust the volume and frequency of the sound.

Listing 9-16. SoundEffect Attributes

```
using System;
using System.Drawing;
using Microsoft.DirectX;
using Microsoft.DirectX.DirectSound;
using Sound = Microsoft.DirectX.DirectSound;
using Buffer = Microsoft.DirectX.DirectSound.Buffer;
```

```
namespace GameEngine
{
    /// <summary>
    /// Summary description for SoundEffect
    /// </summary>
    public class SoundEffect : IDisposable
    {
        #region Attributes
        private SecondaryBuffer soundBuffer = null;
        private Buffer3D soundBuffer3D = null;
        private Object3D m_source = null;
        private string m_FileName;
        private bool looping = false;
        private int min_freq = 22050;
        private int max_freq = 22050;
        private float current_freq = 0.0f;

        private static int master_volume = 0;
        #endregion
```

The SoundEffect class will expose a number of properties (shown in Listing 9-17) to provide programmatic control of the effects. The first three are read/write properties to provide access to the looping flag and the frequency range for the sound. The property for the current frequency is also read/write but includes logic in the set function to ensure that the value is clamped within the proper range of values. The DirectSound classes have the concept of a minimum and maximum range. Any sound within the minimum range between the sound source and the listener will be at its maximum value. Any sound that is further than the maximum range from the listener will not be heard at all. These ranges default to a minimum range of 1 and a maximum range of 100,000,000. Since the default value for maximum range is so large, it is a good idea to set this for each sound as it is loaded to improve performance.

Listing 9-17. SoundEffect Properties

```
        #region Properties
        public bool Looping { set { looping = value; } get { return looping; } }
        public int  MinFreq { set { min_freq = value; } get { return min_freq; } }
        public int  MaxFreq { set { max_freq = value; } get { return max_freq; } }
        public float Frequency {
            set {
                current_freq = value;
                if ( current_freq > 1.0 ) current_freq = 1.0f;
```

```
        if ( current_freq < 0.0 ) current_freq = 0.0f;
    } get { return current_freq; } }
  public float  MinDistance { set { soundBuffer3D.MinDistance = value; }
                                get { return soundBuffer3D.MinDistance; } }
  public float  MaxDistance { set { soundBuffer3D.MaxDistance = value; }
                                get { return soundBuffer3D.MaxDistance; } }

  public static float Volume {
    set { master_volume = (int)(-4000 * (1.0f - value)); } }

  private static int MasterVolume { get { return master_volume; } }
  #endregion
```

We will provide two static properties for the volume. The first property is a write-only property that allows the user to set the master volume to a floating-point value between zero and one as we did for the music and jukebox. The second property is private, which limits its use to within this class. This is the property that will be used to retrieve the integer attenuation value that actually controls sound volume.

The constructor for the SoundEffect class (shown in Listing 9-18) is fairly simple. It saves the sound file's path to the m_FileName attribute and calls the LoadSoundFile to actually perform the file loading. Since we may need to reload the sound at a later point, it is better to encapsulate this functionality in a separate private method.

Listing 9-18. SoundEffect Constructor

```
  public SoundEffect( string FileName)
  {
    m_FileName = FileName;
    LoadSoundFile();
  }
```

The implementation of the LoadSoundFile method is shown in Listing 9-19. Just as the Listener class has a description class to define its properties, SoundEffect has such a class as well. We can use a number of different algorithms to process sounds for three-dimensional representation. The four choices for the algorithms can be found in the DirectSound documentation. We will use Guid3DalgorithmHrtfLight, which provides a good middle of the road between performance and sound quality. We will also set flags within the description to indicate that we want three-dimensional processing and that we may also be modifying both frequency and volume.

Listing 9-19. SoundEffect LoadSoundFile Method

```
private void LoadSoundFile()
{
    BufferDescription description = new BufferDescription();

    description.Guid3DAlgorithm = DSoundHelper.Guid3DAlgorithmHrtfLight;
    description.Control3D = true;
    description.ControlFrequency = true;
    description.ControlVolume = true;

    if (null != soundBuffer)
    {
        soundBuffer.Stop();
        soundBuffer.SetCurrentPosition(0);
    }

    // Load the wave file into a DirectSound buffer.
    try
    {
        soundBuffer = new SecondaryBuffer(m_FileName, description,
                Listener.Device);
        soundBuffer3D = new Buffer3D(soundBuffer);
    }
    catch ( Exception e )
    {
        GameEngine.Console.AddLine("Exception on loading " + m_FileName +
                ". Ensure file is Mono");
        GameEngine.Console.AddLine(e.Message);
    }

    if (WaveFormatTag.Pcm != (WaveFormatTag.Pcm &
            description.Format.FormatTag))
    {
        GameEngine.Console.AddLine("Wave file must be PCM for 3D control.");
        if (null != soundBuffer)
            soundBuffer.Dispose();
        soundBuffer = null;
    }
}
```

It is possible that this method may be called after the class has been created. If a sound buffer already exists, we will ensure that the sound is not playing before we continue. To actually load the sound from the file, we will create a new secondary buffer using the filename, description, and the DirectSound device created for the Listener. The Buffer3D is generated using this buffer. If the loading fails for any reason (such as the method being unable to find the file or an incorrect file type), an exception will be thrown and a message displayed on the console.

If the file was successfully loaded, we must check the format of the sound data. We can't control the sound in three dimensions unless it is in PCM format. This won't tend to be a problem, since this is the most common WAV file format. If the data is not in PCM format, we will post a message to the console. If we have a sound buffer, we will dispose of it and set the reference to null.

It is possible that during the course of the game, the game application may lose focus and the sound buffer may be lost. The private RestoreBuffer method (shown in Listing 9-20) will check to see if this has happened. If the buffer has not been lost, it will simply return a false to flag the calling method that everything is fine. If the buffer was lost, though, we need to restore the buffer before proceeding. We will loop and call the Restore method of the buffer until the BufferLost flag is cleared. We then return a true so that the calling method will know that the file needs to be reloaded.

Listing 9-20. SoundEffect RestoreBuffer Method

```
private bool RestoreBuffer()
{
    if (false == soundBuffer.Status.BufferLost)
        return false;

    while(true == soundBuffer.Status.BufferLost)
    {
        soundBuffer.Restore();
    }
    return true;
}
```

The sounds are activated using the PlaySound method shown in Listing 9-21. The BufferPlayFlags enumeration defines the choices that may be made when playing a sound. We will be concerned with two of the values of the enumeration. If we are not looping, we will take the default settings for playing the sound. Otherwise, we will use the Looping flag in the enumeration. Before playing the sound, we need to ensure that the buffer is still valid. We will call the RestoreBuffer method that we described earlier. If it returns a true value, then we must reload the sound file. We will also ensure that the position within the buffer is set back to

the beginning in case there is leftover data for the buffer position. The Play
method of the buffer starts the sound playing. If an exception occurs at any
point in this procedure, we will post a message to the console.

Listing 9-21. SoundEffect PlaySound Method

```
public void PlaySound()
{
    try
    {
        BufferPlayFlags flags;
        if ( looping )
        {
            flags = BufferPlayFlags.Looping;
        }
        else
        {
            flags = BufferPlayFlags.Default;
        }

        if (RestoreBuffer())
        {
            LoadSoundFile();
            soundBuffer.SetCurrentPosition(0);
        }
        soundBuffer.Play(0, flags);
    }
    catch ( Exception e )
    {
        GameEngine.Console.AddLine("Exception on playing " + m_FileName);
        GameEngine.Console.AddLine(e.Message);
    }
}
```

Normally, we will let sounds continue until they have finished on their own.
This only works, of course, if we are not looping the sound. For sounds that we
might wish to terminate early or are looping, we include a method to stop the
sound. The StopSound method (shown in Listing 9-22) commands the buffer to
stop playing and resets the position within the buffer back to the beginning. This
prepares the sound for reactivation in the future.

Listing 9-22. SoundEffect StopSound Method

```
public void StopSound()
{
    soundBuffer.Stop();
    soundBuffer.SetCurrentPosition(0);
}
```

Just as the Listener class has an Update method to refresh the position of the listener, the sound effect needs a similar method (shown in Listing 9-23). The code within the method will be wrapped in a Try/Catch block to protected against exceptions during the update procedure. We will begin by calculating the range of frequencies between the minimum and maximum values. If the range is nonzero, then this sound has a varying frequency. We will calculate the value for this point in time by interpolating between the values in the range based on the current_freq value. We will also copy the master volume into the buffers volume. Finally, if a source object has been defined, we will set the buffer's position to that of the object.

Listing 9-23. SoundEffect Update Method

```
public void Update()
{
    try
    {
        int freq_range = max_freq - min_freq;
        int freq_now;

        if ( freq_range > 0 )
        {
            soundBuffer.Frequency =
                min_freq + (int)(freq_range * current_freq);
        }

        soundBuffer.Volume = MasterVolume;

        if ( m_source != null )
        {
            soundBuffer3D.Position = m_source.Position;
        }
```

```
        }
        catch ( Exception e )
        {
            GameEngine.Console.AddLine("Exception while updating " + m_FileName);
            GameEngine.Console.AddLine(e.Message);
        }
    }
}
```

The `Dispose` method for the `SoundEffect` class (shown in Listing 9-24) has two attributes that need to be disposed. One is the sound buffer and the other is the `Buffer3D`.

Listing 9-24. SoundEffect Dispose Method

```
    public void Dispose()
    {
        soundBuffer.Dispose();
        soundBuffer3D.Dispose();
    }
  }
}
```

Putting 3D Sound to Work in a Game

We have completely defined the two classes that we will need for three-dimensional sound. To use these classes, we will employ two excerpts from the `Ownship` class in the game application. The first excerpt (shown in Listing 9-25) is from the `Ownship` class constructor. We instantiate a copy of the `Listener` class attached to our `Ownship` vehicle. There will be three sound effects related to this vehicle. The first will be our engine sound. This will be a variable frequency effect that loops. You will see that we create the sound with our base idle sound and set the looping flag and the frequency range. Two different sounds are created for two different types of crash events. The thump sound will represent hitting minor objects that do not damage the vehicle. The crash sound is for collisions that will cause damage.

Listing 9-25. Ownship Class Constructor Excerpt

```
        ears = new Listener(form, this);
        engine_sound = new SoundEffect("car_idle.wav");
        engine_sound.Looping = true;
```

```
engine_sound.MinFreq = 9700;
engine_sound.MaxFreq = 13500;
thump = new SoundEffect("thump.wav");
crash = new SoundEffect("crash.wav");
```

The second excerpt (shown in Listing 9-26) is from the Update method of the Ownship class. This is where we will update the listener and active effects. If this is the first time the Update method has been called, we start the engine sound. The listener's Update method is called and the engine sound's frequency is updated based on the current throttle setting, and its Update method is called as well. Later in the Update method, there are checks to see if the vehicle has collided with anything. If the vehicle has collided with something, we will check the object's name to see what it was that we hit. If we hit one of the red or blue marker posts or the small cactus, we will trigger the thump sound. Collision with any other objects (vehicles or palm trees) will trigger the crash sound.

Listing 9-26. Ownship Class Update Method Excerpt

```
if ( first_pass )
{
   first_pass = false;
   engine_sound.PlaySound();
}

ears.Update();

engine_sound.Frequency = Gas;
engine_sound.Update();

if ( Collide(test_obj) )
{
   if ( test_obj.Name.Substring(0,3) == "red"   ||
        test_obj.Name.Substring(0,4) == "blue" ||
        test_obj.Name.Substring(0,6) == "cactus" )
   {
      thump.PlaySound();
   }
   else
   {
      crash.PlaySound();
   }
}
```

Summary

This chapter has covered the different ways in which audio is used within a game. The Music class provides the means for playing a single song. The Jukebox class takes this a step further by holding a collection of Music entries and cycling between them for a complete soundtrack to the game. We also defined the Listener and SoundEffect classes, which provide everything that is needed within a game for three-dimensional sound effects.

CHAPTER 10

Game Physics: Keeping It Real

ONE THING THAT CAN MAKE or break the believability of a game is the physics implementation. Physics is the science of the physical world. It provides the mathematical representation of all dynamic objects. Through this math, we can determine how an object should move realistically.

This chapter will explore two applications of physics. The first is the dynamics involved within an automobile. This will include the interactions between the wheels, the ground, and the suspension, which, coupled with a simulation of an engine and transmission, provides a simple but believable simulation of a car for our racing game.

The second application of physics for our game engine will be an example of the physics of cloth. The math behind the simulation of cloth may be applied to flexible systems within a game such as flags, clothing, hair, and even grass. We will apply this type of physics to a rectangular section of cloth for use as a flag that flutters as the force of wind passing along it interacts with the cloth.

Physics is an extensive and diverse subject. We can only touch on a small part of the subject in this chapter. Entire books have been devoted to this subject, and additional books and online resources for physics can be found by searching the Web. A recent online search for "game physics" returned over 2000 entries. Another search for "vehicle dynamics" returned over 14,000 entries. If you are serious about applying physics within your games, I highly recommend that you think of this text as simply a springboard and that you do further research into this vast subject. For instance, one of the many links that I have found takes you to an interesting article that explains the physics behind the ballistics of a projectile (http://www.pixelate.co.za/issues/3/3/articles/game_physics/intro.htm).

Looking at Vehicle Dynamics

Vehicle dynamics is the subset of physics concerning the motion of vehicles (planes, trains, automobiles, boats, etc.) through space as well as how they interact with other objects. Other objects include the medium that they are moving through or on as well as anything that they might collide with. The mathematics involves the mass of the vehicle as well as the forces that act upon the vehicle.

NOTE *You might remember from high school physics class that mass is not the same as weight. Weight is the force that mass exerts when the acceleration of gravity is applied.*

The key equation of motion in physics is the basic force equation that follows and its derivatives. In order to make an object move from one location to another in a realistic manner, we must apply forces to the object. Those forces create an acceleration of the object along some vector. By integrating the acceleration we can determine the object's new velocity, and by integrating the velocity we can determine a change in position.

Force = Mass * Acceleration

Acceleration = Force / Mass

Multiple forces will be involved in our vehicle dynamics. Gravity will apply a downward force on our vehicle. Assuming that the vehicle's tires are in contact with the terrain, an upward force will be applied to the tires by the ground surface. When the engine is causing the tires to rotate, a frictional force between the tires and the ground will create a linear force that will serve to accelerate or decelerate the vehicle. As the vehicle moves through the air, the friction between the vehicle and the air will create a drag force that serves to limit the vehicle's maximum speed. As we proceed through the chapter, we will address these forces as well as others to develop a basic dynamics model for our game.

Defining Supporting Classes

Before we dive into the actual physics code, we need to look at a few support classes that will be used in the `CarDynamics` class. The `VehicleDynamics` assembly is a stand-alone library that will be used by the game engine. As such, it is designed to exist separately from DirectX and could be used just as easily with an OpenGL rendering engine. Because it was written this way, we will need to redefine two classes that we have been working with in the game engine.

Redefining the Vector Class

The first of these classes is the `Vector` class. Within the game engine we were able to rely on the Vector3 class that comes with DirectX 9. Listing 10-1 contains the entire definition of the `Vector` class that is used within this library. Within the vehicle dynamics library, we will work almost exclusively with double-precision floating-point variables. The mathematics of physics tend to rely on a greater level of precision than we find necessary within the game engine itself.

I will not be describing the class in Listing 10-1 to the same level of detail that I've used for the game engine. Suffice it to say that the class holds three doubles and provides a number of properties and methods for manipulating the three values as a vector. It is included here for completeness. Although you could enter all of this code manually from the book, I urge you instead to download all of the sample code from the Apress Web site (http://www.apress.com).

Listing 10-1. Vector Class

```
using System;

namespace VehicleDynamics
{
    public class  Vector
    {

        public    Vector() {x=0.0; y=0.0; z=0.0;}
        public    Vector ( Vector other ) {x-other.x; y-other.y; z-other.z;}
        public    Vector ( double new_x, double new_y, double new_z )
        {x=new_x; y=new_y; z=new_z;}
        ~Vector () {}

        // Operator functions
        public static bool operator <( Vector first, Vector second )
        {
            return (first.x < second.x && first.y < second.y && first.z < second.z);
        }
        public static bool operator >( Vector first, Vector second )
        {
            return (first.x > second.x && first.y > second.y && first.z > second.z);
        }
        public   static  bool operator ==(Vector first, Vector second )
        {
            return first.x==second.x && first.y==second.y && first.z==second.z;
        }
        public   bool Equals( Vector second )
        {
            return x==second.x && y==second.y && z==second.z;
        }
    }
```

```
public  static  bool operator !=(Vector first, Vector second )
{
   return first.x!=second.x || first.y!=second.y || first.z!=second.z;
}

public  static  Vector operator -(Vector first)
{
   return new Vector(-first.x, -first.y, -first.z);
}
public  static  Vector operator - (Vector first, Vector second)
{
   return new Vector(first.x - second.x, first.y - second.y,
         first.z - second.z);
}
public  static  Vector operator + (Vector first, Vector second)
{
   return new Vector(first.x + second.x, first.y + second.y,
         first.z + second.z);}
public  static  Vector operator / (Vector first, float value)
{
   return new Vector(first.x/value, first.y/value, first.z/value);
}
public  static  Vector operator * (Vector first, float value)
{
   return new Vector(first.x*value, first.y*value, first.z*value);
}
public  static  double operator * (Vector first, Vector second)
{
   return (first.x*second.x + first.y*second.y + first.z*second.z);
}

// Accessor functions
public double X  { get {return x;} set { x = value; } }
public double Y  { get {return y;} set { y = value; } }
public double Z  { get {return z;} set { z = value; } }

// Set functions
public    Vector Set ( double new_x, double new_y, double new_z )
{
   x= new_x; y= new_y; z= new_z; return this;
}
public    Vector SetX ( double new_x )
```

```
{
   x= new_x; return this;
}
public    Vector SetY ( double new_y )
{
   y= new_y; return this;
}
public    Vector SetZ ( double new_z )
{
   z= new_z; return this;
}
public    Vector SetToZero ()
{
   x= 0; y= 0; z= 0; return this;
}

// Limiting functions
public    Vector Limit( Vector value, Vector limit )
{
   return new Vector( Math.Min( limit.X, Math.Max( limit.X, value.X) ),
      Math.Min( limit.Y, Math.Max( limit.Y, value.Y) ),
      Math.Min( limit.Z, Math.Max( limit.Z, value.Z) ) );}

public    Vector Limit ( Vector limit )
{
   LimitX( limit.X );
   LimitY( limit.Y );
   LimitZ( limit.Z ); return this;
}

public    double LimitX ( double min_value, double max_value )
{
   return Math.Min( max_value, Math.Max( min_value, x) );
}
public    double LimitX ( double value )
{
   return Math.Min( value, Math.Max( -value, x) );
}
public    double LimitY ( double min_value, double max_value )
{
   return Math.Min( max_value, Math.Max( min_value, y) );
}
```

```
public    double LimitY ( double value )
{
   return Math.Min( value, Math.Max( -value, y) );
}
public    double LimitZ ( double min_value, double max_value )
{
   return Math.Min( max_value, Math.Max( min_value, z) );
}
public    double LimitZ ( double value )
{
   return Math.Min( value, Math.Max( -value, z) );
}

public    Vector Delta ( Vector from )
{
   return new Vector(x - from.x, y - from.y, z - from.z);
}
public    double DeltaX ( Vector from )
{
   return x - from.x;
}
public    double DeltaY ( Vector from )
{
   return y - from.y;
}
public    double DeltaZ ( Vector from )
{
   return z - from.z;
}
public    Vector ABSDelta ( Vector from )
{
   return new Vector(Math.Abs(x - from.x), Math.Abs(y - from.y),
         Math.Abs(z - from.z));
}
public    double ABSDeltaX ( Vector from )
{
   return Math.Abs(x - from.x);
}
public    double ABSDeltaY ( Vector from )
{
   return Math.Abs(y - from.y);
}
```

```
public    double ABSDeltaZ ( Vector from )
{
   return Math.Abs(z - from.z);
}


protected double x;
protected double y;
protected double z;


private double DistanceFrom ( Vector from )
{
   return Math.Sqrt((x-from.x)*(x-from.x) + (y-from.y)*(y-from.y) +
          (z-from.z)*(z-from.z));

}

public double otherXYDistanceFrom ( Vector from )
{
   return Math.Sqrt((x-from.x)*(x-from.x) + (y-from.y)*(y-from.y));
}

public double otherDistanceFrom ()
{
   return Math.Sqrt( (x*x) + (y*y) + (z*z) );
}

public double DistanceFrom ( )
{
   return Math.Sqrt( (x*x) + (y*y) + (z*z) );
}

public double XYDistanceFrom ( Vector from )
{
   return Math.Sqrt((x-from.x)*(x-from.x) + (y-from.y)*(y-from.y));
}

public double XYDistanceFrom ()
{
   return Math.Sqrt( (x*x) + (y*y) );
}
```

```
public double otherXYDistanceFrom ()
{
   return Math.Sqrt( (x*x) + (y*y) );
}

public Vector Normalize ()
{
   float temp = (float)Math.Sqrt(x*x + y*y + z*z);
   if ( temp != 0.0f )
      return new Vector( x/temp, y/temp, z/temp );

   return new Vector (0.0f, 0.0f, 0.0f );

}

Vector CrossProduct ( Vector that)
{
   return new Vector(y*that.z - z*that.y, z*that.x - x*that.z,
         x*that.y - y*that.x);
}

public double otherElevBrg ( Vector other )
{
   double xy_length= XYDistanceFrom( other );
   double elev_brg= Math.Atan2( DeltaZ( other ), xy_length );

   while ( elev_brg > Math.PI ) elev_brg -= Math.PI;
   while ( elev_brg < -Math.PI ) elev_brg += Math.PI;

   return elev_brg;

}

public double otherRelBrg ( Vector other )
{
   return Math.Atan2( Y-other.Y, X-other.X );
}

bool otherIsParallelWith ( Vector other )
{
   return CrossProduct(other) == new Vector(0.0f, 0.0f, 0.0f);
}
```

```
    public void IncrementX(double value)
    {
       x += value;
    }

    public void IncrementY(double value)
    {
       y += value;
    }

    public void IncrementZ(double value)
    {
       z += value;
    }

  };
}
```

Redefining the Attitude Class

The second class that is somewhat a redefinition from the game engine is the
Euler class, which is an expansion of the Attitude structure used within the game
engine. This class holds not only the heading, pitch, and roll values (psi, theta, and
phi), but also the sines and cosines of these values as well as a rotation matrix
based on these values. The goal of this class is to be as efficient as possible and to
take advantage of the interrelations between the angular values and the methods
that rely on them. That is why the trigonometric values and the rotation matrix are
included within the class. Rather than rebuild the matrix each pass based on the
latest angular information, it can check a flag to see if the matrix is current. The
rotation matrix is only recalculated if an angle has changed and the flag has been
cleared indicating that the matrix needs to be recalculated. The same holds true
with the sine and cosine of each angle. Rather than calling the computationally
expensive trigonometric functions every pass, they are called only when the associated angle is modified.

Listing 10-2 is the complete Euler class. Because it is a support class that is
not specific to the game engine, I will not go into a more complete explanation
of this code. All of the properties and methods within this class are quite simple
and should be readily understandable. The only methods that are not obvious at
a glance might be the AEPCPI methods, which are angle end-point check methods
that maintain an angle between zero and two pi.

Listing 10-2. Euler Class

```csharp
using System;

namespace VehicleDynamics
{
    public class Euler
    {

        private  double   psi;
        private  double   theta;
        private  double   phi;
        private  double   cpsi;
        private  double   ctheta;
        private  double   cphi;
        private  double   spsi;
        private  double   stheta;
        private  double   sphi;
        private     double[,]   mat = new double[3,3];
        private     bool    matrix_current;

        // The default class constructor
        public    Euler() {psi = 0.0; theta=0.0; phi=0.0;}

        // A constructor that accepts three floats defining the angles
        public    Euler(double x_psi, double x_theta, double x_phi )
        {Psi = x_psi; Theta=x_theta; Phi=x_phi;}

        // A copy constructor
        public    Euler (
           Euler x_angle
           ) {psi = x_angle.Psi; theta=x_angle.Theta; phi=x_angle.Phi;}

        // The class destructor
        ~Euler () {}

        // Calculates the difference between two copies of the class
        public    Euler Delta ( Euler from    )
        { return new Euler( psi - from.psi, theta - from.theta, phi - from.phi ); }

        public    double DeltaPsi ( Euler from    )
        { return psi - from.psi; }
```

```
public    double DeltaTheta (  Euler from   )
{ return theta - from.theta; }

public    double DeltaPhi (  Euler from   )
   { return phi - from.phi; }

public    Euler ABSDelta (  Euler from   )
   { return new Euler( Math.Abs(psi - from.psi),
   Math.Abs(theta - from.theta),
   Math.Abs(phi - from.phi) ); }

public    double ABSDeltaPsi (  Euler from   )
   { return Math.Abs(psi - from.psi); }

public    double ABSDeltaTheta (  Euler from   )
   { return Math.Abs(theta - from.theta); }

public    double ABSDeltaPhi (  Euler from   )
   { return Math.Abs(phi - from.phi); }

public  static  Euler operator * (Euler first, float value)
{return new Euler(first.psi*value, first.theta*value, first.phi*value);}
public  static  Euler operator + (Euler first, Euler second)
{return new Euler(first.psi+second.psi, first.theta+second.theta,
         first.phi+second.phi);}

// Accessor functions
public    double Psi
{
   get {return psi;}
   set
   {
      matrix_current = psi == value;
      psi = value;
      cpsi=(float)Math.Cos(psi);
      spsi=(float)Math.Sin(psi);
   }
}
public    double Theta
{
   get {return theta;}
   set
```

```
        {
           matrix_current = theta == value;
           theta = value;
           ctheta=(float)Math.Cos(theta);
           stheta=(float)Math.Sin(theta);
        }
     }
     public      double Phi
     {
        get {return phi;}
        set
        {
           matrix_current = phi == value;
           phi = value;
           cphi=(float)Math.Cos(phi);
           sphi=(float)Math.Sin(phi);
        }
     }
     public      double cosPsi { get {return cpsi;} }
     public      double cosTheta { get {return ctheta;} }
     public      double cosPhi { get {return cphi;} }
     public      double sinPsi { get {return spsi;} }
     public      double sinTheta { get {return stheta;} }
     public      double sinPhi { get {return sphi;} }
     public      double PsiAsDegrees { get {return (psi*180.0/Math.PI);} }
     public      double ThetaAsDegrees { get {return (theta*180.0/Math.PI);} }
     public      double PhiAsDegrees { get {return (phi*180.0/Math.PI);} }

     // Set functions
     public    Euler SetToZero () {psi= 0; theta= 0; phi= 0; return this;}
     //====================================================================
     public    Euler SetPsiAsDegrees (
        double x_psi
        ) {Psi = (x_psi*Math.PI/180.0); return this;}
     //====================================================================
     public    Euler SetThetaAsDegrees (
        double x_theta
        ) {Theta = (x_theta*Math.PI/180.0); return this;}
     //====================================================================
     public    Euler SetPhiAsDegrees (
        double x_phi
        ) {Phi = (x_phi*Math.PI/180.0); return this;}
     //====================================================================
     public    float AEPCPI( float angle)
```

```
{
    while ( angle > (Math.PI+Math.PI) )
        angle -= (float) (Math.PI+Math.PI);
    while ( angle < 0.0f )
        angle += (float) (Math.PI+Math.PI);
    return angle;
}
//=====================================================================
public   double AEPCPI( double angle)
{
    while ( angle > (Math.PI+Math.PI) )
        angle -= (float)Math.PI;
    while ( angle < 0.0 )
        angle += (Math.PI+Math.PI);
    return angle;
}
//=====================================================================
public void Limits ()
{
    // Flip heading and roll when we go over the top or through the bottom.
    if ( theta > (Math.PI/2.0) )
    {
        theta = Math.PI - Theta;
        psi = AEPCPI( Psi + Math.PI );
        phi = AEPCPI( Phi + Math.PI );
    }
    else if ( theta < -(Math.PI/2.0) )
    {
        theta = -Math.PI - Theta;
        psi = AEPCPI( Psi + Math.PI );
        phi = AEPCPI( Phi + Math.PI );
    }
    else
    {
        psi = AEPCPI( Psi );
        phi = AEPCPI( Phi );
    }

} // End Limits
//=====================================================================
public void Limits ( Euler results )
{
    // Flip heading and roll when we go over the top or through the bottom.
    if ( results.Theta > (Math.PI/2.0) )
```

```
      {
         theta = (float)Math.PI - results.Theta;
         psi = (float)AEPCPI( results.Psi + (float)Math.PI );
         phi = (float)AEPCPI( results.Phi + (float)Math.PI );
      }
      else if ( results.Theta < -(Math.PI/2.0) )
      {
         theta = -(float)Math.PI - results.Theta;
         psi = (float)AEPCPI( results.Psi + (float)Math.PI );
         phi = (float)AEPCPI( results.Phi + (float)Math.PI );
      }
      else
      {
         theta = results.Theta;
         psi = (float)AEPCPI( results.Psi );
         phi = (float)AEPCPI( results.Phi );
      }

   } // End Limits
   //=======================================================================
   public void Limits ( float x_psi, float x_theta, float x_phi )
   {
      // Flip heading and roll when we go over the top or through the bottom.
      if ( x_theta > (Math.PI/2.0) )
      {
         theta = (float)Math.PI - x_theta;
         psi = (float)AEPCPI( x_psi + Math.PI );
         phi = (float)AEPCPI( x_phi + Math.PI );
      }
      else if ( x_theta < -(Math.PI/2.0) )
      {
         theta = -(float)Math.PI - x_theta;
         psi = (float)AEPCPI( x_psi + Math.PI );
         phi = (float)AEPCPI( x_phi + Math.PI );
      }
      else
      {
         theta = x_theta;
         psi = (float)AEPCPI( x_psi );
         phi = (float)AEPCPI( x_phi );
      }
```

```
} // End Limits
//=====================================================================
public float AngularDifference( float ang1, float ang2 )
{
   float result;

   result = ang1 - ang2;

   if ( result < 0.0 )
   {
      result *= -1.0f;
   }

   return result;
}
//=====================================================================
public void RotateAtoE( Vector num )
{
   double[] temp = new double[3];

   if ( !matrix_current ) CalcMatrix();

   temp[0] = mat[0,0] * num.X + mat[0,1] * num.Y + mat[0,2] * num.Z;
   temp[1] = mat[1,0] * num.X + mat[1,1] * num.Y + mat[1,2] * num.Z;
   temp[2] = mat[2,0] * num.X + mat[2,1] * num.Y + mat[2,2] * num.Z;

   num.X = temp[0];
   num.Y = temp[1];
   num.Z = temp[2];
}
//=====================================================================
public void RotateEtoA( Vector num )
{
   double[] temp = new double[3];

   if ( !matrix_current ) CalcMatrix();

   temp[0] = mat[0,0] * num.X + mat[1,0] * num.Y + mat[2,0] * num.Z;
   temp[1] = mat[0,1] * num.X + mat[1,1] * num.Y + mat[2,1] * num.Z;
   temp[2] = mat[0,2] * num.X + mat[1,2] * num.Y + mat[2,2] * num.Z;
```

```
        num.X = temp[0];
        num.Y = temp[1];
        num.Z = temp[2];
    }
    //=========================================================================
    public void CalcMatrix()
    {
        mat[0,0] = ctheta * cpsi;
        mat[0,1] = sphi * stheta * cpsi - cphi * spsi;
        mat[0,2] = cphi * stheta * cpsi + sphi * spsi;

        mat[1,0] = ctheta * spsi;
        mat[1,1] = sphi * stheta * spsi + cphi * cpsi;
        mat[1,2] = cphi * stheta * spsi - sphi * cpsi;

        mat[2,0] = -stheta;
        mat[2,1] = sphi * ctheta;
        mat[2,2] = cphi * ctheta;

        matrix_current = true;
    }
};
}
```

Adding Support for Data Curves

There is one more support class to investigate before we get into the actual
dynamics code: the LFI class. LFI is short for linear function interpolation. At
times a calculation is based on physical information supplied in the form of
a data curve. Some sample uses for this can be found in coefficient of lift-and-
drag data versus angle of attack for flight equations of motion. We will use this
interpolation for the engine torque curve for our car dynamics.

Data points along the curve are supplied to the class with two values. The
class assumes that the index axis of the data curve is linear and based at zero,
with as many as 100 data points along this axis. In order to achieve these requirements, the class includes a slope and intercept value that may be set to scale the
index values into this range.

The code for this class is shown in Listing 10-3. To calculate the return value,
the input value is first scaled using the slope and offset. The integer portion of
this number is the index into the data table. The fractional portion of this number is the portion of the delta between this index value and the next.

Listing 10-3. LFI Class

```csharp
using System;

namespace VehicleDynamics
{
    ///<summary>
    ///Class for linear function interpolation
    ///</summary>
    public class LFI
    {
        private double[] data = new double[101];
        private double   slope = 1.0;
        private double   intercept = 0.0;

        public double Slope
        {
            get { return slope; }
            set { slope = value; }
        }
        public double Intercept
        {
            get { return intercept; }
            set { intercept = value; }
        }


    ///<summary>
    ///Method to place curve data into the class
    ///</summary>
    public bool SetDataPoint(double index_value, float data_point)
{
    bool result = false;
    int index = (int)(index_value / slope - intercept);

    if ( index >= 0 && index <= 100 )
    {
        data[index] = data_point;
        result = true;
    }
        return result;
    }
```

```
///<summary>
///Method to interpolate linearly to get a value from a data curve
///</summary>
public double Interpolate( double index_value )
{
    double delta;
    double result = 0.0;

    try
    {
        double scaled_value = index_value / slope - intercept;
        int index = (int)scaled_value;
        delta = data[index+1] - data[index];
        result = data[index] + delta * (scaled_value - index);
    }
    catch ( Exception e )
    {
        System.Diagnostics.Debug.WriteLine(e.Message);
    }

}
};
}
```

Getting Dynamic—Car Physics Classes

Now we are ready to get into the actual dynamics classes.

Putting Wheels on Our Car

The first of these classes will be the Wheel class, which represents one wheel of a vehicle and its associated suspension. All aspects of the wheel are tracked and manipulated through this class. The attributes for the Wheel class are found in Listing 10-4. The class includes an enumeration that declares which corner of the vehicle the wheel belongs in. As you can see from the enumeration, this class assumes a four-wheeled vehicle. If we wanted to support tractor-trailers with this class, we would need to expand the enumeration.

Listing 10-4. Wheel Class Attributes

```
using System;

namespace VehicleDynamics
{
    public enum WhichWheel { LeftFront=0, RightFront, LeftRear, RightRear };

    public struct Wheel
    {
        public      Vector          offset;
        public      Vector          earth_location;
        private     double          rel_heading;
        public      double          radius;
        public      double          ground_height;
        public      double          altitude;
        public      double          height_above_ground;
        private     double          weight_over_wheel;
        private     double          static_weight_over_wheel;
        public      double          suspension_offset;
        public      double          max_suspension_offset;
        private     double          upwards_force;
        public      double          friction;
        private     double          stiction;
        private     double          sliding_friction;
        public      bool            bottomed_out;
        public      bool            touching_ground;
        public      bool            squealing;
        public      bool            sliding;
        public      bool            drive_wheel;
        public      WhichWheel      position;
```

The offset attribute denotes the position of the wheel relative to the center of gravity of the vehicle. The earth_location attribute is the wheel location relative to the terrain frame of reference. We need this position when we want to query the terrain for the height of the ground beneath the wheel. The rel_heading attribute is the relative heading between the vehicle and the wheel itself. The Car class would adjust this if this were one of the front wheels as a function of the steering actions.

The origin for the wheel is at its point of rotation in the center. The radius attribute lets us know how far below this point we would be contacting the ground. The ground_height attribute is the height of the ground beneath the wheel. The vehicle's position plus the earth_location offset minus the radius gives us the altitude attribute. Together with the ground_height attribute, it can determine if the wheel is in contact with the ground, off of the ground, or currently pressed into the ground (which would demand additional force upwards on the suspension).

We need to figure out the various forces working on the wheel. One of the most important considerations is how much weight is pressing down on the wheel. Two attributes are used to represent this. The static_weight_over_wheel attribute represents the portion of the vehicle's weight the wheel supports when the vehicle is at rest. The weight_over_wheel attribute, on the other hand, is the amount of weight that the wheel is currently supporting. You will see later in this chapter how external forces working on the vehicle can change the distribution of weight on the wheels.

The next set of attributes to consider involves the forces that oppose the force of the weight. These are the suspension forces. The suspension_offet attribute represents the current position of the suspension referenced from its static position. This attribute can go both positive and negative, since the spring can be either stretched or compressed depending on the forces working against it. The max_suspension_offset attribute represents the limit to which the suspension can be stretched or compressed. The upwards_force attribute is the force created by the suspension. This is normally in the upward direction opposing the weight of the vehicle, unless the vehicle has lost contact with the ground. If contact has been lost, there would be a negative force until the suspension reached its static position or contact is restored.

The final forces acting on the wheel are the friction forces. Three types of friction are involved:

- The friction of the surface that the wheel is moving over is represented by the friction attribute.

- The static friction of the wheel is represented by the stiction attribute.

- Finally, a reduced friction value occurs if the wheel has lost adhesion to the ground surface and is now sliding across the surface. This attribute is called sliding_friction.

All of these friction values are expressed as the number of gravities (Gs) of force that the friction supplies.

A number of status flags are also held within the structure. The bottomed_out flag is true if the suspension has been compressed to its limit and may be used by the game code to trigger an appropriate sound effect. The touching_ground flag is true if the wheel is in contact with the ground. The squealing attribute is also made available for use in triggering sound effects. If the wheel is on the verge of sliding, it will start to make a squealing sound. If it has broken loose, the sliding flag is set. There is also a flag that indicates whether this wheel is a drive wheel or not. If the car is front-wheel drive, this flag will be set for the front tires and cleared for the rear. Finally, the WhichWheel enumeration value indicates the wheel's position on the vehicle.

Several properties for the Wheel class, shown in Listing 10-5, enforce read-only or write-only status for several of the attributes. The RelHeading property provides write-only access to the corresponding attribute. On the other hand, the UpwardsForce property is read only. The Stiction property not only sets the stiction attribute, but also sets sliding_friction to 60 percent of the static friction.

Listing 10-5. Wheel Class Properties

```
#region Properties

public double RelHeading { set { rel_heading = value; } }
public double UpwardsForce { get { return upwards_force; } }
public double WeightOverWheel {
        set { weight_over_wheel = value; }
        get { return weight_over_wheel; } }
public double StaticWeightOverWheel {
        set { static_weight_over_wheel = value; } }
public double Stiction
{
    set
    {
        stiction = new_value;
        sliding_friction = 0.6f * stiction;
    }
}
#endregion
```

The constructor for the Wheel structure (shown in Listing 10-6) is fairly straightforward. It simply initializes each of the attributes to a reasonable initial value. The vehicle class that has the wheels must set most of these values. That class (or a parent class that holds an instance of the class) will have the knowledge to set them to the proper values for that vehicle. We will assume that the vehicle begins with all of the wheels touching the ground.

Listing 10-6. Wheel Class

```
public Wheel(WhichWheel where)
{
    position = where;
    offset = new Vector(0.0, 0.0, 0.0);
    earth_location = new Vector(0.0, 0.0, 0.0);
```

```
        rel_heading = 0.0;
        radius = 0.5;
        circumference = 0.0;
        height_above_ground = 0.0;
        rpm = 0.0;
        ground_height = 0.0;
        friction = 1.0;
        weight_over_wheel = 0.0;
        static_weight_over_wheel = 0.0;
        suspension_offset = 0.0;
        max_suspension_offset = 0.25;
        altitude = 0.0;
        bottomed_out = false;
        drive_wheel = false;
        sliding = false;
        sliding_friction = 0.0;
        squeeling = false;
        stiction = 1.0;
        upwards_force = 0.0;
        touching_ground = true;
    }
```

The method that performs that actual work for the wheels is the Process method shown in Listings 10-7a through 10-7e. Listing 10-7a shows the arguments to the method as well as the calculations of the wheel's position. The first argument (delta_t) is the amount of time that has passed since the last time this method has been called. It will be used for integrating values as a function of time. The remaining arguments provide the status of the vehicle that the wheel belongs to. This includes the vehicle's attitude, position velocities, and accelerations.

Listing 10-7a. Wheel Class Process Method

```
public void Process(float delta_t, Euler attitude, Vector acceleration,
    Vector velocity, Vector position)
{
    double   temp;
    double   susp_delta;
    double   squeel_force;
    double   slide_force;
    double   grab_force;
    double   tire_side_force;
```

```
earth_location.X = offset.X;
earth_location.Y = offset.Y;
earth_location.Z = offset.Z + suspension_offset;
attitude.RotateAtoE( earth_location );

altitude = position.Z + earth_location.Z - radius;

height_above_ground = altitude - ground_height;

touching_ground = height_above_ground <= 0.0f;
```

Taking the body-relative offsets and the current suspension offset and rotating it into earth frame using the vehicle's current attitude calculates the location of the wheel in the terrain frame of reference. The altitude at the base of the tire is this offset applied to the vehicle's height minus the radius of the wheel. The height above the ground is the difference between the ground elevation and the bottom of the tire. The tire is touching the ground if the height above the ground is less than or equal to zero.

The next section of the Process method (shown in Listing 10-7b) deals with determining the new suspension offset. If the wheel is touching the ground, the offset will be the inverse of the height above ground. In other words, we will compress the suspension enough that the base of the wheel will be resting on the surface of the ground in the next frame. If the wheel has lost contact with the ground, the weight of the wheel will extend the suspension to its negative limit. A suspension delta is calculated as the integrated sum of the suspension offset and the height above the ground. This delta is applied if the upward force applied to the vehicle is at least 2 pounds greater than the weight of the vehicle applied to the wheel. This will give us a small increase in the suspension extension to help balance out the forces. The suspension offset is limited to the range of plus and minus the maximum suspension offset. The suspension on the wheel has bottomed out if it has reached the positive limit of its movement.

Listing 10-7b. Wheel Class Process Method (Continued)

```
if ( touching_ground )
{
    suspension_offset = -height_above_ground;
}
else
{
    suspension_offset = -max_suspension_offset;
}
```

```
susp_delta = (suspension_offset + height_above_ground) * delta_t;
if ( Math.Abs(upwards_force - weight_over_wheel) < 2.0 )
{
   suspension_offset -= susp_delta;
}
if ( suspension_offset > max_suspension_offset )
{
   suspension_offset = max_suspension_offset;
}
else if ( suspension_offset < -max_suspension_offset )
{
   suspension_offset = -max_suspension_offset;
}
bottomed_out = suspension_offset == max_suspension_offset;
```

The next section of the method (shown in Listing 10-7c) is the simplified calculation of the force that the wheel is exerting on the vehicle. The `temp` value
represents the fractional portion of the vehicle's weight that is being countered
by the wheel and its suspension. It is calculated as 90 percent of the ratio of the
suspension offset squared to the maximum offset squared. Squaring the suspension offset removes the direction of the offset. If the offset is negative, the value
of `temp` is negated. If the suspension is roughly centered, `temp` will be set to zero,
since this is the offset from the static force required to hold up the vehicle. One
is then added to the value to get the complete percentage of the base force that
will be applied this time. If the wheel is not in contact with the ground, then
there will be no upward force applied by the wheel. The actual force is the static
weight over the wheel multiplied by the value of `temp`.

Listing 10-7c. Wheel Class Process Method (Continued)

```
temp = ( 0.9f * ( suspension_offset * suspension_offset ) /
   (max_suspension_offset * max_suspension_offset ) );
if ( suspension_offset < 0.0f )
{
   temp *= -1.0f;
}
if ( Math.Abs(suspension_offset) < 0.3f )
{
   temp = 0.0f;   // Suspension neutral
}
temp += 1.0f;
if ( !touching_ground )
```

```
{
    temp = 0.0f;
}


upwards_force = static_weight_over_wheel * temp;
```

The next section of the method (shown in Listing 10-7d) is a second adjustment to the suspension offset based on the new upward force. If the upward force is at least 2 pounds greater than the actual weight over the wheel, then the suspension is extended at the rate of .5 per second. Likewise, if the weight is at least 2 pounds greater, then the upward force the suspension is compressed at the same rate.

Listing 10-7d. Wheel Class Process Method (Continued)

```
if ( (upwards_force - weight_over_wheel) > 2.0f )
{
    suspension_offset -= 0.5f * delta_t;
}
else if ( (upwards_force - weight_over_wheel) < -2.0f )
{
    suspension_offset += 0.5f * delta_t;
}
```

The final section of the Process method (shown in Listing 10-7e) deals with the forward and lateral forces applied to the wheel and the interaction of the wheel with the ground. The force required to make the wheel slide is the product of the ground friction and the tire static friction converted from Gs to acceleration. The wheel will begin to squeal at 90 percent of the sliding value. The acceleration at which the wheel will stop sliding is the sliding friction converted from Gs to acceleration.

Listing 10-7e. Wheel Class Process Method (Conclusion)

```
 slide_force = 32.0f * stiction * friction;
squeel_force = 0.9f * slide_force;
 grab_force = 32.0f * sliding_friction;

if ( (acceleration.Y > 0.0f && rel_heading > 0.0f ) ||
    (acceleration.Y < 0.0f && rel_heading < 0.0f ) )
{
    tire_side_force = (float)Math.Abs(acceleration.Y *
        (1.0f - Math.Cos(rel_heading)));
}
```

```
            else
            {
                tire_side_force = (float)Math.Abs(acceleration.Y *
                    Math.Cos(rel_heading));
            }

            squeeling = false;
            if ( drive_wheel && acceleration.X >= slide_force )
            {
                sliding = true;
            }
            if ( (acceleration.X < -squeel_force && acceleration.X > -slide_force) ||
                (tire_side_force > squeel_force && tire_side_force < slide_force) )
            {
                squeeling = true;
            }
            if ( acceleration.X <= -slide_force || tire_side_force >= slide_force )
            {
                sliding = true;
            }
            if ( Math.Abs(acceleration.X) < grab_force &&
                Math.Abs(acceleration.Y)< grab_force &&
                tire_side_force < grab_force )
            {
                sliding = false;
            }
        }
    };
}
```

The side force applied to the tire is a function of the lateral acceleration of the vehicle and any relative heading applied to the wheel. If the wheel is turning into the direction of the acceleration, the wheel is turning somewhat with the force, and the force is reduced based on the amount of the relative heading. If the tire is steering away from the force, the tire sees much more of the acceleration as side force.

If the wheel is a drive wheel and the forward acceleration is greater than the slide force, the tire will start to slide (i.e, laying rubber, spinning, etc.). If the forward acceleration is between the squeal force level and the sliding force level or the side force is between those same extremes, then the tire will squeal. If either the forward or the lateral forces exceed the slide force level, then the wheel will be sliding rather than gripping the surface. If any of these accelerations drop below the grab force threshold, the wheel will grab the surface again and stop sliding.

Simulating the Car

That completes our look at the `Wheel` structure. Now we get down to the serious work of vehicle dynamics with the `CarDynamics` class. The attributes and enumerations for this class are shown in Listings 10-8a and 10-8b. The `IgnitionState` enumeration in Listing 10-8a defines the current position of the "key" in the ignition. This allows the class to support the ability to start and stop the vehicle's engine. The second enumeration, `GearState`, defines the state of the transmission. Our sample game will only utilize the drive gear of the transmission, but the class will support either an automatic or three-speed manual transmission.

Listing 10-8a. CarDynamics Enumerations and Attributes

```
using System;
using System.Threading;
using System.Diagnostics;

namespace VehicleDynamics
{
    public class CarDynamics : IDisposable
    {
        public enum IgnitionState { IgnitionOff, IgnitionOn, IgnitionStart };
        public enum GearState { Park=0, Reverse=1, Neutral=2, Drive=3,
            FirstGear=4, SecondGear=5, ThirdGear=6 };

    #region Attributes
        private    Euler        attitude = new Euler();
        private    Euler        attitude_rate = new Euler();
        private    Euler        ground_slope = new Euler();
        private    Vector       position = new Vector();
        private    Vector       velocity = new Vector();
        private    Vector       earth_velocity = new Vector();
        private    Vector       acceleration = new Vector();
        private    Vector       body_gravity = new Vector();
        private    Wheel[]       wheel = new Wheel[4];
        private    double       weight;
        private    double       cg_height;
        private    double       wheel_base;
        private    double       wheel_track;
        private    double       wheel_angle;
        private    double       wheel_max_angle;
        private    double       weight_distribution;
        private    double       front_weight;
        private    double       back_weight;
```

```
private    double         wheel_pos;
private    double         throttle;
private    double         brake;
private    double         engine_rpm;
private    double         wheel_rpm;
private    double         wheel_force;
private    double         net_force;
private    double         drag;
private    double         rolling_resistance;
private    double         eng_torque;
private    double         mph;
```

The Attitude attribute holds the current heading, pitch, and roll of the vehicle. Attitude_rate is the rate of change of each of these angles. The ground_slope attribute represents the current pitch and roll of the ground under the vehicle in the vehicle's frame of reference. This will be important since the impact of gravity is a function of this slope so that the vehicle will tend to accelerate while going downhill and slow when going uphill.

Five vectors are held by the class. These vectors contain the position, velocities, and accelerations for the vehicle. We also have the gravity vector in the vehicle's body frame as well as an array of four wheels for our car. The weight attribute is the overall weight of the car. The cg_height attribute, which represents the height of the car's center of gravity above the ground, is used in calculating the offset of the wheel's positions based on the car in its static condition. The wheelbase of the vehicle is the side-to-side separation between the wheels, and the wheel track is the forward-and-back separation between the wheels. It is assumed that the wheels are evenly distributed around the center of the vehicle.

The wheel angle is the current relative heading of the front wheels due to steering inputs. The wheel_max_angle attribute represents the limits to which the front wheels may be turned. The weight_distribution attribute is the fraction of the vehicle's overall weight that is over the rear wheels when the vehicle is not moving. Accelerations will result in the actual weight distribution to shift once the vehicle starts moving. These accelerations will cause the front_weight and back_weight to change dynamically. These weights will be divided up and passed to each wheel as the weight over that wheel.

The next three attributes are the control values passed in from the parent class that control the basic driving of the vehicle. The wheel_pos attribute is the steering wheel position normalized to ±1 with positive steering to the right. The throttle is the gas pedal position normalized, with 0 meaning no depression of the pedal and 1 being pedal to the metal. The brake attribute works the same way for the brake pedal, with 0 being pedal up and 1 being pedal fully depressed.

The engine_rpm is the current speed of the engine. This value is a function of the throttle position and any losses fed back from the interactions with the road.

If the vehicle is going uphill, for example, the vehicle will slow and reduce engine speed until the transmission drops to a lower gear. The wheel_rpm indicates how fast the wheels are turning based on the engine RPM and the current transmission gear ratio. The wheel_force specifies the amount of the force developed by the engine that is passed to the wheels to move the vehicle. The engine torque (in the eng_torque attribute) is the force developed by the engine. The net_force attribute, calculated from the summation of all of the forces acting on the vehicle, defines the net force that changes the vehicle's acceleration. The drag attribute, which acts to slow the vehicle due to air impacting the front of the vehicle as it is moving, is one of several forces that act to limit the top speed of a vehicle. Another force acting against the movement of the vehicle is the rolling resistance. This is energy that deforms the tires as they rotate. The mph attribute is the vehicle's speed in the forward direction expressed in miles per hour.

The remaining attributes are shown in Listing 10-8b. The brake_torque and engine_loss attributes are two forces that act in opposition to the engine torque. The normal RPM when the engine is idling is held in the idle_rpm attribute, and the maximum RPM is contained in the max_rpm attribute. The target_rpm indicates the engine speed that is currently being demanded by the throttle position. The engine_horsepower and max_engine_torque determine how much power the engine can produce.

Listing 10-8b. CarDynamics Enumerations and Attributes (Conclusion)

```
private    double        brake_torque;
private    double        engine_loss;
private    double        idle_rpm;
private    double        max_rpm;
private    double        target_rpm;
private    double        engine_horsepower;
private    double        max_engine_torque;
private    double        air_density;
private    double        drag_coeff;
private    double        frontal_area;
private    double        wheel_diameter;
private    double        mass;        // In slugs
private    double        inverse_mass;        // In slugs
private    float         centripedal_accel;
private    bool          running;
private    bool          front_wheel_drive = false;
private    GearState     gear;
private    GearState     auto_gear = GearState.Drive;
private    double[]      gear_ratio = new double[7];
```

```
            // percent max torque - index by % max RPM * 10
            private    LFI              torque_curve = new LFI();
            private    IgnitionState    ignition_state = IgnitionState.IgnitionOn;
            private bool                was_sliding = false;

            private Thread              m_process_thread;
            private bool                thread_active = true;
            private Mutex               mutex = new Mutex();

        #endregion
```

The next three attributes calculate the aerodynamic drag against the vehicle. The air_density is the thickness of the air that the vehicle is passing through. The standard value for air density at sea level is 14.7 pounds per square inch. The air_density attribute will hold the inverse of this value (0.068). The drag coefficient (drag_coeff) is a factor representing the amount of drag that a given shape has when moving through the atmosphere. Without a physical model of our vehicle and a wind tunnel, it is difficult to determine a specific number for this coefficient. Instead, we will just pick a value and adjust it until everything seems realistic. The last factor in the calculation is the frontal area of the vehicle, the cross-section of the vehicle that impacts the air as it moves forward.

The diameter of the wheels is involved in the calculations for wheel torque as well as for passing the radius of the wheel to each wheel for its own calculations. The mass of the vehicle is required to change the forces working on the vehicle into accelerations. Remember that acceleration is force divided by mass. To make the calculation more efficient, we will also hold the inverse of the mass so we can multiply instead of divide. The acceleration that works laterally on the vehicle due to inertia is called *centripetal acceleration*. Flags will also exist that state whether or not the engine is running and if the vehicle has front-wheel or rear-wheel drive.

There are two instances of the GearState enumeration. The first attribute, gear, is the gear that has been selected by the driver. A second attribute, auto_gear, is the state of the automatic transmission. This is because an automatic transmission shifts between the forward gears as a function of engine RPM and torque. The gear ratios in each of the transmission's gears are held within an array of double-precision variables. There is also an instance of the LFI class, which holds the torque curve for the engine. The data in the curve is the percentage of maximum engine torque as a function of the engine RPM. We also have an instance of the IgnitionState enumeration, which indicates the current state of the engine's ignition. A flag indicates whether the vehicle's tires were sliding on the previous pass.

The final attributes in the class manage a separate processing thread for the class. There is a reference to the thread itself, a flag that controls if the thread should continue to cycle, and a Mutex object for thread-safe data transfers between the thread process and the remainder of the class.

The properties for the CarDynamics class (shown in Listing 10-9) provide the public interface for the class. All of the control inputs from the containing class will come in through these properties. The SteeringWheel property sets the wheel position as a double-precision value between ±1. The Throttle property specifies the gas pedal position and the Brake property does the same for the brake pedal. The Gear property is used for shifting gears and the Ignition property for turning the key. A bit of logic is involved with the Ignition property; it checks the current gear and starts the engine if the Start value is set and the gear is set to Park or Neutral. Likewise, if the Off state is requested the engine is stopped. There are also properties to retrieve the current RPM and running state.

Listing 10-9. CarDynamics Properties

```
#region Properties
    public double SteeringWheel {
        get { return wheel_pos; }
        set { wheel_pos = value; } }


    public double Throttle { get { return throttle; } set { throttle = value; } }


    public double Brake { get { return brake; } set { brake = value; } }


    public GearState Gear { get { return gear; } set { gear = value; } }


    public IgnitionState Ignition { get { return ignition_state; }
        set
        {
            ignition_state = value;
            if ( ignition_state == IgnitionState.IgnitionStart &&
                ( gear == GearState.Park || gear == GearState.Neutral ) )
            {
                running = true;
            }
            else if ( ignition_state == IgnitionState.IgnitionOff )
            {
                running = false;
            }
        }
    }


    public double EngineRPM { get { return engine_rpm; } }


    public bool EngineRunning { get { return running; } }
```

```
public double Roll {
    get { return attitude.Phi; }
    set { attitude.Phi = value; } }
public double Pitch {
    get { return attitude.Theta; }
    set { attitude.Theta = value; } }
public double Heading {
    get { return attitude.Psi; }
    set { attitude.Psi = value; } }

public double North {
    get { return position.X; }
    set { position.X = value; } }
public double East {
    get { return position.Y; }
    set { position.Y = value; } }
public double Height {
    get { return position.Z; }
    set { position.Z = value; } }

public double NorthVelocity {
    get { return earth_velocity.X; }
    set { velocity.X = value; } }
public double EastVelocity {
    get { return earth_velocity.Y; }
    set { velocity.Y = value; } }
public double VerticalVelocity {
    get { return earth_velocity.Z; }
    set { velocity.Z = value; } }

public double ForwardVelocity { get { return velocity.X; } }
public double SidewaysVelocity { get { return velocity.Y; } }
public double WheelRadius {
    get { return wheel[(int)WhichWheel.LeftFront].radius; }
    set
    {
        wheel_diameter = value * 2.0;
        wheel[(int)WhichWheel.LeftFront].radius = value;
        wheel[(int)WhichWheel.LeftRear].radius = value;
        wheel[(int)WhichWheel.RightFront].radius = value;
        wheel[(int)WhichWheel.RightRear].radius = value; }
}
```

```
    public double HorsePower {
        get { return engine_horsepower; }
        set { engine_horsepower = value; } }


    public double LFGroundHeight {
        set { wheel[(int)WhichWheel.LeftFront].ground_height = value; } }
    public double RFGroundHeight {
        set { wheel[(int)WhichWheel.RightFront].ground_height = value; } }
    public double LRGroundHeight {
        set { wheel[(int)WhichWheel.LeftRear].ground_height = value; } }
    public double RRGroundHeight {
        set { wheel[(int)WhichWheel.RightRear].ground_height = value; } }


    public double MPH { get { return mph; } }
    public bool Running { get { return running; } }
```

#endregion

Various properties get and set the vehicle's attitude and position within the world. There are also properties to access the vehicle's velocities in both the world frame of reference as well as the body frame.

NOTE *Notice that we are using North, East, and Vertical instead of X, Y, and Z for the world-related values. The X, Y, and Z values have different meanings in different places. In physics equations, we tend to think of X going to the north, Y moving to the east, and Z moving up. DirectX, on the other hand, uses a different axis convention. To eliminate confusion, we use a public interface that employs world-related terms.*

The property that accesses the size of the wheels assumes that all four wheels of our vehicle are the same size. Therefore, we can return the left-front wheel's radius in the Get method and set all wheels to the same value in the Set method. We also set the diameter of the wheel with the same property. The HorsePower property changes the power of the engine for the vehicle being simulated. The height of the ground under each tire is likely to be different. Because of this, a separate property exists for each wheel. There are also properties to access the vehicle's speed in miles per hour and a flag that indicates whether or not the engine is running.

The constructor for the class (shown in Listing 10-10) initializes the attributes that do not change over time. This includes the horsepower of the engine as well as the engine's torque curve. It also resets the members of the wheel array so that each wheel is initialized knowing its position on the vehicle. The constructor then calls the Reset method to complete the initialization. Placing the other attribute initialization in a separate method allows us to reset the vehicle to a know state when needed. The final task for the constructor is to create and start the thread that will perform the dynamics processing. The integrations involved in these calculations tend to be very rate dependent. If they are not processed quickly enough, they can become unstable and oscillate out of control. To prevent this from happening, we will run the dynamics processing in a separate thread that will cycle at a nominal 100 hertz.

Listing 10-10. CarDynamics Constructor

```
public CarDynamics()
{
    engine_horsepower = 70.0f;
    torque_curve.SetDataPoint(  0, 0.0f );
    torque_curve.SetDataPoint(  10, 0.13f );
    torque_curve.SetDataPoint(  20, 0.32f );
    torque_curve.SetDataPoint(  30, 0.5f );
    torque_curve.SetDataPoint(  40, 0.72f );
    torque_curve.SetDataPoint(  50, 0.9f );
    torque_curve.SetDataPoint(  60, 1.0f );
    torque_curve.SetDataPoint(  70, 0.98f );
    torque_curve.SetDataPoint(  80, 0.89f );
    torque_curve.SetDataPoint(  90, 0.5f );
    torque_curve.SetDataPoint( 100, 0.13f );
    wheel[(int)WhichWheel.LeftFront]  = new Wheel(WhichWheel.LeftFront);
    wheel[(int)WhichWheel.RightFront] = new Wheel(WhichWheel.RightFront);
    wheel[(int)WhichWheel.LeftRear]   = new Wheel(WhichWheel.LeftRear);
    wheel[(int)WhichWheel.RightRear]  = new Wheel(WhichWheel.RightRear);
    Reset();
    m_process_thread = new Thread(new ThreadStart(Process));
    m_process_thread.Start();
}
```

The method that will run in the processing thread is the Process method (shown in Listing 10-11), which has no arguments. Since the thread will be running at about 100 hertz, the time delta will be the inverse of the frequency, or 0.01 seconds per pass. The method will iterate until the thread_active flag becomes cleared. Each pass, it will call the normal Process method and then sleep for 10 milliseconds. It is this idle time produced by the Sleep method that gives us the iteration rate we want.

Listing 10-11. CarDynamics Thread Process Method

```
public void Process()
{
    float delta_t = 0.01f;

    Debug.WriteLine("car physics thread started");
    while ( thread_active )
    {
        Process( delta_t );
        Thread.Sleep(10);
    }
    Debug.WriteLine("car physics thread terminated");
}
```

The Reset method (shown in Listing 10-12) places the state of the dynamics into a basic starting condition. The attitude, velocities, and accelerations are all reset to zero. The maximum wheel angle defaults to 40 degrees. Since all angular work within the software is done in radians, we will set it to the radian equivalent of 40 degrees. The maximum RPM for the engine will be set to 7000 with the idle speed set to 10 percent of this maximum. The current RPM will be set to zero since it will be recalculated when the engine starts.

Listing 10-12. CarDynamics Reset Method

```
public void Reset()
{
    wheel_max_angle = 0.69813170079773183076947630739545; // 40 degrees
    idle_rpm = 700.0f;
    max_rpm = 7000.0f;
    engine_rpm = 0.0f;
    attitude.Theta = 0.0f;
    attitude.Phi = 0.0f;
    attitude.Psi = 0.0f;
    attitude_rate.Theta = 0.0;
    attitude_rate.Phi = 0.0;
    attitude_rate.Psi = 0.0;
    position.X = 0.0;
```

```
            position.Y = 0.0;
            position.Z = 0.0;
            velocity.X = 0.0;           // Body velocity
            velocity.Y = 0.0;           // Body velocity
            velocity.Z = 0.0;           // Body velocity
            earth_velocity.X = 0.0;       // Earth velocity
            earth_velocity.Y = 0.0;       // Earth velocity
            earth_velocity.Z = 0.0;       // Earth velocity
            acceleration.X = 0.0;        // Body accelerations
            acceleration.Y = 0.0;        // Body accelerations
            acceleration.Z = 0.0;        // Body accelerations
            cg_height            = 2.0f;
            wheel_base           = 5.0;
            wheel_track          = 8.0;
            weight               = 2000.0f;
            wheelRadius        = 1.25;
    wheel[(int)WhichWheel.LeftFront ].offset.Set( wheel_track / 2.0f,
        -wheel_base / 2.0f,
        -cg_height + wheel[(int)WhichWheel.LeftFront].radius );
    wheel[(int)WhichWheel.RightFront].offset.Set( wheel_track / 2.0f,
        wheel_base / 2.0f,
        -cg_height + wheel[(int)WhichWheel.LeftFront].radius );
    wheel[(int)WhichWheel.LeftRear  ].offset.Set(-wheel_track / 2.0f,
        -wheel_base / 2.0f,
        -cg_height + wheel[(int)WhichWheel.LeftFront].radius );
    wheel[(int)WhichWheel.RightRear ].offset.Set(-wheel_track / 2.0f,
         wheel_base / 2.0f,
        -cg_height + wheel[(int)WhichWheel.LeftFront].radius );
            for ( int i=0; i<4; i++ )
            {
                wheel[i].SetStaticWeightOverWheel(weight / 4.0f);
            }
            weight_distribution   = 0.5f;
            front_weight          = weight * ( 1.0 - weight_distribution);
            back_weight           = weight * weight_distribution;
            wheel_pos             = 0.0f;
            throttle              = 0.0f;
            brake                 = 0.0f;
            engine_rpm            = 0.0f;
            wheel_rpm             = 0.0f;
            wheel_force           = 0.0f;
            net_force             = 0.0f;
            mph                   = 0.0f;
            drag                  = 0.0f;
```

```
rolling_resistance     = 0.0f;
eng_torque             = 0.0f;
brake_torque           = 0.0f;
engine_loss            = 0.0f;
air_density            = 0.068;
drag_coeff             = 0.4f;
frontal_area           = 20.0f;
mass                    = weight * 0.031080950172;       // In slugs
inverse_mass           = 1.0 / mass;
running = true;
front_wheel_drive = false;
gear = GearState.Drive;
gear_ratio[(int)GearState.Park]          = 0.0f;
gear_ratio[(int)GearState.Reverse]       = -80.0f;
gear_ratio[(int)GearState.Neutral]       = 0.0f;
gear_ratio[(int)GearState.Drive]          = 45.0f;
gear_ratio[(int)GearState.FirstGear]     = 70.0f;
gear_ratio[(int)GearState.SecondGear]    = 50.0f;
gear_ratio[(int)GearState.ThirdGear]     = 30.0f;
ignition_state = IgnitionState.IgnitionOn;
max_engine_torque = engine_horsepower * 550.0f;

if ( front_wheel_drive )
{
   wheel[(int)WhichWheel.LeftFront ].drive_wheel = true;
   wheel[(int)WhichWheel.RightFront].drive_wheel = true;
   wheel[(int)WhichWheel.LeftRear  ].drive_wheel = false;
   wheel[(int)WhichWheel.RightRear ].drive_wheel = false;
}
else
{
   wheel[(int)WhichWheel.LeftFront ].drive_wheel = false;
   wheel[(int)WhichWheel.RightFront].drive_wheel = false;
   wheel[(int)WhichWheel.LeftRear  ].drive_wheel = true;
   wheel[(int)WhichWheel.RightRear ].drive_wheel = true;
}
}
```

The height of the center of gravity defaults to 2 feet off of the ground and the wheelbase and track default to 5 feet and 8 feet, respectively. We will also default to a weight of 1 ton, which is 2000 pounds. The offset to each of the wheels is calculated from the wheelbase, wheel track, center of gravity height, and the wheel radius. Since we are assuming that the weight of the vehicle is evenly distributed over the wheels, one quarter of the weight is passed to each wheel as its static weight over the wheel. This also gives us a weight distribution of one half and the associated portions of the weight assigned to the front and rear of the vehicle.

The mass of the vehicle needs to be in slugs for the English system of measurement. The weight is converted to slugs for the mass and inverted for the inverse_mass attribute. We will assume that we reset to a rear-wheel drive vehicle with the engine running and in drive, ready to start racing. The gear ratios are the complete ratio of engine RPM to the corresponding wheel rotation speed. This includes the gearing in the rear hub with the transmission ratios. Note that the value for reverse is negative to reverse the direction of the wheel rotation. The final action in the method is to inform each of the wheels whether or not they are a drive wheel based on the front_wheel_drive flag.

The IntegratePosition method (shown in Listing 10-13) performs the integrations that change accelerations into velocities and velocities into modifications in position. This method of integration is known as *Euler's method*. Since acceleration is feet per second squared and we are multiplying by seconds per pass, we get resulting units of feet per second per pass. Since feet per second represents a velocity, we can add this product to our velocity last pass to get our new velocity. The same holds true for taking our attitude rate in radians per second and integrating with our time delta to get the number of radians each attitude angle changes in a frame. Since we want to ensure that our attitude angles remain in the proper range, we will call the Attitude class's Limit method to handle any integration through zero or the maximum value for a given attitude angle.

Listing 10-13. CarDynamics IntegratePosition Method

```
private void IntegratePosition( float delta_t )
{

    velocity.IncrementX( delta_t * acceleration.X );
    velocity.IncrementY( delta_t * acceleration.Y );
    velocity.IncrementZ( delta_t * acceleration.Z );

    attitude = attitude + (attitude_rate * delta_t);
    attitude.Limits();

    earth_velocity.X = velocity.X;
    earth_velocity.Y = velocity.Y;
    earth_velocity.Z = velocity.Z;
    attitude.RotateAtoE( earth_velocity );
```

```
        position.IncrementX( delta_t * earth_velocity.X );
        position.IncrementY( delta_t * earth_velocity.Y );
        position.IncrementZ( delta_t * earth_velocity.Z );

        mph = (float)velocity.X * 3600.0f / 5280.0f;
    }
```

The terms in the velocity vector are in the vehicle's frame of reference. Before we can integrate our position in the world, we must rotate this vector into the world coordinate system. The vector is copied into another vector that is rotated based on the vehicle's attitude. The earth velocity is integrated to get the change in world position. We will also calculate the miles per hour version of our velocity by taking the forward velocity and converting it from feet per second to miles per hour.

The net force that acts on the vehicle is not being applied through the vehicle's center of gravity (CG). It is actually applied at the interface between the wheels and the ground. Because the force is not being applied at the CG, there is an apparent transfer of the vehicle's weight in both the forward and lateral directions. I'm sure you have experienced this while driving in a car. If the car is accelerated rapidly, the front of the car rises. If you slam on the brakes, the nose of the car dips. If you make a quick turn, the car rolls toward the outside of the turn. These are all examples of weight transfer due to the accelerations acting on the car. Remember that weight is an acceleration. The weight transferred to the front of the vehicle is the forward acceleration multiplied by the ratio of the center of gravity height and the wheelbase. This value is added to the front of the vehicle and subtracted from the rear. The same calculation holds true for the lateral acceleration. Instead of dividing by the wheelbase, though, we will use the wheel track since it is the distance between the tires in the lateral direction. Using these relationships, we can calculate the weight over each of the four tires and pass the values to the associated wheel (see Listing 10-14).

Listing 10-14. CarDynamics CalcWeightTransfer Method

```
    private void CalcWeightTransfer()
    {
        front_weight = (1.0f - weight_distribution) * weight +
          (float)acceleration.X * cg_height / wheel_base;
        back_weight = weight - front_weight;

        wheel[(int)WhichWheel.LeftFront].weight_over_wheel   =
                0.5f * front_weight -
                  (float)acceleration.Y * cg_height / wheel_track;
```

```
        wheel[(int)WhichWheel.RightFront].weight_over_wheel =
                front_weight -
                wheel[(int)WhichWheel.LeftFront].weight_over_wheel;
        wheel[(int)WhichWheel.LeftRear].weight_over_wheel    = 0.5f *
                back_weight - (float)acceleration.Y * cg_height / wheel_track;
        wheel[(int)WhichWheel.RightRear].weight_over_wheel   =
                back_weight -
                wheel[(int)WhichWheel.LeftRear].weight_over_wheel;
    }
```

The SetFriction method (shown in Listing 10-15) provides the interface to set the friction of the surface under a specific wheel. The arguments to the method state which wheel is being set and what the new value should be. This value is simply passed to the requested wheel.

Listing 10-15. CarDynamics SetFriction Method

```
    public void SetFriction(WhichWheel the_wheel, float friction)
    {
       wheel[(int)the_wheel].friction = friction;
    }
```

The SetGearRatio method (shown in Listing 10-16) provides a programmatic way to change the gears in the transmission. This is how the initialization of a class that uses the CarDynamics can tailor the transmission for a specific vehicle. The combination of different horsepower engine and different gear ratios can be used to add vehicles with varying performance.

Listing 10-16. CarDynamics SetGearRatio Method

```
    public void SetGearRatio(GearState state, float ratio)
    {
       gear_ratio[(int)state] = ratio;
    }
```

The current position of a given wheel may be queried using the WheelNorth method shown in Listing 10-17. The enumeration value for a wheel is passed in as an argument and the position in the north axis is returned.

Listing 10-17. CarDynamics WheelNorth Method

```
public float WheelNorth(WhichWheel the_wheel)
{
   return (float)wheel[(int)the_wheel].earth_location.X;
}
```

The east position of a wheel is obtained the same way using the WheelEast method and the vertical position of the wheel with the WheelHeight method. Both of these methods are shown in Listing 10-18.

Listing 10-18. CarDynamics WheelEast Method

```
public float WheelEast(WhichWheel the_wheel)
{
   return (float)wheel[(int)the_wheel].earth_location.Y;
}
public float WheelHeight(WhichWheel the_wheel)
{
   return (float)wheel[(int)the_wheel].earth_location.Z;
}
```

The height of the ground beneath a wheel is set using the SetWheelAltitude method shown in Listing 10-19. The altitude and the selection of which wheel to set are passed in as arguments. The enumeration value is used as an index into the wheel array and the associated wheel's ground height is set to the supplied altitude.

Listing 10-19. CarDynamics SetWheelAltitude Method

```
public void SetWheelAltitude(WhichWheel the_wheel, float altitude)
{
   wheel[(int)the_wheel].ground_height = altitude;
}
```

The SetWheelOffset method (shown in Listing 10-20) adjusts the position of each wheel independently. The three supplied offsets are set within the requested wheel's data structure.

Listing 10-20. CarDynamics SetWheelOffset Method

```
public void SetWheelOffset(WhichWheel the_wheel, float forward,
    float right, float up)
{
    wheel[(int)the_wheel].offset.X = forward;
    wheel[(int)the_wheel].offset.Y = right;
    wheel[(int)the_wheel].offset.Z = up;
}
```

The Dispose method (shown in Listing 10-21) has only one task. Its job is to terminate the processing thread. By setting the thread_active flag to false, the thread will terminate itself when it reaches the end of its while loop. A 20-millisecond sleep is included before the Dispose methods terminates. This is to ensure that the thread has time to terminate before we deallocate the class by passing out of scope.

Listing 10-21. CarDynamics Dispose Method

```
public void Dispose()
{
    Debug.WriteLine("car physics Dispose");
    thread_active = false;
    Thread.Sleep(20);
}
```

NOTE *If we fail to use* Dispose *on a class like this one, which has spawned a thread, it is possible that the thread will not get the message that the application has terminated, and the thread will continue. This will cause the application to remain partially active.*

The Process method (shown in Listings 10-22a through 10-22e) is where the real work of the vehicle dynamics is done. Among the local variables declared for this method is the gravity vector, which is the acceleration in the down direction that will be applied to the vehicle in addition to the other forces that affect the vehicle. The method begins, as shown in Listing 10-22a, by processing the steering of the vehicle. The angular offset of the front wheels is a function of the current steering wheel position and the maximum turn angle for the wheels. This wheel angle is passed to each of the front wheels as their new relative heading. The turn rate for the vehicle is a function of this wheel angle, the distance between the wheels, and the current forward speed of the vehicle. If both of the front wheels are sliding, then we have lost the ability to steer the vehicle, and the turn rate is set to zero. The Greek symbol used to represent heading is psi. The attitude rate for psi is set to this turn rate.

Listing 10-22a. CarDynamics Process Method

```
void Process(float delta_t)
{
    double temp;
    double delta_rpm;
    double current_gear_ratio = 0.0;
    double brake_force;
    double percent_rpm;
    double turn_rate;
    bool  shift_up;
    bool  shift_down;
    double delta_psi;
    Vector   gravity = new Vector(0.0f, 0.0f, 32.0f);

    wheel_angle = wheel_pos * wheel_max_angle;

    wheel[(int)WhichWheel.LeftFront].SetRelHeading( wheel_angle );
    wheel[(int)WhichWheel.RightFront].SetRelHeading( wheel_angle );

    turn_rate = (Math.Sin(wheel_angle) * velocity.X / wheel_track) / 10.0f;

    if ( wheel[(int)WhichWheel.LeftFront].sliding &&
            wheel[(int)WhichWheel.RightFront].sliding )
    {
        turn_rate = 0.0f;
    }

    attitude_rate.Psi = turn_rate;

    delta_psi = turn_rate * delta_t;

    centripedal_accel = (float)(2.0 * velocity.X *
            Math.Sin(delta_psi) ) / delta_t;

    wheel_rpm = 60.0f * velocity.X / (Math.PI * wheel_diameter);

    rolling_resistance = 0.696f * (float)Math.Abs(velocity.X);
```

```
drag = 0.5f * drag_coeff * frontal_area * air_density *
        Math.Abs(velocity.X * velocity.X);


brake_force = brake * 32.0;   // Max braking 1G


if ( mph < 0.0 )
{
   brake_force *= -1.0;
}


if ( wheel[(int)WhichWheel.LeftFront].sliding &&
        wheel[(int)WhichWheel.RightFront].sliding &&
        wheel[(int)WhichWheel.RightRear].sliding &&
        wheel[(int)WhichWheel.RightRear].sliding )
{
   brake_force = 0.0f;
}
```

The centripetal acceleration is a function of the forward speed and the turn rate. The rotational speed of the wheels is a function of the circumference of the wheel and the forward speed of the vehicle. This assumes that the wheels are not slipping. If the wheels were slipping, there would no longer be a direct relationship between forward velocity and tire rotational speed. Instead, the relationship would be between engine RPM and tire rotational speed. The rolling resistance is also a function of the forward velocity. Since the direction of the velocity doesn't affect the resistance, only the magnitude, we can calculate the resistance as the product of a resistance coefficient and the absolute value of the velocity. Likewise, the aerodynamic drag is a function of the drag coefficient, the frontal area of the vehicle, the air density, and the square of the forward velocity. The vehicle's brakes represent another force that will affect the speed of the vehicle. The acceleration that will be applied by the brakes is a function of the brake pedal position and a maximum braking acceleration of 32 feet per second (1 G of acceleration). If the vehicle is traveling backward, the braking force is negated. If all of the wheels are sliding, there is no braking force, and the acceleration is set to zero.

The next section of code, shown in Listing 10-22b, concerns the simulation of the vehicle's transmission. The first thing to do in this section of code is to determine the current percentage of the maximum engine RPM. The percentage of maximum RPM will come into play when deciding the proper time for the automatic transmission to shift. A switch statement based on the current gear determines what the transmission will do. If Park is selected, there will be maximum braking force until the vehicle is almost completely stopped, and then the velocity will be set to zero to complete the process. If Reverse is selected, the associated gear ratio is selected, and the automatic gear is set to the same value. The same holds true for Neutral. If the transmission is in Drive, we must be using an automatic transmission. This means that the transmission will automatically shift up and down through the forward gears as necessary. If the engine RPM is in the top 20 percent of its range, and the automatic gear is less than its top gear, the shift_up flag is set. Likewise, if the automatic gear is in Neutral and the engine is running faster than idle, it will also shift up. The transmission will downshift if the percent RPM drops below 40 percent and the automatic gear is greater than first gear.

Listing 10-22b. CarDynamics Process Method (Continued)

```
percent_rpm = engine_rpm / max_rpm;

switch ( gear )
{
   case GearState.Park:
      if ( mph > 1.0  || mph < -1.0 )
      {
         brake_force = 32.0;
      }
      else
      {
         velocity.SetX(0.0f);
      }
      auto_gear = GearState.Park;
      break;
   case GearState.Reverse:
      auto_gear = GearState.Reverse;
      break;
   case GearState.Neutral:
      auto_gear = GearState.Neutral;
      break;
   case GearState.Drive:
      shift_up = false;
      shift_down = false;
      if ( ( percent_rpm > 0.8 && auto_gear < GearState.Drive ) ||
         ( percent_rpm > 0.1 && auto_gear == GearState.Neutral ) )
      {
         shift_up = true;
      }
```

```
            if ( percent_rpm < 0.4 && auto_gear >= GearState.FirstGear )
            {
                shift_down = true;
            }
    switch ( auto_gear )
    {
        case GearState.Neutral:
            if ( shift_up )
            {
                auto_gear = GearState.FirstGear;
            }
            break;
        case GearState.Drive:
            if ( shift_down )
            {
                auto_gear = GearState.ThirdGear;
            }
            break;
        case GearState.FirstGear:
            if ( shift_up )
            {
                auto_gear = GearState.SecondGear;
            }
            else if ( shift_down )
            {
                auto_gear = GearState.Neutral;
            }
            break;
        case GearState.SecondGear:
            if ( shift_up )
            {
                auto_gear = GearState.ThirdGear;
            }
            else if ( shift_down )
            {
                auto_gear = GearState.FirstGear;
            }
            break;
        case GearState.ThirdGear:
            if ( shift_up )
            {
                auto_gear = GearState.Drive;
            }
            else if ( shift_down )
```

```
            {
                auto_gear = GearState.SecondGear;
            }
            break;
        }
        break;
    case GearState.FirstGear:
        auto_gear = GearState.FirstGear;
        break;
    case GearState.SecondGear:
        auto_gear = GearState.SecondGear;
        break;
    case GearState.ThirdGear:
        auto_gear = GearState.ThirdGear;
        break;
    }
    current_gear_ratio = gear_ratio[(int)auto_gear];
```

Embedded within the Drive state is a second switch based on the automatic gear. If the transmission is currently in Neutral and we are shifting up, the automatic gear is changed to first. It is changed to third gear if we are in Drive and downshifting. If the transmission is in First gear, we can either shift up to Second or downshift to Neutral. If the transmission is in Second gear, we can either shift up to Third or downshift to First. Finally, if the transmission is in Third, we can shift up to Drive or downshift into Second. If the manually selected gear is first through third, than the automatic gear is set to match. The current gear ratio is selected from the gear ratio array based on the current automatic gear.

The next section of the Process method (shown in Listing 10-22c) deals with the speed of the engine and the force that it creates. If the engine is running and the engine is not up to idle speed yet, then we will set idle RPM as our target. On the other hand, if the engine has been turned off, we need to target zero RPM. If neither of these conditions is met, then the target RPM is based on the gas pedal position, demanding an RPM somewhere between idle and maximum RPM. The delta RPM is the difference between the current engine speed and this target RPM. We will limit the change in RPM to 3000 RPM per second. This delta is integrated into the current engine RPM using the time delta.

Listing 10-22c. CarDynamics Process Method (Continued)

```
    if ( running && target_rpm < idle_rpm )
    {
        target_rpm = idle_rpm;
    }
    else if ( !running )
```

```
   {
      target_rpm = 0.0f;
   }
   else
   {
      target_rpm = idle_rpm + throttle * ( max_rpm - idle_rpm);
   }
   delta_rpm = target_rpm - engine_rpm;
   if ( delta_rpm > 3000.0f )
   {
      delta_rpm = 3000.0f;
   }
   else if ( delta_rpm < -3000.0f )
   {
      delta_rpm = -3000.0f;
   }
   if ( delta_rpm < 1.0f && delta_rpm > -1.0f )
   {
      delta_rpm = 0.0f;
   }
   engine_rpm += (delta_rpm * delta_t);
   if ( auto_gear == GearState.Neutral || gear == GearState.Park )
   {
      eng_torque = 0;
   }
   else
   {
      eng_torque = torque_curve.Interpolate(percent_rpm * 100.0) *
            max_engine_torque;
   }

   engine_loss = Math.Max(((engine_rpm/20) * (engine_rpm/20) + 45), 0.0);

   brake_torque = brake_force * mass;

   temp = (eng_torque - engine_loss - brake_torque);

   if ( temp < 0.0 && Math.Abs(mph) < 0.1 )
   {
      temp = 0.0;
   }
```

```
if ( current_gear_ratio != 0.0 )
{
    wheel_force = temp;
}
else
{
    wheel_force = 0.0f;
}
```

If the transmission is in either Park or Neutral, the engine will not produce any torque. Otherwise, we will get the engine's torque from the torque curve LFI based on the engine RPM and the engine's maximum torque. Counteracting the engine torque will be the losses within the engine and the braking force. The engine loss is the sum of a constant loss as well as a portion that increases with engine speed. The braking losses are calculated from the braking acceleration we determined earlier. Since force is mass times acceleration, we need to multiply by the vehicle mass to get the braking torque. An intermediate force is calculated by subtracting these two losses from the engine torque. If this intermediate force is negative, the losses exceed the engine torque, and the speed is close to zero, we will zero this force for stability. If the gear ratio is nonzero, this will become our wheel force. Otherwise, our wheel force is zero, since no force is connecting through to the drive wheels.

The next section of the method (shown in Listing 10-22d) covers the calculation of the net force working on the vehicle. The net force is the wheel force minus the drag and rolling resistance. If the transmission is in reverse, we will negate the force so that it acts in the opposite direction. The next step is to determine the effect of gravity on the vehicle. For this, we rotate a gravity vector from earth to vehicle reference frame. If the car is not in park, we will apply the forces to the vehicle's forward acceleration. We need to divide the net force by the vehicle mass to get the resulting acceleration. From this, we will subtract the braking acceleration and add in the acceleration due to gravity. The vertical component of the gravity is applied to the vertical acceleration. We will assume that the lateral component of gravity is not enough to make a difference and will ignore it. If this iteration's portion of the braking force is greater than the current forward velocity, then we will zero the velocities and accelerations to bring the car to a complete stop.

Listing 10-22d. CarDynamics Process Method (Continued)

```
net_force = wheel_force - drag - rolling_resistance;

if ( gear == GearState.Reverse )
{
    net_force *= -1.0f;       // Force in reverse is in opposite direction.
}
```

```
ground_slope.RotateEtoA( gravity );
body_gravity = gravity;

if ( gear != GearState.Park )
{
    acceleration. X = (net_force / mass - brake_force) + body_gravity.X;
}
acceleration. Z -= body_gravity.Z;

if ( velocity.X < ( delta_t * brake_force ) &&
        velocity.X > ( delta_t * -brake_force ) )
{
    mph = 0.0f;
    velocity.X = 0.0;
    acceleration.X = 0.0;
    brake_force = 0.0;
}
```

The final portion of the method (shown in Listing 10-22e) closes the loop on the engine speed and calls additional methods to complete the processing. The speed of the engine not only creates the power that drives the vehicle, the speed of the vehicle also feeds back to back-drive the speed of the engine. If the transmission is in park or neutral, there is no connection between the wheels and the engine, so the engine speed remains a direct relation to the throttle position. Otherwise, we calculate a value based on the vehicle speed and the current gear ratio. This value is limited between the idle and the maximum RPM, and becomes the new target RPM. To complete the processing, we will call the CalcWeightTransfer method to get the current weight over each wheel. The ProcessWheels method calls the Process method for each wheel and applies the forces from the wheels to the vehicle. The ProcessAttitude method determines the new attitude rate based on the suspension forces. The final step is to call the IntegratePosition method to integrate the new velocity and position.

Listing 10-22e. CarDynamics Process Method (Conclusion)

```
if ( auto_gear == GearState.Neutral || gear == GearState.Park )
{
    temp = idle_rpm + (max_rpm-idle_rpm) * throttle;
}
else
{
    temp = velocity.X * current_gear_ratio;
}
```

```
        if ( temp >= (idle_rpm * 0.9f) )
        {
           if ( temp > max_rpm )
           {
              target_rpm = max_rpm;
           }
           else
           {
              target_rpm = temp;
           }
        }
        else
        {
           target_rpm = idle_rpm;
        }

        CalcWeightTransfer();

        ProcessWheels( delta_t );

        ProcessAttitude( delta_t );

        IntegratePosition( delta_t );
    }
```

The SetAttitude method (shown in Listing 10-23) provides the means of setting the attitude from another class. This would typically be used while initializing the vehicle to a new place prior to starting a new level.

Listing 10-23. CarDynamics SetAttitude Method

```
    void SetAttitude(float roll, float pitch, float heading)
    {
       attitude.Phi = roll;
       attitude.Theta = pitch;
       attitude.Psi = heading;
    }
```

The SetPosition method and SetVelocity method (shown in Listing 10-24) handles the positioning and velocity portion of setting the vehicle to a new position and velocity.

Listing 10-24. CarDynamics SetPosition and SetVelocity Methods

```
void SetPosition(float north, float east, float height)
{
   position.X = north;
   position.Y = east;
   position.Z = height;
}
void SetVelocity(float north, float east, float vertical)
{
   velocity.X = north;
   velocity.Y = east;
   velocity.Z = vertical;
}
```

There are two methods (shown in Listing 10-25) for setting the ground height under the wheels. The first is SetGroundHeight, which can be used to set the height under a specified wheel. The second method, SetAllGroundHeights, takes all four elevations as arguments in order to set the values for all four wheels in one call.

Listing 10-25. CarDynamics SetGroundHeight and SetAllGroundHeights Methods

```
void SetGroundHeight(WhichWheel the_wheel, float height)
{
   wheel[(int)the_wheel].ground_height = height;
}
void SetAllGroundHeights(float left_front, float right_front,
   float left_rear, float right_rear )
{
   wheel[(int)WhichWheel.LeftFront].ground_height = left_front;
   wheel[(int)WhichWheel.RightFront].ground_height = right_front;
   wheel[(int)WhichWheel.LeftRear].ground_height = left_rear;
   wheel[(int)WhichWheel.RightRear].ground_height = right_rear;
}
```

The WheelAngle method (shown in Listing 10-26) provides the means of getting the relative angle of the front wheels in either degrees or radians. If the Boolean argument is true, the return value is converted from radians to degrees.

Listing 10-26. CarDynamics WheelAngle Method

```
double WheelAngle( bool in_degrees )
{
    double result;

    if ( in_degrees )
    {
        result = (wheel_angle * 180.0 / Math.PI);
    }
    else
    {
        result = wheel_angle;
    }

    return result;
}
```

There are similar methods for accessing pitch and roll shown in Listing 10-27. The GetPitch method returns pitch in radians or degrees, and the GetRoll method does the same for roll.

Listing 10-27. CarDynamics GetPitch and GetRoll Methods

```
double GetPitch(bool in_degrees)
{
    double result;

    if ( in_degrees )
    {
        result = attitude.ThetaAsDegrees;
    }
    else
    {
        result = attitude.Theta;
    }

    return result;
}
double GetRoll(bool in_degrees)
{
    double result;
```

```
        if ( in_degrees )
        {
           result = attitude.PhiAsDegrees;
        }
        else
        {
           result = attitude.Phi;
        }

        return result;
    }
```

The IsTireSquealing method (shown in Listing 10-28) provides the ability to query each tire to see if it is currently in a squealing state.

Listing 10-28. CarDynamics IsTireSquealing Method

```
    bool IsTireSquealing(WhichWheel the_wheel)
    {
       return wheel[(int)the_wheel].squeeling;
    }
```

The IsTireLoose method (shown in Listing 10-29) provides similar access to the flag that indicates an individual tire is sliding.

Listing 10-29. CarDynamics IsTireLoose Method

```
    bool IsTireLoose(WhichWheel the_wheel)
    {
       return wheel[(int)the_wheel].sliding;
    }
```

The SetTireStiction method (shown in Listing 10-30) is the means of altering the static friction for the wheels. It is assumed that all four tires are the same and have the same friction characteristics.

Listing 10-30. CarDynamics SetTireStiction Method

```
    void SetTireStiction(float new_value)
    {
       wheel[(int)WhichWheel.LeftFront].SetStiction( new_value );
       wheel[(int)WhichWheel.RightFront].SetStiction( new_value );
```

```
        wheel[(int)WhichWheel.LeftRear].SetStiction( new_value );
        wheel[(int)WhichWheel.RightRear].SetStiction( new_value );


    }
```

The ProcessWheels method (shown in Listing 10-31) was mentioned in the description of the Process method. This is where we update each wheel and its suspension and the resulting forces that act on the vehicle. The lateral acceleration on the vehicle is the opposite of the centripetal force. The method loops through the four tires in the array. Each wheel's Process method is called. The upward force from the four tires is accumulated along with the suspension offsets and ground heights. If any of the wheels have bottomed out or are touching the ground, a local flag is set to reflect this fact. This method also counts the number of tires that are sliding. After all four wheels have been processed, the accumulated suspension offset and ground height are divided by four to get the average values of each. If the suspension is roughly centered, the vertical speed of the vehicle will be reduced by 80 percent to provide damping. If the force is close to zero, we will zero both the force and the velocity. The acceleration is the force divided by the mass. If the wheels are in contact with the ground, we will divide the vertical velocity by two as further damping of the vertical velocity. If any of the wheels have bottomed out, we will set the elevation of the vehicle to ensure that it remains above the ground. If it was moving down when it bottomed out, the vertical velocity will be zeroed as well. The final portion of the method deals with the lateral accelerations on the vehicle. If more than two wheels are sliding and this is the first pass that this has happened, we will break the tires loose and begin moving laterally. If we are sliding to the right, a 1 G acceleration will be applied to the left, representing the friction of the tires serving to slow the slide. If sliding to the left, the acceleration will be applied to the right. If we aren't sliding to the side, the lateral speed and acceleration will be zeroed because the tires are maintaining their grip on the ground.

Listing 10-31. CarDynamics ProcessWheels Method

```
    void ProcessWheels(float delta_t)
    {
        int      i;
        double   accel;
        double   total_upwards_force = 0.0;
        bool   bottomed_out = false;
        bool   on_ground = false;
        int      sliding = 0;
        double   avg_suspension = 0.0;
        double   delta_force;
        double   avg_ground_height = 0.0;
```

```
               acceleration.SetY(-centripedal_accel);

               for ( i=0; i<4; i++ )
               {
                   wheel[i].Process( delta_t, attitude, acceleration, velocity,
                         position );
                   total_upwards_force += wheel[i].UpwardsForce();
                   avg_suspension += wheel[i].suspension_offset;
                   avg_ground_height += wheel[i].ground_height;
                   if ( wheel[i].bottomed_out )
                   {
                       bottomed_out = true;
                   }
                   if ( wheel[i].touching_ground )
                   {
                       on_ground = true;
                   }
                   if ( wheel[i].sliding )
                   {
                       sliding++;
                   }
               }
               avg_suspension /= 4.0f;
               avg_ground_height /= 4.0f;

               if ( Math.Abs(avg_suspension) < 0.1f )
               {
                   velocity.Z = velocity.Z * 0.2;

               }
               delta_force = total_upwards_force - weight;
               if ( Math.Abs(delta_force) < 1.0 )
               {
                   delta_force = 0.0;
                   velocity.Z = 0.0;
               }
               accel = delta_force / mass;
               acceleration.Z = accel;

               if ( on_ground )
               {
                   velocity. Z = velocity.Z * 0.5;
               }
```

```
    if ( bottomed_out )
    {
        position. Z = avg_ground_height + wheel[0].offset.X + wheel[0].radius;
    }

    if ( bottomed_out && velocity.Z < 0.0f )
    {
        velocity. Z = 0.0;
    }

    if ( sliding > 2 && !was_sliding )
    {
        was_sliding = true;
        velocity.Y = acceleration.Y;
    }
    if ( sliding > 2 && velocity.Y > 0.0 )
    {
        acceleration.Y = -32.0;
    }
    else if ( sliding > 2 && velocity.Y < 0.0 )
    {
        acceleration.Y = 32.0;
    }
    else
    {
        velocity.Y = 0.0;
        acceleration.Y = 0.0;
        was_sliding = false;
    }
}
```

The ProcessAttitude method (shown in Listing 10-32) determines the attitude rates based on the suspension offsets and the slope of the ground under the vehicle. The method begins by determining the pitch of the ground under the vehicle. The Terrain class has a method for returning ground slope for a given point. Unfortunately, the slope at a single point on the terrain can give erroneous results compared to the average heights of the four points under the wheels. If, for example, there were a sharp crest in the terrain below the vehicle, the tires could be straddling that point. To get a correct value as experienced by the vehicle, we will take the average height below the front wheels and the average height below the rear wheels. The arcsine of the difference between these heights and the wheelbase of the vehicle is the pitch of the terrain as experienced by the vehicle. The roll angle is calculated the same way. In this case, we will use the arcsine of the difference between the average height on the left and the average height on the right, divided by the wheel track. The attitude rates will be a fraction of the difference between the current attitude angles and those that we just calculated.

Listing 10-32. CarDynamics ProcessAttitude Method

```
void ProcessAttitude(float delta_t)
{
    double avg_front;
    double avg_rear;
    double pitch;
    double avg_left;
    double avg_right;
    double roll;

    // First do ground slope.
    avg_front = (wheel[(int)WhichWheel.LeftFront].ground_height +
                 wheel[(int)WhichWheel.RightFront].ground_height) / 2.0;
    avg_rear  = (wheel[(int)WhichWheel.LeftRear].ground_height +
                 wheel[(int)WhichWheel.RightRear].ground_height) / 2.0;
    pitch = Math.Asin((avg_rear - avg_front) / wheel_base);

    ground_slope.Theta = pitch;

    avg_left = (wheel[(int)WhichWheel.LeftFront].ground_height +
                wheel[(int)WhichWheel.LeftRear].ground_height) / 2.0;
    avg_right  = (wheel[(int)WhichWheel.RightFront].ground_height +
                  wheel[(int)WhichWheel.RightRear].ground_height) / 2.0;
    roll = Math.Asin((avg_right - avg_left) / wheel_track);

    ground_slope.Phi = roll;

    // Now do vehicle attitude
    avg_front = (wheel[(int)WhichWheel.LeftFront].suspension_offset +
                 wheel[(int)WhichWheel.RightFront].suspension_offset) / 2.0f;
    avg_rear  = (wheel[(int)WhichWheel.LeftRear].suspension_offset +
                 wheel[(int)WhichWheel.RightRear].suspension_offset) / 2.0f;
    pitch = Math.Asin((avg_front - avg_rear) / wheel_base);

    attitude_rate.Theta = ((ground_slope.Theta+pitch)-attitude.Theta) * 0.025;
```

```
    avg_left = (wheel[(int)WhichWheel.LeftFront].suspension_offset +
               wheel[(int)WhichWheel.LeftRear].suspension_offset) / 2.0f;
    avg_right = (wheel[(int)WhichWheel.RightFront].suspension_offset +
                wheel[(int)WhichWheel.RightRear].suspension_offset) / 2.0f;
    roll = Math.Asin((avg_right - avg_left) / wheel_track);

    attitude_rate.Phi = ((ground_slope.Phi+roll) - attitude.Phi) * 0.05;

}
```

The `MinorCollision` method (shown in Listing 10-33) will be called whenever the vehicle hits something small that will affect the vehicle's speed only slightly—things like bushes, shrubs, and other small objects. This reduction in speed will be accomplished by making a 10 percent reduction in the vehicle's velocity vector.

Listing 10-33. CarDynamics MinorCollision Method

```
public void MinorCollision()
{
    velocity = velocity * 0.9f;
}
```

When the vehicle hits something major, a `MinorCollision` method won't be enough. The `MajorCollision` method (shown in Listing 10-34) will be used when we hit something that we can't just drive over and continue on our way. In order to react to the object we hit, we need to have some information about the objects involved. We need to know the difference in the velocity vectors of the two objects involved. This will tell us how hard we hit the other object. The other thing we need is the distance vector between the two objects, which gives us the direction between the two objects. Since this library and the game engine use different classes for vectors, we need to pass the components of the vectors individually. The relative velocity vector is built from the velocity components, and a collision normal vector is built from the position delta. Since this needs to be a normal vector, we normalize it so that it will be a unit vector in the direction of the collision.

Listing 10-34. CarDynamics MajorCollision Method

```
public void MajorCollision( float delta_x_velocity,
    float delta_y_velocity,
    float delta_z_velocity,
    float delta_x_position,
```

```
        float delta_y_position,
        float delta_z_position )
    {
        Vector RelativeVelocity = new Vector( delta_x_velocity,
                delta_y_velocity, delta_z_velocity );
        Vector CollisionNormal = new Vector( delta_x_position,
                delta_y_position, delta_z_position );
        CollisionNormal.Normalize();

        double collisionSpeed = RelativeVelocity * CollisionNormal;

        float impulse = (float)(( 2.50 * collisionSpeed ) /
            (( CollisionNormal * CollisionNormal) *
            ( inverse_mass )));

        velocity = ( CollisionNormal * impulse ) * (float) inverse_mass;
        engine_rpm = idle_rpm;
    }
  };
}
```

Normally when a car hits a solid object, we have what is referred to as an *inelastic collision.* The energy of the collision is dispersed by the deformation of the car. Unless we want the game to be over on impact, we need to take a step away from reality for the major collision. Instead, we will have what is called an *elastic collision.* In an elastic collision, the force is expended, driving the objects along the reverse of the normal of the collision. We will in fact exaggerate the force of the collision. This will cause the objects to bounce away from each other.

The first step is to determine how hard the vehicle hit the object. This is the dot product of the relative velocity and the collision normal. The impulse that will be applied to the car would normally be calculated as the impact speed divided by the dot product of the collision normal with itself and divided by the mass of the vehicle. To exaggerate the bounce, we will use two-and-a-half times the force. To convert the impulse into a new velocity for the car, we multiply the impulse by the collision normal vector to put it in the correct direction. We also divide this value by the mass of the vehicle to convert the force to an acceleration that is applied immediately as the vehicle's new velocity.

Waving the Flag

The first part of this chapter has dealt with rigid body dynamics. Now we will look at the dynamics of flexible systems. These techniques can be applied to cloth, hair, grass, or other flexible objects that will move and deform based on forces applied to them. We will use such a system for a rectangle of cloth that happens to be a flag. The flexibility of the object is accomplished by creating an array of control points or nodes as a regularly spaced grid. Each node is connected to its adjacent nodes with a spring/damper connection.

Dividing the Cloth Surface into Nodes

The definition of the Node structure that specifies each of these nodes is shown in Listing 10-35. Each node will have an associated mass. This is the portion of the overall mass of the cloth that is represented by the node. Although the mass is in truth evenly distributed in the spaces between the nodes, we will simplify the problem by isolating the mass at the node locations. As you might guess from this, there is a tradeoff regarding the number of nodes that are used. The greater the number of nodes, the closer the simulation gets to reality. Unfortunately, the amount of processing required increases sharply as the number of nodes increases. For efficiency, we will also hold the inverse of the mass so that we only need to perform the division once during initialization.

Listing 10-35. Cloth Class Node Structure Attributes

```
using System;
using System.Collections;
using System.Drawing;
using System.Threading;
using Microsoft.DirectX;
using Microsoft.DirectX.Direct3D;

namespace GameEngine
{
    /// <summary>
    /// Summary description for Cloth
    /// </summary>
    public class Cloth : Object3D, IDynamic
    {
        private struct Node
        {
            public float   mass;
            public float   inverse_mass;
            public Vector3 position;
            public Vector3 velocity;
            public Vector3 acceleration;
            public Vector3 force;
            public bool    constrained;
```

Each node will have a position in space that will be used when we render the cloth. The velocity of a node is included for integration as well as the acceleration and force vectors that will modify the velocity. Each node also has a flag that defines whether or not the position of the node is constrained. Nodes that are fastened to a parent object will not move due to the forces acting on the rest of the cloth. They will only move as the parent object moves.

The constructor for the Node structure is shown in Listing 10-36. The mass and position of the node are supplied as arguments as well as the flag that defines whether or not the node is constrained to remain in one place. This information is used to initialize each of the attributes of the structure. The velocities, accelerations, and forces are all initialized to zero. If the cloth was in zero gravity and no other forces were applied to the cloth, it would maintain its original rectangular shape. The forces of wind and gravity will change the shape of the cloth.

Listing 10-36. Cloth Class Node Constructor

```
public Node(float mass_, double x, double y, double z,
        bool fixed_in_place)
{
    mass = mass_;
    inverse_mass = 1.0f / mass;
    position.X = (float)x;
    position.Y = (float)y;
    position.Z = (float)z;
    velocity.X = 0.0f;
    velocity.Y = 0.0f;
    velocity.Z = 0.0f;
    acceleration.X = 0.0f;
    acceleration.Y = 0.0f;
    acceleration.Z = 0.0f;
    force.X = 0.0f;
    force.Y = 0.0f;
    force.Z = 0.0f;
    constrained = fixed_in_place;
}
}
```

The springs that connect the nodes will need to know which nodes are at each end of the spring. Since the nodes will be laid out in a grid, we will be able to index them by row and column. The NodeIndex structure (shown in Listing 10-37) will be used for this purpose.

Listing 10-37. Cloth Class NodeIndex Structure

```
private struct NodeIndex
{
    public int row;
    public int column;
}
```

The `Spring` structure (shown in Listing 10-38) will encapsulate the spring/damper system that will connect the nodes. The structure holds two instances of the `NodeIndex` structure that point to the nodes at each end of the spring. There is also a spring constant that defines the force exerted by the spring as it is stretched or compressed and the damping coefficient that counteracts the force of the spring for stability. The last attribute of the structure is the rest length of the spring. When this distance separates the two nodes, there will be no force exerted by the spring.

Listing 10-38. Cloth Class Spring Structure

```
private struct Spring
{
    public NodeIndex node1;
    public NodeIndex node2;
    public float     spring_constant;
    public float      damping;
    public float      length;
}
```

Weaving Our Cloth

Now that we've seen all of the support structures that will be used by the `Cloth` class, we can look at the `Cloth` class itself. We will begin with the attributes and constants for the class (shown in Listing 10-39) that will be used by the class. An array of vertices render the cloth. The node positions will become the positional part of the vertices. The class also includes a vertex and an index buffer. By using the combination of two buffers, we can have each node represented by a single vertex in the buffer. The sharing of the vertices is accomplished by the references to the vertices in the index buffer. Since the contents of an index buffer default to short integers, we will create an array of shorts that will be used to populate the index buffer. The final attribute required for the rendering of the cloth is the texture that will be applied to the cloth. In the case of our sample program, this will be an image of the US flag.

Listing 10-39. Cloth Class Attributes and Constants

```
#region Attributes
private CustomVertex.PositionNormalTextured[]  m_vertices;
private VertexBuffer m_VB = null;  // Vertex buffer
private IndexBuffer  m_IB = null;  // Index buffer
// Indices buffer
private short[] indices;
private Texture      m_Texture; // Image for face
private Node[,] nodes;
private int num_springs;
private int num_faces;
private int num_rows;
private int num_columns;
private int num_nodes;
private Spring[] springs;
private Vector3  m_vOffset = new Vector3(0.0f, 0.0f, 0.0f);
private Attitude m_AttitudeOffset = new Attitude();
private bool m_bValid = false;
private Thread        m_physics_thread;
private bool thread_active = true;
private Mutex mutex = new Mutex();

// Global variables
private static Vector3 wind = new Vector3();

// Constants
private static float gravity = -32.174f;
private static float spring_tension = 40.10f;
private static float damping = .70f;
private static float drag_coefficient = 0.01f;
#endregion
```

The next section of attributes are those required to manage the nodes that control the shape of the cloth. A two-dimensional array of node structures forms the basic grid. We will also keep track of the number of springs that connect the nodes, the number of faces that will exist between the nodes, the number of rows and columns in the grid, and the overall number of nodes. A one-dimensional array will hold all of the springs that connect the nodes.

The final section of normal attributes are those concerned with the attachment of the cloth to a parent object and the updating of the cloth. The Cloth class inherits from the Object3D class. Because of this, it can be attached as a child of another object. We will include a position and attitude offset that may be used to adjust the cloth's placement relative to its parent. If the initialization of the class is successful, the valid flag is set to true. This prevents unneeded processing later if the cloth could not be properly created. As in the CarDynamics class, we must run the dynamics for the cloth at a high iteration rate. This entails spawning a processing thread with its associated active flag and Mutex for safe communications.

One global attribute exists for the Cloth class. A wind vector defines the current wind direction and speed that will affect all instances of the class. The attributes end with a set of static constants that are used in the physics calculations: the acceleration of gravity that will tend to make the nodes fall towards the earth, the spring constant that will work to hold the nodes together, and the damping constant that will prevent the spring forces from oscillating. Finally, we will have a drag coefficient that calculates the force of the wind against the fabric.

The properties for the Cloth class are shown in Listing 10-40. The Offset property is available for checking and altering the object's offset from its parent object, and there are two static properties for controlling the global wind vector.

Listing 10-40. Cloth Class Properties

```
#region Properties
public Vector3 Offset {
    set { m_vOffset = value; }
    get { return m_vOffset; } }

public static float EastWind {
    set { wind.X = value; }
    get { return wind.X; } }
public static float NorthWind {
    set { wind.Z = value; }
    get { return wind.Z; } }
#endregion
```

The constructor for the Cloth class (shown in Listings 10-41a through 10-41e later in this section) is quite involved. Half of the work in simulating a complex spring/damper system is in the initialization. To construct a piece of cloth for our flag, we need a number of arguments. Since the class inherits from Object3D, we need a name for each instance of the class. The name is passed down to the base class. We also need the name of the texture that will be applied to the surface as well as the size of the cloth defined by the number of rows and columns in the node grid and the separation distance between the nodes. Finally, we need the mass of the piece of cloth in order to perform the physics calculations.

The first portion of the constructor is shown in Listing 10-41a. The number of rows and columns are saved away in the associated attributes for later reference and the texture is loaded from the requested file. The working code in the

constructor is enclosed in a Try/Catch block so that errors such as the inability
to load the texture will terminate the constructor without crashing the application. We will consider the rows and columns specified to be the areas between
the nodes. Therefore, we need one more node in each direction. The array of
nodes is allocated with this increased count. The number of faces that will be
rendered is twice the product of the rows and columns, since it requires two triangles for each square piece of the cloth. The number of springs required is even
greater. Springs will connect each node with its neighbors in the vertical, horizontal, and diagonal directions. Once the required number of springs is calculated,
the array of springs will be allocated. We will also clear the global wind vector
within the constructor so that there will be no wind unless specifically set by the
game application.

Listing 10-41a. Cloth Class Constructor

```
public Cloth(string name, string texture_name, int rows, int columns,
            double spacing, float mass) : base(name)
{
   try
   {
      num_rows = rows;
      num_columns = columns;
      m_Texture =
         GraphicsUtility.CreateTexture(CGameEngine.Device3D,
         texture_name);
      nodes = new Node[rows+1,columns+1];
      num_nodes = (rows+1) * (columns+1);

      num_faces = rows * columns * 2;
      num_springs = columns * ( rows+1) + rows * (columns+1) +
         columns*rows*2;
      springs = new Spring[num_springs];

      wind.X = 0.0f;
      wind.Y = 0.0f;
      wind.Z = 0.0f;
```

The next section of the constructor (shown in Listing 10-41b) allocates the
array of vertices and all of the nodes. The array of vertices is allocated to be as
large as the total number of nodes that we will be using. The vertex format
includes position, normal, and texture coordinate information. The mass at each
node is also calculated. Since we stated that the mass would be evenly distributed
across the nodes, this is simply the total mass divided by the number of nodes.

Listing 10-41b. Cloth Class Constructor (Continued)

```
m_vertices = new CustomVertex.PositionNormalTextured[num_nodes];

float mass_per_node = mass / num_nodes;

for ( int r=0; r<=rows; r++ )
{
   for ( int c=0; c <=columns; c++ )
   {
      nodes[r,c] = new Node(mass_per_node, -(c*spacing),
            -(r*spacing), 0.0, c==0 && (r==0 || r == rows));
   }
}
```

To construct the nodes, we will loop through all of the rows and columns of our grid. The position of each node is a function of the row and column number and the spacing distance. We will constrain the top and bottom nodes of the first column. Since we are modeling a flag, these will be the points at which the flag is attached to the parent object.

The next section of the constructor (shown in Listing 10-41c) covers the creation and population of the index and vertex buffers. These are buffers that are allocated on the video card if at all possible. The vertex buffer is created large enough to hold one vertex for each of the nodes. The index buffer is large enough to hold the indices of the three vertices for each face making up the surface of the cloth. The indices array that holds the local image of the index buffer is also allocated as an array of short integers the same size.

Listing 10-41c. Cloth Class Constructor (Continued)

```
// Create a buffer for rendering the cloth.
m_VB = new VertexBuffer(
   typeof(CustomVertex.PositionNormalTextured), num_nodes,
   CGameEngine.Device3D, Usage.WriteOnly,
   CustomVertex.PositionNormalTextured.Format,
   Pool.Default );

m_IB = new IndexBuffer(
   typeof(short), num_faces * 3, CGameEngine.Device3D,
   Usage.WriteOnly, Pool.Managed);
indices = new short[num_faces * 3];
m_IB.Created += new System.EventHandler(this.PopulateIndexBuffer);
this.PopulateIndexBuffer(m_IB, null);

m_VB.Created += new System.EventHandler(this.PopulateBuffer);
this.PopulateBuffer(m_VB, null);
```

An event handler will be set up to repopulate the buffers if they become re-created at some point in the future. To complete the initial population of the buffers, we will call these event handlers manually at this point.

The next section of the constructor (shown in Listing 10-41d) initializes all of the springs that connect the nodes. To do this, we will loop through all the rows and columns of our grid again. If the current column is not the last column, we attach a spring between the current node and the one in the next column. The row and column indices of the two nodes are recorded, and the spring and damping constants are copied into the structure. We need to know the rest length of the spring. It is the magnitude of the distance vector that connects the two nodes. We will connect another spring down to the node below this one if the current node is not in the last row. Another spring will be connected diagonally down and to the right if the current node is not in the last row or column. One last spring will be connected to this node down and to the left if there is a node in that direction. This will give us springs connecting every node with every adjacent node in each direction, which will be what holds the fabric of our cloth together.

Listing 10-41d. Cloth Class Constructor (Continued)

```
// Create the springs
int index = 0;
for ( int r=0; r<=rows; r++ )
{
    for ( int c=0; c <=columns; c++ )
    {
        if ( c < columns )
        {
            springs[index].node1.row = r;
            springs[index].node1.column = c;
            springs[index].node2.row = r;
            springs[index].node2.column = c+1;
            springs[index].spring_constant = spring_tension;
            springs[index].damping = damping;
            Vector3 length = nodes[r,c].position - nodes[r,c+1].position;
            springs[index].length = length.Length();
            index++;
        }
        if ( r < rows )
        {
            springs[index].node1.row = r;
            springs[index].node1.column = c;
            springs[index].node2.row = r+1;
```

```
         springs[index].node2.column = c;
         springs[index].spring_constant = spring_tension;
         springs[index].damping = damping;
       Vector3 length = nodes[r,c].position - nodes[r+1,c].position;
         springs[index].length = length.Length();
         index++;
     }
     if ( r < rows && c < columns )
     {
         springs[index].node1.row = r;
         springs[index].node1.column = c;
         springs[index].node2.row = r+1;
         springs[index].node2.column = c+1;
         springs[index].spring_constant = spring_tension;
         springs[index].damping = damping;
         Vector3 length = nodes[r,c].position -
                 nodes[r+1,c+1].position;
         springs[index].length = length.Length();
         index++;
     }
     if ( r < rows && c > 0 )
     {
         springs[index].node1.row = r;
         springs[index].node1.column = c;
         springs[index].node2.row = r+1;
         springs[index].node2.column = c-1;
         springs[index].spring_constant = spring_tension;
         springs[index].damping = damping;
         Vector3 length = nodes[r,c].position -
                 nodes[r+1,c-1].position;
         springs[index].length = length.Length();
         index++;
     }
   }
}
```

The final portion of the constructor (shown in Listing 10-41e) fires off the thread that will calculate the movement of the cloth. A new thread is created that will use the DoPhysics method as its code. The thread is then started. If we have reached this point without throwing an exception, then we know that the cloth has been successfully initialized. The validity flag can now be safely set. If an exception is thrown during the construction, a message will be posted to the console

Listing 10-41e. Cloth Class Constructor (Conclusion)

```
            m_physics_thread = new Thread(new ThreadStart(DoPhysics));
            m_physics_thread.Start();
            m_bValid = true;
        }
        catch (DirectXException d3de)
        {
            Console.AddLine("Unable to create cloth for " + name);
            Console.AddLine(d3de.ErrorString);
        }
        catch ( Exception e )
        {
            Console.AddLine("Unable to create cloth for " + name);
            Console.AddLine(e.Message);
        }
    }
```

The PopulateBuffer method that is called by the constructor and will be called any time the vertex buffer changes is shown in Listing 10-42. The method loops through all of the nodes, copying the position of the node into the corresponding entry in the local vertex array. The texture coordinates for each vertex can be calculated as the ratio of the current row and column with the maximum value of each. Once the local array of vertices has been filled, we need to transfer the data to the vertex buffer in the video card's memory. For thread safety, we don't want to do this while the card's vertex buffer is in use. To prevent this, we will set the Mutex object. Once the Mutex object is locked for us by its WaitOne method, we can copy the data safely to the vertex buffer. When the copying is completed, we will release the Mutex object to signal we are done.

Listing 10-42. Cloth Class PopulateBuffer Method

```
    public void PopulateBuffer(object sender, EventArgs e)
    {
        VertexBuffer vb = (VertexBuffer)sender;

        int index = 0;
        for ( int r=0; r<(1+num_rows); r++ )
        {
            for ( int c=0; c <(1+num_columns); c++ )
            {
                m_vertices[index].SetPosition(nodes[r,c].position);
                m_vertices[index].SetNormal(new Vector3(0.0f, 0.0f, 1.0f));
```

```
        m_vertices[index].Tv = (float)r / (float)(num_rows);
        m_vertices[index].Tu = (float)c / (float)(num_columns);
        index++;
      }
    }
    // Copy vertices into vertex buffer.
    mutex.WaitOne();
    vb.SetData(m_vertices, 0, 0);
    mutex.ReleaseMutex();
}
```

The PopulateIndexBuffer method (shown in Listing 10-43) works in a similar manner. In this case, the data that is placed in the local index buffer is calculated from the row and column numbers themselves. Two sets of three indices are placed in the buffer for each face. Once the local buffer has been filled, the data is copied over to the card's index buffer using the same procedure we followed for the vertex buffer.

Listing 10-43. Cloth Class PopulateIndexBuffer Method

```
public void PopulateIndexBuffer(object sender, EventArgs e)
{
    int index = 0;

    IndexBuffer g = (IndexBuffer)sender;
    for ( int r=0; r<num_rows; r++)
    {
        for ( int c=0; c<num_columns; c++)
        {
            indices[index]   = (short)((r)  *(1+num_columns) + (c));
            indices[index+1] = (short)((r+1)*(1+num_columns) + (c));
            indices[index+2] = (short)((r)  *(1+num_columns) + (c+1));

            indices[index+3] = (short)((r)  *(1+num_columns) + (c+1));
            indices[index+4] = (short)((r+1)*(1+num_columns) + (c));
            indices[index+5] = (short)((r+1)*(1+num_columns) + (c+1));
            index += 6;
        }
    }

    mutex.WaitOne();
    g.SetData(indices, 0, 0);
    mutex.ReleaseMutex();
}
```

The Render method of the Cloth class (shown in Listing 10-44) is an override of the method from the base class. The method will not render anything if the class does not complete construction and set itself as valid. If it is valid, the process begins by determining the world matrix required to render the cloth in the proper location. If a parent exists, we will use the product of the class's matrix with the parent's matrix. Otherwise, we will just use the class's matrix. This matrix is passed to the device so it may translate the vertices we will send to the correct location. A plain white material, the texture, and the buffers are passed to the device. We will wrap the actual rendering call with the Mutex code to ensure that we don't try to render with buffers that are being changed. Since the class not only can be a child but may also have children of its own, we need to render any children held by the class. If children exist, we loop through the list of children and call the Render method for each one.

Listing 10-44. Cloth Class Render Method

```
public override void Render( Camera cam )
{
    if ( m_bValid )
    {
        Matrix world_matrix;

        if ( m_Parent != null )
        {
            world_matrix = Matrix.Multiply(m_Matrix, m_Parent.WorldMatrix);
        }
        else
        {
            world_matrix = m_Matrix;
        }

        CGameEngine.Device3D.Transform.World = world_matrix;

        Material mtrl = new Material();
        mtrl.Ambient = Color.White;
        mtrl.Diffuse = Color.White;
        CGameEngine.Device3D.Material = mtrl;
        CGameEngine.Device3D.SetStreamSource( 0, m_VB, 0 );
        CGameEngine.Device3D.VertexFormat =
                CustomVertex.PositionNormalTextured.Format;

        CGameEngine.Device3D.RenderState.CullMode = Cull.None;
```

```
// Set the texture.
CGameEngine.Device3D.SetTexture(0, m_Texture );

// Set the indices.
CGameEngine.Device3D.Indices = m_IB;

// Render the face.
mutex.WaitOne();
CGameEngine.Device3D.DrawIndexedPrimitives(
    PrimitiveType.TriangleList, 0, 0, num_nodes, 0, num_faces);
mutex.ReleaseMutex();

if ( m_Children.Count > 0 )
{
    Object3D obj;
    for ( int i=0; i<m_Children.Count; i++ )
    {
        obj = (Object3D)m_Children.GetByIndex(i);
        obj.Render( cam );
    }
}
    }
  }
}
```

The Update method (shown in Listing 10-45) is another method that is declared by the base class and needs to be overridden for completeness. The update process for the cloth itself is done in the processing thread. If an additional Update method has been attached to the cloth, it will be called from this method. If the class has any children, then their Update method will be called as well.

Listing 10-45. Cloth Class Update Method

```
public override void Update( float DeltaT )
{
    if ( m_UpdateMethod != null )
    {
        m_UpdateMethod( (Object3D)this, DeltaT );
    }
    if ( m_Children.Count > 0 )
    {
        Object3D obj;
        for ( int i=0; i<m_Children.Count; i++ )
```

```
            {
                obj = (Object3D)m_Children.GetByIndex(i);
                obj.Update( DeltaT );
            }
        }
    }
```

The DoPhysics method that runs in the processing thread (shown in Listings 10-46a through 10-46d) is where the actual cloth dynamics takes place. The method has a local vector that will hold the inverse speed of the parent if a parent exists (see Listing 10-46a). This represents the apparent wind caused by the movement of the parent. An instance of the System.Random class is instantiated. Random numbers are generated to represent turbulence in the wind interacting with the cloth. This method loops within the thread until the thread_active flag is cleared. The code within the loop is encapsulated within a Try/Catch block to make sure that any exceptions are caught and don't terminate the thread prematurely. If the class has a parent, its velocity is inverted and saved as the parent_wind as mentioned earlier. A world translation matrix based on the object attitude, offsets, and position is created next.

Listing 10-46a. Cloth Class DoPhysics Method

```
private void DoPhysics()
{
    Vector3 parent_wind = new Vector3(0.0f, 0.0f, 0.0f );
    System.Random rand = new System.Random();

    while ( thread_active )
    {
        try
        {
            if ( m_Parent != null )
            {
                parent_wind = m_Parent.Velocity * -1.0f;
            }
            m_Matrix = Matrix.Identity;
            m_Matrix = Matrix.RotationYawPitchRoll(Heading+
                m_AttitudeOffset.Heading,
                Pitch+m_AttitudeOffset.Pitch,Roll+m_AttitudeOffset.Roll);
            Matrix temp = Matrix.Translation(m_vPosition);
            m_Matrix.Multiply(temp);
```

Making the Cloth Move

The next section of the DoPhysics method (shown in Listing 10-46b) concerns the external forces that are acting on the cloth. It begins by zeroing the force vector for every node. We will be accumulating forces into this vector. We will then loop through all of the nodes again. If the node is constrained, we will not calculate forces for the node. We will start by adding in the force due to gravity in the vertical direction. Next, we will calculate the drag force acting on the node. The first step is to get the normal of the velocity vector inverted to point in the direction opposite the current velocity of the node. We will do this because drag is always in opposition with the current velocity. The drag force is the square of the magnitude of the velocity times the drag coefficient applied along this normalized vector.

Listing 10-46b. Cloth Class DoPhysics Method (Continued)

```
for ( int r=0; r<=num_rows; r++ )
{
    for ( int c=0; c <=num_columns; c++ )
    {
        nodes[r,c].force.X = 0.0f;
        nodes[r,c].force.Y = 0.0f;
        nodes[r,c].force.Z = 0.0f;
    }
}

// Process external forces
for ( int r=0; r<=num_rows; r++ )
{
    for ( int c=0; c <=num_columns; c++ )
    {
        if ( !nodes[r,c].constrained )
        {
            // Gravity
            nodes[r,c].force.Y += (float)(gravity * nodes[r,c].mass);

            // Drag
            Vector3 drag = nodes[r,c].velocity;
            drag.Multiply(-1.0f);
            drag.Normalize();
            drag.Multiply((nodes[r,c].velocity.Length() *
                nodes[r,c].velocity.Length()) * drag_coefficient);
            nodes[r,c].force += drag;
```

```
                            // Wind
                            Vector3 turbulence = new Vector3(
                                (float)rand.NextDouble(), 0.0f,
                                (float)rand.NextDouble());
                            Vector3 total_wind = wind + turbulence + parent_wind;
                            nodes[r,c].force += total_wind;
                        }
                    }
                }
```

The final external force acting on the nodes is any wind. A turbulence vector is created using three random numbers. This turbulence along with global wind and the wind from the parent form the total wind force acting on the node.

The internal forces from the springs are calculated in the next section of the method shown in Listing 10-46c. This section loops through the array of springs. It begins by getting the indices of the nodes at each end of the spring. The distance vector between the two nodes is calculated. The magnitude of this vector is the current length of the spring. A copy of this distance vector is divided by this length in order to normalize the vector. A vector based on the difference in the velocities of the two nodes is also computed. The force due to the spring is calculated as the product of the spring coefficient and the deviation of the spring length from its rest length. The damping force that opposes the spring force is the damping coefficient times the dot product of velocity delta vector and the distance vector divided by the current spring length. The sum of these two forces, oriented with the normalized vector, becomes the force acting on one of the nodes. The inverse of the force acts on the other node. The nodes are either pulled together by the spring force or repelled, depending on whether the spring is stretched or compressed. If the nodes are not constrained, the associated force is applied to each of these nodes.

Listing 10-46c. Cloth Class DoPhysics Method (Continued)

```
            // Spring forces
            for ( int i=0; i<num_springs; i++ )
            {
                int row1    = springs[i].node1.row;
                int column1 = springs[i].node1.column;
                int row2    = springs[i].node2.row;
                int column2 = springs[i].node2.column;

                Vector3 distance = nodes[row1,column1].position -
                        nodes[row2,column2].position;
                float spring_length = distance.Length();
                Vector3 normalized_distance = distance;
```

```
        normalized_distance.Multiply( 1.0f / spring_length );
        Vector3 velocity = nodes[row1,column1].velocity -
                nodes[row2,column2].velocity;
        float length = springs[i].length;

        float spring_force = springs[i].spring_constant *
                (spring_length - length);
        float damping_force = springs[i].damping *
                Vector3.Dot(velocity,distance) / spring_length;

        Vector3 force2 = (spring_force + damping_force) *
                normalized_distance;
        Vector3 force1 = force2;
        force1.Multiply(-1.0f);

        if ( !nodes[row1,column1].constrained )
        {
            nodes[row1,column1].force += force1;
        }

        if ( !nodes[row2,column2].constrained )
        {
            nodes[row2,column2].force += force2;
        }
    }
```

The final step in the processing is shown in Listing 10-46d. This step is to apply the forces to the nodes and integrate the new accelerations, velocities, and positions for each node. Once again, we loop through all of the nodes. The new acceleration is calculated by multiplying the current force by the inverse of the node's mass. Since we are iterating at a nominal 100 hertz, we will calculate the new velocity by adding in .01 of the acceleration. The position is changed by .01 of the new velocity. The last thing we need to do is update the vertex buffer with the new node positions. We have reached the end of the processing for one pass and will sleep for 10 milliseconds before starting it all again.

Listing 10-46d. Cloth Class DoPhysics Method (Conclusion)

```
// Integrate position
for ( int r=0; r<=num_rows; r++ )
{
    for ( int c=0; c <=num_columns; c++ )
```

```
                      {
                          float x;
                          Vector3 accel = nodes[r,c].force;
                          accel.Multiply( nodes[r,c].inverse_mass);
                          nodes[r,c].acceleration = accel;
                          nodes[r,c].velocity.X += accel.X * 0.01f;
                          nodes[r,c].velocity.Y += accel.Y * 0.01f;
                          nodes[r,c].velocity.Z += accel.Z * 0.01f;
                          nodes[r,c].position.X += nodes[r,c].velocity.X * 0.01f;
                          nodes[r,c].position.Y += nodes[r,c].velocity.Y * 0.01f;
                          nodes[r,c].position.Z += nodes[r,c].velocity.Z * 0.01f;
                          x=1;
                      }
                  }
                  PopulateBuffer((object)m_VB, null);

              }
              catch (DirectXException d3de)
              {
                  Console.AddLine("Unable to update a Model " + Name);
                  Console.AddLine(d3de.ErrorString);
              }
              catch ( Exception e )
              {
                  Console.AddLine("Unable to update a Model " + Name);
                  Console.AddLine(e.Message);
              }

              Thread.Sleep(10);

          }
      }
```

The last method in the class is the `Dispose` method shown in Listing 10-47. The only task for this method is to terminate the processing thread. Clearing the thread_active flag and waiting 100 milliseconds to ensure that the thread has terminated accomplishes this.

Listing 10-47. Cloth Class Dispose Method

```
public override void Dispose()
{
    thread_active = false;
    Thread.Sleep(100);
}
}
}
```

Summary

This chapter has covered a couple aspects of physics as they apply to our sample game. Other aspects of physics might come into play in other games. Weapons or nonpropelled objects in flight would use the area of physics known as ballistics. Flying vehicles would employ aerodynamics. Boats would use hydrodynamics. All of these branches of physics boil down to the calculation of forces and the resulting accelerations, both linear and rotational, that they create. I hope that this introduction to physics sets you on the path to understanding and implementing physics as required for your games.

Tools of the Trade

THE FIRST TEN CHAPTERS OF this book covered the development of a simple game engine. We'll wrap up with a look at the tools you will need for building the sample game engine as well as any games created with this engine. We will also look at some of the tools you can use to build the artistic content for your games. This includes three-dimensional models, collections of models to form a scene, textures and other two-dimensional content, and audio files. In each of these categories, we will look at not only the more professional tools that are available, but also the free or inexpensive tools that are available to the novice or hobbyist developer.

Setting Up Your Development Environment

You are never going to get anywhere in your game development if you can't build the software. The software development tools include not only the compiler for the software, but also tools to debug and profile the software. You will also need to have the .NET Framework and the DirectX 9 SDK installed on your development machine. Both of these packages are free to download from Microsoft. The .NET Framework can be found at http://msdn.microsoft.com/netframework. The latest version of DirectX can be downloaded from http://www.microsoft.com/directx. When downloading DirectX, be sure that you get the SDK. There is also a download at this site that contains only the runtime components. These components will allow you to execute the DirectX application but do not include all of the headers and tools required to build DirectX applications. When installing the SDK, be sure to install the debug libraries. Your software will execute a bit slower with these libraries, but they provide invaluable information when chasing a problem in your software.

In order to run the .NET Framework, you must have at least the Windows 98 version of Microsoft Windows. I would recommend either Windows 2000 or Windows XP. To get the most out of DirectX, you should also have a fairly recent graphics card and get the latest drivers for the card. As of this writing, only the latest cards from nVIDIA and ATI are fully DirectX 9 compatible.

Driving the Cadillac—Visual Studio

The quickest way to develop game software is with a good integrated design environment (IDE). An IDE brings all the software development tools together in one place. This includes the editor, the debugger, and other tools. The best IDE on the market for C# development is Visual Studio 7. This is a somewhat pricey package for the novice and hobbyist developer, but it does provide everything that a developer needs. In addition to the basic IDE components already mentioned, it has an integrated object browser. The object browser gives you the ability to browse through the classes and structures in any .NET assembly. Since the Microsoft documentation for Managed DirectX 9 is somewhat behind the C++ documentation, you may occasionally need to do a bit of digging to figure out exactly what the API is doing. The solution is to become familiar with the C++ documentation. You must then supplement that information with the limited C# documentation and looking directly at the classes in the object browser.

Visual Studio also provides a DirectX Wizard that will create the graphical equivalent to a "Hello World" application for you. It uses the same underlying framework that was the used in this book's sample game engine. It also adds references to the project for the DirectX components requested. If you don't use the wizard or if you decide that you need additional components later, you must add references to those assemblies. References are added to a project within the workspace by right-clicking the References folder for the project in the Solution Explorer pane. The Add Reference dialog box will appear, and the DirectX assemblies will be displayed on the .NET tab of the dialog box. Simply select the desired assembly, and click the Select button followed by the OK button. The assembly will then be displayed in the project's References folder.

Visual Studio also provides complete debugging capabilities. One of the important capabilities of the debugger is the ability to perform unmanaged debugging. The debug libraries of DirectX provide what is referred to as "debug spew." This "spew" is a stream of status and fault information that is provided by the debug version of the libraries, which is one reason why the debug libraries run slower than the release versions. If unmanaged debugging is activated, this information is routed to Visual Studio's output pane. Unmanaged debugging is disabled by default. To enable it, you must open the property window for the project. Under Configuration Properties you will find a selection for debugging. On this page appears a property labeled Enable Unmanaged Debugging. Setting this property to true enables this capability. With unmanaged debugging enabled, any DirectX commands that fail will send useful information to the output pane.

Visual Studio is the Cadillac of development tools when it comes to developing Managed DirectX. This level of capability comes at a price, though. The C#-only version costs at least $100. The full version of Visual Studio costs over $800. While this is not out of line for professional developers, it could be a bit pricey for hobbyist developers.

Getting There in a Yugo—Free Tools

Luckily for hobbyist developers, there are other options open for developing C# and managed DirectX applications. The first option is supplied with the .NET

Framework itself. The framework comes with a command line C# compiler. In fact, it is this compiler that is invoked by Visual Studio when building applications. You can edit your source code with your favorite text editor and then invoke the compiler to build the application. Some developer's editors include the capability to invoke compilers from within the editor environment. This provides the ability to build the applications but not to debug them. Luckily, Microsoft has provided some debugging tools with the DirectX SDK. The first of these tools is DBMon. DBMon is a DOS window that acts like the Output pane during unmanaged debugging. The DBMon window displays the same "debug spew" from the debug libraries.

Another option is available that is closer to the Visual Studio experience: an open source project, called SharpDevelop, available at `http://www.sourceforge.net/projects/sharpdevelop` or `http://www.icsharpcode.net`. This is a C# IDE written entirely in C#. Since SharpDevelop is an open source project, the full source to the compiler is also available. This application provides the entire IDE experience. You can edit your code, compile, and debug. It uses the command line compiler provided by the .NET Framework to perform the actual compiling. The one thing that it does not support so far is the display of the DirectX "debug spew." For that, you still need to use the DBMon application.

Three-Dimensional Modeling Tools

A three-dimensional game requires three-dimensional objects within the environment. Although it is possible to design an object on graph paper and manually enter all of the vertices for that object using a text editor, it is an arduous effort. Luckily, there is a wide range of modeling tools available.

Professional Modeling Tools

A number of professional-grade modeling tools are available on the market. Some of the more popular packages are Maya by Alias|Wavefront, 3D Studio Max by Discreet, and Creator by MultiGen-Paradigm. Each of these packages is an incredibly powerful suite of modeling tools for creating three-dimensional models. All of that power and capability comes at a price. A license for one of these package costs thousands of dollars. If you can afford these tools, this is the way to go. Information on these tools can be found on the following Web sites:

- `http://www.aliaswavefront.com`

- `http://www.discreet.com`

- `http://www.multigen.com`

Discreet also offers a free modeling tool called gmax. In some ways, this tool could be thought of as "3D Studio Lite." It has a similar user interface and many of the same basic features. Discreet designed gmax as an enabling tool for game developers. The concept was for a free tool that could be used by game owners to create additional content for the game that they have purchased. Game development companies can purchase a gmax developer kit that allows them to create import/export filters between their game's model format and the gmax model format. For that reason, gmax may not be used to generate DirectX format models directly. It is possible, though, to export to Quake format models using the Tempest gmax plug-in for Quake. Once you have models in the Quake format, there are tools available to convert them into the DirectX format.

Hobbyist Modeling Tools

If you are not an industry professional, you will likely find the professional tools beyond your price range. Numerous low-cost and free tools are also available, however. One of the best of the inexpensive modeling programs that I have encountered is trueSpace by Caligari. The latest version of the software is only $595. Older versions of this program are available for as little as $99. All of these versions can directly read and write DirectX-format model files. In addition to the three-dimensional modeling capability, it includes animation and shader support. Information regarding this tool can be found at `http://www.caligari.com`.

If trueSpace is still a little too expensive for you, you have a couple of shareware/freeware options available for download from the Internet. One is MilkShape 3D available at `http://www.swissquake.ch/chumbalum-soft` from chUmbaLum sOft. MilkShape 3D is a shareware product with a modest registration fee of $25. It does not have the ability to import DirectX format models, but it is able to export to DirectX through a free third-party plug-in.

The second alternative is Blender, available at the Blender Foundation site (`http://www.blender.org`). Blender is an open source freeware application. It also is unable to import DirectX models and uses a downloadable plug-in for exporting to DirectX format. Blender is more than just a modeling tool—it actually has game engine features built within the applications.

If you are unable to afford one of the professional packages, I recommend that you download and try out each of these applications. The trueSpace application has a demonstration version that can be downloaded for evaluation. It is fully functional with the exception of saving the models that you create. MilkShape 3D has a 30-day evaluation period before registration is required. Each package has its own style of user interface, and by evaluating each one you can determine which fits your style the best.

Converting Model Formats

In addition to creating your own models from scratch, you have the option of downloading free three-dimensional models from the Internet. A search with your favorite Internet search engine will provide numerous sites dedicated to free models. Unfortunately, most of the models will not be in DirectX format. Most models are in either the 3D Studios format (.3DS) or in Autocad format (.DXF). To use these models, you would need to either write an importer for your game engine or convert the models into DirectX format. A conversion program like the ones we will take a look at next is a must-have for your game development toolkit.

One of the premier professional conversion packages is PolyTrans by Okino (http://www.okino.com). This package lists for just under $400 for the PC platform and is able to translate between most model formats. There are a few formats that require a plug-in at an extra cost. Luckily, the DirectX format is not one of these. You can check out Okino's Web site for details.

Another option for model conversion is Deep Exploration by a company called Right Hemisphere (http://www.righthemisphere.com). This is a nice package that lists for $249. It not only provides the capability of converting models between formats, but is also a good visualization tool for models and two-dimensional images. It has a user interface similar to that of the Windows Explorer. It also has the ability to select and play any animations that are a part of a 3D model file.

If you are a hobbyist developer without the budget for one of these tools, there is still an option left to you. A freeware package called CrossRoads provides limited model conversion capability. It may be downloaded from the creator's Web site at http://home.europa.com/~keithr/Crossroads/. It has some export capability for DirectX format models, though it can be somewhat buggy at times.

The final option for the hobbyist is the conv3ds application from Microsoft. The DirectX 8 SDK and earlier included the application to convert 3D Studios format files into the DirectX format. Although conv3ds doesn't come with the DirectX 9 SDK, luckily it is still available on a number of Web sites. One such site is http://www.microtower.com. The conv3ds application works from a DOS command line interface.

Level Editors

One tool that tends to be specific to each game engine is the level editor. This is a tool that is used to create each of the levels within a multilevel game. The gmax editor was designed primarily as a level editor. Its ability to edit three-dimensional models is actually an additional feature. A game level is a set of both the fixed (e.g., terrain and building) objects and the moving objects as well as win/loss criteria that define one playable subset of a game. Commercial games that ship with gmax plug-ins provide the ability for players to create their own levels for use within the game. Think of the levels as the content that is executed by the game engine.

Even if you have no intention of releasing a level editor with your game, you may wish to either adapt an existing level editor for your game or create one. Our example game contained only a single level. Because of this, we were able to code the loading of the level components within the application. If your game will have more than a single level, it is better to create a level loader for the game engine. A number of level editors are available for existing games that you may use if you do not have the resources to create your own or the finances to purchase the gmax developer kit. The level editor to choose depends mostly on the genre of your game engine. If you are writing a third-person strategy game, the level editor for a first-person shooter will probably not work well for you.

Editing Images

Over the course of this book, you have seen images used for a wide variety of purposes including textures for objects, terrain height maps, splash screen backgrounds, and buttons. In order to create and manipulate these images, you will need one or more image editing tools.

Editing Images in General

Every copy of Microsoft Windows comes with the Paint program. This program provides simple editing capability. Although Paint does provide the ability to edit an image, it is limited in the file formats it supports—numerous types of Windows bitmap (.BMP and .DIB) files as well as JPEG, GIF, TIFF, and PNG format files—and the tools it supplies. One of the major features that it lacks is the ability to manipulate transparency information in an image.

NOTE *If you choose to use the Windows bitmap formats, be sure to use the 24-bit color version. The other two color formats use either 4 or 8 bits per pixel and require palette management. The 24-bit style contains all of the color information for each pixel within the image data. When you add the transparency data, you move up to 32 bits with the 8 bits of alpha information.*

To get serious about image editing requires a more powerful tool. The tool of choice is Adobe Photoshop (http://www.adobe.com). This package is not cheap at a list price of $609, but it provides any image editing feature you could think of. This includes a wide range of filtering options as well as the ability to work with each color channel and the alpha transparency channel individually.

Creating Textures

The creation of textures for models and billboards is the most common use for the image editing tool. If you do have Photoshop, you have everything that you need. You can create any transparent areas needed within a texture.

 NOTE *Remember to create your textures with dimensions that are a power of two. Video cards can manage the textures much more efficiently if both dimensions of the texture meet this requirement.*

If you do not have Photoshop, you are not out of luck. You can still create textures with Microsoft Paint and add the alpha channel using the texture tool provided by Microsoft with the DirectX SDK (DxTex.exe). The texture tool can work with any of the texture formats that Paint can create with the exception of the GIF format. It also has its own format (DirectDraw Surface, or DDS) that it can read and write. The DDS format is a 32 bit per pixel format that includes the alpha transparency information.

To create a texture with transparency requires that you create two images with Paint. The first image is the normal view of the image with the color information. The second image is a gray-scale image the same size of the first. You load the first image into the texture tool. You then open the second image in the alpha channel within the tool. Any pixels that are white in the second image will be opaque in the composite image. Any pixels that are black in the second image will be completely transparent. Gray values will be partially transparent based on the intensity of gray. The composite image may then be saved into a DDS file for use by the game.

Creating Height Maps

Remember in Chapter 4 that we used a height map image to control the shape of the terrain. The height map is a gray-scale image. The intensity of each pixel in the image represents the elevation of the corresponding point in the terrain. This height map can be generated either manually or programmatically. Any image editing tool will work for this. A tool like Photoshop will provide a smoother looking terrain since it has the ability to apply color gradients to an image. It also includes a blurring filter to smooth transitions between manually applied colors.

There are several automated approaches to creating a height map. The Microsoft DirectX 9 SDK includes a C++ sample called Fractal. This sample uses fractal mathematics to create a height map and then render it to the screen as terrain. This sample could easily be ported to C# and coupled with the screen-shot code used in the sample game to save the generated height map images.

An excellent freeware height map generator is also available at SourceForge (`http://hme.sourceforge.net`). Since this is an open source project, it comes with the source code so that you may modify and expand it to meet your needs.

Audio Tools

There will be times when the audio files that you wish to use for sound effects are not in the format that you need. One prime example is a sound that you want to use with three-dimensional sound that is in a stereo format. Remember that all sounds used with 3D sound must be mono, since the sound system automatically performs the left/right mixing for the sounds. Numerous shareware and professional packages are available to solve this problem.

The best package that I have located for audio editing is Audio Edit by E-Soft (`http://www.e-soft.co.uk`). It is available in a wide range of languages and costs a modest $19. Audio Edit is able to work with both WAV and MP3 format sound files. In addition to its ability to convert a sound from stereo to mono, this package provides a wide range of effects that may be applied to any portion of a sound.

Summary

This chapter has provided you with a small selection of the many development tools that are available to you. You will need tools like these in order to develop the content that will be used in conjunction with your game engine to create a game. The tools that I have mentioned in this chapter are the ones that I have found useful. There are many more tools to choose from. Finding the right one is a matter of searching for solutions to any need you encounter and selecting the solution that works best for you.

I hope that you have found this book to be a good introduction to the basic concepts of a three-dimensional game engine. Once you have mastered these basics, you will be ready to expand the power and capability of your game engine. Some of the more advanced topics that you will move up to include animation and the use of the programmable pipeline.

Index

Numbers and Symbols